# A-Z
## of Trade Unionism
## and Industrial Relations

## Jack Jones and Max Morris

HEINEMANN : LONDON

William Heinemann Ltd
10 Upper Grosvenor Street London W1X 9PA
LONDON MELBOURNE TORONTO
JOHANNESBURG AUCKLAND

First published 1982
© Jack Jones and Max Morris
434 90900 9

Typeset by Preface Ltd, Salisbury, Wilts.
Printed in Great Britain by The Pitman Press, Bath

# A-Z

## of Trade Unionism
## and Industrial Relations

# Preface

This book has been written in response to what we believe to be a genuine and important need. Our experience of the trade union movement and contact with people interested in industrial relations with all its political and economic overtones, has shown up the absence of an easily accessible, *single* source of basic information on what may be broadly described as the world of labour. Not a day passes without reference in the press or media to events whose proper understanding demands some knowledge of trade unionism, industrial relations and the political and economic problems associated with them. Names, terms and initials are freely used in reporting and discussing a wide range of activities affecting the working lives of the community. Accurate knowledge of their meaning is normally assumed although in fact it frequently does not exist among members of the general public or even among those directly involved, for example trade unionists, shop stewards, personnel officers, teachers, employers.

A great deal of excellent information is available in a large and growing volume of literature produced by trade union education departments, research organizations, publishers and Government Departments. What we have attempted to do, however, is to produce for easy reference, in a handy form under a single cover, the kind of information which will help to guide readers through the maze of material, official and otherwise, that exists. Some of the information we have expressed in simple definitions of a line or two. On the other hand, there are matters of great complexity which require detailed treatment. There are also issues of sharp controversy which need some explanation. We have tried to be accurate and comprehensive consistent with not overloading the reader with every detail of some of the items included; although, regrettably, accuracy has sometimes demanded the repetition of official and legalistic formulations, we have tried to cut these to a minimum.

Naturally many of the issues we deal with are capable of conflicting interpretations. In such circumstances, while striving for objectivity and accuracy on the presentation of facts, we have nevertheless approached the issues from the point of view which can be broadly described as that of the trade union movement with which we have both been closely identified all our working lives. But we believe that this will be helpful also to those who, even if they do not accept the trade union point of view, should be well briefed on what it is.

We have not written for specialists. Our aim has been to reach a wide public including teachers in schools and further education who are being increasingly pressed to deal with the world of labour in their curricula.

Some of the entries deal with controversies still current at time of writing and probably even of publication; some, e.g. social security, youth training, and trade union legal immunities, are actually in process of legislative and administrative changes. Here we have striven to be as up to date as possible, indicating, sometimes at length, what the issues under discussion are.

We have received a great deal of help which we acknowledge but any views expressed, unless otherwise indicated, are our own for which we take responsibility.

*Jack Jones*
*Max Morris*

# Acknowledgements

In preparing this book we have used many sources of information. We are particularly indebted to the TUC and the large number of trade unions (listed below) who generously provided us with copies of their own excellent educational material; to the Department of Employment, ACAS and the Department of Health and Social Security for their official publications; to the indispensable Labour Research Department on whose publications we have drawn widely; and to the numerous organizations mentioned in the text who sent us their official documents or pamphlets.

We have received generous help from individuals and would like to mention: Mrs. Noreen Branson of the LRD, Mr. Roy Jackson and Mr. John Monks of the TUC, Mr. Barry Fawcett, Mr. Graham Clayton, Miss Jean Farrel and Miss J. Jarvis, all of the NUT, Mr. Alan Gronow, then of LACSAB, Mr. Jan Toporowski for help on the economic entries, Mr. Jim Mortimer, then of ACAS, Mr. W. Boaden and Mr. H. E. Houghton, Mrs. C. Ellacott for help in typing and documentation, and Mrs. Margaret Morris for general help and advice.

Trade Unions who sent us their material:

APEX, ASLEF, ASTMS, AUEW, AUEW(TASS), BIFU, COHSE, CPSA, CSU, EIS, GMWU, ISTC, NALGO, NATFHE, NUM, NUPE, NUR, NUT, POEU, SCPS, T & GWU, UCATT, UCW, USDAW and the GFTU.

# Contents

# A

**ABILITY TO PAY**   An element in trade union claims for higher wages and improved conditions. Trade union negotiators usually aim to prove that the concessions they seek can be met by employers on the basis of their financial position and general viability. In this way it is claimed that prosperous undertakings should share their prosperity with the workforce. Pressure by trade unions to secure full information has been increasing in recent years and the Employment Protection Act (1975) obliged employers to disclose to representatives of recognized independent trade unions information required for collective bargaining. (*See* Disclosure of Information.)

**ABSENTEEISM**   Absence from work not due to unavoidable causes; could be mentioned as ground for dismissal. Ill feeling among workers has been created by the use of the term in relation only to workers' absences, ignoring absenteeism among management, especially top management, for social reasons, e.g. long weekends, attendance at Ascot etc.

**ACAS, ADVISORY, CONCILIATION AND ARBITRATION SERVICE**   The 'Conciliation and Arbitration Service' was established and financed by the Labour Government in 1974, given the name ACAS in 1975, and put on a statutory basis by the Employment Protection Act as from 1st January, 1976. Its duty under the Act is to promote the improvement of industrial relations and in particular to encourage the extension of collective bargaining and to develop, and where necessary to reform, collective bargaining machinery. Its five main functions are: collective conciliation, individual conciliation, arbitration, advisory work and extended investigation into industrial relations problems.

The Service is directed by a Council whose Chairman and nine members are appointed by the Secretary of State for Employment. Three of the members are nominated by the Trades Union Congress (TUC), three by the Confederation of British Industries (CBI). The three others are university professors with considerable experience of industrial law and industrial relations. The first Chairman was

1

# ACAS

Mr. Jim Mortimer, a well known trade unionist; he was replaced on retirement in 1981, by the present government, by the former Personnel Director of British Leyland, Mr. Pat Lowry.

ACAS offers a service independent of any Government Department and has been frequently involved in resolving major industrial disputes. Its services are available to trade unions, employers or individuals to whom it can offer advice, information and practical assistance on any question concerning industrial relations, free of charge. Normally it will not be called on for help until all stages in any agreed procedure which is involved have been exhausted and have failed to result in a settlement.

Conciliation by ACAS is voluntary. The officer concerned cannot impose a settlement; it must be agreed by the parties to the dispute. ACAS also offers a voluntary service in which the arbitrator(s), having heard both sides, can make an award, which though it is not legally binding is normally accepted. It can also, if requested, mediate, for example in a pay dispute, and recommend terms for a settlement.

More specifically it is responsible for providing conciliation on complaints of unfair dismissal, on equal pay and sex or race discrimination brought under the relevant Acts of Parliament. Here again settlements must be voluntary by the parties concerned.

Other services offered include drawing up Codes of Practice aimed at improving industrial relations. Among its Codes, of great importance is one on the Disclosure of Information by employers to unions for the purpose of collective bargaining and one on Time Off from Work of elected officials for trade union activities. It is noteworthy that ACAS felt unable to endorse the Thatcher government's (1980) Codes of Practice on Picketting and the Closed Shop.

ACAS performs a valuable service in investigating industrial relations problems and suggesting remedies. Its help is invited by both sides of industry, for example on problems of personnel management, redundancy procedures, procedural agreements and job evaluation. It may help if requested on problems of union recognition, a sphere in which it had statutory obligations until they were abolished by the Employment Act, 1980.

Longer term enquiries include investigations into industrial relations in particular industries or individual factories or companies in order to find the facts, pinpoint the problems and suggest solutions.

The services offered are made more easily accessible by the existence of ACAS Regional Offices able to deal with local problems. Though there is a substantial full-time staff, necessary to deal with the numerous calls for its services, ACAS also uses the services of part-time academics and others to carry out various activities on its behalf.

**ACCIDENT BOOK**   Under the 1975 Social Security Act employers must keep readily accessible a book for recording details of any accident causing personal injury. The book must be in a 'form approved by the Secretary of State for Employment'. Approved accident books can be obtained from HMSO. Any accident should be recorded even if no time is lost from work. Employers are required to preserve accident books, when they are filled, for a period of 3 years from the date of the last entry in the book. Employees are responsible for notifying accidents causing personal injury as soon as practicable after an accident – an entry in the accident book will be enough for this purpose.

These rules apply in premises covered by the Factories Act, Mines and Quarries Act *or* where more than 10 insured people work.

Apart from the compilation of statistics it is essential for employees that all accidents should be recorded. To claim industrial injury benefit, or to sue for damages, an employer needs to show that any injury resulted from an accident at work. Failure to record even apparently minor accidents could have serious consequences – for example if a harmless-looking cut turned badly septic, or a 'sprain' turned out to be a broken bone. A minor accident, such as a cut on the face, may indicate the danger of more serious injury, for example the loss of an eye. (*See* Industrial Injuries Benefit.)

**AFFILIATION**   If a trade union connects or attaches itself to another body whether trade union, political or social, by *ad hoc* decision or through its rules, it is said to affiliate to that body. Affiliations are normally made to organizations with similar, related or allied objects, or organizations towards which the union wishes to show sympathy, or in order to secure necessary support and added power for the union's activities. They may involve observance of or conformity with the organization's rules and the acceptance of conditions of affiliation as well as the payment of either a single fee or a subscription based on the union's membership.

Thus trade unions can affiliate, e.g. to the TUC or to the Labour Party or to various national bodies or at more local level, e.g. to a

# Agreements

Trades Council or a Community Relations Council. The particular affiliation must not be in conflict with the union's rules, e.g. the National Union of Teachers may not affiliate to any political party. Affiliation of unions to a political party must be in accordance with the relevant legislation. (*See* Political Levy.)

**AGREEMENTS (GENERAL, INCLUDING PROCEDURE AGREEMENTS)** Informal agreements between workers and employers may exist in an establishment, which are not written down in any precise way or even at all but embody an understanding based on custom and practice over a period. More commonly, trade unions negotiate *substantive agreements* with employers on a variety of issues. Normally they are signed and cover, for example, a twelve-month period, but they may be open-ended and may be amended at any time by mutual agreement. It is customary today for individual employees to receive copies of relevant agreements as part of their contract of employment. Most unions consult their members before signing an agreement on their behalf. Collective agreements are not legally binding unless so stated in writing. But they are binding on individual employees to the extent that they are incorporated in their contracts of employment.

Of great importance are *Procedure Agreements*. These are essentially mutually acceptable arrangements between both sides in any unit of industry to deal with industrial relations. They specify the conditions for dealing with issues that are likely to arise whether in the field of pay or conditions of work. Procedure Agreements can cover details of membership for whom the union has negotiating rights, recognition of the appropriate committees for dealing with issues and the facilities provided for them, the stages by which claims are progressed, procedures for dealing with grievances, and provisions for the amendment of the agreement.

In different unions agreements can be made at different levels within the union according to its rules. Trade unionists should study the rules and check with their union office in order to know what powers are given at different levels, and so avoid unnecessary frustration.

Types of agreement concluded by collective bargaining cover issues such as: union recognition, closed shop, check off, disciplinary procedures, disclosure of information, health and safety. Job and income security agreements may include sick pay, maternity pay, guaranteed week, redeployment and redundancy procedures. Yet again agreements may deal with time off for trade union and public duties and conditions for other kinds of leave with or without pay, early retirement provisions, equal opportunities, avoidance of sex and race discrimination.

A key feature of agreements is normally a 'status quo' clause where applicable, that is the position prevailing prior to any change giving rise to a grievance or a dispute shall prevail or be restored until the procedure for settlement has been exhausted. Similarly it is essential that any change in the procedures for settlement of any issue must be agreed by both sides.

Good agreements will also try to prevent delaying tactics e.g. by specifying time limits for various stages in dealing with issues.

**AGRICULTURAL WAGES BOARD FOR ENGLAND AND WALES, SCOTTISH AGRICULTURAL WAGES BOARD** These Boards have the power to determine minimum rates of pay and some conditions of employment for ordinary workers and premium rates for craftsmen and employees with supervisory and/or managerial responsibilities. They are composed of equal numbers of workers' and employers' representatives plus independent members appointed by the Secretaries of State for Agriculture, Fisheries and Food and the Secretaries of State for Wales and Scotland. For England and Wales the employees' representatives are five from the National Union of Agricultural Workers*, three from the T&GWU*; for Scotland the T&GWU represents the employees. Employers are represented by the National Farmers' Union for England and Wales and Scotland. *(merged in 1982).

When there is a failure of the employees' and employers' representatives to agree, the independent members can impose a settlement which becomes statutorily applied.

The Boards may make Wages Orders (*see* Wages Councils) which are enforceable. Below the Board for England and Wales there are County Agricultural Wages Committees similarly composed as the Board. Among their duties are the issue of craft certificates to enable workers to apply for craftsmen's rates and approving premium agreements between workers in training and their employers.

It should be emphasized that the Boards regulate *minimum* wages and local rates may exceed these.

5

# Aims of Industry

**AIMS – THE FREE ENTERPRISE ORGANIZATION (AIMS OF INDUSTRY)**   Aims, more commonly known under its original name, Aims of Industry, is an organization devoted to making propaganda for 'free enterprise industry and a free market economy'. It was established by industrialists and is financed by company contributions. Its activities include the production of material for 'parliament, press, television, the trade unions, the public, the universities and schools and people whose decisions affect and influence industry'. This latter group is identified as 'companies, federations and associations' for whom 'important services are provided'.

Operating through advertising, poster, and press campaigns, Aims has attacked nationalization and claims to have fought successful battles against 'attempts to nationalize many industries'. It also campaigns against 'bureaucratic control of industry by government' and fights 'for small businesses and for just taxation'. Among its more specific objectives is opposition to local authorities' direct labour building departments.

Aims also provides its own members, as well as members of Parliament, with 'facts and figures on trade and industry' and answers questions from them on specific subjects. It has a staff which includes 'experts in business economics and journalism' and in addition can call on the services of specialists in economic and industrial subjects. These presumably include trade unions and industrial relations.

In all these activities, Aims 'acts as a watchdog for free and private enterprise'. It warns companies of the approach of 'unwarranted government intervention' and fights it with all the power that can be brought to bear, in the communications media, in parliament and 'wherever public opinion finds expression'. It claims that its coverage in provincial papers is 'probably second to none'.

Believing that 'it is vital that we should start early in teaching the principles of business and free enterprise economics and countering left wing bias', Aims provides material on these subjects, including tapes and teaching programmes, 'for millions of school children'. It claims to have played a part in the 'swing away from socialism in the universities'.

Aims claims to be non-party-political, to have no 'special panel of M.P.s', to have 'wide contacts' with all major parties and never to have 'supported any political party' but its activities are clearly directed against the Labour Party. At election times is spends money on anti-public-ownership propaganda which is obviously anti-Labour because of the Labour Party's association with nationalization. Thus in the period preceding the general elections of 1974 it tried to raise half a million pounds to be used in propaganda against Labour.

Though the organization has a Council that includes 'leaders of industry, business and the professions', the names of the Council members officially listed are nearly all industrialists.

Among a large number of publications listed by the organization are included: *Reducing the Growth of Civil Servants*; *Power on the Shop Floor*; *Co-operation, Control or Chaos*; *Reds Under the Beds*.

**ALDINGTON–JONES REPORT** Known alternatively as the 'Jones-Aldington' Report this related to the Special Committee on the Ports set up in 1972 to deal with the problem of surplus labour in the docks arising from containerization and other aspects of modernization of the British ports. The Committee consisted of Docks union representatives and the Chairmen of the major ports and was presided over by Lord Aldington (Chairman of the Port of London Authority) and Jack Jones (General Secretary of the Transport and General Workers Union). It recommended total abolition of casual employment for registered dockworkers by abolishing the 'temporarily unattached register' in the ports covered by the Dock Labour scheme. It also recommended that the loading and unloading of containers should be dealt with at the ports by registered port workers, as far as possible. Improved training and pension schemes were called for as also was a review of the work conducted in the smaller ports.

Under the report a new departure in the level of amounts offered for voluntary severance was secured. The Government itself accepted responsibility for the expenditure of £30 million to finance the voluntary severance scheme. (*See* Decasualization.)

**'ALL-IN' RATE** This is simply a way of expressing a total time wage or salary method of payment. That is to say, employees work for employers for an agreed sum of money per week or per annum. With manual workers this is normally broken down to an hourly 'all-in' rate as distinct from the practice in some industries of having the time wage made up of a number of factors e.g. base rate, lieu rate, merit rate, and possibly a bonus element in addition. (*See* Allowances; Bonuses.)

# Allowances

**ALLOWANCES**    Regular payments made to workers in addition to their basic wages are normally called allowances. There are a great variety of allowances paid under different wage and salary agreements. These include, for example, allowances paid in particular industries and occupations to employees living in the London area, travelling allowances, lodging allowances, dirty money, danger money, allowances for moving house, meals allowances, allowances for dependants, for rent, for free coal, for purchase of tools, etc. Trade unions may attempt to consolidate some allowances into the basic wage structure, so increasing wage rates. (*See* London Weighting, Danger Money, Dirty Money, Tool Allowance.)

**AMALGAMATIONS & TRANSFERS OF ENGAGEMENTS, TRADE UNIONS**    Normally 'amalgamation' means that each union loses its identity as a union and becomes merged in a new union under a new name.

A 'transfer of engagements' is a transfer of the obligations of one union (transferor) to another (transferee) and an assumption of those obligations by the latter.

Members of all unions involved in a proposed 'amalgamation' should be given the opportunity to vote but in the case, however, of a proposed 'transfer of engagements' the voting is confined to the members of the 'transferor' union.

The object of amalgamation or transfer is to strengthen the bargaining power of the workers concerned by creating larger and more powerful units and eliminating conflicting policies which may exist between unions and which may therefore weaken union power in negotiating with employers. The movement towards amalgamations has intensified in recent years and continues, the tendency being to create fewer and larger unions. Amalgamations have been encouraged and assisted by the TUC.

The 1964 Trade Union Amalgamations etc. Act made it easier for mergers and transfers of engagements between trade unions to take place. The principal provisions are: Two or more trade unions may amalgamate and become one trade union, with or without a division or dissolution of the funds of any of the Unions involved.

In the case of each of the Unions desiring amalgamation, a resolution which approves an instrument of amalgamation acceptable to the Certification Officer (see p. 34) must be passed on a vote within the Union subject to the following:

(a) Every member of the Union must be entitled to vote on the resolution.
(b) Every member of the Union must be allowed to vote without interference or constraint and must, so far as is reasonably possible, be given a fair opportunity of voting.
(c) The method of voting must involve the marking of a voting paper by the person voting.
(d) All reasonable steps must have been taken by the Union to secure that, not less than seven days before voting on the resolution begins, every member is supplied with a notice in writing approved for the purpose by the Certification Officer.

With regard to the notice distributed to members the intention of the Act is to ensure that they see the proposed 'instrument of amalgamation or transfer' and that they have enough information to enable them to form a 'reasonable judgement of the main effects of the proposed amalgamation or transfer'.

The 'instrument of amalgamation or transfer' together with a copy of the notice it is intended to issue to the members must be submitted to the Certification Officer for his approval before they are conveyed to the members for voting upon.

A simple majority of those voting is sufficient to approve an instrument of amalgamation or transfer and when that is secured application can then be made to the Certification Officer for the amalgamation or transfer to be registered. The registration will not take effect 'before the expiration of a period of six weeks beginning with the date on which the application was sent to the Certification Officer'.

The same procedure applies in the case of 'amalgamation' or 'transfer'. The difference is that in the case of 'amalgamation' each of the Unions concerned must vote while in the case of 'transfer of engagements' only the members of the Union transferring are required to vote.

**APPEALS, APPEALS PROCEDURE** Disciplinary and grievance procedures normally allow of a right of appeal to a third or higher body if one of the parties to a dispute is dissatisfied with or does not wish to accept the decision reached under the procedures. The appeal and its result then become the final stage in the process. Trade unions normally ensure that a right of appeal is written into disciplinary and grievance procedures.

Within trade unions themselves there are normally appeals procedures provided for in their rules for settling internal disciplinary

# Apprenticeship

matters e.g. suspensions, expulsions or fines. In some cases an appeal may be made to the TUC Independent Review Committee. (*See* Grievance Procedure, Independent Review Committee).

**APPRENTICESHIP**    On the job training for young workers aspiring to become skilled craftsmen has existed for centuries and is called (craft) apprenticeship. The training, normally coupled with some form of vocational education, begins when the young person enters employment at the age of 16 or 17 and normally lasts about four years. Most apprenticeships for young men are in engineering, construction, printing and motor vehicle servicing. There are far fewer apprenticeships for girls, mostly in hairdressing. The term has, in the recent past, been used to include similar training at other levels than crafts. Thus, there are now comparatively small numbers of:

(a) technician apprenticeships which involve training for technician levels with appropriate qualifications
(b) student apprenticeships for positions of higher technical responsibility with higher education qualifications
(c) graduate apprenticeships for holders of university degrees and their equivalents which enable the trainee to qualify for membership of professional institutions.

There are also a few commercial apprenticeships for administrative jobs in commerce or in accounting.

Craft apprenticeship schemes are normally administered by national bodies representing employers and trade unions in an industry.

The vocational education which is the normal part of apprenticeship schemes is either recommended or required and involves part-time day (normally one day or two half-days throughout the year) or block release (full-time release for a specified period each year, usually 12 weeks or less, for several years) in further education colleges by the employer in working hours with pay, but additional attendance on one or two evenings may also be required. It is not usual for any final examination or test of competence to be passed. Serving the necessary time – normally 4 years, but ranging from 2 to 5 – usually leads to acceptance as a craftsman by both the employer and the union. The vocational education schemes, however, do involve appropriate examinations (normally City and Guilds of London Institute – CGLI), though they do not affect the apprentice's craftsman's status.

Numbers of apprenticeships, already low compared to some European industrialized countries, most of whom have considerably greater vocational educational provision, have been dropping substantially in recent years, including those available in major industries. This is a symptom of the unemployment situation and fears have been expressed on the future of the skilled manpower 'pool' in Britain. While, before the recession, 120,000 apprentices could be recruited in a good year, only about half this number has been estimated by the Manpower Services Commission (MSC) to have been recruited in 1981–2; there have been sharp drops in the engineering, construction and road transport industries. The MSC spent £40 million in 1981 on supporting apprenticeships, particularly in engineering.

The apprenticeship system has come under close scrutiny as part of the continuing public discussion taking place on the whole issue of industrial training and its relationship with both the development of industrial skills and the education service. Apprenticeship has been criticised as teaching skills which are becoming less necessary and not teaching those most in demand and relevant to changing technology. Of some importance, too, is the reconsideration of the rules on age of entry for craft and technician apprenticeships which are criticised as too inflexible, and of the 'time serving' basis of apprenticeship, rather than one based on skilled performance. The extension of education and training to cover very many more young people, especially girls, is in the centre of the argument.

What is at issue is the modernization of a traditional system and its greater flexibility in response to changing demands in industry and changing educational patterns among young people. (*See* Industrial Training: White Paper, Manpower Services Commission, Youth Opportunities Programme.)

**ARBITRATION**   When collective bargaining has failed to produce a settlement, either entirely or on particular issues, or when the interpretation of a settlement is in dispute, either one or both sides in the dispute may wish to refer the matters to the arbitration of a third party, a person or persons whom they find acceptable. If both sides agree to do this the process is one of voluntary arbitration. It is customary then for both sides to accept the findings of the arbitrator(s) though this may not always be the case. ACAS – or occasionally the Department of Employment itself – is always prepared to help by providing the names of people with experience from whom both parties may choose agreed arbitrators. There is frequently a panel with one person nominated by each side and an ACAS appointed chairman with power of decision.

Before arbitration can operate the terms of reference of the arbitrator(s) must be agreed, that is he or they must be given very clear information and instruction on what are the precise issues in dispute on which he is to arbitrate. How the arbitrator operates can vary from case to case but it is usual for both sides to present their case in writing and then for the arbitrator to see and question both parties either separately or together. This can be done privately or publicly according to whatever is agreed should be the procedure. The arbitrator(s) then considers the case and makes his award usually giving reasons for his decision.

Compulsory arbitration differs from voluntary in that both sides are not required to agree before arbitration is adopted. It may be that under rules agreed in the industry, or under the law there has to be arbitration when there is a failure to agree. Or the rules may provide that one side alone may secure the operation of arbitration. An example of the former is the railway industry where, on failure to agree on a settlement, disputes are referred to the Railway Staffs National Tribunal (RSNT). Here, however, the recommendations of the RSNT are not binding as was evidenced when the British Railways Board rejected a major RSNT recommendation in July, 1981, leading to a strike threat and the reopening of negotiations.

Compulsory arbitration called into operation by one side has been criticised as inhibiting the full process of negotiation before it has been completely exhausted and so creating dissatisfaction on one side or the other. (*See* ACAS, Central Arbitration Committee.)

**ASSETS AND LIABILITIES**    In a firm's Balance Sheet there will be a statement of assets and liabilities. The firm's assets are its possessions upon which values are placed. These include cash in hand and in the bank, stocks of goods held, investments and money owing to it. These are known as current assets. In addition there are fixed assets: buildings and other properties owned and their contents including furniture, equipment and machinery and vehicles.

Current liabilities are what the firm owes, such as debts to creditors, interest on bank overdrafts and loans, taxation and dividends payable.

Net current assets are the difference between current assets and current liabilities.

**AWARDS**    The findings of arbitration machinery employed in the settlement of disputes can be described as awards. In the case of at least one set of salary negotiating machinery, the Burnham Committees, the final settlement is traditionally known as the award. Whether awards are binding or not depends on the arrangements under which arbitration takes place.

# B

**BACK PAY (RETROSPECTIVE PAY)**    When a settlement is made on a wage increase between an employer and a union the increase may be paid from a date preceding the signature of the agreement. Similarly an arbitrator or tribunal may award an increase from a date preceding the award, e.g. from the time of the commencement of a dispute. Sometimes negotiations can continue after the normal date when an increase is due under agreed procedures. Payment is then normally backdated to the date the increase became due, and the procedures will in these circumstances make provision for such 'retrospective payment'. Such provisions can be double-edged in that while they allow negotiations or arbitration procedures to operate without undue haste, they may also spin out negotiations unnecessarily, and in times of inflation can reduce the value of the increase when ultimately paid.

The term 'back pay' may also be used to describe payments to individual workers in a variety of circumstances in which payment due in the past was not made.

**BALANCE OF PAYMENTS, BALANCE OF TRADE**    The Balance of Payments consists of two elements:

(a) The Balance of Trade. This is the relationship between *visible* exports and imports, that is the expression in terms of money of the difference between the value of physical goods exported and physical goods imported. The balance is judged to be favourable if exports are greater than imports and unfavourable if imports exceed exports. In this context the term 'goods' means actual merchandise, e.g. vehicles and other manufactures and raw materials, e.g. oil or grain. This is, however, only part of the country's trading activities making up the Balance of Payments.

# Balance of Payments

(b) For a complete picture it is necessary to take into account *invisible* exports and imports. These are trading operations which do not involve actual merchandise. They refer to payments made to people or institutions in this country and abroad for services rendered. For example tourists going abroad transfer British money to other countries just as tourists coming into Britain bring foreign money into Britain. Again when British money has been invested abroad the resulting interest or profits coming into Britain count as invisible exports, as the effect is the same as though actual goods were exported which bring money into the country. On the other hand foreign investment in Britain can lead to payments to other countries and so count as invisible imports. Another example of invisible imports is the country's expenditure on the upkeep of British troops abroad, e.g. West Germany, because it involves the exchange of British for foreign currency. The reference in this section is to actual payments made or received and not to the capital sums invested which give rise to these payments.

The sum total of visible and invisible exports and imports balanced against one another is technically called the Balance of Payments on Current Account and can be favourable or unfavourable at any particular time. The difference between the value of exports and imports of all goods and services, visible and invisible, is sometimes also described as the 'trade gap' if the balance is unfavourable. If it is favourable the situation is sometimes described as showing a 'trade surplus'.

In addition there is the Balance of Payments on Capital Account. These cover the actual sums transferred for investment abroad, e.g. to manufacture there, or sums flowing into British banks, for example, to take advantage of high interest rates, or money invested in Britain by foreign firms to build factories and make some of their goods here. These are known as movements of capital and affect the balance of payments on Capital Account which may be favourable or unfavourable.

The Current and Capital Account balance along with Government balancing transactions, e.g. money from the International Monetary Fund, all taken together is known as the Total Currency Flow and gives a fuller picture of trading performance than any of the balances described above.

Bankruptcy

Overall trading performance of course affects both employment and the level of incomes. Use is often made of the various facets of the Balance of Payments situation by the major employers' organizations in their general approach to industrial relations and especially to the level of wages and employment. Similarly, trade unions advocate their own policies on these questions in the interests of their members. (*See* International Monetary Fund.)

**BALANCE SHEET**    This is a statement prepared once a year for the annual report of a union and is submitted to the conference or annual general meeting of the organization. It should show the overall financial position and should contain both a statement of income and expenditure showing any balance (surplus) or deficit, and provide full information on the union's assets (what it owns) and its liabilities (what it owes). For example, if a union has its own building the value of the building and its equipment, less depreciation, must be included in the assets. If the union has borrowed money the outstanding debt must be shown as a liability.

The balance sheet must be audited by auditors under arrangements provided for in the rules. Balance sheets of local organizations are usually fairly simple statements audited by members appointed annually to do the job who receive from the treasurer or other appropriate officer all the necessary documents (receipts for payments etc.). The auditors may make any relevant comments they wish on the handling of the accounts and finances of the organization.

**BANK RATE**    *See* Minimum Lending Rate.

**BANKRUPTCY**    When a business cannot pay its debts, the owners themselves or those to whom they owe the money, the creditors, may go through a procedure which results in a declaration of bankruptcy in respect of the business. The procedure involves petitioning the (Bankruptcy) Court for a 'receiving order' which if granted places an Official Receiver in charge of the business. He will call a creditors' meeting where the business can be declared bankrupt. Such assets as the business has will be sold and the proceeds divided among the creditors. In place of a declaration of bankruptcy the creditors may accept payment of a proportion of their debts.

Bankrupts may apply to the Court for an order of 'discharge' from their bankruptcy after the disposal of assets has been completed. If granted this releases the debtors from obligations on the debts concerned.

Employees have certain rights of payment of debts e.g. in 1982 arrears of pay for 8 weeks up to £135 a week, holiday pay up to £130 a week etc. when the employer has become insolvent. These rights are detailed in Department of Employment, Pamphlet No. 3 on the Employment Protection Act, available from any office of the Department of Employment. Application forms for such payment are available from the Receiver or the employer's representative (e.g. liquidator, trustee) and application should be made as soon as possible after employment has ended, the forms being returned to the employer's representative. The employee has also certain rights in respect of any occupational pensions scheme.

As the provisions regarding employees' rights are detailed and complex, advice in case of the employer's insolvency should immediately be sought from the employee's trade union so that the employee's rights are fully safeguarded.

**BENEFITS, SOCIAL SECURITY**   *See* Social Security.

**BENEFITS, TRADE UNION**   Traditionally trade unions have placed a great deal of emphasis on the provision of cash benefits to members. The mutual aid element was very important in the operations of the earlier trade societies, from the payment to travelling members of money for bed and food to superannuation benefits and sickness, unemployment, death and funeral benefits introduced long before legislation and industrial agreements moved into those areas.

With the growth of trade union membership and political influence combined with collective bargaining over an ever-widening field there has been a diminished interest in trade union cash benefits of the insurance and Friendly Society type though some have been retained. And most unions make provision for payments to be made during strikes or lockouts or in the event of victimization, though these payments vary widely in size.

In recent years with the increasing, complexity of industry and industrial relations problems trade union benefits have made a sharp turn towards educational and legal services.

Payment of insurance type benefits may be made from a fund into which under the rules part of the members' subscriptions are paid, in which case the member is 'in benefit' as long as his subscription is up to date. Alternatively members may pay voluntarily into a separate fund and receive benefits according to the sums they subscribe. There is normally a qualifying period before benefits are paid. Other types of payment or service do not require any special financial arrangement; they are part of the normal 'benefit' union members receive in return for their subscriptions.

Union benefits are a supportive service additional to payments made under the social security regulations. Their general scope can however be very wide and include for example assistance with house buying and the right to use union convalescent or holiday homes. They may form a substantial attraction to potential members, and encourage the retention of members.

**BLACKING**    Trade unionists 'black' or boycott goods or services manufactured or provided by a firm when they refuse to handle the goods or provide the services of a firm involved in a trade dispute either with their own or another union. 'Blacking' can also mean refusal to supply materials or components to the firm or to transport them. Similarly, a job or post regarding which there is a dispute can be 'blacked' by a union – that is, trade unionists are advised or instructed not to apply for it and to have nothing to do with it. In addition, goods or services of a firm may be 'blacked' because the firm, not involved in the dispute, is considered to have influenced the course of the dispute adversely.

Some forms of 'Blacking' constitute a breach of contract and may lead to disciplinary action against individual employees. Organizers are immune from liability unless the breach is induced when there is no trade dispute, or where there is a trade dispute against an employer who is not associated with the employer in dispute or is not his immediate customer or supplier.

**BLACKLEG (SCAB)**    A term commonly and traditionally used to describe someone who is involved in strikebreaking, whether by refusing to observe a strike call by the union or by crossing a union picket line or by assisting the employer in any way during a strike or lockout. It is an emotive term reflecting the force of the principle of trade union solidarity and is sometimes more loosely used in describing violations of trade union decisions democratically agreed in other than strike situations. The even more emotive term 'scab' can be used as synonymous with blackleg. Scab or blackleg labour is the description commonly given to workers continuing to work during a dispute or drafted into an establishment to replace workers on strike or locked out. (*See* Strike, Lockout.)

**BLACKLIST**    A list, occasionally kept by an employer or group of employers or an organization financed by employers, of workers whom it is considered undesirable to employ because of their known trade union or political activity at their place of work. If kept by an organization, the Blacklist is made available for consultation by employers as required. It is quite normal for employers to deny the existence of such lists and it is difficult to prove that they do exist and that they are used to deny jobs to particular trade unionists. The trade union movement as a whole has always strongly opposed such methods as designed to weaken trade union power. (*See* Victimization.)

**BLOCK VOTE**    This is the system of voting for example at the TUC and the Labour Party Annual Conference whereby in a card vote the entire vote of a union, constituency Labour Party or affiliated organization is cast for one side or the other following the debate on a motion, or in the case of elections to the TUC General Council or the relevant sections of the Labour Party Executive. The decision on how to cast the block vote is made by each union under its own procedures. Criticism of the block vote usually centres on the fact that it takes no account of what may be substantial minorities e.g. within the union or within union delegations to Congress or Annual Conference. This is countered by the argument that trade union decisions are made by majority vote under their particular procedures and these decisions must be accepted by minorities, or trade union power is undermined. Block votes normally have regard to union policies as agreed by the union's own policy-making procedures.

Block votes may also operate in unions in respect of branch votes at the annual conference and in federations of unions, e.g. the Confederation of Shipbuilding and Engineering Unions in respect of affiliated unions.

**BLUE BOOK – WHITE PAPER – GREEN PAPER**    These are names which describe the different status of various government documents, and are so called because of the colour of the cover in which the document appears.

A *Blue Book* is an official report authorized by Parliament or the

Privy Council. The name is sometimes confined to the National Income and Expenditure Blue Book.

A *White Paper* is a statement of Government policy on an issue and may precede either legislation or arrangements by regulation or otherwise that the Government intends to make. Details of policy contained in White Papers may be subject to negotiations with or representations from interested bodies so that policy contained in a White Paper is not necessarily unalterable. Examples are proposals on housing or education policy.

A *Green Paper* is a statement issued by the Government for discussion on a matter on which policy has not been decided. It is normally circulated among interested bodies whose opinions are invited as a preliminary to policy making. An example is the government document on Trade Union Immunities.

**BLUE COLLAR WORKERS**   A description sometimes given to manual as distinct from clerical and administrative workers. (*See* White Collar Workers.)

**BONA FIDE**   Literally this means 'in good faith' and is an expression used e.g. to describe an offer made informally by either side in a negotiation or dispute which it is intended to honour. The term is also sometimes used to describe recognized or independent trade unions, that is unions accepted as such by other unions or by the TUC. 'Company Unions' are not regarded by the trade union movement as *bona fide* trade unions. (*See* Company Unions.)

**BONUSES**   A term used to describe additional payments above the normal wage or salary e.g. incentive bonus, premium bonus, attendance (for good time-keeping) bonus, Christmas bonus, sales bonus, merit bonus, production bonus, annual bonus, holiday bonus, cost of living bonus, etc.

In incentive systems of payment the amount earned above the basic rate may be described as 'piece-work bonus' or 'direct-workers bonus' relating to the workers employed directly on production. A bonus may also be paid to ancillary workers and others not engaged directly in the production process; this may be called 'indirect bonus'. Bonuses are sometimes also paid to executives and supervisors and usually bear a relationship to the earnings of employees under them.

**BOOM**   A period of flourishing economic activity marked by increasing production and employment, higher profits, wages and prices. (*See* Depression.)

**BRANCHES AND BRANCH LIFE, TRADE UNION**  The basic unit of organization in a trade union is the branch though this title is not universal; in some unions it is called an association or division or (in printing) chapel or lodge. Union branches may be based in a local workplace or may be organized on the basis of areas where their members live, or the class of member covered. They may be known by number or by the name of the area, the factory etc. Their method of organization and the powers they have within the union are laid down within the national rules.

Throughout the trade union movement, branches operate for the most part in a broadly similar way for the conduct of their business. For this purpose, the rules may be laid down in the Union's general rule book or in some unions each branch has its own rules, normally drawn up by its own members according to its own procedures. Uniformity may also be secured by the provision from national headquarters of Model Rules with which branch rules must agree in all essential respects. Local variations from model rules may not contradict any national rules and to ensure that this is so it is normal for local rules to be approved by the union's national authority.

Thus branch rules usually follow a common pattern. They state the name or number of the branch and the area or institution or firm and the kind of membership covered. There follow the aims and objects of the branch which may contain both excerpts from the national rules and such local aims and objects as are appropriate. A great variety of provisions normally follow, including clear statements on who are eligible to be members and how membership is applied for and agreed under national rules and the national subscription and any local fee applicable. If there is a local scheme for deduction of subscription by the employer at source this would be indicated as well as other methods of payment.

Rules normally contain a list of the officers who must be elected to run the branch, e.g. chairman, secretary, treasurer and any other officer customary in or laid down by the particular union, and the regulations for their election, e.g. procedure for nomination, dates for issue of voting papers if election is by a postal ballot, or details of any other method of election, e.g. at a branch meeting, normally the annual general meeting. Provision is also normally made for filling casual vacancies. Rules must also be there for the election of a committee which along with the officers normally runs the branch between general meetings. The duties and powers of officers and committee may be prescribed.

Conditions under which general meetings are held, often including a rule for a minimum number in a year and also for holding committee meetings are customary as well as rules for a quorum, that is a minimum number of members necessary in attendance before business can be conducted. Notice of a certain number of days or weeks is normally necessary for the summoning of general meetings and rules should be clear on the procedure for calling special meetings, e.g. by decision of the officers and/or on receipt of a minimum number of signatures from members. Sometimes meeting dates are fixed by rule.

Branches may have an annual general meeting (AGM) at which the results of elections are announced or elections take place and at which the chief officers will deliver, orally or in writing, their annual reports. At the AGM, also, the accounts and balance sheet for the year will be presented by the treasurer after having been audited by authors appointed at the previous AGM who usually hold no other official position in the branch.

It is customary for a section of the rules to be devoted to relationships (including financial) with higher bodies of the union, for example election of delegates to the annual conference, relationships with county or regional bodies and the means of communication with the union Executive. A section may also deal with the duties of official representatives of the branch at their workplaces if this is applicable. There may be rules dealing with unauthorized activities and the conditions under which industrial action may be asked for or taken. Conditions for political affiliations may also be laid down.

It is unusual for a branch officer to be paid a wage for the job but many unions make provision for the payment of honoraria as compensation for time spent on union business. In some unions the branch officers may be concerned with time-consuming case work and this may be provided for in the rules.

Conditions under which resolutions may be brought forward at meetings (notice etc.) are laid down. A section is frequently devoted to detailing the order of business at the AGM which is normally conducted with greater formality than ordinary meetings. It is customary that only business indicated in the rules can be carried out though provision may be made for emergency business. It is also customary that changes of rule, under clearly specified conditions, take place only at an AGM.

**BRANCH OFFICER**   The chairman leads the team of officers and committee and is usually their spokesman on any public occasion or in local negotiation and consultation with the employer if this is part of the functions of the branch. Above all in conducting the branch business he must act impartially as the elected leader of the whole branch. At the same time it is his duty to act according to the decisions of the majority. Branches are democratic organizations which frequently decide on contentious issues after democratic debate in which minority opinions have full rights to be expressed.

It is the duty of the branch secretary to conduct the correspondence of the branch and to keep its records. He is the channel of communication between the branch and higher bodies of the union and between the officers and committee and the membership. He also communicates on behalf of the branch with the employer where this is applicable under the powers of the branch. The responsibility is his for dealing with the day-to-day business of the branch and for seeing that agendas of meetings are properly prepared and sent out in time. He may be responsible for keeping minutes or records of meetings unless there is a specially appointed minuting secretary for this job. There is often an assistant secretary to help him as well as other assistants for special aspects of the work e.g. membership records, press, social activities etc. The secretary normally prepares the annual report for the AGM. He is also responsible for initiating action following upon decisions of meetings.

The Treasurer is responsible for handling all matters concerned with the branch finance. He keeps the books, has records of all payments and receipts, keeps the bank account as well as any petty cash and signs cheques, sometimes as the sole signatory, sometimes with another designated member, often the secretary or chairman. It is also his duty to prepare and present the annual financial statement to the branch AGM after it has been audited by auditors who are not normally committee members or officers. In some unions the branch secretary also acts as treasurer. The auditors have access to all financial documents of the branch. (*See* Conduct of Meetings.)

**BRIDLINGTON AGREEMENT**   Among its many roles the Trade Union Congress regulates relationships between its affiliated unions and has laid down a code of conduct for this purpose popularly known as the 'Bridlington Agreement', a set of principles approved at the Trades Union Congress in Bridlington in 1939, which were supplemented by the Croydon Declaration adopted by a special Trades Union Congress in 1970.

They were established because trade unionists realized that in situations where more than one union could represent a particular grade of worker, it was necessary to avoid too great a proliferation of unions if a stable form of union organization and collective bargaining machinery was to be developed. The principles and the machinery established within the TUC to enforce them has limited poaching between unions and prevented breakaway unions, while more recently they have effectively dealt with demarcation problems between unions.

Most inter-union disputes fall into one of four categories:

1 a difference about the union to which a particular individual or group of workers should belong (membership);
2 a difference about which union should organize (recognition);
3 a difference about which members should carry out particular work (demarcation);
4 a difference about the policy which should be pursued in respect of terms and conditions of employment.

A Disputes Committee set up by the TUC can require Unions to attend a hearing and can make an Award or Recommendation. An Award made by a Disputes Committee and approved by the TUC General Council is binding on affiliated unions and any union failing to comply faces immediate suspension from the TUC.

**BRITISH INSTITUTE OF MANAGEMENT**  This is a body concerned with promoting 'the art and science' of management and increasing the effectiveness of management by the exchange of information and ideas. It also represents people involved, interested and concerned in management problems. There are over 50,000 managers in membership including accountants, engineers, production and marketing executives, hospital administrators and local and national government officials. The Institute is governed by an elected council and its activity is organized by a Director General and staff.

**BRITISH STANDARDS INSTITUTION**   This is a body concerned with the technical standards of products and provides its members with information on standards at home and abroad. Its functions also include the testing of products in relation to established standards.

**BRITISH TECHNOLOGY GROUP**   The National Enterprise Board and the National Research Development Corporation are now operating under the title British Technology Group 'to provide a major new force for promoting innovation and investment in British industry'. The Group combines the skills and expertise of both organizations and offers a wide range of support including finance to companies and individual entrepreneurs for technical innovation e.g. in micro electronics, robotics, biotechnology etc., etc. It also funds research projects at British universities and polytechnics and is the primary channel for developing and exploiting technology derived from UK public sector sources. It has local offices in the Assisted areas for handling investment proposals.

Its Council consists of members of both organizations as a joint management team. The organizations continue to operate also as separate bodies (1981). (*See* NEB, NRDC.)

**BULLOCK REPORT**   The Government Committee on Industrial Democracy headed by Lord Bullock was set up in 1975 and reported in January 1977.

The main recommendation was that there should be equal representation of employees and shareholders on company boards. They proposed equal numbers of employee and shareholder representatives plus the co-option of additional independent directors (the '2x'+'y' formula). The 'y' element was to comprise less than a third of the total board and be an uneven number greater than one. The report stated 'the co-option of additional directors will also enable people with a broader view of the Company's affairs to take seats on the board . . . We recognize that the normal process of decision making on a board is by consensus rather than by voting, but if there were any tendency towards block voting, the presence of co-opted directors would act against it'. It was also recommended that the Chairman should come from the group of shareholder representatives, although this could change eventually.

The Bullock Committee rejected the view that workers' representatives on the board could be based upon an alternative structure to trade unionism, e.g. works councils. It pointed out the dangers of divorce from the collective bargaining machinery. 'Given the rapid and continuing development at the workplace, an attempt to by-pass this structure would be seen as an attack on trade unions and collective bargaining and would be fiercely resisted.' The link with the trade union channel 'would give the necessary strength and back-up to employee directors and provide an established channel of communication to and from the shop floor through which they could keep in touch with their constituents'.

Non-union employees should not receive any special provisions; the report argued that if an employee organization was neither 'independent' under the terms of the 1975 Employment Protection Act nor recognized by management, then it should not be granted any rights in law on industrial democracy.

All employees in a company would participate in the initial 'trigger-mechanism' by which workers could vote on whether they wished to participate in a scheme of board-level representation. A simple majority on a turnout of at least a third of the workforce would be necessary to set the process in motion. The right to request such a ballot would rest with the independent trade unions in a company. There would also be an 'escape clause' by which after five years, any union or unions which constitute at least a fifth of the workforce could request another ballot to be held on whether board representation should continue.

A committee of the trade unions in the company (known as the Joint Representation Committee) would negotiate with the existing board on the size and structure of the new board and would have to reconcile the conflicting claims of trade unions for seats. Any disputes would be referred to the Industrial Democracy Commission which the Bullock Committee proposed should be set up.

Employee representatives would come from the company involved and would receive no fees other than financial loss payments. They could be removed, in exceptional circumstances, when the accredited representatives of all the unions on the board demanded their dismissal. They would initially report back to the JRC, which would determine the means of reporting back further down the company e.g. to the shop-floor.

The Report recommended that the proposals should apply, in the first place, to enterprises employing 2,000 or more people in the UK, roughly 1,800 separate companies. These companies were on average 70 per cent unionized, compared with a figure of 50.4 per cent for the economy as a whole.

The function of the Industrial Democracy Commission would be to provide information and advice on the operation of industrial democracy legislation and to provide conciliation and arbitration. Recommendations were also made on the formal training and education for prospective employee representatives.

The change of Government in May 1979 put an end, for the time being, both to the Bullock Proposals and to any action on the Labour Government's White Paper on the Report.

**BURNHAM COMMITTEES** Negotiations for teachers' salaries in England and Wales are conducted in two committees, called Burnham, after the man who was their chairman when they were first set up. There is a Burnham for teachers in primary and secondary schools and one for teachers in further and higher education establishments excluding universities. These committees differ from the overwhelming majority of pay negotiating bodies in that they have a statutory basis. They now operate under the Remuneration of Teachers Act (RTA) 1965, which lays down their constitution and powers. Thus they deal only with pay, though government proposals to amend the Act to include in their remit conditions of service for teachers in primary and secondary schools have been announced but have been postponed due to pressure from teachers' unions. The National Union of Teachers (NUT) favours a separate National Joint Council for this purpose.

*Primary and Secondary Committee* This deals with the salaries of teachers in maintained schools though its decisions are normally followed by most schools in the independent sector. Its Chairman is appointed by the Secretary of State for Education and Science as an independent person and he presides over the two sides representing management and teachers' organizations, the composition of each side being determined by the Secretary of State. There are 28 members on the Management Panel including representatives of the Department of Education and Science (DES), the Association of County Councils, the Association of Metropolitan Authorities, and the Welsh Joint Education Committee.

Though the DES has only 2 out of the 28 members its voting power is weighted to give it 15 votes and therefore considerable – in practice usually decisive – influence on the management side.

# Burnham Committees

On the teachers' side, consisting of 32 members, the NUT has 16 seats, the National Association of Schoolmasters/Union of Women Teachers (NAS/UWT) 7, the Assistant Masters and Mistresses Association (AMMA) 4, The National Association of Headteachers (NAHT) 2, the Secondary Heads Association (SHA) one, the Professional Association of Teachers (PAT) one, and the National Association of Teachers in Further and Higher Education (NATFHE) one. Seats are loosely related to membership numbers with the NUT having an overall majority among the school teachers' organizations. Each organization on either side appoints its own members and the Committee has joint Secretaries from management and teachers.

An annual claim is presented by the Teachers' Panel to the Management Panel and if agreement is reached it is transmitted to the Secretary of State by the Chairman. The Secretary of State is then obliged to give it statutory effect and the local authorities, who are the teachers' employers, must pay the salaries agreed. All details of the new salaries and any conditions attaching to them, e.g. discretionary elements, are contained in a document drafted by the DES after consultation with the Burnham Committee, known as the Burnham Report.

If agreement cannot be reached the issues can go to arbitration only if both sides agree to ask for it. Terms of reference must be agreed, or decided by the chairman in default of such agreement. The arbitration body is set up by ACAS with an independent chairman mutually agreed and two others, one each from panels nominated by each side. The findings of the arbitrators are binding on both sides and on the Secretary of State who must give statutory effect to them unless certain steps are taken. If he wishes to vary the recommendations in any way he must have the authority of a Resolution passed by both Houses of Parliament that national economic circumstances do not permit of the recommendation being accepted. In that case the Secretary of State has the power, after consultation with the Burnham Committee, to give effect to any new scales he thinks are appropriate. Up to the present this power has not been used.

Though the Burnham system as described has been in operation since 1965 it has been the subject of controversy in certain respects. Among both teachers and local authorities the presence of government representatives on the management panel and the way this operates is the main bone of contention. Thus a 'concordat' exists between the local authorities and the government that no offer must be made and no claim accepted unless the Secretary of State has agreed the global sum involved. Secondly, should there be disagreement within the management panel over the *distribution* of any sum agreed then the weighted vote of the DES described above may be used. This of course substantially limits the room for manoeuvre of the management in any negotiations and arises from the fact that the Government pays such a large part of local authority expenditure through the Rate Support Grant and therefore claims a substantial say in how the money is spent.

On the teachers' side there is strong feeling, e.g. in the NUT, that the Government should not be represented on the management side, feelings echoed among sections of the management, as this inhibits free negotiation and leads to unsatisfactory agreements. This situation has led to the setting up of special official committees of enquiry into teachers' salaries, which have recommended substantial increases which the Government has had to accept.

**BURNHAM FURTHER EDUCATION COMMITTEE** The committee, under the RTA 1965, negotiates salaries of both part- and full-time teachers in all maintained establishments of further and higher education including teachers in adult education establishments. This effectively includes all further education colleges and institutions and polytechnics. It does not include universities. As for school teachers the composition is determined by the Secretary of State. The Chairman has normally been the same independent person as for the school teachers' committee and the management panel is drawn from the same associations of employers and the DES. The seventeen representatives of the teachers' side are drawn from the National Association of Teachers in Further and Higher Education (12), The Association of Principals of Colleges (2), The National Society for Art Education (1), The Association of Agricultural Education Staffs (1), the Association of Polytechnic Teachers (1). There are joint Secretaries, from management and teachers.

Procedures for achieving agreement and the resort to arbitration are as in the school teachers committee, as are the powers of the Secretary of State to vary an arbitration award.

In Further Education, unlike in primary and secondary, there is a

National Joint Council for Further Education Teachers in England and Wales which deals with conditions of service.

**BUSINESS EDUCATION COUNCIL, BEC**    Set up in 1974 following the recommendations of the Haslegrave Report the BEC is concerned with 'craft' and 'technician' levels of business education, that is education for work in industry, commerce, local and central government apart from technical and scientific work which is the concern of the Technician Education Council. Its job is to plan, administer and review a unified system of non degree courses; to devise suitable courses and approve, i.e. validate others; to establish standards of performance and assess them and to award certificates and diplomas accordingly.

BEC courses take place in Colleges of Further and Higher Education and lead to three levels of awards, General, National and Higher National with entry requirements ranging from none to O and A Levels respectively. There is a Certificate or Diploma for each level. The General Certificate and Diploma level courses aim to provide a broad educational foundation with emphasis on literacy and numeracy and may lead on to National Certificate and Diploma courses which in turn may lead on to Higher National qualifications. Minimum entry requirements may be waived in certain circumstances. BEC awards of the appropriate standard are recognized for entry to degree courses.

BEC is administered by the City and Guilds of London Institute through a representative machinery including business, local authority, teacher and Government interests, set up for the purpose. There is a separate Scottish counterpart. (*See* CGLI.)

# C

**CA' CANNY**    The name used at the end of the last century to indicate slow working as a form of industrial action. In the Seaman's Chronicle of October 24th 1896, 'ca' canny' was described as 'a handy phrase for a new instrument or policy which may be used by the workers in place of a strike'. Various descriptions have been applied to 'ca' canny' such as 'go-slow', 'slow-gear strike', 'lazy strike' — and ca' canny methods have been used in a variety of circumstances, for example a limitation of output by workers in order to keep up piecework prices — a response to management attempts to reduce piecework prices.

**CAPITAL**  Though economists have many definitions of 'capital' and describe many varieties of 'capital', in common usage it describes either money invested in a business for the purpose of producing goods or services or the actual physical goods themselves (capital goods) used in production e.g. buildings, machinery, sources of power, means of transport, stocks of raw materials or products used in manufacture of a final product, in fact everything involved in production except labour and land. In the former case people subscribing money to a company will receive 'shares' and the total subscribed is the 'share (or issued) capital'. The physical goods used in production e.g. buildings and machinery are sometimes called 'fixed capital' or 'real capital' as distinct from raw materials which may be described as 'circulating capital' (though this term has other uses).

Trade unionists in negotiation will demand the disclosure of all details concerning the company's capital in its various forms in order to make a true assessment of the company's wealth as well as its annual income.

Capital may appreciate, i.e. grow in value, or depreciate, i.e. drop in value e.g. through age or obsolescence. Companies set aside capital sums to cover depreciation and provide capital for replacement. Increases in value of capital, e.g. in the price of shares, may result in a 'capital gain' when sold.

**CAPITALISM**  This is best described as the system in which land, industry, commerce and services are privately owned for the purpose of private profit-making. Today state intervention in the economy is so widespread in one form or another that industrial economies are one way or another 'mixed' i.e. a combination of private and public ownership or public control directly or indirectly, wholly or partly. Capitalism is sometimes described as the 'free market' economy or an economy overwhelmingly based on 'private enterprise' as for example in the USA, though the 'free market' is subject to government controls of one kind or another.

The trade union movement, while working within a capitalist economy to do the best for their members, has traditionally espoused policies aiming at the extension of public ownership and control or the replacement of private by public ownership and control, usually described as nationalization.

Capitalism is also used by the Labour Movement as a term describing the political system based on a capitalist economy.

**CARD, MEMBERSHIP OF UNION**    A numbered card certifying paid-up membership of the union, or on which trade union subscriptions are entered.

**CARD CHECK, CARD INSPECTION**    Different unions have different methods and procedures for checking which workers in an establishment (or sometimes at a meeting) are paid-up members. Such members are said to be 'in compliance'. Card checks may take place periodically under the union rules, or *ad hoc*.

**CARD VOTE**    Though the commonest form of voting at both the TUC and trade union conferences is by show of hands, provision normally exists in the rules for a card vote to be demanded by delegates or ordered by the Chairman. This means that instead of the decision being determined by a majority of *delegates* it is determined by adding up the membership figures each delegate represents and declaring a majority according to the membership that delegates voting represent. A card vote is conducted by an authorized delegate of the union handing a card, on which the officially agreed membership is written or printed, to official tellers or scrutineers who then tot up the totals.

**CASE WORK**    When a union acts in defence of an individual or group of its members where particular problems have arisen with management which do not, in the first instance at any rate, involve or need not involve collective action (e.g. industrial action) the negotiation is in some unions described as case work. A great deal of a union's work is of this kind and matters may be settled by case work which obviate the need for further action. Case work may sometimes lead to legal action through the courts in defence of members.

**CASH LIMITS (FOR LOCAL AUTHORITIES ETC.)**    Cash Limits are a major device of the Government for controlling public expenditure and operate mainly in the system of grant aid to local authorities and in pay negotiations with its own employees.

Before 1976 when the device was first operated, if, for a justifiable reason such as a greater rate of inflation than anticipated or a higher

# Cash Limits

level of salary and wage increases than expected, the grant allotted proved inadequate to carry out the approved programme then a supplementary grant could be sought for and voted by Parliament. Under the cash limits systems, however, this is no longer the case. Now a fixed allowance is made in advance for estimated inflation and for wage and salary increases. Though these allowances may be well below the actual increases in prices and pay, the ceiling of grant initially fixed cannot be exceeded, so creating severe difficulties for local authorities, unless the Government is prepared to alter its policy.

Since Local Authorities are responsible for the wages and salaries of a large section of the workforce, the cash limit imposed has clearly an important influence on the course of collective bargaining. Until the Local Government Planning and Land Act, 1980, it was always open to local authorities to supplement the grant received, if it was found inadequate to meet programme costs of services or wage and salary agreements by increasing rates. Under the Act, however, this power is severely inhibited by the method of paying grant which penalizes local authorities if they exceed levels of expenditure which the Government considers right on any of their services or other activities.

The Treasury is now able to exercise a very strict control on the provision of services and on pay settlements irrespective of what local authorities consider to be necessary in the exercise of their proper and legal responsibilities. This, clearly, can also have a serious influence on whether or not redundancies take place.

An important consequence of the cash limits policy has been to cause local authorities to be over-cautious in what they do, leading to underspending and so to unnecessary curtailment of activities to the detriment of essential services. The policy also places great power in the hands of the Treasury administrators so that major cuts can take place without parliamentary discussion.

At the same time, as the result for example of the overall grant to allow for wage increases in 1981 and the 4% suggested for 1982, an incomes policy can in effect be put into operation without any discussion let alone agreement with the trade unions. The TUC has consistently opposed the cash limits policy. In operation it has served to erode the Welfare State. (*See* Rate Support Grant, Welfare State.)

**CASTING VOTE**    When votes including the vote of the chairman for and against a motion or amendment are equal, the chairman has the right to a second vote, which he may exercise if he wishes. It is called a casting vote and gives a majority to one side or the other.

**CASUAL LABOUR**    Casual employment tends to occur where there is a fluctuation in demand for labour because of the nature of the industry. This can be seasonal in the case of the racing industry for example. The construction and ship repair industries also have problems arising from short term contracts. Casual employment haunted the docks for a long time. In effect it means that labour may be taken on for a day, or days, or a week or so, but without any guarantee of regular employment or benefit of employment protection legislation. Before the second World War, most manual workers did not have guaranteed employment and could be dismissed or 'laid-off' at very short notice. During the second World War, legislation introduced the principle of guaranteed employment over a wide field and industry built on that foundation after the war. In the docks industry decisive steps were taken, over a period, to achieve decasualization.

Some casual work attracts 'moonlighting' (people in regular jobs taking up occasional work in other occupations); examples are mini-cab drivers and temporary bar-staffs. (*See* 'Decasualization', 'The Aldington-Jones Report'.)

**CENTRAL ARBITRATION COMMITTEE (CAC)**    The Central Arbitration Committee was set up under the Employment Protection Act (1975) replacing the previous Industrial Arbitration Board and is made up of representatives of the TUC and CBI under an independent chairman. Though there is no direct relationship between ACAS and the CAC, if other steps have failed ACAS may refer disputes to it provided the parties agree. The CAC also has powers, for example, to deal with claims concerning disclosure of information by employers to unions for the purpose of collective bargaining; and with collective agreements which it is alleged are in breach of the Equal Pay Act and so are alleged to involve discrimination; and with issues arising from the operation of the Fair Wages Resolution.

If employers fail to comply with CAC recommendations it has powers, after various procedures have been followed, to make an enforceable award. Although in many cases the CAC is concerned with applying the law, it seeks to achieve agreement between the parties in dispute, taking into consideration the importance of achieving or maintaining good industrial relations. Thus it must take into account relevant parts of the Codes of Practice issued by ACAS, and in the case of Codes issued by the Department of Employment it may do so. The Codes are not legally binding but their provisions are admissible as evidence before the CAC. (*See* Arbitrators, Fair Wages Resolution, Codes of Practice.)

**CENTRE FOR POLICY STUDIES**    This was formed in 1974 to promote 'the methods available to improve the standard of living, the quality of life and the freedom of choice of the British people, with particular attention to social market policies' (i.e. virtually free market policies). Its first President and Chairman were Mrs. Margaret Thatcher and Sir Keith Joseph respectively. The Centre is widely regarded as an adjunct to the policy-making apparatus of the Tory Party and has financial backing from big business. While sometimes giving the appearance of objectivity it produces policy studies on current issues in line with Conservative Party thinking.

**CERTIFICATION OFFICER (FOR TRADE UNIONS AND EMPLOYERS' ASSOCIATIONS)**    The Certification Office was established in 1976. Under the Trade Union and Labour Relations Act 1974 and the Employment Protection Act 1975, the Certification Officer is responsible for:

- maintaining lists of trade unions and employers' associations;
- determining the independence of trade unions;
- seeing that trade unions and employers associations keep accounting records, have their accounts properly audited and submit annual returns;
- ensuring the periodical examination of members' superannuation schemes;
- securing observance of the statutory procedures for transfer of engagements, amalgamations and changes of name;
- supervizing the statutory requirements as to the setting up and operation of political funds and dealing with complaints by members about breaches of political fund rules.

Under the Employment Act 1980 the Certification Officer is, in addition, responsible for:

- administering payments towards expenditure incurred by trade unions in conducting secret ballots.

The Certification Officer's staff, accommodation and finance are provided by ACAS, but in exercising his functions the Certification Officer is not subject to any direction by the Service, or by any Minister of the Crown. He publishes an annual report.

**CHAPEL**   Trade union branches, based on workplace, in the printing and newspaper industry are known as chapels. The term covers all the printing unions, craft and general. The spokesman or shop steward of the chapel is known as the Father of the Chapel.

**CHECK-OFF**   Unions largely rely on having their contributions collected at the place of work. Some have official collectors or 'corresponding members'. The rules of other Unions require members to pay their contributions at their appropriate branch while it is not unusual now for trade unionists (mainly professional/white collar) to pay by banker's order.

An increasing number of trade unionists, however, have their trade union contributions deducted from their wages or salary by their employer. This system, known as the 'check-off' (a title first used in the United States) is spreading and about 75 per cent of trade unionists in manufacturing industry are now covered by it.

Because it makes for efficiency by avoiding differences over Union arrears payment problems, and the loss of time involved in the older system of union collectors, both sides of industry recognize its advantages.

There are, however, divergent views about the desirability of the 'check-off' and some trade unionists do not like the idea of employers handling their trade union contributions and knowing who is in the Union. This attitude has tended to diminish as the Unions have grown stronger.

**CHILD BENEFIT**   *See* Social Security.

**CITY   AND   GUILDS   OF   LONDON   INSTITUTE (CGLI)**   Known popularly as 'City and Guilds' the CGLI is an independent body, operating under a Royal Charter, which aims to develop vocational education and industrial training mainly for young people in industry. It helps them acquire knowledge and skills needed in their future careers by the provision of courses for use in further education colleges (and more recently, still to a very small extent, in schools).

These courses are at different levels based on standards accepted by the various industries and occupations concerned. They measure the young worker's achievement against these standards and their successful conclusion leads to Awards and Certificates which are generally accepted qualifications throughout industry. There are for example, Vocational Education Certificates based on C & G courses and assessments at FE Colleges; Industrial Achievement Awards based on tests of specific industrial skills developed by C & G within industry; Combined Certificates, for achievement combining vocational education and industrial training in preparation, for a career in for example the Motor Vehicle or Electronics industries.

Courses are developed for those at a more advanced level including highly specialized technologies and management skills and there are senior Awards available at the professional and equivalent stage. C & G also provides administrative services to the Technician and Business Education Councils and for a number of Joint Committees for National Certificates and Diplomas. Its technician courses are, however, in the process of being withdrawn as TEC develops its work, though they will continue to operate overseas.

Entry into C & G courses at 16 plus is not normally dependent on possession of GCE O Level or CSE certificates. Success in the courses is measured by both paper tests and assessment of practical work examined either by specialist teachers or people working in the industry.

Expertise and the maintenance of standards is guaranteed by the C & G Council and its specialist committees which are representative of employers, trade unions and professional organizations, teachers and LEA's, Government Departments and Industrial Training Boards. The actual teaching is done in colleges, HM Forces, Government Skillcentres and some schools. (*See* BEC, TEC.)

**CIVIL SERVICE ARBITRATION TRIBUNAL (CSAT)**     Until 1981, when there was a failure to agree, arbitration was normally available under the Whitley system to either side, in the case of staff, through either recognized associations or the Trade Union Side, national or departmental. Recourse to arbitration could be on certain matters affecting conditions of service with certain limitations and was through the Civil Service Arbitration Tribunal set up in 1925.

The Tribunal has an independent chairman and individuals chosen from panels representing both sides. Claims that can be referred to the Tribunal are questions of pay and allowances, weekly hours of work and leave. Individual cases are excluded as are questions of superannuation and numbers of staff employed. Pay includes all emoluments— bonuses, overtime rates, subsistence rates, travel and lodging allowances. Any pay claim above the maximum of the Principal's rate, however, can only go to arbitration if both sides agree. The National Trade Union Side has gone to arbitration only infrequently since the war.

Arbitration claims were submitted through the Department of Employment normally on agreed terms of reference; hearings were in public and the procedure was informal. If the members of the Tribunal disagreed the chairman could make an 'Umpire's Award'. The Government could refuse arbitration on 'grounds of policy', which gave it an advantage over the Trade Union Side but this right of refusal was not, it is claimed, often used. In addition, the Government was not itself obliged to go to arbitration when it wished to alter conditions of service. Its view was expressed in the words: 'It would be the negation of all government to submit to the view that the Executive has no right to take action in the public interest before this outside authority (the CSAT) has first of all prescribed what action it should take'.

The refusal of the Government to accept arbitration in the case of the 1981 pay claim overrode in practice the normal process of negotiation. Arbitration was conceded, however, in the 1982 claim.

**CLAUSE IV**    Trade unions with political and social aims affiliated to the Labour Party have been concerned in the past with controversy around Clause IV of the Labour Party's constitution. This states the Party's National objects as:

1 To organize and maintain in Parliament and in the country a Political Labour Party.
2 To co-operate with the General Council of the Trades Union Congress, or other kindred Organizations, in joint political or other action in harmony with the Party Constitution and Standing Orders.
3 To give effect as far as may be practicable to the principles from time to time approved by the Party Conference.

# Clause IV

4 To secure for the workers by hand or by brain the full fruits of their industry and the most equitable distribution thereof that may be possible upon the basis of the common ownership of the means of production, distribution, and exchange, and the best obtainable system of popular administration and control of each industry or service.
5 Generally to promote the Political, Social and Economic emancipation of the People, more particularly of those who depend directly upon their own exertions by hand or by brain for the means of life.
6 To co-operate with the Labour and Socialist organizations in the Commonwealth Overseas . . .
7 To co-operate with the Labour and Socialist organizations in other countries . . .

Shortly after the 1959 General Election when the Conservative Party increased its majority and Labour had lost three elections in a row, at a Special Conference of the party in November, 1959, Hugh Gaitskell, the party leader in a major speech referred to the party constitution 'written over forty years ago'. It needed, he said, to be brought up to date and he made specific reference to section 4 of Clause IV which dealt with common ownership etc. 'It implies', he said, 'that the only precise object we have is nationalization . . . It implies that we propose to nationalize everything, but do we? Everything? – the whole of light industry, the whole of agriculture, all the shops – every little pub and garage? Of course not. We have long ago come to accept . . . for the foreseeable future, at least in some form, a mixed economy; in which case, if this is our view . . . had we not better say so instead of going out of our way to court misrepresentation?'

These remarks sparked off what has been known as the Clause IV controversy, a major political argument on whether Clause IV should be revised. The controversy continued throughout the months that followed and finally ended with Clause IV left unamended at the 1960 Labour Party Conference. The conference, however, agreed to accept a statement that the party's social and economic objectives 'can be achieved only through an expansion of common ownership substantial enough to give the community power over the commanding heights of the economy'. The statement however also 'recognized' that 'both public and private enterprise have a place in the economy' and that further extension of common ownership should be decided from time to time in the light of these objectives and according to the circumstances 'with due regard for the views of the workers and consumers concerned'.

This has been generally interpreted as acceptance by the Labour Party of what is described as a 'mixed economy'. The basic issues of the Clause IV controversy are still the subject of political argument within the trade union and labour movement and a bone of contention between left and right wing activists, between those who want more and those who want less socialism.

**CLEGG COMMISSION**    *See* Comparability, Pay.

**CLOSED SHOP (UNION MEMBERSHIP AGREEMENTS — UMA)**    The closed shop takes two forms. In a pre-entry closed shop a person has to be a member of an appropriate trade union before he can work in the establishment. In a post-entry closed shop a person is obliged to join an appropriate union within a specified time after being accepted for employment. The term formally used for the closed shop is 'union membership agreement' (UMA). About a quarter of the total workforce were in closed shops in 1979 though only a minority of these were in pre-entry closed shops.

Closed shops are the subject of sharp controversy. They developed as a means of defending pay and conditions won by the unions from being undermined by persons willing to work for worse pay and conditions. They are backed up by the argument that the benefits from union-negotiated agreements go to all workers irrespective of union membership and it is not known that non members refuse these benefits; such non members are sometimes perjoratively called 'free riders'. Though some employers oppose closed shops many see the advantage of negotiating with unions representing the entire workforce and the stability this gives to industrial relations.

The Donovan Commission found the convincing union arguments for the closed shop to be that in some industries 'it is impossible or difficult for a union to establish effective and stable organization without it, and it may be needed to display the workers' bargaining strength to the full'. Conditions for the operation of closed shops are governed by recent Labour legislation. This deals with the possibility of dismissal of a worker, or action short of dismissal against a worker, for non membership of a union. Under the Employment

# Closed Shop

Protection Act 1975, dismissal was not unfair if there is a union membership agreement for employees of the particular class concerned and the worker is not a member of the specified union or has refused to join, unless he genuinely objected on religious grounds to trade union membership of any kind. Sometimes in such circumstances the employee has been expected to pay the equivalent of the union fee to charity. Some agreements provide that certain categories of worker need not be members of unions named in the agreement. In practice the great majority of UMAs allow for new entrants to claim exemptions on one or more grounds and impose no obligation on those who were not union members at the time the UMA was reached to join a trade union.

Under the Employment Act, 1980, amendments were made to the closed shop conditions hitherto operative. Thus the provision for religious objection has been extended to include 'grounds of conscience or deeply held convictions'. Since these grounds are obviously hard to define the amendment must be regarded as intended to weaken closed shop agreements. Other instances where dismissal is now 'unfair' are: where the worker was not a member of the relevant union when the union membership agreement took effect; where in the case of agreements made subsequent to the 1980 Act they are not approved by a ballot with the support of at least 80 per cent of all the workers concerned; where the worker, already employed, was not a member of a relevant union at the time of or after the holding of the ballot. These, like the conscience clauses, can only serve to weaken the growth of closed shops. They leave the way open for litigation, with liability to pay compensation in the case of an adverse decision for the trade union concerned.

The 1980 Act also provides through an industrial tribunal for a person employed in, or seeking to join a firm with, a closed shop agreement not to be unreasonably refused membership of the union or be expelled from it. There is an Independent Review Committee set up by the TUC to consider appeals from workers who have been dismissed as the result of being excluded from or refused admission to a union in closed shop establishments.

A Code of Practice on Closed Shop Agreements and Arrangements was issued in December, 1980 by the Department of Employment and has been critically commented on by the TUC which accuses the Government of aiming seriously to weaken trade union organisation. ACAS felt unable to endorse the Code.

# Codes of Practice

In January 1982, in the Employment Bill 1982, the Government has proposed legislation designed to limit closed shops. (*See* Employment Bill 1982.)

In addition the Government announced the decision that closed shop agreements should be reviewed every 5 years. This provision could be introduced in relation to existing closed shops either one or two years after passage of the Bill. Continuation of closed shops would require support of 80 per cent of those covered or 85 per cent of those voting.

**CODES OF PRACTICE**    Codes of Practice aim to set standards in various fields of industrial relations with a view to their improvement. Provision for issuing them is now contained in the Employment Protection Act. This enables ACAS to issue Codes and requires them to do so in the case of disclosure of information for the purposes of collective bargaining and time off for trade union duties and activities. A third code issued by ACAS under the Act deals with disciplinary procedures and practices in employment.

In addition, the Employment Act 1980 gives the Secretary of State for Employment powers to issue codes for the improvement of industrial relations and Codes have been issued on Picketting and the Closed Shop which have been strongly criticized by the TUC and which ACAS felt unable to endorse. Both the Commission for Racial Equality and the Equal Opportunities Commission are also empowered to issue codes in their respective fields as far as employment is concerned. So too the Health and Safety Commission is empowered, with the consent of the Secretary of State to issue *approved* codes of practice giving guidance on the operation of the Health and Safety at Work Act.

Codes of Practice are not legally binding and failure to observe them will not render anyone liable to legal proceedings. ACAS and Dept. of Employment Codes are nevertheless admissible in evidence in industrial tribunal cases and in hearings of the Central Arbitration Committee which must take into account any relevant provision of a code. In the case of a code issued by the Secretary of State the provisions may be admissible in evidence before the courts as well as before industrial tribunals and the CAC.

ACAS is obliged to publish a draft of any code for consultative purposes. After any revisions have been made the draft goes to the Secretary of State for Employment and if he approves it, it must then be laid before both Houses of Parliament. After parliamentary authority is given ACAS may issue the Code which becomes operative by order of the Secretary of State.

Before publishing the consultative draft of a code of his own, the Secretary of State must first consult ACAS.

It should be noted that where there is an 'approved' Code of Practice, as in the case of the Health and Safety Codes, a court is *required* to admit in evidence any of its relevant provisions, failure to observe which may be taken as proof of non-compliance with the Act.

Codes of Practice, though not legally binding, play an increasingly important part in industrial relations as points of reference though their provisions, as in the case of the Department of Employment's Codes of Picketting and the Closed Shop, can be the subject of sharp controversy. Agreements between unions and employers may establish conditions superior to those in a code but in general the codes carry great weight. (*See* Closed Shop, Health and Safety, Picketting).

**COLLECTING STEWARD**   The person appointed within a trade union branch to collect contributions, normally at the place of work.

**COLLECTIVE BARGAINING**   Collective bargaining in all its current complexities is the bread and butter activity of trade unions, their lifesblood, what their members regard as the reason for their existence, the normal means of defending their interests and maintaining and improving their living standards. The term covers the various negotiating methods and procedures generally used to reach agreement between employers and unions at all levels, from plant to industry, whether local, regional or national, or between single unions and employers or groups of unions and employers' federations.

The procedures vary from industry to industry and normally result from voluntary agreement though in some cases they may be dictated by the law (e.g. teachers). They normally set out the different stages of the negotiating process between management and unions, the occasion for the use of conciliation or arbitration machinery, the reference of issues to third parties or committees agreed by both sides or laid down by legislation.

When collective bargaining fails to produce a settlement the situation becomes one of industrial dispute which may lead to industrial action or arbitration in one form or another.

Collective agreements are not legally binding unless so stated in writing. But they are binding on individual employees to the extent that they are incorporated in their contracts of employment.

**COMBINE COMMITTEES**    *See* Shop Stewards.

**COMMISSION ON INDUSTRIAL RELATIONS (CIR)**    An institution set up by the Labour Government in 1969. Under the Conservative Government of 1970 it was given statutory powers and enlarged functions to settle disputes over procedure agreements and bargaining agents. With its enlarged authority it became an institution of the Industrial Relations Act of 1971 and was boycotted by the TUC affiliated trade unions. The CIR was abolished under the measures adopted by the Labour Government elected in 1974 to repeal the Industrial Relations Act.

**COMPANY**    When a group of people join together to form a business, whether to produce goods, or provide services or lend money, they form a company. Companies are of various kinds regulated by the law. The commonest form is a Joint Stock Company where the money (capital) is raised by issuing shares and the shareholders have limited liability, to the extent of their investment only, for the company's debts. Such companies are normally Public Companies issuing shares to the public. Companies may be Private and their shares may not be offerred to the public but are privately subscribed, e.g. by a family. A Private Company may have limited liability as above or its members may have unlimited liability, that is they are liable for debt beyond their share in the company to include their whole wealth.

All companies have to register with the Registrar of Companies, have to provide audited accounts at the end of each financial year, and are subject to the Disclosure of Information provisions of the Employment and Protection Act. All limited companies must make available for public scrutiny information about their activities as laid down by law and must circulate their accounts to the shareholders. Private unlimited companies are less regulated in this respect. Parent companies are obliged to file accounts not only for themselves but for their subsidiaries.

# Company Taxation

Companies are administered by Boards of Directors (or sometimes a Director) who issue an annual report. They must hold an annual meeting at which shareholders may be present. Voting strength of shareholders is according to the extent of their holding. It is increasingly common for shareholders even with negligible voting power to raise questions on company policy at the annual meeting and at other times as a form of pressure and publicity.

Later figures available (end 1981) show the 15 largest (by turnover) British companies as in Table 1.

**Table 1**

| Rank by turnover | COMPANY | Main activity |
|---|---|---|
| 1 | British Petroleum Co. | Oil industry |
| 2 | 'Shell' Transport & Trading | Oil industry |
| 3 | BAT Industries | Tobacco, retailing, paper & cosmetics |
| 4 | Imperial Chemical Industries | Chemicals, fibres, paints, etc. |
| 5 | Unilever Ltd. | Food products, detergents, etc. |
| 6 | Imperial Group | Tobacco, food, drink and packaging |
| 7 | Ford Motor Co. | Motor vehicle manufacturers |
| 8 | Esso Petroleum Co. | Oil industry |
| 9 | Shell UK | Oil industry |
| 10 | BL | Motor vehicle manufacturers |
| 11 | Rio Tinto-Zinc Corporation | Mining & industrial — metals & fuel |
| 12 | General Electric Co. | Electrical engineers |
| 13 | Allied Breweries | Brewers, vintners, hoteliers, etc. |
| 14 | Rothmans International | Tobacco manufacturers |
| 15 | Grand Metropolitan | Hotel props, milk prds. brewers, etc. |

(*Source*: *Labour Research Department.*)

**COMPANY TAXATION**   Company taxation is a crucial factor for trade unions assessing a company's ability to pay in wage negotiations and in a union's demand for the fullest disclosure of information on its financial position.

The main tax levied on companies is Corporation Tax which is payable at the rate of 52% for companies with profits over £200,000 and 40% for companies with profits less than £80,000 with a sliding scale for those in between those figures. In practice, however, companies do not pay as much on the pre-tax profits shown in their annual reports.

Thus, before paying Corporation Tax, the company is allowed to deduct in any year the cost of machinery bought in that year (and frequently in previous years too!) instead of merely deducting a sum for depreciation, though the annual report will show a deduction for depreciation only. This is known as the *capital allowance*. For other capital assets the deductions allowed are less. Tax avoidance occurs on a large scale when non-manufacturing companies buy machinery which they then lease to manufacturing companies.

Again, there is a Stock Appreciation allowance whereby the full value of stocks held is not taxable. There are also tax concessions for companies whose stocks have fallen during the recession. The various plant and stock allowances (including leasing) cost the Exchequer over £9 billion in 1980/1.

Liability to pay tax is also reduced when companies increase dividends to shareholders. These are paid net of tax to the shareholders and the company pays the tax at the more advantageous standard rate. This 'Advance Corporation Tax' is deducted from the amount of Corporation Tax paid.

Other concessions include reduced prices for gas and electricity for bulk users, tax and loan benefits for small businesses and relief in certain cases for industrial and commercial buildings, development land tax and rates on commercial and industrial property. There are also tax advantages for companies (and individuals) which invest in small businesses. The March 1982 Budget, in new provisions affecting capital gains, gave further substantial relief to companies including relief involving Corporation Tax.

Because of the various allowances and of tax avoidance, less than 40 per cent of companies paid corporation tax. The tax in 1980/1 yielded less than 3 per cent of the national revenue.

**COMPANY UNION**  Independence of the employer is the crucial characteristic of bona fide trade unionism. A company union is a union which is either created or organized directly or indirectly by the employer or with his connivance or whose expenses may either be paid or subsidized by the employer, or which acts under the decisive influence of the employer. Company unions are seen as identifying themselves with the interests of the employer and not of the employees. They may be organized in order to prevent or forestall the creation of an independent union.

If employees belong to an independent union they find that the company union may then be the union recognized by the employer for the purpose of negotiation. Company unions will be opposed to industrial action against the employer in all circumstances. They cannot be considered as part of the trade union movement. They are sometimes called 'scab' unions. In the banking industry for example there are some bona fide unions which compete with a number of 'unions' in particular banks which are accused of being company unions.

**COMPARABILITY**    Comparability is a principle which has operated in regulating pay in certain occupations for a considerable time. It has also been invoked from time to time in the public service, the most recent example being the appointment by the last Labour Government of the Clegg Commission to examine the terms and conditions of workers in the public services and to report on the possibility of establishing acceptable bases of comparison with terms and conditions for other comparable work. Its terms of reference were 'to assess the appropriate forms of comparisons with terms and conditions in other sections of the economy and identify relevant comparators'. The motivating force behind demands for comparability in the public service has been the view of the trade unions concerned that public service workers are disadvantaged in comparison with similar workers in the private sector.

The Clegg Commission (abolished in 1980 by the Thatcher government though its reports were accepted by it) covered the cases, for example, of Local Authority manual workers, National Health Service workers, ambulance workers, university manual workers, and teachers in primary, secondary and further education. Though in all cases improvements in pay were recommended and accepted by government, employers and unions, the unions continued to argue that though they clearly showed that public service pay lagged behind the private sector, the problem of low pay in the public service was not solved by the reports of the commission on comparability. The unions representing the low-paid manual workers asked that in determining decisions on comparability the principle of 'indexation' linked with the rise in average earnings of male manual workers or the level of social security benefits should be adopted.

Unions representing nurses and teachers argued for the updating of pay awards to the real level of previous awards which had been made in an attempt to solve the problem of comparability.

Neither approach was, however, adopted by the Commission. Instead it operated on the basis of 'job comparison', something very difficult to estimate satisfactorily. In the case of the low-paid the unions' objection was that comparison of low-paid with other low-paid inevitably meant the low-paid ending up low-paid. In the other case, e.g. teachers, the difficulty exists of finding genuinely comparable jobs and then of how to make the comparisons. The Commission found this impossible to do satisfactorily and finally used its judgement in adopting other methods of comparison.

The principle of comparability is also in common use as a negotiating factor in all sections of industry.

**COMPOSITE RESOLUTION, COMPOSITING**   At trade union conferences and at the TUC there are frequently resolutions on a topic which are very similar or have a number of features in common. To facilitate discussion and save time it is customary for the branches or unions concerned to be called together in order to reach agreement on a wording acceptable to all in a single resolution. This process is called compositing and the new resolution is known as a 'composite'. In some unions compositing is carried out by a committee empowered to do so.

**CONCILIATION**   When a dispute threatens or after it has occurred and negotiations have broken down on an issue, a third party may be called in, in the hope of getting the parties to the dispute round the table again, so re-opening the possibility of a settlement with the aid of the third party. This process is known as conciliation and conciliators, who are available from ACAS — which has the statutory responsibility for providing conciliation — are considered to be independent and neutral persons trusted to act impartially and acceptable to both sides. Conciliation does not normally take place until the agreed procedures for negotiation have been exhausted. Requests for conciliation may come from unions or employers, separately or jointly. The conciliator cannot impose a settlement; this is the responsibility of the parties concerned.

Conciliation is essentially an informal process. It is therefore flexible and can work in a variety of ways, for example through confidential discussions, either separately with each party or jointly. It is

# Conduct of Meetings

not the conciliator's job to pronounce on the merits of the case, though he may make suggestions about how a dispute may be solved and will provide any necessary information, for example on the legal position, towards that end. The conciliator depends on his powers of persuasion based on his assessment of the issue after gathering all the available information from both sides. The very fact that he has been called in indicates a degree of reasonableness on both sides and a wish to avoid or end industrial action.

Conciliation may occur in a dispute between an individual worker and his employer as well as in a collective dispute between the employer and the union.

Examples of the former may include disputes concerning unfair dismissal, equal pay, race or sex discrimination, guarantee payments, trade union activities, maternity rights including maternity pay, redundancy matters etc. In such cases attempts at conciliation usually precede recourse to tribunals, although the right of the individual remains to have the case referred to an industrial tribunal if conciliation fails. The settlement of an individual's claim through ACAS conciliation is, however, final; no application may then be made to a tribunal. If, however, an individual dispute gives rise to a collective one which may be resolved by conciliation, the right to go to a tribunal remains even if it is not invoked, because it is statutory.

**CONDUCT OF MEETINGS**   In addition to rules, constitutional authorities in unions, e.g. branches, will have Standing Orders for the orderly conduct of meetings. These are pretty much of a standard pattern throughout the trade union movement. They would make provision for the order of business on a meeting's agenda (unless this is provided for in the rules) and may also indicate times of starting and finishing business.

Meetings normally begin with apologies for absence which have been notified, go on to approval of the 'minutes' (records) of the previous meeting and any matters arising from the minutes that are not on the agenda as separate items. This may be followed by any correspondence from Head or regional office, from within branch, or from recognized outside bodies. Correspondence may be commented upon and may sometimes give rise to resolutions if this is provided for. Then there are various reports from officers, the committee and any sub-committees if relevant. Conditions are laid down for the time that may be taken in moving and seconding resolutions and amendments to resolutions, for speakers in the discussion, and for moving the closure of a debate if this is applicable.

Standing Orders lay down the powers of the chairman, particularly his power to interpret the rules if they are called into question. They also lay down the conditions under which the chairman's ruling may be challenged by a member and in which he may exercise a casting vote if there is a tie in the vote on any resolution or amendment. Provision is also made for the suspension of standing orders, usually for the purpose of altering the notified agenda in some way, and for the taking of emergency motions.

Standing Orders will also deal with rules on the interruption of speakers in debate, on 'points of order' which can be asserted only if the chairman agrees that the speaker has either strayed unjustifiably from his subject or has broken a standing order or rule of the branch. In such cases the speaker must be asked to keep to the point or to the rule. Speakers may not (unless special provision for this exists) be interrupted on 'points of information', which can be misused as a device for members to intervene in an otherwise orderly debate. Some standing orders allow for a 'balance of debate', that is, speakers called in turn for and against a resolution; others simply take speakers in order of request. Debates are normally closed either when there are no more speakers or when the 'closure' is carried. This is done by the meeting agreeing to take the vote, on someone moving this or proposing 'that the question be put'. A discussion (though not normally a debate on a motion) may be closed by someone moving 'next business' which is then put to the vote of the meeting.

A debate on a motion may be closed without a vote if 'the previous question' is carried. Debate on this, if moved, must take precedence over any other amendment on motions before the meeting. The effect of the 'previous question' being carried is that the meeting has agreed to take no decision on the motion concerned one way or the other. Standing orders may also provide for a motion or a report to be 'referred back'. Reference back means that the matter under discussion be reconsidered and brought forward on a later occasion.

Business in progress may be interrupted if the agenda provides for some other issue to be discussed at a fixed time as 'fixed business' or 'timed business'. Again, if business at a meeting is not concluded, the meeting is sometimes, if the rules permit, adjourned to a later date. In that case the meeting is formally concluded only after the adjourned meeting is held.

In meetings much depends on the quality of chairmanship. A good chairman controls a meeting with good humour and friendliness. While having an eye on the time and seeing that things move along briskly, he should try to make no-one feel left out who wishes to speak, as long as they are acting within the rules and conventions of the union. If people make mistakes he should be sympathetic and helpful and explain where they have gone wrong. He himself must know the rules and standing orders accurately and be able to refer to them if necessary. He should be thoroughly familiar with the agenda of any meeting and have studied in advance the various possible outcomes and their consequences so as to guide the meeting if necessary or if requested. It is common for the chairman and officers to approve the agenda before it is issued by the secretary (see above).

The chairman is responsible for seeing that meetings start and finish on time and that any decisions reached are as clear as possible in the circumstances.

**CONFEDERATION OF BRITISH INDUSTRY (CBI)**  The CBI is the most important and best-known organization of emp- loyer on such bodies as ACAS and the National Economic Develop- man of British employers in industry and commerce and is regarded as the opposite number of the Trades Union Congress (TUC), speak- ing on behalf of workers. It is financed by its membership which includes individual firms, nearly all the nationalized industries, and trade and employers' associations, in total amounting to over 200,000 companies employing some 10 million workers. It is an independent body which is generally taken to reflect its members' views on major matters of economic and industrial relations policy and is regularly consulted by the government. It represents the emp- loyer on such bodies as ACAS and the National Economic Develop- ment Council and nominates members to a wide variety of public organizations to represent the viewpoint of the management side of industry and commerce. It also appoints members to industrial tri- bunals.

The CBI is governed by a Council made up of over four hundred members from all sections of its membership and has as chairman the President. Guiding the Council is the President's committee, consisting of leading industrialists, which advises the President on all important issues and reports to the Council. Although the President is nominally the chief public representative of the CBI, the main spokesman is more frequently the Director General who is a paid official and occupies an important place in British public life.

There are over thirty standing committees of the Council as well as many working parties and study groups covering numerous aspects of industry and commerce, and aspects of British life of concern to industry and commerce. The committees are serviced by six policy directorates which do the groundwork necessary for the confederation's policy-making. These directorates are for Company Affairs, Economic Matters, Education, Training and Technology, Smaller Firms, Social Affairs, and Overseas Problems.

A network of Regional Councils covers the UK. This keeps the CBI informed of what is happening locally and regionally, is concerned with local and regional industrial problems, and keeps in touch with local authorities and local MPs.

**CONFEDERATIONS & FEDERATIONS OF UNIONS**  Apart from the TUC itself which is a grand 'Confederation of trade unions' there are numerous joint bodies in the trade union movement formed for mutual assistance with some exercising a negotiating function. These include:

The General Federation of Trade Unions (GFTU)
The Confederation of Shipbuilding and Engineering Unions (CSEU)
The Council of Civil Service Unions (CCSU)
The National Federation of Professional Workers (NFPW)
The National Affiliation of Carpet Trade Unions
The National Association of Unions in the Textile Trade
The Northern Counties Textile Trades Federation
The Scottish Council of Textile Trade Unions
The Confederation of Entertainment Unions
The Federation of Broadcasting Unions
The Federation of Theatre Unions
The National Federation of Furniture Trade Unions
The Confederation of Insurance Trade Unions
The Joint Committee of Light Metal Trade Unions
The National Craftsmen's Co-ordinating Committee (Iron and Steel)

The Council of Post Office Unions
The British Seafarers' Joint Council

In addition to the foregoing, the Industrial Committees of the TUC perform co-ordinating functions in the Transport, Construction, Fuel and Power, Health Services, Health and Catering, Local Government, Printing, Steel, Textiles, Clothing and Footwear industries. In many industries there are Trade Union sides of Joint negotiating bodies which co-ordinate union activities and negotiating policies, e.g. the joint negotiating bodies in big companies like ICI and Fords. (*See* GFTU, CSEU, CCSU, NFPW.)

**CONFEDERATION OF SHIPBUILDING & ENGINEERING UNIONS (CSEU)**   This body is numerically the largest trade union grouping outside the TUC. It was formed in 1935 and has 23 unions in affiliation, with a total membership of approximately 2.5 million members. The main function of the CSEU is to co-ordinate the various trade unions for negotiating purposes in dealing with the Engineering Employers, the Shipbuilding Employers and British Rail (for railway workshops). In addition it serves as a representative spokesman in dealings with Government and Governmental institutions in matters affecting trade unionists in the industries concerned.

*Affiliated unions:*

1 Boilermakers, Shipwrights, Blacksmiths and Structural Workers, Amalgamated Association of (ASBSBSW)
2 Clerical, Technical and Supervisory Staffs, Association of (ACTS – the white-collar section of TGWU)
3 Construction, Allied Trades and Technicians, Union of (UCATT)
4 Domestic Appliance and General Metal Workers, National Union of (NUDAGMW)
5 Electrical, Electronic, Telecommunication and Plumbing Union (EETPU)
6 Electrical and Engineering Staffs Association (EESA – the white-collar section of EETPU)
7 Engineering Workers, Amalgamated Union of (Constructional Section)
8 Engineering Workers, Amalgamated Union of (Engineering Section)

9 Engineering Workers, Amalgamated Union of (Foundry Section)
10 Engineering Workers, Amalgamated Union of (Technical and Supervisory Section)
11 Furniture, Timber and Allied Trades Union (FTAT)
12 General and Municipal Workers, National Union of (GMWU)
13 Managerial, Administrative, Technical and Supervisory Association (MATSA – the white-collar section of GMWU)
14 Metal Mechanics, National Society of (NSMM)
15 Metalworkers' Union, Associated (AMU)
16 Patternmakers and Allied Craftsmen, Association of (APAC)
17 Professional, Executive, Clerical and Computer Staff (APEX)
18 Scalemakers, National Union of (NUS)
19 Screw, Nut, Bolt and Rivet Trade Union (SNBRTU)
20 Scientific, Technical and Managerial Staffs, Association of (ASTMS)
21 Sheet Metal Workers, Coppersmiths, Heating and Domestic Engineers, National Union of (NUSMWCHDE)
22 Transport and General Workers' Union (TGWU – Power Group)
23 Transport and General Workers' Union (TGWU – Vehicle Building and Automotive Group)

**CONGLOMERATE**    The name given to a business organization, normally large, where a parent or holding company controls a number of satellite companies engaged in widely varying activities, industrial or commercial, which may have little or no common link apart from the financial control of the parent company. Companies must under the law list their subsidiary and associate companies in their annual reports and accounts. Such information is valuable to trade unions in collective bargaining and should be demanded in negotiations.

**CONSPIRACY (THE CONSPIRACY AND PROTECTION OF PROPERTY ACT, 1875)**    In early trade union history trade unions were harassed when they undertook action in furtherance of their demands by the operation of laws which were interpreted to charge them with 'conspiracy', a common law crime. Thus the Criminal Law Amendment Act of 1871 allowed the operation of criminal conspiracy charges against strikers even though it repealed an earlier law which had allowed other criminal charges. As the result of trade union pressure a new Act was passed in 1875, the Conspiracy and Protection of Property Act, which provided legal immunity for strikers from charges of conspiracy when they acted in furtherance of a trade dispute. This was an important step in strengthening the power of unions to act in defence of their members and became the basis for further protective legislation. The Act still prohibits strikes without notice endangering life or property. (*See* Immunities.)

**CONSTRUCTIVE DISMISSAL**   *See* Unfair Dismissal.

**CONTINUOUS EMPLOYMENT**   Various rights (e.g. redundancy, maternity and guarantee payments, protection against unfair dismissal, re-instatement rights) enjoyed by employees depend on a qualifying period of 'continuous employment' and this, in turn, depends on working normally for a certain minimum of hours each week. Rules are laid down by employment law for deciding what counts towards continuous employment and on the calculation of working hours when the worker's contract does not provide for normal working hours. Rules are also laid down for calculating a week's pay for the purpose of determining an individual's rights. The main rules are as follows:

Employment is worked out in weeks, the week ending with a Saturday. Any week in which the employee works for 16 hours or more and any week in which the worker is under contract normally to work for 16 hours or more, counts towards a continuous period of employment. Spells of absence through sickness, injury or pregnancy, temporary lay-offs and holiday breaks and temporary short-time working, provided the basic contract remains unchanged, count towards continuous employment even if, as a result, actual hours worked are less than 16. Workers with five years or more service who work on the same basis at least 8 hours a week have the whole of their service counted. Workers whose contracts are changed so as to reduce their hours below 16 but more than 8, can count all their service if the contract is revised subsequently within twenty-six weeks to raise the hours back to 16 or more. Finally, any right once acquired by a period of continuous service is not lost as long as the working hours remain 8 or more.

A week may also count in some circumstances even if there is no contract of employment during the course of it. This applies if the employee is away for all or part of the week:

(a) through sickness or injury, so long as the absence is not more than 26 weeks, for example if the employee is re-engaged after having had the contract ended during the period of absence
(b) through temporary cessation of work
(c) in circumstances in which, by custom or arrangement, the employment is regarded as continuing
(d) wholly or partly through pregnancy or confinement; this can occur where a woman has no contractual right to maternity leave and goes off her employer's books while she is away having a baby, but returns within 29 weeks in the exercise of her statutory right to return.

The law also covers a number of special circumstances. Important among these are the consequences of a finding of unfair dismissal. If this is upheld and the employee is subsequently re-instated or re-engaged, then all the weeks which fall between the date when the dismissal happened and the date when work is resumed count towards continuous employment.

Although weeks in which workers are on strike do not count in calculating the *number* of weeks of continuous employment, strikes after 5 July, 1964 do not break the *continuity* of the period of employment. Lock-outs do not normally terminate the contract and, therefore, normally create no problem. Those that do terminate the contract which then has to be revived are treated like strikes if they occurred after 5 July, 1964. Time spent on strikes and lock-outs before 5 July 1964, however, does count, and continuity is not broken.

The various provisions outlined earlier do not apply to registered dock workers engaged in dock work; they have special provisions. If a registered dock worker moves to other work for the same employer and becomes entitled to various rights, his previous dock work will count.

Similarly, if a worker has worked abroad for an employer and later worked for him in this country and become eligible for various rights, then his foreign service counts.

Normally continuous service applies only to service with the current employer. But it operates if the business is transferred to another employer and in a number of other special circumstances. *See* Department of Employment Pamphlet No. 11 for the detailed rules for calculating a week's pay and for a comprehensive statement of all matters concerning continuous employment.

**CONTRACTS OF EMPLOYMENT: NOTICE OF TERMINATION OF EMPLOYMENT**    The provision for periods of notice is made by the Employment Protection (Consolidation) Act 1978, Section 49.

(1) From the Employer

The periods of notice differ according to length of service and are set out below:

Up to 4 weeks service ............................................. none
After 4 weeks but less than 2 years ........................ 1 week
After 2 years service ......................................... 2 weeks
Then 1 week for each year's continuous service up to the maximum of 12 weeks.

(2) From the Employee

Notice given by an employee who has been employed for 4 weeks or more shall not be less than 1 week.

*No Right to Notice*

Employees normally working less than 16 hours a week, but those employees with 5 years service who work at least 8 hours a week and workers whose working hours are dropped from over 16 to less than 16, but more than 8, and this drop lasts for no more than 26 weeks, will have the same rights as if they worked 16 hours each week.

*Pay in Lieu of Notice*

Entitlement to notice can be waived and wages taken in lieu. But if wages are refused, the contract continues until notice expires. In a disputed dismissal where reinstatement is hoped for it is therefore advantageous not to accept wages in lieu, and to continue to turn up for work. This would apply especially in cases of dismissal for union activity.

The law in no way affects the right of either party to terminate the contract without notice if the conduct of the other justifies it. If the justification is disputed, either party can take action through the County (or, in Scotland, the Sheriff) Court for breach of contract, or through an industrial tribunal which deals with dismissals.

Not all employees are covered by the Act. Not covered are: registered dock workers engaged in dock work; crown servants; most employees on fixed term contracts. It should be noted that the reason for a category being excluded, e.g. dock workers or crown servants, is normally that such categories are covered by other arrangements. Again, if a contract of employment gives rights to longer notice than the minimum in the Act, then the longer period of notice applies. Thus teachers, for example, are subject to considerably longer periods of notice than those stipulated in the Act.

The Act gives a number of guarantees on notice to employees. Thus a worker who is dismissed as redundant is still entitled to receive due notice of termination under a contract of employment or under the Act whichever is the greater. Similarly the Act guarantees minimum pay during notice according to what an employee would have expected to earn during normal working hours subject to certain conditions. Sick or holiday pay, if in operation during the notice period, may be deducted by the employer from the notice pay. The employee also has certain rights of payment, if the employer is insolvent, from the Department of Employment.

The rights to notice and minimum pay are enforceable in the County and Sheriff Courts if either employer or employee wish to bring an action in cases where they consider they have incurred loss. (*See* Redundancy Payments.)

**CONTRACTS OF EMPLOYMENT, WRITTEN STATEMENT** All employees should have a contract of employment. Such a contract in fact exists as soon as the employee proves his acceptance of an employer's terms and conditions of employment by starting work. The contract may be written, oral or implied except in the case of apprentices and merchant seamen whose contracts must be in writing. Both employer and employee are bound by the terms offered and accepted, which are enforceable in the civil courts whether the contract is in writing or not. The contract may be of indefinite duration or for a fixed period.

A number of terms of employment are implied by common law. For example the employer is obliged to provide a safe system of work. Just as the employer must pay wages, so the employee must observe the lawful and reasonable orders of his employer and the conditions of any collective agreement. He cannot, however, be required to do a job outside his own competence or skill or to start a new job a long distance away from his present job unless the contract so provides. Again, the employee should not at any time work for a

# Contracts of Employment

competitor while he is employed by a particular employer.

The Employment Protection (Consolidation) Act 1978 (Sections 1—7):

(a) gives both employers and employees rights to minimum periods of notice to terminate employment, and
(b) lays a duty on employers to give their employees a written statement of their main terms of employment. This must be done by thirteenth week of continuous service.

The written statement must include the following, though employees may be referred to a reasonably accessible document on some of these items:

1 Names of Employer and Employee
2 Date employment began and whether any previous service is continuous
3 Rate of pay, or method of calculating it
4 Whether paid monthly, weekly, or at some other interval
5 Hours of work, with and without overtime
6 Entitlement, if any, to annual holidays, holiday pay, and public holidays
7 Conditions relating to sickness, injury and sick pay, if any
8 Particulars of disciplinary and grievance procedure
9 Periods of notice
10 Any Pension arrangements.

Apart from a few Wages Council industries (where legal minimums are laid down) there is no statutory obligation to provide holiday and sick pay, or overtime at premium rates. These are matters for individual contract or collective agreement at local or national level.

The written statement can be used as important evidence of the terms and conditions of an oral contract.

The employer should make clear, before the employee is engaged, whether he is being employed on a written or oral contract. Where the contract is oral and a written statement is provided as detailed above, the employee should be careful not to sign any form of words which might imply agreement with the statement (although he may sign that he has *received* it) because the statement may not contain *all* the terms and conditions contained in the oral contract but only its important parts.

Part-time employees working 16 or more hours a week, or 8 hours if they have been employed for at least five years, must also be given written statements.

If the employer wishes to change the terms and conditions of the contract or of the written statement, either the employee's consent is necessary or the agreement of the union, where there is a collective agreement; and written notice must be given to the employee within one month of the change. If, however, the particulars are stated in the collective agreement and the written statement refers the employee to it, it is sufficient then to alter the collective agreement. (*See* Dismissal, notice of.)

**CONTRACTING IN AND OUT**    'Contracting in and out' refers to the legal provisions which have been applied to trade unions wishing to give financial assistance to the Labour Party. Since many fewer members 'contract out' than would be the case if they had to 'contract in' the issue has historically been a bone of contention involving the power of the Labour Party. The 1913 Trade Union Act empowered trade unions to apply a political levy to all their members with the exception of those who 'contract out'. The 1927 Trades Disputes Act altered this power so that it applied only to members who 'contracted in'. The previous practice was however restored in 1947 when the 1927 Act was repealed. Trade Unions operating a political levy must make available forms for 'contracting out' to members who wish to do so. Generally, the number of members taking this action are very small.

The terms 'contracting in' and 'contracting out' are also used to describe the action of employers with occupational pensions schemes, under the pension scheme introduced on April 5th 1979. (*See* Occupational Pensions, Political Levy.)

**CONVERTIBILITY (EXCHANGE CONTROL)**    This is the term applied when a currency can be exchanged for another freely, though it is usually used to mean full convertibility, that is unrestricted exchange for all currencies. International convertibility used to be at fixed rates which were originally defined in terms of a fixed quantity of gold. This was known as being on the Gold Standard. Britain was on the Gold Standard before the First World War and again from 1925 till 1931. There then followed a period of floating exchange rates, i.e. when the value of the pound sterling varied according to day-to-day demand on the international money market.

# Cooling Off Period

Convertibility ceased after the outbreak of the Second World War and when it was restored fixed rates were again adopted, but the rate was fixed in terms of dollars, not gold. This was known as the neo-Gold Standard.

The advantage of the Gold Standard or any other system of fixed exchange rates is that it provides stable prices for international trade. Problems arise if a country's real economic position changes or even if international financiers think a country is falling behind or losing control of its economy. Then a crisis of confidence occurs, that is, *bankers'* confidence in the country's economic policy declines, forcing governments either to take stringent measures of internal deflation or else to devalue. This happened in Britain in 1931 and again in 1949 and 1967 – all years when Labour Governments were in power in Britain, which in itself weakened the confidence of international financiers in Britain's 'soundness' – a potent capitalist weapon against any socialist government of a country as dependent as Britain is on international trade.

After a series of international financial crises in the late 1960s and early 1970s fixed exchange rates were abandoned in many countries including both Britain and the U.S.A. The pound sterling is therefore now floating again although the Bank of England tries to manipulate the international money market to reduce extreme fluctuations. E.E.C. countries, however, have tied their currencies to each other, flexibly within a narrow band. This is known as the European Monetary System, to which Britain does not belong.

The real issue for trade unionists is not fixed or floating rates but the issue of free convertibility or control. International capitalist agencies such as the IMF aim at full convertibility. Trade unions, however, regard exchange control as an essential tool of economic policy which should be operated in the interests of employment and democratic control of the economy. (See IMF.)

**COOLING OFF PERIOD**  Proposals for labour legislation have from time to time suggested that where there is a labour dispute there should be a 'cooling off' period, after a deadlock has been reached in negotiations, before strike or lock out action can be taken by employees or employers. The object of the 'cooling off' period is to allow of further consideration of the issues by either or both sides including the possible resort to conciliation or mediation.

**CO-OPERATIVES**   A co-operative or co-operative society is a voluntary organization set up, owned and controlled by its members
and which is normally concerned with the production, marketing or
distribution of goods or services.

(a) *Consumers' Co-operatives*: The commonest type of co-operative in
Britain is the Consumers' Co-operative which can be a single
shop or a chain of stores. Membership is open to all who wish to
join and who buy one or more shares in the society usually of a
nominal value of £1.00. Co-operative shops operate like most
other commercial shops and are open to all shoppers whether
members or not. They aim to keep prices as low as possible
though goods may also be sold at the same prices as in other
shops and such profits as are made are distributed to the members in one form or another. Some of the profits, however, may
be used for educational or political purposes associated with the
Labour Movement, and some may as in any commercial concern
be ploughed back into the business so that the Society's capital
may consist of both the members' share contributions and some
of the trading profits.

Co-operative societies have a democratic organization through
which members elect the directors responsible for running the
business, and decide on what other activities the society undertakes and what committees shall be responsible for them.

The extent of Co-operative Society trading makes them a very
large element in the country's retail trading operations.

(b) *Co-operative Wholesale Society (CWS)*: The CWS is an important
part of the Consumers' Co-operative movement. It acts as a
major supplier to the retail co-operative trading organizations in
England and Wales. There is a separate Scottish CWS operating
in Scotland.

(c) *Production co-operatives*: There have been production co-
operatives, in one form or another, in Britain since the middle of
the last century. Two examples are boot-making and printing
but there have been many others. The idea that workers collectively own a business and operate it on a co-operative principle
has much to commend it. There have been many successful
experiments overseas, particularly in Spain, France and Italy. In
those countries there has been considerable state support and

banks have generally been willing to give aid. Even in the United States there have been experiments; a report on plywood co-operatives in the USA stated:

'The main sources of productivity in the mills are low over-heads (there are no high salaried executives), elimination of management (there are no first line supervizers) greater flexibility in manpower (all workers learn many jobs . . .) and quality control (through responsible handling, the worker-owners make productive use of cheaper materials that in conventional plants might be broken or disregarded).'

Renewed interest in production co-operatives has arisen in Britain with the increase in the number of factory closures, and the growth of unemployment. Workers have sought to turn redundant plants into co-operatives to maintain employment and have thus created a small number of islands of worker-owned capital. A number of Local Authorities have given financial aid to promote co-operatives but State involvement has been very little in contrast to the very positive support measures given for example in France.

The British Government now has powers, under the Industrial Common Ownership Act, to give financial assistance to co-operatives, and other assistance and other advice aid can be provided by the Co-operative Development Agency set up by the Labour Government (1974–9) but in both cases the help given has been extremely modest. The Agency, for example, with financial help from the European Social Fund and the Manpower Services Commission, has assisted in setting up a Co-operative Enterprise Centre in Hartlepool where there is high unemployment.

**CO-OPTION**   This is the addition to an elected body, e.g. a committee, of members elected by the body itself. Thus a committee elected by a trade union branch or association may co-opt a certain number of additional members if this is permitted by the rules. Co-option is normally defined for specific purposes or under specific conditions. Numbers of co-options permitted are also normally laid down to ensure that elected members remain in a clear majority on the body. Co-opted members normally have the same speaking and voting rights as elected members.

**CO-PARTNERSHIP**   The term describes a system of production in which employees are, under a formal agreement, shareholders along with the private owners of the enterprise. It also assumes some scheme for sharing the profits, proportionate to the small number of shares usually allotted. But it need not involve employees participating in the management of the enterprise although it may not exclude this. It is usually advocated both as a way of increasing incentives for the workforce and as a recipe for industrial harmony, sometimes even as an alternative to trade unionism. It is not widespread. It must be distinguished from the practice of offering top management shares in the business.

Trade unions have criticized co-partnership on two grounds. First, such schemes do not in reality provide any genuine control over the managerial decisions. Even if shares with voting rights are distributed, this would have to be on a fairly massive scale before any real control were vested in the workers or shareholders. Most workers involved in such schemes regard the annual·profit share-out as no more than a useful annual bonus. Secondly, there is no advantage to workpeople in tying up their savings in the firm that employs them, since this increases their insecurity if the firm goes bankrupt.

There has been some experimentation in Scandinavian countries with the idea of capital sharing at the national level based on a national fund administered by the trade union movement but there has been little interest among British unions in this idea.

**COST BENEFIT ANALYSIS**    It has been increasingly common in recent years for a project to be analysed in order to estimate its social impact either before it is undertaken or when it has been in operation for some time. The procedure and its techniques are known as cost benefit analysis. It is very complex and not always susceptible to precise calculation, as it goes far beyond direct and immediate financial calculations to estimate, for example, the impact of a proposed public work such as an airport, a particular high-rise building or a motorway, on the environment and to balance the expected gains and losses. Cost Benefit Analysis must therefore be viewed with some scepticism. Trade unionists are especially concerned with the procedure's impact on employment projects as well as with, for example, the assessment of stress and strain on workers involved.

**COST OF LIVING INDEX**    *See* Retail Price Index.

**COUNCIL OF CIVIL SERVICE UNIONS**    *See* National Whitley Council, Civil Service.

# Courts of Inquiry

**COURTS OF INQUIRY**     A statutory provision for the settlement of disputes was included in the Industrial Courts Act of 1919 and is still operative. Under this Act the Secretary of State for Employment may establish a Court of Inquiry to inquire into any trade dispute with a view to establishing the facts and making recommendations. Since the establishment of ACAS, which under the Employment Protection Acts may itself set up an inquiry into a dispute, the power to set up a Court of Inquiry has been little used.

When used, Courts of Inquiry have been set up on an *ad hoc* basis, always with an independent chairman, usually accompanied by experienced persons representative of employers and workers.

**CREDIT, CREDIT SQUEEZE**     When goods or services are supplied without immediate payment, they are given 'on credit'. Postponement of payment may not involve any charge additional to the cost of the goods or services but more usually some form of interest is paid. Hire purchase is a common form of credit in which a downpayment is made and the total costs when payments are complete are greater than if the goods or services had been paid for outright. Credit arrangements are normal within industry between, for example, suppliers of components and manufacturers or manufacturers and traders.

Money loaned by banks to individuals or firms is a crucial feature of modern trade and industry. The rate of interest charged is therefore of considerable importance in affecting economic activity. Credit control is thus of great concern to governments, which frequently operate either to limit or to facilitate the expansion of credit facilities. High interest rates serve to restrict credit and economic activity and coupled with other more direct restrictions are described as a 'credit squeeze'. This has been the policy of the Thatcher government and has been an important factor in increasing unemployment.

High interest rates and consequent domestic credit restriction have the effect, too, of attracting foreign money deposits into British banks and so of strengthening the pound (raising its value in terms of foreign currencies). This however has an adverse effect on exports and increases imports – another consequence of the Thatcher government's policy. (*See* Minimum Lending Rate.)

**CRIMINAL INJURIES COMPENSATION**     Compensation may be payable for injuries caused by criminal action suffered in the course of employment, e.g. in passenger transport or the public services. The scheme for such compensation, financed by the government, and which covers all crimes of violence whether at work or not, is administered by the Criminal Injuries Compensation Board composed of thirteen legally qualified members appointed by the Home Secretary and the Secretary of State for Scotland. It does not cover Northern Ireland where a separate scheme exists.

Claims may be made to the Board for an *ex gratia* payment (either by the victim himself or by his spouse or dependent if he has died) where the victim has suffered injury from a criminal attack or its psychological consequences. Compensation will not normally be paid while the assailant is awaiting trial.

The scheme is limited to injuries valued at £250 at least (1981) and to cases where the assailant is prosecuted or the police are notified without delay. It does not apply to cases where the assailant and victim are living together as part of the same family, where the injury is the result of a traffic offence, or where the victim has voluntarily entered into a fight unless the fight developed unexpectedly into the assailant's using a knife or gun.

Compensation is paid in a lump sum assessed on the basis used by the court for awarding damages but taking into account wage loss and social security benefit entitlement or payment and any compensation received from another source. e.g. the courts or insurance. As claims may take up to a year to settle, interim awards may be made.

Union advice and assistance should be sought on how to make application in pursuing the compensation. After enquiries by the Board's staff, the case is presented to a member of the Board who will decide on the justice of the claim and the amount of compensation. If he cannot decide, he may refer the case to a hearing before three members of the Board. If the decision is made by the single member there is a right of appeal to the three members. The trade union's help should be sought in making and presenting any appeal. Hearings are more informal than in a court.

Compensation comes from government funds, although it has been suggested that these be added to by pooled money from fines, forfeitures and confiscations from the criminals, to enable abolition of the minimum sum for a claim and interim payments to be made while cases are being heard.

In the financial year 1980/1 more than £21 million was paid out to over 25,000 applicants, according to the Board's Annual Report in which can also be found its guidelines for compensation payments.

**CRIMINAL LAW CONSPIRACY ACT, 1977**    This Act contains several provisions that could affect trade union activity, which throughout the history of the movement has been linked from time to time with 'conspiracy'. The Act reforms the law of conspiracy and increases the penalties that can be imposed for 'conspiracy' offences. It is now laid down that 'conspiracy' will consist of an agreement to commit a criminal offence. Although this means that conspiracy to trespass (used against trade union activity in the past) has been abolished, the Act creates other offences relating to trespass which could affect industrial action. Thus it is an offence to use or threaten violence to secure entry to premises (e.g. for a sit-in or occupational picket) if you know that there is someone inside opposed to the action (as there is bound to be) and the possible definitions of violence, e.g. to property, are also very wide. Similarly, once on the premises it is an offence to have a 'weapon of offence' with you and here again the possible definitions of such weapons are many and wide.

It is possible for the Act to be invoked in respect of people engaged in organizing activities which would lead to a commission of any of the offences.

The TUC has rejected the introduction of criminal law in these ways into the law of trespass and the possibility that as a result trade unionists, in pursuance of what has hitherto been regarded as a legitimate form of industrial action, could be penalized under the criminal law. (*See* Conspiracy.)

**CUSTOM AND PRACTICE**    At works level, in an industrial undertaking, it is common for works representatives (e.g. shop stewards) and local management (e.g. foremen) to arrive at understandings over detailed conditions of employment. These might include the allocation of work, allowances for specific jobs, arrangements for overtime, etc. These arrangements are usually not written down, but become reinforced in time through habit and custom and are known as 'custom and practice'.

# D

**DANGER MONEY – DIRTY MONEY – HEIGHT MONEY** 'Danger money', 'Height money' and 'dirty' (or 'dirt') money are examples of special payments made to manual workers in certain circumstances. Workers in the construction, docks and steel erection industries are often entitled to such payments which are part of the collective agreement. In some industries the term 'plus payments' is used, others will specify 'abnormal conditions allowance' and 'arduous conditions payment'. Whatever the conditions are, careful examination normally takes place by management when application is made for the payment by trade union representatives.

**DECASUALIZATION** The fight against casual employment has been a major issue with trade unions in a number of industries over a long period. It is still a problem for example in the building and construction industry. But the most significant effort to remove the fear of employment insecurity has been made in the docks industry, dating back to the 1889 dock strike when one of the slogans used by the strikers was 'work or maintenance'.

Up to the 1889 strike labour on the docks was hired for as little as one or two hours. After the strike hiring was on the basis of a four hour minimum. From that limited gain great progress was made over the years but full permanent employment for registered dock workers was not secured until 1972 when the Aldington–Jones Committee insisted that all registered port workers must have a permanent employer and be guaranteed permanent employment, carrying with it the elimination of a 'temporary unattached' register.

The casual basis of employment in dockland was related to the nature of the industry itself. Variations in foreign trade, both imports and exports, can be effected by industrial, commercial, political and weather conditions. Demand for labour therefore tended to fluctuate as ships arrived or left ports. As long as workers could be picked up on the dockside as and when required, employers were reluctant to offer permanent employment to more than a very small proportion of their labour force.

With the growth of trade unionism in the ports demands for permanent employment and a regular wage were pressed forward in dockland, but progress was slow. Registration of labour, to restrict

# Decasualization

the number of workers available for work, was the first attempt, made on the Merseyside in 1912. Known as the 'clearing house' scheme a register of qualified dockers was established and the men were issued with 'tallies' by the Board of Trade. Port employers had to give them preference for work and because men might work for a variety of employers (usually small stevedoring and portering companies) during the week, their wages were paid through a clearing house. This arrangement also made possible the deduction of insurance contributions and enabled the 'casual' dock workers to participate in the unemployment insurance scheme.

Time after time the Unions, led by Ernest Bevin, demanded the end of casual employment. He put the case succinctly at the Shaw Enquiry in 1920:

'The easiest thing to get rid of is the human. He has not been sufficient trouble. If he had only been more audacious and more aggressive, then possibly they would have found other means but the reason why casual labour has been perpetuated is because it has been the easiest method of dealing with shipping up to this point . . . But there is another motive behind it too. I am convinced that the employers have always had at the back of their minds that economic poverty producing economic fear was their best weapon for controlling labour. I do not think that a civilization built upon that is worth having. We believe in developing self discipline as against maintaining control by economic poverty and economic fear.'

Despite that appeal and recommendations from the Shaw Enquiry of 1920, and the MacLean Committee of 1924, regular employment was only conceded to dock-workers during the Second World War through the Essential Works Order for the docks. Casual employment returned after the war but attempts to limit its use were made with the introduction of the Dock Workers (Regulation of Employment) order of 1947. This set up the Dock Labour Scheme with a National Dock Labour Board and local Dock Labour Boards all having equal representation from dock-workers and dock employers. This new system of joint control allocated surplus dockers to work, operated a system for paying wages and dealt with discipline and other matters, but still did not manage to provide permanent employment. What it did do was to ensure that men could not be removed compulsorily from the register except for disciplinary reasons. With the development of palletization, packaged timber and containerization, together with other labour-saving equipment, the demand for dock labour fell dramatically but the Unions insisted that this was a problem for the employers. An Enquiry under Lord Devlin in 1966 supported this view and recommended the allocation of all men on the register to permanent employers. This view was carried forward and implemented by the Special Committee on the Ports, known as the Aldington–Jones Committee, which brought to an end casual employment for registered dock workers.

Building Trade Unions have demanded a similar scheme – so far without success. (*See* Aldington–Jones Report.)

**DEDUCTIONS** Deductions from the weekly or monthly pay of workers should be properly notified in writing on or before payment and be industrially agreed, apart from statutory deductions i.e. national insurance, PAYE (for income tax). Examples of deductions would be: trade union contributions, payments to charities, repayment of loans, payments to sports club etc. Fixed deductions may be covered in an agreed annual statement.

**DEFLATION** This means the adoption of measures aimed at reducing the rate and level of inflation, in order by bringing prices down to make the economy more competitive in exports and to curtail imports. Such measures adopted by the Thatcher Government (whose policy is accepted as deflationary) included efforts to diminish the rate of increase in the money supply by increases in interest rates, an over-valued currency, the reduction of public expenditure including aid to industry and increasing indirect taxation. Implicit in deflation is therefore a fall in production, rapidly rising unemployment ('shaking out labour') and control of the public sector to keep wages down. This deflation of the economy has had cumulative effects since the progressive reduction of purchasing power that has resulted has further reduced economic activity and put more people out of work. Prices, however, have not fallen as intended; the main impact of the policy has been on employment.

**DEINDUSTRIALIZATION** This is the process which has been taking place since the Second World War, whereby employment has tended to shift from the manufacturing sector to the service sector. This has not been a healthy development of the economy since the growth of other sectors of the economy has not compensated adequately for the loss of jobs involved or for the loss of Britain's manufacturing strength, some $3\frac{1}{2}$ million jobs in manufacturing in the last decade. Even during the 'recession' from 1979, while investment in manufacturing has declined, it has increased in the distributive and service sector (3 per cent in 1981 and an estimated $3\frac{1}{2}$ per cent for 1982).

By March 1981 the number of workers employed in manufacturing industry had fallen by 970,000 or 14 per cent to 6.1 millions since mid-1979, the biggest percentage drop being in metal manufacturing and textiles. Facts like these have led, since the coming to power of the Thatcher Government, to the use of the term as a description of a major feature of the present depression in Britain. This is the contraction of the country's industrial base through the shutting down of large sections of important industries. Even if the pace of the process is slowing down, as is officially claimed, it is still continuing and is not compensated for by the rate of opening of new industries which provide employment.

The effect of deindustrialization is particularly severe in the areas of the old basic industries where any diversification taking place is relatively minor. Industries severely hit have included those suffering from international competition (because of the strong and, it is argued, overvalued pound) and newer major industries developed since the war in the old heavy industry areas. Deindustrialization has also affected hitherto relatively prosperous areas with lighter industry in the South East.

**DEMARCATION DISPUTES**   Traditionally, unions in industries like shipbuilding and printing had difficulties in securing mutual agreement as to which trade or grade of workers should undertake particular types of work. Disputes arose over lines of demarcation and involved different unions claiming the work for their members. The TUC can now (since 1969) intervene in such inter-union disputes with a view to resolving the issue. To the credit of the trade union movement, demarcation disputes are now few and far between.

**DEPRESSION (SLUMP)**   These are synonyms, used to describe a sharp, continuous and lengthy decline in economic activity marked by widespread unemployment, falling production and profits and reduced international trade. In the past, slumps were also characterized by falling prices but since the 1960s this has not been the case. In recent years, slumps have been co-existent with inflation.

Before the Second World War slumps followed booms – that is periods of rising employment, production and profits. But in the post-war period, until recently, what was called the 'trade cycle' (boom . . . slump . . . boom) has largely been controlled by economic policies that managed to avoid the deep troughs of unemployment known earlier. Today in Britain, Government policies have actually been directed to increase unemployment and intensify falling production, with its consequence of large numbers of business bankruptcies and shut-downs.

The trade union movement has refused to accept the inevitability of the trade cycle and has demanded economic policies that, it claims, could maintain full employment and avoid slumps, including increased public expenditure, exchange controls, a major investment policy in manufacturing, and import and price controls. These are based on the view that the fundamental cause of slumps is falling demand, which therefore has to be stimulated while at the same time inflation is avoided by the use of other controls.

**DEVALUATION**   A currency is 'devalued' when government action reduces its exchange value in relation to other currencies. This has happened twice in Britain since the second world war, in 1949 and in 1967, both under Labour Governments. On both occasions the devaluation was the result of balance of payments difficulties and was intended to give a boost to exports by lowering the value of the pound and so making exports more competitive and imports more expensive.

Because of the possible 'loss of confidence' internationally in a currency (i.e. speculative selling of that currency by financiers in anticipation of its lower value) which is threatened with devaluation it is generally a matter of acute controversy and used by Governments as a last resort when other measures to deal with the problem have proved inadequate. There is also the danger to be faced that other countries may devalue their currencies to meet the new situation so that devaluation may not succeed in its immediate objective. And devaluation, by making imports dearer, may increase the cost of living, giving rise to additional wage demands which may in turn raise the price of exports. Since 1971 the pound sterling has been allowed to float, that is its value has been allowed to fluctuate within bounds set by Government policy. Devaluation is advanced as a measure to help solve the present (1982) crisis, among proposals for alternatives to current economic policy.

**DIFFERENTIALS**    Differences in pay or rates of pay between one section of workers in an industry and another are usually described in terms of 'differentials'. Thus within an industry it will be customary for the more skilled to have a 'differential' over the pay of the less or the unskilled. Similarly people with greater experience or doing special, dangerous or dirty work or work with greater responsibilities, may be paid a 'differential'. As the result of differentials, the pay structures of various industries and occupations can be very complicated and require complex negotiations.

**DILUTION (OF LABOUR)**    The history of the trade union movement shows the tenacity with which skilled workers protect their skills and their exclusive right to do the jobs which require them. Attempts by employers to have these jobs done by workers less skilled, either by training or experience, is described as dilution and has been a bone of contention throughout industrial history, leading to industrial action because of the desire of workers to protect both skilled jobs and skilled rates of pay. Rapidly changing technology has made the issues more complex and the borderlines between various levels of skill often more difficult to define. The issues however remain important in union negotiations.

During the First and Second World Wars, legislation was passed, in co-operation with the unions, to permit dilution of skilled work subject to its registration and the restoration of pre-war practices at the end of hostilities. (*See* Restrictive Practices.)

**DIRECT LABOUR**    The system whereby some local authorities establish their own organization for building, sewerage and highway work and/or maintenance work. In 1980 there were over 500 Direct Labour Organizations (DLO) employing just under 20 per cent of building workers. Under the Local Government (Planning and Land) Act 1980, of the Conservative Government, which took effect from April 1981, use of DLOs has been greatly circumscribed. They must bid for a substantial proportion of their work in competition with tenders from the private sector; must earn a prescribed rate of return (the target is 5 per cent) on capital and must publish their results. The Secretary of State for the Environment now has the power to close down DLOs which consistently fail to achieve the target.

Most direct labour is, in fact, employed on maintenance and it represents only a small proportion of the output of the building industry. In maintenance work, too, all DLO contracts over £10,000 must go out to tender. In addition, it is now the rule that, provided the Council does repair work of £300,000 or more, at least 30 per cent of jobs costing less than £10,000 must go out to tender, as must road maintenance contracts costing more than £50,000.

Direct Labour Organizations work only for the local authority and do not compete for building and maintenance work outside. They rarely, as is common in the private sector, employ casual labour and therefore have the advantage of offering continuous and regular employment in an industry which is notorious for irregular employment. Their employees work under conditions of service common to other local government manual employees as regards, for example, sick pay and pensions.

DLOs are also responsible for training their own apprentices without subvention from the Construction Industrial Training Board. Labour costs, therefore, tend to be higher than in the private sector of the building industry as a result of what are, in effect, better conditions of work. Trade union membership is also much higher than in the private sector of the industry.

Within the trade union movement there is considerable support for the principle of Direct Labour being employed both by local and central government. On the other hand, DLOs are the object of frequent attack by employers in the private sector and by right-wing politicians who regard it as a form of socialism.

Central government maintenance work which is not contracted out to private employers is undertaken by direct labour. The Government is itself a direct employer of labour, e.g. the Ministry of Defence and the Department of the Environment.

**DIRECTORS' PAY** While pay curbs are the order of the day for employees in the public service and private industry, company chairmen, managing directors and directors continue to receive very high salaries with substantial annual increases. The case of Michael Edwardes of BL (a 52 per cent increase in 1981) is far from being untypical. A sample of seventy big companies show salaries in 1980 ranging from about £50,000 (Tesco) to £203,000 (NCL) a year, and

# Dirty Money

the Chief Executive of the BOC Group earned £477,100 in 1981. The sample includes, as well as manufacturing companies, breweries, press, insurance, retailing and banking companies. Figures for 1981 show a similar pattern. The Charterhouse Group's guide to top management pay (October 1981) showed that the number of chairmen or directors earning over £75,000 a year was 42. A gross salary of £100,000 was becoming the norm for chairmen and chief executives of major companies, and a number receive £200,000 or more. For the 12 months to September 1981, the average rise in Directors' pay was 14 per cent, compared to a 9.3 per cent increase in average earnings. (*See* Fringe Benefits, Perks.)

**DIRTY MONEY**    *See* Danger Money.

**DISABLEMENT (AND INDUSTRIAL DISEASES) BENE-FITS**    *See* Industrial Injuries Payments.

**DISCIPLINARY PROCEDURES**    Normally in industry disciplinary procedures are laid down in a collective agreement between employers and unions. Under the law employers must provide employees with a written statement of the main terms and conditions of employment. These must include any disciplinary rules applicable to them and indicate the person to whom they should apply if they are dissatisfied with any disciplinary decision, and the further steps that may be taken for dealing with grievances or disciplinary decisions.

The relevant ACAS Code of Practice makes clear that while management is responsible for maintaining discipline within a workplace, if rules are to be fully effective they must be seen as reasonable by the workers. Therefore the more the workers and their representatives are involved, if they wish to be, in formulating rules the better. Agreement is at all events desirable for establishing procedural agreements and in seeing that they are used fairly. The Code emphasizes that disciplinary procedures should not be viewed simply as a means of imposing sanctions or punishments but should aim at smooth and acceptable relationships. At the same time employees should be in no doubt about the consequences of breaking rules especially if this could mean dismissal.

The Code suggests for example that the procedures should provide for matters to be dealt with quickly, should specify who can take particular decisions, should ensure that workers are fully informed of any complaints against them and are given full opportunity to state their case, and be accompanied by a TU Representative or friend so that the case is fully investigated, and should provide a right of appeal. Very important is the provision that dismissal should be the responsibility of senior management and should never follow a first offence unless the misconduct is 'gross'. The Code does not define this. Trade Unions would normally seek to spell it out. The TUC advises opposition to the imposition of fines or deductions from pay as disciplinary measures.

Good procedure, it is suggested, involves grades of severity of penalty according to the gravity of the offence. These can range from informal oral warnings to formal or written ones leading to written warning of suspension without pay or transfer, according to the nature of the misconduct if the contract of employment allows for these measures. The final step would be dismissal.

Warning is given of the need to allow in the procedure for special circumstances, e.g. conditions of night work where no trade union representative may be immediately available, or action against a worker who is also a trade union official, where it can be misinterpreted as action against the union. In the latter case oral warnings are recommended until the matter has been discussed with a senior trade union representative or paid official. Again, if a worker is convicted of a crime outside his employment, this should not be treated as automatically leading to dismissal. The main consideration ought to be whether the offence is one that makes the individual unsuitable for his work or unacceptable to other employees.

Good practice would ensure that accurate records of cases are kept and that they are confidential. It is also good practice to disregard breaches of rule after a specified period or satisfactory conduct.

It must be noted that the whole question of ensuring discipline at work can be the subject of controversy. Thus trade unions may refuse to take part in drawing up disciplinary rules and prefer to use the grievance procedures backed up by industrial action. But a clear distinction must be made between rules and procedures. The latter set out the steps that must be taken before disciplinary action is taken and unions are normally involved in agreeing procedures in order to safeguard their members from disciplinary actions which could endanger their jobs. The normal trade union aim is to ensure that while the stages of a procedure are being followed, the *status quo* should be maintained, i.e. the worker should not be penalized in any

# Disclosure of Information

way pending the resolution of the issue. This is particularly important where suspension is the penalty.

**DISCLOSURE OF INFORMATION**    If collective bargaining is to be fully effective, the trade unions must have access to accurate information on the employers' financial and economic position, their 'ability to pay'. This is given to them to a certain extent under the Employment Protection Act which requires the employer to disclose to representatives of an independent trade union, recognized for collective bargaining, information without which their bargaining power would be impeded and which should be disclosed. In the interest of good industrial relations ACAS gives guidance to both sides in a Code of Practice suggesting information which might be disclosed.

This includes information under five headings:

(a) *Pay and Benefits* which covers everything to do with, for example, hours and wages, job evaluation and grading systems, bonuses and allowances, details of fringe benefits etc.
(b) *Conditions of Service* which includes policies on recruitment, redundancy, training, promotion, health, welfare and safety, equal opportunities, redeployment.
(c) *Manpower*: numbers employed analysed by grade, sex, etc., labour turnover, absenteeism, overtime and short time, manning standards, planned changes in work methods, investment plans, etc.
(d) *Performance*: productivity and efficiency data, return on capital invested, state of the order book and sales.
(e) *Finances*: gross and net profits, assets, liabilities, details of government assistance, etc.

One important exception is that the information can be withheld if in the opinion of the employer it would cause him substantial injury commercially. In such cases he would have to prove that there was a likelihood that the union would actually leak the information. Other exceptions include information given to the employer in confidence, or whose disclosure would be against the interests of national security. But refusal to disclose can be referred to the Central Arbitration Committee which usually refers the matter to ACAS for conciliation. If this fails the CAC considers the complaint and if it finds it justified it makes a Declaration to that effect and sets a period within

# Distribution of Wealth and Income

which the employer ought to disclose. Where the employer does not disclose the union can make a further complaint to the CAC and may also claim terms and conditions for the employees concerned. If this is upheld the CAC can make an award which is binding on the employer.

Clearly the most satisfactory situation is one where the ACAS Code is followed as an example of good industrial relations practice, making reference to the time consuming, CAC legal procedures unnecessary. The value of the EPA's provisions has been to lay the basis for creating an atmosphere in which reasonable disclosure is normal, collective bargaining procedures facilitated and unnecessary disputes consequently avoided. But the provisions have been criticised by trade unionists as not being effective enough in practice.

In the Companies Act, 1981, regarding the general requirements of companies to publish financial information on their activities, in order to harmonize the presentation and publication of company accounts in the EEC, no statutory requirement is included for companies to provide full accounts for their employees, although the Companies Act of 1980 says that directors have the same duties to employees as to shareholders (S.46). This is in effect a disclosure duty. The new exemptions of full disclosure of information by small companies effectively weaken the value of the Disclosure of Information provisions of the EPA for many trade unionists who work in small companies.

In addition employers are required under legislation to provide information affecting Health and Safety, terms and conditions of individual workers, redundancy, etc. (*See* Company, Company Taxation.)

**DISMISSAL, NOTICE OF**   *See* Contracts of Employment, Notice of Termination of Employment.

**DISTRIBUTION OF WEALTH AND INCOME**   The Report of the Royal Commission on the Distribution of Income and Wealth published in 1975 is the most comprehensive information still available on the subject, although it refers only to the period up to 1973. It shows that in 1972, of the adult population in Great Britain, the top one per cent owned more than a quarter of the nation's personally owned wealth, the top 5 per cent owned more than a half, the top 10 per cent owned about two thirds, the top 20 per cent over four-fifths, while the bottom 80 per cent owned less than one-fifth.

# Distribution of Wealth and Income

The Report also showed that since just before the First World War, the share of the top one per cent had substantially declined although the decline was taking place more slowly after 1960 than before. At the same time the share of the bottom 90 per cent had more than doubled from a mere 8 per cent by 1960 but had been increasing more slowly since.

In more detail the Report showed that in 1973 less than one per cent of the adult population owned about 70 per cent of all the company shares in personal ownership and 72 per cent of the land; and about $3\frac{1}{2}$ per cent of the adult population owned about 90 per cent of these two forms of property. The ownership of homes is, however, more equally distributed and this represents a trend towards greater equality of wealth, especially as the price of houses has risen relative to the price of shares in industry. A provisional estimate for 1973-4 showed a drop in the share of the top group of wealth owners, probably because of this latter factor.

As far as personal incomes are concerned, the top 10 per cent received over a quarter of the total personal incomes before tax in 1972-3 while the bottom 50 per cent received just under a quarter. Thus the inequality in the distribution of *income* is not as great as in the ownership of *wealth* but the Royal Commission's view was that there had been only slight changes in the distribution of income over the previous fifteen years; there had been only a small change in the share of those at the top while the share of the bottom 50 per cent had hardly risen. If one takes income after tax, the share of the top one per cent is sharply reduced but, apart from this group, income tax was shown to have only a moderate equalizing effect on income distribution. Later official figures, for income after tax for 1976, show that the bottom 50 per cent had gained very little in their share of the distribution since 1949, less than one half per cent. The movement away from the top income groups was to the advantage of the group between these and the bottom 50 per cent.

On the latest official basis for calculation, the share of wealth of the top one per cent rose from 22.5 per cent in 1974 to 24 per cent in 1977 with similar increases for the top 5 per cent.

Other calculations, by Professor Townsend in his *Poverty in the UK*, show that in 1963 the top 4 per cent took 64.7 per cent of distributed personal income after tax, but in 1977-8 the figure had changed to only 64.2 per cent, while the bottom 50 per cent's gain was from 11.8 per cent to only 12.4 per cent. During the same period

# Diversification of Industry

the top 10 per cent's share of personal wealth dropped from 73.3 per cent to 62.4 per cent while the bottom 90 per cent's share increased from 26.7 per cent to 37.6 per cent. This would bear out the continuance, in spite of change, of massive inequalities.

Information published by the Inland Revenue for 1979 shows hardly any change in distribution of personal wealth since 1974, the share of the top one per cent being 24 per cent; of the top 5 per cent, 45 per cent; of the top 10 per cent, 59 per cent; and of the top 25 per cent, 82 per cent; while that of the bottom 25 per cent was 18 per cent. The 1980 figures from the Central Statistical Office on net income distribution of households, after allowing for *both taxes and benefits*, show that the share of the bottom 40 per cent fell during 1976–80 from 20.4 per cent to 19.1 per cent, while that of the top 40 per cent rose from 71 per cent to 72.4 per cent.

This point is emphasized by a study (1982) by the European Commission which states that the proportion of people living in poverty has not changed since the Welfare State began and this position may worsen through operation of current economic policies.

**DIVERSIFICATION OF INDUSTRY**    The term may be used in two ways. It is applied to the development of different industries within an area which has been hitherto mainly or almost entirely dependent on a single industry e.g. coal or steel. As such, diversification has been encouraged by governments from time to time, especially when a particular major industry in a locality has been in difficulties, as a means of maintaining employment. In such circumstances new industries may be subsidized, especially at their development stage, by state intervention. Such diversification has been part of the Labour Movement's industrial policies.

Diversification also describes the branching out of a one-product firm into other industrial or commercial activities, sometimes related to the original product but not necessarily so. It may take place through the desire of a company to expand its activities and spread its risks, to anticipate falling demand for the original product, as the result of mergers with other companies, in order to utilize fully the skills and experience available in the company or for other reasons. In general the main reason is to take advantage of profits in other markets. It is also a feature of large organizations, such as multinationals, which may operate over very wide and disparate industrial and commercial fields, sometimes through the control of complex financial management. (*See* Conglomerate.)

# Dock-labour Scheme

**DOCK-LABOUR SCHEME**   Fluctuation in the demand for labour is a characteristic of the docks industry due to the movement of international trade, the weather, technological changes etc. Efforts were made over many years by the port trade unions (mainly the Transport and General Workers Union) to overcome the problems of casual employment in the industry and a major change came during the Second World War. In order to ensure an adequate supply of qualified dock labour the Government introduced the Dock Labour Scheme, a statutory instrument which gave dock-workers representation in overlooking their industry.

The scheme has been amended and strengthened from time to time and basically provides for a system of registration of dock-workers in the major ports. The register is maintained and controlled jointly by equal numbers of representatives of the dock-workers (through their trade union – mainly the TGWU) and the port employers, on the local Dock Labour Board. The Board decides on issues affecting the increase or decrease in the dock labour force in the port concerned.

There is a National Dock Labour Board which overlooks the work of the local Dock Labour Boards, deals with voluntary severance schemes, training and re-training, and the provision of welfare and medical services in the ports. The Chairman and Deputy Chairman of the National Dock Labour Board are appointed by the Government and the remaining members of the Board consist of equal numbers of dock-worker and employer representatives.

The Dock-Labour scheme is financed by levy from the registered port employers.

**DONOVAN COMMISSION**   The Labour Government in 1965 set up a Royal Commission on Trade Unions and Employers Associations under Lord Donovan. Its report was issued in 1968. The Commission's central recommendation was that the informal system of industrial relations (e.g. local bargaining) should be more effectively regulated through the medium of *formal* plant agreements (or company agreements in multi-plant companies) which, in companies above a certain size, should be registered with the Department of Employment. An Industrial Relations Commission should be set up to investigate issues arising from these agreements and to conduct inquiries, including the examination of trade union recognition problems. The Commission urged that collective bargaining should be encouraged; no employee should be prevented from belonging to a trade union, and employers should reconsider their attitudes towards the unionization of white collar workers. The Commission expressed the view that their recommended reform of collective bargaining machinery was the key to dealing with unconstitutional strikes. It took the view that the application of legal sanctions to individual persons for striking in breach of a procedure agreement or to unions for being party to such strikes would be ineffective and counter-productive, although it did note that legal sanctions might have to be reconsidered if circumstances changed. It also recommended against the introduction of compulsory strike ballots and a compulsory 'cooling-off period'.

On individual rights the Commission made a series of proposals. Employees should be protected against unfair dismissal and statutory machinery to adjudicate in such cases should be created. The closed shop should not be prohibited, though workers dismissed because of a closed shop should be able to complain to an industrial tribunal, and an independent review body should be established to hear cases where people had been excluded from a union. This body should also deal with complaints about alleged irregularities in union elections, mergers or union rules.

The Commission's proposals also covered the structure of unions, their registration, and their legal immunities which, it thought, should be retained and slightly extended. Multi-unionism should be reduced, and unions should be encouraged to form joint union committees, or to conclude spheres of influence agreements. Union branch structures should be revised to focus on the plant and formally incorporate shop stewards.

Much of the work of this Commission influenced subsequent legislation and also experiments like the Commission for Industrial Relations. Its recommendations on informal systems reflected changes which were already in process and would doubtless have continued in the direction indicated by the Commission, even if the Commission had not sat. Nevertheless the Report and findings of the Commission still have much relevance.

# E

**EARNINGS, SOURCES OF INFORMATION** Comparisons between what workers actually earn in different occupations and

# The Economic League

jobs can be a major factor in negotiations as, for example, the work of the Clegg Comparability Commission, appointed by the Callaghan Government and continued by the Thatcher Government, has shown. Trade unions therefore, in making their case, can use a number of different official sources giving statistics of the movement of earnings.

(a) *The New Earnings Survey* (NES): This gives very comprehensive information on payments made to a sample of one per cent of the workforce randomly selected from all PAYE contributors employed in early April. Its information is published at various times in the year and includes data for the whole sample on major collective agreements in different industries, regions and age groups in both the public and private sectors; overtime earnings and hours worked by different groups; and hours and earnings of part-time women workers.

Publication, which is by the Department of Employment, from whom the information is available, has the disadvantage that information is often out of date by anything from six months to two years. This weakness can be partly made good by using:

(b) *The Monthly Index of Average Earnings*: This deals with all employees, covers all industries and shows the movement of average earnings industry by industry, compared with the previous year and with a January 1976 base. These figures can be helpful in updating information from the NES but they do not distinguish between the earnings of men and women, age groups, part- and full-time workers. The monthly index also includes information on basic wage rates which are an inadequate source of information in many respects since they do not include overtime, bonuses or the results of local bargaining on top of basic rates.

(c) *The October Survey*: This provides information on manual workers only in respect of weekly and hourly earnings and hours worked in different regions by industry. Here again the information is not full enough for use in a comparability exercise.

There are other surveys of particular industries, e.g. Coal, Rail, Shipbuilding, Agriculture, Chemicals and Engineering, published in the *Employment Gazette* of the Department of Employment.

**THE ECONOMIC LEAGUE** This is an independent, non-profit-making organization financed by voluntary subscriptions from companies in industry and commerce, and from individuals. It was founded to work against 'all subversive forces' and 'for the preservation of personal freedom and free enterprise'. Although it claims to be non-party-political, it is opposed to nationalization and its propaganda, largely conducted through mass publication of leaflets, has a strong anti-Labour flavour, aiming to educate workers against socialism and 'extreme' trade unionism. It distributed 18 million leaflets at factory gates in 1980.

It claims 'to expose the real intentions of extremists in industry and by so doing to alert people in industry – management and shop floor alike – to the dangers of allowing extremists to gain influence'. Among its ways of doing this is giving private information to employers about 'subversive' employees, which in practice can simply mean active trade unionists, socialists and communists. Its publications have also named left-wing activists. It has been alleged that it keeps blacklists aimed to prevent the employment of certain people. Its activities against trade unionists have been strongly opposed by the TUC.

It has a substantial budget and its Council's composition reflects powerful interests in business and the media. Among its backers are the four big banks. It works both centrally and through regional offices.

**EMBARGO**   This is a term widely used to describe the action of a union in stopping, normally as part of a dispute, a particular practice or activity, e.g. overtime. The term can also be used when goods or services are 'blacked' or boycotted. (*See* Blacking.)

**EMERGENCY POWERS ACT**   The Emergency Powers Act (1920), passed by the Lloyd George coalition government during a miners' dispute, permits the Government to intervene in industrial disputes and to declare a 'State of Emergency' where the circumstances are such 'as to be calculated, by interfering with the supply and distribution of food, water, fuel, or light, or with the means of locomotion, to deprive the community, or any substantial proportion of the community of the essentials of life'. The Act gives considerable powers to the Government to make orders and military forces can be used to do the work normally done by the strikers. While the Act does not ban strikes or picketing its use usually undermines the strike. Although a 'state of emergency' may be proclaimed when Parliament is not sitting, approval must be given by Parliament within five days for the use of the Emergency Powers Act, and its operation is subject to monthly renewal by Parliament.

Emergency Powers have been brought in eleven times since 1920. Since the Second World War they were used by Labour Governments in 1948 and 1949 (Docks industry dispute) and 1966 (seamen's dispute). More recently the Conservative Government brought them in twice in docks disputes, 1970 and 1972, in the electricity supply industry in 1970, and in mining disputes in 1972 and 1973. In fact the powers were used sparingly and were generally kept in the background to encourage a settlement.

**EMPLOYMENT ACT 1980**   The Employment Act became law on August 1st 1980 as an amending Act, by the Thatcher Government, to previous Labour legislation. Its main provisions are as follows:

*Secret Ballots (s.1 & 2)*: Public money is to be made available to trade unions to offset the cost if they decide to hold secret ballots on starting and ending strikes, the election of shop stewards and full-time officials, changing rule books, and mergers with other unions. Employers with more than twenty members are obliged to give a recognized union a place on the company's premises to carry out the poll.

*Codes of Practice (s.3)*: The Secretary of State for Employment is empowered to issue such Codes. The first two, issued in August 1980, covered picketing and the closed shop.

*Unfair Dismissal (s.6, 8, 9, 15)*: The onus will be on the worker to show that an employer acted unreasonably in dismissing an employee. Industrial Tribunals will take into account the size and resources of the company in making a decision. Companies with twenty or fewer employees are exempt from unfair dismissal rules when the employee has worked less than two years. The basic award can be reduced by a tribunal if there is evidence that the employee behaved unreasonably. Workers receive a general right to stop employers taking action short of dismissal in order to make them join a union. The union may also be liable to pay some of the compensation if it is held to have pressurized the employer into taking such action.

*Maternity (s.11, 12, 13)*: A woman can now be fairly dismissed if it is not reasonably practicable for her to return to her former job and she turns down suitable alternative employment. An employer with five or fewer workers can be exempt from any such responsibility as he can claim that it was not even reasonably practicable to offer another job.

*Repeal of Schedule 11 (s.19)*: Under Schedule 11 of the previous Labour Government's Employment Protection Act unions were able to go to arbitration to secure recognized terms and conditions and in the absence of them to demand for groups of workers the general level obtaining in a particular area or industry. In addition, repeal of the remaining parts of the 1938 Road Haulage Act has abolished similar procedures specific to that industry.

*Trade Union Recognition (s.19)*: The statutory procedure under which unions in dispute over recognition could apply for an official investigation operated by ACAS is also removed.

*Coercive Recruitment (s.18)*: Action by trade unionists to force workers at another company to belong to their union (or one or more particular unions) is outlawed.

*Closed Shop (s.4, 5, 7 & 19)*: The right of individuals is established not to be unreasonably expelled from or refused admission to a trade union where a closed shop operates. The procedure for such cases lies through Industrial Tribunals and then appeal to the Employment Appeal Tribunal (EAT). If union membership is still refused the EAT would be able to award compensation of up to £16,000. New closed shops must have the support of 80 per cent of the workers involved (not just those voting in a ballot) to be immune from unfair dismissal claims if an employee loses his job through the operation of a closed shop agreement.

The statutory religious conscience clause has been widened from religious belief to objections on other grounds of conscience or deeply held personal belief to joining any trade union or to joining a particular trade union. In addition non-unionists employed at the time a closed shop agreement arrangement came into operation are exempt from compulsion to join the Union.

*Picketing (s.16)*: the section removes immunity from civil action from persons who picket at places other than their own place of work, with the exception of trade union officials and dismissed workers who are to be allowed to join picket lines.

*Sympathetic Industrial Action (s.17)*: Immunity (embodied in the Trade Union and Labour Relations Act 1974) is removed where there is secondary industrial action unless

(a) the purpose of the secondary action is to interfere directly with the flow of goods or services to or from the employer in dispute (and the action is likely to achieve that purpose), or

(b) its purpose is to interfere directly with the flow of goods or services of an associated employer (e.g. a subsidiary company or one under the same ownership or control) and the goods or services are in substitution for the goods or services normally supplied to or by the employer in dispute (and the action is likely to achieve that purpose), or

(c) the secondary action involves picketing within the new and narrower definition of picketing in section 16 of the Employment Act.

Eighteen months after the Act became law, official monitoring of its operation showed that the provisions regarding picketing have rarely been invoked by an employer, and those regarding closed shops and secret ballots not at all. The Act, however, continues to have an adverse affect on industrial relations between union and government.

**EMPLOYMENT APPEAL TRIBUNAL**    *See* Industrial Tribunals.

**EMPLOYMENT BILL, 1982**    A new Employment Bill was introduced in the House of Commons at the end of January, 1982 which it is intended should become law well before the end of the year. The Bill makes major alterations in the law concerning closed shops, trade union immunities, trades disputes etc. and has created a sharply antagonistic reaction in the trade union movement. Some of the main provisions, as outlined by the Department of Employment, are:

*Compensation for closed shop victims*

*Clause 1* enables the Secretary of State for Employment to pay compensation to people who were dismissed for non-membership in closed shops between the coming into force of the 1974 Act and the coming into force of the 1980 Employment Act and who were either existing employees of their employer before the closed shop agreement took effect in their firm or who objected to union membership on grounds of conscience or other deeply-held personal conviction.

*Dismissal for non-membership of a trade union*

*Clause 2* enlarges the circumstances in which dismissal for non-membership of a trade union in a closed shop is to be regarded as unfair, where a closed shop agreement which took effect before 15 August 1980 has not in the five years preceding the dismissal been supported in a secret ballot by 80 per cent of the employees covered by it or 85 per cent of those voting.

*Clause 5* enables an employee who is claiming to have been dismissed unfairly for not being a member of a trade union to claim compensation for the unfair dismissal wholly or partly against the union or other person rather than against the employer.

*Selective dismissal in a strike*

*Clause 7* applies to an employee who is dismissed while taking part in a strike. An employee will not be able to claim unfair dismissal provided that his employer has given notice to every employee on strike that any employee who does not return to work within a specified period of at least four working days may be dismissed.

*Action short of dismissal*

*Clause 8* extends an employee's right not to have action short of dismissal taken against him by his employer, in order to compel him to be a trade union member, to the additional circumstances in which his dismissal for non-membership of a trade union would be unfair under the new provisions of Clause 2.

*Clause 9* extends the new provisions described under clause 5 to cases of action short of dismissal for non-membership of a trade union.

*Union labour only requirements*

*Clause 10* makes void any term in a commercial contract requiring the contractor to use only union labour (or only non union members) in fulfilling the contract. It also makes it unlawful to terminate a contract, to exclude from a tender list or to refuse to invite tenders from or make a contract with a person on the grounds that anyone employed or likely to be employed to fulfil the contract is, or is not a union member.

*Clause 11* removes the legal immunities from trade unions and other persons who put pressure on an employer to act contrary to Clause 10. It also removes the immunities from those who organize action by employees which interferes with the supply of goods

# Employment Bill, 1982

or services on the ground that work done in connection with the supply of those goods or services is or has been performed by non-union or union members.

## Trade union immunities

*Clause 12* repeals Section 14 of the Trade Union and Labour Relations Act 1974. This brings the legal immunities for trade unions (and employers' associations) into line with those for individuals, with the effect that trade unions may be held liable for unlawful acts committed outside a trade dispute and for action which is already made unlawful by the Employment Act 1980. The clause describes the circumstances in which a trade union is to be regarded as liable for the unlawful acts of its officials.

*Clause 13* puts upper limits on damages which may be awarded against a trade union in civil proceedings (except in some cases of personal injury or connected with the ownership of property). The limits are defined by reference to the number of members in a trade union:

| | |
|---|---|
| fewer than 5,000 members | £ 10,000 |
| 5,000– 24,999 | £ 50,000 |
| 25,000–100,000 | £125,000 |
| more than 100,000 | £250,000 |

*Clause 14* specifies certain property from which damages costs or expenses may not be recovered in any proceedings against a trade union or employers' association.

## Trade dispute

*Clause 15* amends the definition of a 'trade dispute' in Section 29 of the 1974 Act. It specifies that a trade dispute must be between workers and their employer, and removes from Section 29 disputes between workers and workers. It requires that a trade dispute must relate wholly or mainly to the subjects in Section 29(1) of the 1974 Act, rather than merely be connected with them.

TUC COMMENTS ON THE BILL

*Industrial action*: First, the Employment Bill affects the lawfulness of – and the potential liability of unions and their officials for – industrial action. By narrowing the legal definition of what constitutes a 'trade dispute' in furtherance of which industrial action is lawful, the Bill removes 'immunity' from a wide range of categories of industrial action. To be lawful, industrial action will have to arise from disputes 'between workers and their employer', and will have to be 'wholly or mainly' related to the narrow issues of their terms and conditions of employment. Industrial action arising from disputes between 'workers and workers' and most disputes relating to matters occurring outside the UK is specifically made unlawful. Disputes in which Government policy is a factor, for instance on 'privatization' or public expenditure cuts, might be interpreted by the courts as not being 'wholly or mainly' related to industrial issues; the consequence is that the lawfulness of much industrial action, particularly by public sector workers, could be at risk.

In practical terms, this means that unions will run the risk of legal action where they take industrial action in situations in which important grievances justify it despite the non-involvement of the workers directly concerned. It is unclear whether this would affect industry-wide disputes between unions and employers' associations; solidarity and sympathy action would also appear to be at grave risk.

Industrial action resulting from disputes in which there is conflict between employers and various unions but also between the unions and between groups of workers may also be caught by the Bill. Although many of these disputes are labelled 'inter-union', the reality is that the employer is rarely, if ever, a disinterested and 'innocent' third party. These disputes occur in the main because employers change work allocations, technology and pay structures, and the removal of 'immunity' from trade union action in these fields would have widespread effects. Moreover, the restriction of the lawfulness of industrial action in solidarity with trade unionists in other countries appears to be designed to cut off the limited countervailing pressure that union organisations are currently able to exert on multi-national companies.

On top of this, the Government is to make it possible for unions to be sued for injunctions, and for their funds to be exposed to claims for damages as a result of unlawful action organised by their officials. For the first time since 1906 (except during 1971–74 under the Industrial Relations Act) union funds will be at risk where employers claim that they have been hit by unlawful industrial action and sue for damages. Larger unions will be liable to damages of up to £250,000 where a legal action is successful.

The cumulative effect of these provisions will be to restrict severely the range of actions trade unionists can lawfully take to bring pressure to bear on employers in dispute. A wide range of traditional and hitherto accepted forms of union action will potentially be affected.

The withdrawal of 'immunity' from certain types of industrial action by the 1980 Employment Act, and the new Employment Bill's narrowing of the definition of 'trade dispute' from which the 'immunities' stem, are likely to make it far easier for injunctions to be obtained against those conducting industrial action if its lawfulness is challenged in the courts. Moreover, the sheer complexity of the new statutory provisions will open the way to speculative court actions by employers and others, and give a hostile judiciary the opportunity to encroach even further on unions' dramatically reduced legal rights.

What is more, the fact that, in many circumstances, a union itself may be liable for unlawful industrial action — in addition to or instead of the officials conducting the action — may encourage employers and others to proceed more frequently to a full trial in order to claim damages. Hitherto in practice this has been extremely rare — an employer's usual objective would be to stop the industrial action, not to sue for damages. But with the exposure of union funds to damages claims this could change. If this were to happen, the amounts involved could be very large indeed, and any single dispute could potentially give rise to a number of separate legal cases and separate claims for damages.

Employers have the discretion whether or not to use the new legislative provisions, and many employers will realise that to do so could cause serious damage to their industrial relations. From 1971 to 1974, under the comparable provisions of the Industrial Relations Act, very few employers chose to launch damaging legal actions against trade unionists, and many of those who did attracted criticism from other employers. However, the decision whether or not legal action should be taken will not be under the sole control of the employer in dispute. It may be open to customers, suppliers and other parties claiming that they have been affected, to initiate legal actions for injunctions and damages against the official or union conducting industrial action – parties who will not have the same concern as the employer in dispute for industrial relations in that company.

*Trade union organization* The Bill also attacks trade union organization and union membership agreements and arrangements. The grounds on which compensation can be obtained by workers who refuse to join a union and are sacked will be widened, and the sums involved increased massively, in some cases up to £20,000 or more. A £2 million fund is being set up to compensate people who were dismissed under union membership agreements between 1974 and 1980 when the Trade Union and Labour Relations Act was in force. For the sacking of any non-unionist to be treated as fair, the union membership agreement concerned will have to be ratified every five years by an 80 per cent majority of those covered or an 85 per cent majority of those voting; without such ratification an employer will be liable to pay compensation to an employee dismissed for non-membership of a union. Unions themselves could be liable and responsible for paying compensation if they press employers to dismiss workers in such circumstances. Other measures include outlawing any arrangement or action to ensure that contract work is done only by unionized labour.

No trade unionist should be under the illusion that he or she will be totally unaffected by these provisions. The five or six million trade unionists who are covered by union membership agreements or arrangements face the possible disruption of their established practices and procedures. If the employer decides to hold a ballot as required under the proposed legislation, a union will be faced with the choice between not co-operating with the ballot – and thereby risking awards of compensation for sacked non-unionists — and co-operating and engaging in regular and strenuous campaigns to secure the very high majorities necessary. Although these majorities could no doubt easily be secured in many workplaces, there is a strong likelihood that such ballots could cause disruption, and the dissatisfaction of a minority of members with, say, a pay agreement could well surface in a campaign of this kind and result in undermining the union membership agreement. Some individuals will also be tempted by the 'pools-win' sums which are on offer to those who are dismissed for not being union members.

Many workers in the engineering, construction and printing industries, in local government and in other public services, among others, will have their terms and conditions placed in jeopardy by the proposed ban on 'union labour only' clauses in commercial contracts, or indeed on action by workers themselves refusing to work alongside non-unionists or refusing to handle work from non-union companies. The Government's aim here is

# Employment Bill, 1982

to encourage the flow of work to non-union contractors and labour who can undercut the tenders and charges of unionized firms by undercutting rates of pay and conditions that unions have won for their members.

In sum, by promoting periodic ballots on long-established as well as new union membership agreements, and by massively increasing the compensation obtainable by dismissed non-unionists, the intention of the Bill is to destabilize existing union membership arrangements and encourage individuals to drop out of union membership. This unjustified legal onslaught on union membership agreements, as well as the outlawing of 'union labour only' practices, could well lead to serious industrial relations problems for employers as well as unions. It could also undermine the TUC Disputes Principles and Procedures and exacerbate problems of multi-unionism.

*Selective dismissal*: The Bill proposes that employers will be able to threaten to dismiss all workers on strike at the end of a four days' notice period, and thereafter to dismiss all who have not returned to work without those persons having any right of recourse to an industrial tribunal. This provision is designed to encourage employers to issue ultimatums. It is an invitation to get rid of shop stewards and other activists who resist management threats.

*Trade Union Immunities*: The new restrictions proposed on workers will turn an already highly complex area of the law into an impenetrable legal morass. They open a wide range of industrial actions to challenge in the courts, irrespective of whether they result from unjust treatment, employers' provocation and other legitimate grievances. Moreover, the confused and confusing legal situation the Government would be causing would open the way for speculative court actions by employers and others. On past experience the judiciary may well use such actions to encroach even further on the legal right to withdraw labour.

In conjunction with these changes, unions will become liable for damages for the 'unlawful' actions of any of their officials. Trade unions are not corporate bodies. They are representative bodies which rely in large measure on lay officers, not full-time employees of the union, to conduct much of the union's administrative and negotiating work.

The use of the law as proposed will not provide any solution to industrial conflict: it is more likely to aggravate industrial disputes if resorting to the courts for injunctions and damages to coerce trade unionists back to work becomes a tactic used by employers.

*Dismissals During Strikes*: In proposing amendments to the present statutory position concerning selective dismissals during strikes, the Government appears to be giving legal encouragement to employers for the discriminatory sacking of employees, including shop stewards and active trade union members, who resist such divisive management threats and remain on strike.

*Conclusions*: The proposals represent a further step in the Government's sustained legal offensive against essential trade union rights and against the mutual support which is the hallmark of free trade unionism. They are rooted in the Government's deep seated hostility to trade union activity, and its distorted analysis of industrial relations, which ignores the power of business and the role of management in precipitating industrial disputes.

It has been further argued that the Employment Act, 1980, has not been in operation long enough (some 18 months) to 'prove the need' for stronger anti-union proposals. Even the Government's own Green Paper that preceded the Bill had reservations about the advisability of withdrawing the provision for trade union immunities which date from 1906, while the changes in the statutory definition of a trade dispute will place excessive powers in the hands of judges with no experience of industrial relations. This will inhibit unions from taking action on behalf of their members for fear that legitimate and reasonable action could be declared unlawful.

**EMPLOYMENT MEDICAL ADVISORY SERVICE**  This service consists of approximately a hundred full time doctors and nurses employed under the Health and Safety Commission and has the task of identifying health hazards relating to employment by monitoring studies and surveys, acting as a central information bank, advising trade unions and employers on how to deal with health hazards, and acting as a focus for medical aspects of employment problems, particularly in areas such as disablement and rehabilitation. (*See* Health and Safety.)

**EMPLOYMENT PROTECTION ACT (EPA) 1975**  The Employment Protection Act was the attempt by the Labour Government of that period to put right the wrongs inflicted by the Industrial

# Employment Protection Act 1975

Relations Act of 1971 in addition to the repeal legislation contained in the Trade Union and Labour Relations Act of 1974 (TULRA). The EPA was basically designed to strengthen collective bargaining and improve the rights of workers.

The Act was divided into five parts, which were:

(a) the improvement of industrial relations
(b) the rights of employees
(c) the reform of Wages Councils
(d) the procedure for handling redundancies
(e) other provisions.

Its approach to *improving industrial relations* was to put ACAS (the Advisory, Conciliation and Arbitration Service) on a statutory basis in keeping with the philosophy of 'conciliation not confrontation'. In addition to its role in the encouragement of collective bargaining, ACAS was empowered to issue Codes of Practice concerning practical guidance for promoting good industrial relations. For example it issued codes on disciplinary procedures, disclosure of information and time off for trade union activities. The EPA established the post of Certification Officer to take over the functions of the Chief Registrar of Friendly Societies and to 'ensure the development of trade unions which are financially independent of employers'. Another feature was the setting up of the Central Arbitration Committee.

A considerable extension in the *rights of employees* was given, including the introduction of Guarantee Payments; various measures for the protection of pregnant mothers (maternity leave, maternity pay, reinstatement rights, restrictions on dismissal); provisions for securing trade union recognition; disclosure of information; strengthened measures on unfair dismissals; improved arrangements governing periods of notice related to termination of contracts of employment; provision for itemized pay statements to be given to employees; guidance on disciplinary procedures by ACAS; protection of the right of employees to join and take part in the activities of a certified trade union; introduction of Government support for time off from work with pay for employees in certain circumstances including trade union activities and seeking new employment or training when working out redundancy notices. The Employment Appeal Tribunal was also established.

On the *reform of Wages Councils* the Act widened the powers of the Councils to determine *all* terms and conditions of employment and not only basic pay and holidays which was the case previously. This also applied to the Agricultural Wages Board which was allowed to make orders with retrospective effect. ACAS was empowered to investigate the whole area of Wages Councils. Not least, Schedule 11 was brought in to enable an independent trade union to secure an award from the Central Arbitration Committee against a 'black sheep' employer who failed to observe the general level of terms and conditions accepted by other employers in the same trade or industry, where conditions are similar.

Measures to minimize the hardship suffered by employees facing *redundancy* were introduced, including safeguards for employees of bankrupt firms, notification of impending redundancies and provisions for consultation with trade unions.

*Other provisions* in the Act dealt with payment of unemployment benefit to those laid off as a result of a strike; standardization of licensing for private employment agencies; appointment of safety representatives only by independent trade unions; and the extension of employment legislation generally to those working on oil rigs and the sea bed in the British sector of the North Sea.

The EPA was amended by the Employment Act, 1980. (*See* Employment Act 1980.)

**EMPLOYMENT PROTECTION (CONSOLIDATION) ACT 1978** This Act consolidated *individual* employment rights drawn from previous legislation: Trade Union and Labour Relations Act (1974) and (1976), the Employment Protection Act (1975), Contracts of Employment Act (1972) and Redundancy Payments Act (1965).

The 'rights' were: the right to a written statement of the main terms and conditions of the employment; the right to a minimum period of notice; the right to an itemized pay statement; the right to a guarantee payment; the right to payment while on suspension from work on medical grounds; the right to time off work for trade union duties and activities, for public duties, to look for work or to arrange training prior to redundancy; the rights of an expectant mother; the right not to be unfairly dismissed; the right to be provided with a written statement of the reasons for dismissal; the right to receive a lump sum payment if dismissed as redundant; the right of employees not to have action short of dismissal taken against them because of trade union membership or activities; the right to payments which an employer cannot make because of insolvency. The Act was amended by the Employment Act 1980. (*See* Employment Act, 1980.)

**EMPLOYERS' ASSOCIATIONS**     There are over 350 organizations of employers registered with the Certification Officer as Employers' Associations. Apart from the CBI they normally link together employers in a particular industry and/or region. These bodies exist for the purpose of consultation, self protection, the exchange of information, and often the collective regulation of wages and conditions of employment in negotiation with their opposite numbers in the trade unions. Some of them are very wealthy and are able to deploy considerable resources jointly subscribed by their members.

Among the wealthiest and largest Associations are: the Engineering Employers' Federation, the National Farmers' Union, the British Shipping Federation, the Freight Transport Association, the Electrical Contractors, the Road Haulage Federation, the National Federation of Builders, the Chemical Industries Association, and the British Printing Industries Federation.

In addition there are regional and local Chambers of Commerce and other associations concerned with commerce as well as various national associations concerned with technical objectives. (*See* Confederation of British Industries.)

**EMPLOYERS' LIABILITY**     In addition to the liability an employer may have towards the community at large, i.e. his public liability, he has special obligations to those he employs. The employer may have towards the community at large, i.e. his public gence towards his work people and, because of what the law describes as vicarious liability, he has to answer for the negligent acts of persons he may employ.

Certain Acts of Parliament impose direct obligations upon employers, many of which can be regarded as absolute duties. The Factories Act and the Mines and Quarries Act are clear examples. These Acts of Parliament require employers to take certain measures and precautions to guard against accidents to their workpeople. If the employer fails to comply then he is guilty of a statutory breach of responsibility and is clearly liable for damages to anyone injured as a result of his neglect.

The broad outline of the employer's duty to his employee is, among other things, to provide:

(a) proper plant, machinery, equipment and premises in reasonable condition having regard to the nature of the work to be carried out;

(b) reasonably competent fellow servants;
(c) adequate supervision and instruction when any dangerous work or dangerous machinery is involved;
(d) a reasonably safe system for carrying out the work generally.

If injury to a workman occurs as a result of a breach of one or more of these duties a claim for damages may result. The fact that an accident has happened does not in itself show the method of work to be unsafe. Custom, practice and past happenings all are factors to be taken into account. The employer's liability, if a wrong is done, applies even if he delegates responsibility to someone else e.g. manager, foreman, or supervisor, for putting into effect the necessary safety measures and the person so deputed fails to carry them out.

On the same principle an employer may be held responsible for accidents due directly to negligent acts of his employees. For example if employee A is injured because of employee B's negligence the employer may have to meet a damages claim by employee A. In such circumstances the act of alleged negligence must be capable of proof.

Trade Unions are very much involved where employer's liability claims are being made because proof is sometimes difficult to establish and the pursuit of claims, particularly through the Courts, can be very costly. The mere fact that an accident has occurred does not automatically mean that negligence is involved, no matter how serious the accident may be. Industrial Injuries legislation provides for payments to be made to employees injured at work irrespective of whether claims are made against employers for negligence or not. (*See* Industrial Injuries/Payments.)

**ENGINEERING COUNCIL** This is a Council set up under Royal Charter in 1981, aimed at strengthening the engineering profession. It will have powers to set professional qualifications and create a register of accredited engineers. It will control the accreditation of academic engineering courses and engineering training programmes. The title of Chartered Engineer, at present granted by the Council of Engineering Institutions (CEI) will be available for grant by the new Council three years after its formation if its activities have received the approval of the CEI. There is to be a major transfer of power and responsibility from the CEI to the new body but not until the end of 1983.

The Council is initially being funded by the Government but is intended to be self-supporting. Its membership will be drawn from

# Equal Pay

industry, the engineering professions and institutions and academics. At least half of the members will have to have practical experience of engineering as employers or managers.

No special provision is made for trade union representation although two trade union leaders are among the first list of appointments made by the Department of Industry.

**EQUAL PAY**   This phrase is used in the sense of equal remuneration for equal work without distinction of sex. The Equal Pay movement developed in order to change the position where, in many occupations and jobs, women performing the same duties as men were paid at a lower rate simply because they were women, even though they could be employed by the same employer and in the same locality as their male fellow-workers. In the years after the war, women, in a number of instances (e.g. in the Civil Service and the teaching profession), won equal pay mainly by trade union action. But throughout industry the position remained very largely one of unequal pay. In 1970 the Labour Government passed the Equal Pay Act in order to remedy the situation by law.

The Act (operative since 1976) aims to eliminate discrimination between men and women in all forms of pay and other terms of their contracts of employment, e.g. holidays and sick leave. The work must be broadly similar or be of equal value, as determined by a job evaluation scheme, if it is different. Discrimination in collective agreements, employers' pay structure, and statutory Wages Orders, can be referred to the Central Arbitration Committee which can order the removal of the discrimination. Individual women alleging discrimination should seek union assistance and have the ultimate right to apply to an industrial tribunal. The Act provides, too, for men to receive equal treatment with women. Job evaluation may be used to determine 'equal value'.

Equal treatment, it should be said, does not necessarily mean identical treatment. It means that each term in a woman's contract must not be less favourable than the corresponding term in a man's, e.g. in respect of holidays. The comparisons can be made only between people working for the same or an associated employer. It is known that employers may resist realistic skill gradings, to the detriment of women, in order to maintain a *status quo* practising discrimination. Thus the Act in itself has not created equal pay; its successful application depends on the initiative and persistence of the unions on behalf of their women members, and on their skill in interpreting the provisions of the Act in manifold circumstances.

Criticism of the Equal Pay Act and other forms of sex discrimination in employment has been made by the TUC and the Equal Opportunities Commission (EOC). The TUC has represented to the European Commission that the Act does not comply with Community (EEC) law in that it does not give a clear definition of equal pay for work of equal value and this helps discrimination to continue. But the Government's view is that the legislation is adequate in spite of criticisms already made by the Commission.

In its fifth annual report, 1980, the EOC states that 'progress towards equality, e.g. in terms of earnings, had come to a halt. We have now begun to report that the position of women in this respect has begun to worsen'. It added that unless the law was amended, women would continue to earn about 73 per cent of men's pay, due to the difficulty of comparing what may be in practice exclusively female jobs with male jobs. In fact there was a very slight increase in women's (full-time) hourly earnings from $73\frac{1}{2}$ per cent to 75 per cent of men's between April 1980 and April 1981 and a similar increase for weekly earnings, according to the New Earnings Survey, 1981. But the Survey also showed that in 17 selected occupations where women predominate, only 5 had achieved greater equality since 1975 while in 8 the inequality had worsened.

Part-time women workers (of whom there were over $3\frac{1}{2}$ million in June 1981) are the worst-paid workers compared with both full-time men and full-time women workers. This position has remained unchanged since 1975. Unequal pay is, however, only one aspect of discrimination in employment. Other aspects are dealt with in the Labour Government's Sex Discrimination Act, 1975. (*See* Sex Discrimination.)

**EUROPEAN MONETARY SYSTEM (EMS) – THE 'SNAKE'**   The system whereby a number of European Economic Community (EEC) Central Banks (including the French, West German, Italian, Belgian, Dutch) commit themselves to buy and sell each other's currencies in such a way as to maintain fixed exchange rates (the so-called Snake) between them. A small amount of variation (normally 5 per cent) is allowed in these exchange rates. The UK has not joined the EMS and is not a party to the Snake arrangements.

# European Social Fund

**EUROPEAN SOCIAL FUND**    The European Social Fund is an employment fund under the EEC and its purpose is described in Article 123 of the Treaty of Rome as follows:

'to improve employment opportunities for workers in the Common Market and to contribute thereby to raising the standard of living . . . (by) rendering employment of workers easier and . . . increasing their geographical and occupational mobility'. In practice this means that it provides financial support for schemes of training, retraining and resettlement, to help mainly the unemployed and underemployed.

The scope can be very wide. In 1981 the East Leeds Women's Workshop received a grant of over £100,000, spread over three years, towards the cost of running a creche while mothers trained for jobs. For 1982, £100.5 million has been earmarked to support a wide range of job projects in Britain.

To be eligible for assistance from the Fund, a scheme must have financial support from a public authority, that is it must be wholly or partly financed by public funds.

The Social Fund can meet up to half the cost of a project where the scheme is run by public authorities. In the case of a scheme run by a private organization the Social Fund may match the public authority support.

In the United Kingdom the Department of Employment is the point of contact with the EEC Social Fund Administration and all applications have to be sent through the Department.

**EXCHANGE CONTROL**    *See* Convertibility.

**EX GRATIA PAYMENT**    Employers sometimes may make a payment to employees which is outside and over and above any money the employees are due as the result of an agreement and which in no way affects or alters the agreement. Such 'ex gratia' payments may include a Christmas bonus or extra money in gratitude for a job specially well done, e.g. fulfilling an export order in good time. Such special payments may also be made in case of injury or accident at work or to a worker's family.

# F

**FACILITIES FOR TRADE UNION REPRESENTATIVES**
*See* Time off for Trade Union representatives.

**FAIR TRADING ACT 1973**    Until this Act, alleged monopolies
and monopoly practices could be referred to the Monopolies and
Mergers Commission only by the Secretary of State for Trade. The
1973 Act created the office of Director General of Fair Trading with
powers to investigate trading activities and refer alleged monopolies
and monopolistic practices to the Commission. His power does not
extend to referring mergers except that he can advise the Minister
regarding them. Restrictive labour agreements can also be referred
to the Commission by the Minister although he cannot statutorily
stop them as the result of an investigation.

A wide range of commercial restrictive practices comes under the
jurisdiction of the Director General who, in the interests of protecting consumers, can recommend action to the Secretary of State for
Prices and Consumer Protection. His recommendations are vetted
by the Consumer Protection Advisory Committee. Cases may come
before the Restrictive Practices Court; he may also ask for an undertaking from an offending firm to discontinue the relevant practice
and publish such undertaking.

The Secretary of State for Consumer Protection has powers to
issue Statutory Orders against restrictive trade practices. (*See*
Monopolies.)

**FAIR WAGES RESOLUTION**    The Fair Wages Resolution of
1946 of the House of Commons established the principle that workers in government employ either directly or through government
contractors must be offered terms and conditions at least as good as
those offered in the trade in the district by private employers or if
there are no such comparisons available, then the generally accepted
standards for the industry for similar jobs. Also established was the
right of the workers to join a union of their choice. A weakness of the
Resolution is that it can be interpreted as establishing *minimum* standards–which could in practice become *maximum*.

It must be noted that the Resolution is *not* an Act of Parliament. It
has nevertheless been generally taken as a rule to be observed. Complaints on failure to observe the principles of the Resolution are
made to the Department of Employment who in practice refer them

# Family Expenditure Survey

to the Central Arbitration Committee. Though the CAC has no power to make a binding award its decisions usually are accepted in practice.

The principles of the Resolution apply statutorily also to most nationalized industries, e.g. coal, gas, electricity, atomic energy, civil aviation and to beet sugar refining, film making, TV, road haulage, road transport, and the National Health Service. Local authorities also normally include a fair wages clause in their agreements with contractors. In the above cases claims go the CAC via ACAS. (*See* Going Rate.)

**FAMILY EXPENDITURE SURVEY** This is a survey, published annually by the Government, based on information about the expenditure of some 7,000 families selected as representative of the population. Its purpose is to show the ways in which families of different kinds and economic levels spend their incomes. Comparisons are also made possible as between one year and another.

It provides data on the expenditure of all households on items such as rent, rates, water, fuel, food, clothing, household goods, transport, vehicles. Information is included on the expenditure of pensioners, low and high earners, class of dwellers in council houses and owner-occupied homes, the cost of items in the various regions, the number of earners in a family, etc.

The survey makes it possible to assess the different percentage of their total income different kinds of family spend on basic necessities and all other items that are common in current patterns of expenditure today such as cars, entertainment, holidays etc., and so provides valuable information for negotiators. For example in 1979 the average gross family income was £120.45 a week but 55 per cent of families received less than that and 26 per cent had incomes of less than £60 a week.

**FAMILY INCOME SUPPLEMENT** *See* Social Security.

**FINES** Many trade unions have disciplinary rules involving the payment of fines, suspension or expulsion. Some of the older craft trade unions can impose fines for non-attendance at meetings or for leaving a meeting without the permission of the chairman. Such rules tend to be honoured 'in the breach' these days. On the other hand most trade unions can and do impose fines on members 'acting against the interests of the Union' or for working during an official dispute. If a member fails to pay a fine properly applied under the Union's rules the amount may be counted as though the member is in arrears of payment of union subscription, with all the consequences that this may entail. Members of unions may appeal against such penalties through the machinery laid down in the Union's rules.

**FLYING PICKETS**   These are pickets who move from one site to another in the course of an industrial dispute with the object of exercising pressure usually through the customers of the firm or organization in dispute with the union. Thus in a famous incident miners in dispute with the Coal Board sent pickets to a power station using coal to try to prevent it from doing so. The 1980 Employment Act has severely circumscribed picketing including the possibility of utilizing flying pickets. (*See* Picketing.)

**FREE HEALTH SERVICE TREATMENT**   *See* Social Security.

**FREE RIDERS**   This is a pejorative term applied to those working in an establishment or an industry or occupation where wages, salaries, and other terms of employment or conditions of service are negotiated on their behalf by unions but they nevertheless refuse to join. They are accused of accepting the protection and benefits won by the unions but refusing to pay their share of the costs by subscribing to the union or adding to the strength of negotiators.

**FREEDOM ASSOCIATION (FORMERLY NATIONAL ASSOCIATION FOR FREEDOM, NAFF)**   The NAFF, later renamed the Freedom Association, was founded in 1975 'to campaign on a non-party political basis . . . for the preservation, maintenance and extension of freedom and free enterprise'. It was registered as a company limited by guarantee without share capital in 1977. In its Memorandum of Association it refers to 'the concept of active citizenship . . . namely that it is the duty of responsible citizens to organize for the defence of freedoms that are under attack'. It is commonly regarded as an extreme right wing political organization opposed to trade unionism. The Freedom Association has a Council which includes industrialists, financiers, military men and some Conservative MPs. It is financed by individual subscription and donations from business firms and it publishes a fortnightly paper, Free Nation. Among its activities have been involvement in legal proceedings including injunctions against a number of trade union actions.

**FREEDOM OF ASSOCIATION**   The International Labour Organization (ILO) in its Convention No. 87 provided that 'workers' and employers' organizations shall have the right to draw up their constitutions and rules, to elect their representatives in full freedom, to organize their administration and activities and to formulate their programmes' and that the 'public authorities shall refrain from any interference which would restrict this right or impede the lawful exercise thereof'. This principle of 'Freedom of Association' was reinforced in another ILO Convention No. 98 which provides that 'workers shall enjoy adequate protection against acts of anti-union discrimination in respect of their employment' and, more particularly, that this protection shall apply in respect of acts calculated to 'make the employment of a worker subject to conditions that he shall not join a union or shall relinquish trade union membership' or to 'cause the dismissal of or otherwise prejudice a worker by reason of trade union membership or because of participation in union activities'.

Both these Conventions have been ratified in the United Kingdom and were given statutory backing, in particular, by the legislation passed by the 1974–79 Labour Government.

The ILO has special machinery known as the Committee on Freedom of Association, for the impartial investigation of allegations of infringements of freedom of association so that it may, if necessary, make recommendations to the Governments concerned, or take other appropriate action.

**FRINGE BENEFITS** In addition to wages and salaries employees at both shop floor and management levels may receive some of a wide range of additional benefits and services generally described as fringe benefits. At shop floor level these can include e.g. occupational pensions, travelling allowances, luncheon vouchers, advances free of interest to pay for season tickets, social and recreational facilities, special holiday payments, cheap purchase of the firm's goods or cheap or free access to the organization's services (e.g. rail or air travel) etc.

On the higher management level fringe benefits can include generous pension schemes and widow's protection benefits, lavish expense accounts often difficult to monitor, the use of a company car (according to the Inland Revenue there were in 1980 about 750,000 private users of company cars), free petrol, subsidized lunches, medical insurance involving access to private health treatment, assistance with school fees, profit-sharing and share purchase option schemes, loans at favourable interest rates, help with mortgage purchases, substantial redundancy compensation, etc. For executives earning over £8,500 a year (1981) many of these benefits are taxable but their financial value remains very substantial and constitute in effect a major tax-free addition to the actual salary paid.

Increased taxation on company cars, taxation on company petrol for private use, tax-free season tickets and taxation of certain credit card arrangements between executives and their employers, were all pledged by the Government in 1980 for early imposition. Some tax will be paid on privately used petrol from April 1982.

In the Charterhouse Group's annual survey of benefits and conditions for company directors, reported in the Times, a generalized description is given of larger companies: 'The director . . . will . . . have a company Daimler or Jaguar. . . . He is likely to have most of his private petrol costs paid with a credit card for running costs, and possibly a second car.

'The company will contribute more than 20 per cent of his earnings to his pension plan, while he contributes about 5 per cent. He will have free life assurance cover of four times his salary and his widow will continue to receive at least half his pension.

'Other benefits include generous medical insurance, with a guaranteed salary for a year; a service contract of three years or more, free meals and newspapers, help with telephone rental and calls, free financial advice . . . chauffeurs, club subscriptions, company accommodation, share options, and even a job-with-car for the director's wife.' (*See* Perks.)

**FULL EMPLOYMENT**   Following the Second World War, with the experience of pre-war mass unemployment in mind, the post-war Labour Governments pledged themselves to policies aiming at full employment, i.e. an approximate balance between those seeking jobs and jobs available. This was also the bi-partisan objective of the White Paper on Employment produced by the coalition Government during the war in 1944. The term allows for a small amount of temporary unemployment as people switch from one job to another or for seasonal unemployment or to cover changes and developments which may take time to settle down. But it is also sometimes interpreted so as to allow for a 'low' level of unemployment, perhaps from 2 to 5 per cent.

Full employment ceased to be the major priority it had previously been after the devaluation crisis of 1967 and the levels of unemployment have risen sharply in the 70s, especially under the Thatcher

Government since 1979. Under this government full employment no longer has any priority as an objective of economic policy; it features, however, in the alternative economic strategies being advocated by the Labour and Trade Union movement.

Full employment places trade unions in a strong position in bargaining for better terms of employment, espcially wages, as employers find it harder to fill vacancies. On the other hand it tends to reduce the operation of restrictive practices as workers are less inclined to cling to clearly demarcated jobs when other alternatives are readily available.

# G

**GENERAL FEDERATION OF TRADE UNIONS (GFTU)** This consists of 37 unions nearly all of whom are also affiliated to the TUC and was created in 1899 as the result of a resolution passed at the 1898 TUC. The affiliated membership amounts to less than half a million, mainly in small unions, the largest group of which are in the textile trades. The membership has been declining due to the run down of industries in which many of the unions concerned operate.

Unlike the TUC, the Federation has funds to which its affiliates contribute for the purpose of gaining financial relief when involved in industrial disputes. It also operates a Research Service and organizes trade union educational activities.

The objects of the GFTU are:

(a) To do anything necessary to promote the interests or perfect the working of all or any of its affiliated organizations or to improve the conditions and protect the interests of the individual members of any such organizations and in particular to improve the conditions of employment, rates of wages and hours of labour of such members individually or collectively, to regulate the relations between employer and employed and to impose restrictive conditions on the conduct of any trade or business, to settle or obtain the settlement of disputes between employer and employed. Generally to do all such other acts and things as shall be considered to be for the furtherance of the objects in this rule and all other trade union, social or educational purposes.

(b) To provide benefits for its affiliated organizations and to give to all or any of them financial or other assistance. To make advances of money by way of loan to all or any of its affiliated organizations.

(c) To provide and make financial provision for educational facilities and instruction in accordance with any scheme or schemes which may from time to time be approved by the Governing Body.

(d) To assist any affiliated organization either financially or otherwise in any legal proceeding or dispute or other matter or in the provision of legal advice.

(e) To inaugurate and maintain schemes for the provision of pensions or grants of money for the Officers and Staff of the GFTU and for Officers and Staff of all or any of its affiliated organizations.

(f) To provide and maintain any sanatorium, convalescent home, club or other institution for the use of members of affiliated organizations and for their Officers and Staff and for the Officers and Staff of the GFTU.

**GENERAL STRIKE**   The idea of a universal stoppage of work as a means of raising the position of the working class was first put forward in Britain in the early 19th century. Later versions of the idea saw it more explicitly as a means of bringing about the revolutionary overthrow of capitalism – the General Strike was the centre of the strategy of the pre-1914 syndicalist movement – but it was also advocated as a way of forcing governments to concede more limited political changes. The British General Strike of 1926 was called by the TUC in order to defend the miners who were being locked out by the coal owners until they would accept lower wages and longer hours.

The General Council were very anxious to insist that it was a sympathetic industrial action and not a 'General Strike' (i.e. with political aims) at all but the Government's attack on the strike as a challenge to the Constitution undermined the will of the General Council, who, despite a magnificent response by the rank and file of the trade union movement, called off the strike without helping the miners.

**GO SLOW**   *See* Ca'Canny, Work to Rule.

# Going Rate

**GOING RATE: SCHEDULE 11 CLAIMS (COMPARABILITY CLAIMS)** Trade Unions strive to prevent the cutting by employers of wage rates below what is claimed to be the general level for a particular trade or industry. Where an employer is observing terms and conditions of employment less favourable than 'the recognized terms and conditions', parity could, until 1980, be claimed by reference to ACAS to investigate the matter. Claims that ACAS felt should be pursued could be heard by the Central Arbitration Committee (CAC). This procedure could also operate where there were no such *recognized* terms and conditions but it was claimed that wage rates were below the relevant 'general level' operating in the trade or industry. Recognized terms and conditions are those established by district or national agreements by unions and employers or by arbitration awards. The right to pursue such claims was contained in Schedule 11 of the Employment Protection Act and such claims were generally known as Schedule 11 or comparability claims to establish the 'going rate' for the trade or industry.

When Schedule 11 was in operation in the case of a particular claim where there was no district or national agreement, for purposes of comparability the claim could be judged with reference to the 'general level' of terms and conditions in the industry or trade. The general level did not mean the highest level but, normally, an average level, observed in the same industry or section of industry in the same district, and the circumstances of the employers had to be similar. This latter point was capable of wide interpretation.

Awards made by ACAS became part of the worker's contract so that employers could be sued for breach of contract if the terms were not observed.

These provisions were, however, repealed by the Employment Act, 1980, which was strongly opposed by the trade union movement. The issue is of some importance since comparability claims could deal not only with basic wage rates but also with other terms and conditions of employment including shift rates, overtime payments, holiday pay, London allowance, hours of work, sick pay, meals allowances and pensions. In dealing with such claims the CAC had to take into account all the terms and conditions operating in the trade or industry, not simply isolated elements. As the CAC is not a court but an arbitration body, its decisions did not, however, set precedents for other cases.

Section 11 of the EPA did not apply to workers in Crown employment, e.g. Civil Servants, or to workers whose terms and conditions are covered by other legislation, such as certain Health Service employees, teachers, and probation officers. But apart from these, employees of public and local authorities were covered.

Certain other workers, those employed by contractors to government departments, nationalized industries, and local authorities, are covered by the Fair Wages Resolution of 1946, which still applies. Under this, contracts can be withdrawn from employers who fail to observe the 'going rate' as described above, thus giving unions a means of redress against offending employers. (*See* Fair Wages Resolution.)

**GOLD STANDARD**    *See* Convertibility.

**GOLDEN HANDSHAKE**    'Golden handshakes' mean the payment of large sums of money to individuals in management, usually top management, on the termination of services or contractual obligation for one reason or another. The money may be paid under various guises but it is in effect a type of redundancy (voluntary or compulsory) pay for top management, of far greater value than the redundancy payments made to workers under the law. This is why 'golden handshakes' have aroused considerable controversy and opposition from trade unions.

Companies are required by law to disclose such payments in aggregate only, i.e. the individuals concerned need not be identified. But such identification has often been made officially or become known. Directors of companies have been paid very large sums (apart from pension payments and other 'perks'), often more than £150,000, and overall payments have been as high as £750,000 in one case and close to £400,000 in another. In contrast, the average statutory redundancy pay received between July and September 1981 by over 220,000 employees was reported in the Employment Gazette as £119.

Until the March 1982 Budget, no tax was payable on the first £25,000 of a Golden Handshake and the rest was taxed in effect at 30 per cent. From April 1982, tax relief on sums over £25,000 is on sliding scale, the full tax rate (60 per cent) being reached only for sums over £75,000.

**GREEN PAPER**    *See* Blue Book.

**GRIEVANCES AND GRIEVANCE PROCEDURE**    Problems

may arise at the workplace, concerning an individual employee or a group of employees, which require speedy solution but which do not necessarily involve the consideration of industrial action and which can be solved without such action by other methods. In these circumstances the existence of a Grievance Procedure for individual cases and a Disputes Procedure for collective cases is desirable, indeed necessary, for handling such issues.

'Grievances' include individual or group pay grievances (calculation of pay, deductions, gradings, etc.); failure to give time off for union activities; changes not according to union agreements in work practices, e.g. increased workload without corresponding adjustment of pay; personal difficulties with the supervisor or other charges of unfair treatment; and unfair allocation of overtime. Collective disputes may cover safety problems, any changes in work organization introduced without consultation with the union, alleged breach of agreements etc.

It is necessary that the procedures for solving such problems, which may arise from day to day, should be clearly formulated in writing and that they should specify in detail the precise manner of dealing with them, by whom, at what level in each type of case and the higher level of reference if necessary, the time limits within which the grievance must be dealt with and, of great importance, the operation of a *status quo* clause which means that while the grievance is being dealt with, the conditions which operated before the alleged grievance occurred will operate and, equally, no recourse to industrial action will be made. Grievance procedures may allow of outside conciliation and of arbitration as a final stage.

Both management and shopfloor representatives require training in recognizing grievances, estimating their importance, and operating the procedures, if grievances are to be sensibly handled so that they do not blow up unnecessarily into larger issues.

**GROSS DOMESTIC PRODUCT (GDP); GROSS NATIONAL PRODUCT (GNP)**    The GDP is a money estimate of the value of the output of goods and services produced in the country in any year, normally at market prices. If depreciation is taken into account we have the *net* Domestic Product. The GNP adds to the GDP income from overseas investment and property but does not include income from investment or property owned by foreigners and going outside the country. It is common to estimate the share that expenditure on services such as education or health or defence takes of the GDP or the GNP.

## GUARANTEE PAYMENTS FOR LAY-OFF OR SHORT-TIME WORKING

*Workers' Rights to Payment*: Under Sections 12–18 of the Employment Protection (Consolidation) Act, 1978, a worker, if he is not provided with work on a normal working day, is entitled to a guarantee payment from his employer.

This is except where:

(a) suitable alternative work has been offered to and is refused by that worker
(b) the employer's inability to provide work is caused by a trade dispute involving other workers of the same or of an associated employer.

*Basis and Limits of Payment*: Payment due is based on the worker's normal daily earnings, subject to a maximum payment of £9.15 a day (in 1982) and to an entitlement of up to 5 days only in a 3-month period. A worker's right to guarantee payment under contract may, however, be offset against his statutory right to payment.

A full day's work must be lost (but not through a trade dispute) for a guarantee payment to fall due, and there will be no entitlement to guarantee payments if the worker affected has not been employed for four weeks by the employer involved and does not ensure that his services are available for the kind of work he normally does, on the day in question. He must have worked for at least 16 hours a week or, if he has had 5 years' service or more, for at least 8 hours a week.

*Exemption Under Contractual Provisions*: An exemption order may be issued by the Secretary of State, releasing from the statutory requirements parties to a collective agreement that provides for guarantee pay, should they apply for exemption and the Secretary find their request reasonable. Both statutory and collectively agreed schemes may operate concurrently, however, and this may prove to be to the workers' advantage.

*Appeals Procedure*: A worker failing to obtain a guarantee payment from his employer may appeal to an industrial tribunal, which may order the employer to make the payment due. His appeal must be made within 3 months of the lay-off day where this is practicable.

The following workers are not covered by the Guarantee Payments provisions:

> members of the police and armed forces,
> an employee who is the husband or wife of the employer,
> registered dock workers engaged on dock work,
> share fishermen who are paid solely by a share in the profit or gross earnings of a fishing vessel,
> employees who under their contracts of employment ordinarily work outside Great Britain,
> employees employed for a fixed term of twelve weeks or less or to perform a specific task not expected to last more than twelve weeks, unless in either case the employee is in fact continuously employed for more than twelve weeks – the provisions would then apply from the thirteenth week,
> an employee who has no normal working hours prescribed by his contract of employment, for example some insurance agents and sales representatives.

Employment on offshore installations in British Territorial waters and certain work in British designated areas of the Continental Shelf are also covered by the provisions.

Trade unions may negotiate *pro rata* payments for part time lay-offs, payment without the four-week qualifying period, or disregarding industrial action outside the actual establishment in which the worker is employed, or for more days than provided for by the statutory provisions. Workers are entitled to payment under the Act or under an agreement, whichever is the more favourable. (*See* Suspension on Medical Grounds etc.)

# H

**HEALTH AND SAFETY AT WORK**    The Health and Safety at Work Act came into operation on July 31 1974. It requires all employers to ensure, insofar as is reasonably practicable, the health, safety and welfare at work of all their employees. It empowers the Secretary of State for Employment, acting through the Health and Safety Commission – a body set up in October 1974 – to draw up detailed regulations and codes of practice on specific health and safety matters. The main purpose of the Act was to provide for one comprehensive and integrated system of law dealing with the health, safety and welfare of workpeople and safety of the public as affected by work activities. In effect it took over the Factories Act, the Mines and Quarries Act, the Shops and Railway Premises Act and similar legislation, and extended them.

The Act re-organized and unified the various government inspectorates into a body called the Health and Safety Executive Inspectorate with powers to enforce the Act. The Act lists three main ways in which employers can be forced to provide and maintain a safe and healthy place of work: the issuing of improvement notices and prohibition notices, the imposition of heavy fines and the threat of imprisonment.

When the Inspectorate serves an improvement notice, the employer must act to put things right within a specified time. If he does not, a prohibition notice may be issued stopping the operation which gives rise to the hazard.

An Inspector also has power to issue an immediate prohibition notice stopping an operation if there is a risk of immediate danger to workers or the general public. Appeals against these notices must be made to an Industrial Tribunal. An appeal can lead to a stay of execution of an improvement notice, but there can be no delay in the implementation of a prohibition notice if the Inspector believes that the risk of personal injury is acute.

In cases where the Inspector thinks there is no immediate risk, he may give some time for remedial action to be taken, i.e. a deferred prohibition notice.

Non-compliance with these notices is an offence and can lead to a heavy fine on conviction at a magistrate's court, or up to two years imprisonment in the case of trial by indictment. In addition to these penalties there could be a continuing fine of £50 per day for every day of non-compliance.

The Health and Safety Commission is composed of an independent chairman who is full-time and nine part-time commissioners, three of whom are nominated by the TUC and three by the CBI. The Commission possesses comprehensive powers to make new regulations and to draw up proposals for extension, revision or replacement of existing legislation concerning the protection of the safety and health of workpeople.

The following is a summary of the Act:

# Health and Safety at Work

*Section 1* states the general purpose of Part 1 of the Act which is aimed at (a) maintaining or improving standards of health, safety and welfare of people at work; (b) protecting other people against risks to health and safety arising out of work activities; (c) controlling the storage and use of dangerous substances; and (d) controlling certain emissions into the air from certain premises.

*Section 2* begins by laying down the general duty of the employers to take reasonable care of their employees and makes provision for the appointment of workers' safety representatives by recognized trade unions. These regulations came into force on October 1 1978 and the functions of the safety representatives are: (a) to carry out inspections of the work area at least three-monthly; (b) in the event of a notifiable accident or dangerous occurrence to carry out an inspection; (c) to inspect any documents which are relevant to health and safety; (d) to enter a record of inspection in a register provided by the employer.

The name of the safety representative shall be posted in the workplace. It is the duty of every employer to establish safety committees at the request of the appointed safety representatives. The committee must keep under review measures taken to ensure workers' safety and health.

*Section 3* places a general duty on employers and the self-employed to ensure that their activities do not endanger anybody and, in certain circumstances, to provide information to the public about any potential hazards to health and safety.

*Section 4* places a duty on anybody responsible for places of work to ensure that the premises themselves, as well as plant and machinery in them, do not endanger people using them.

*Section 5* provides that controllers of the premises of a prescribed class must use the best practicable means for preventing the emission into the atmosphere of noxious or offensive substances and for rendering harmless and inoffensive such substances as may be emitted.

*Section 6* places duties on anyone who designs, manufactures, imports or supplies an article or substance for use at work to ensure, so far as reasonably practicable, that the article or substance is safe when used in accordance with information supplied by him. The duty extends to the provision of necessary information and the carrying out of necessary testing, inspection and research. Those who install plant are also obliged to ensure that it is safely installed.

*Section 7* places duties on employees to take reasonable care to

114

ensure that they do not endanger themselves or anyone else who may be affected by their work activities, and to co-operate with employers and others in meeting statutory requirements.

*Section 8* places a duty on everyone not to misuse anything provided in the interest of health or safety at work under a statutory requirement.

*Section 9* provides that no employer may charge his employees for anything done, or equipment provided, for health or safety purposes under a statutory requirement.

*Section 10* lays down that in their annual reports to shareholders, directors must give information about what their companies are doing in safety and health matters.

*General note*: Employers have a wide general duty to provide health and safety information to all their employees. They are also required to provide trade union safety representatives with extensive information to enable them to carry out their functions. This information includes, for example, plans, performances, and future changes in the workplace and technical information issued to subcontractors and home workers. The Act also requires designers, manufacturers and suppliers to provide employers with full information about hazards and precautions associated with their products as well as the results of any relevant research.

Inspectors of the Health and Safety Executive are obliged to supply safety representatives with technical information, factual information obtained during visits (i.e. survey results, notices of prosecution and correspondence relating to and copies of any improvement or prohibition notices issued to their employer.

**HEALTH AUTHORITIES (THE NATIONAL HEALTH SERVICE – NHS)** Within the National Health Service there are various levels of Authority for England and Wales on which the trade union movement is represented.

Regional Health Authorities (RHA), appointed by the Secretary of State for the Department of Health and Social Security, are responsible for planning health services in a Region within general guidelines laid down by the DHSS. TUC Regional Councils nominate for seats on the RHA in consultation with county associations of trades councils and local trades councils.

Below these there were ninety Area Health Authorities (AHA) which were abolished in 1982 but which were responsible for

# Height Money

planning and providing hospital and community services in an area. Regional Councils of the TUC nominated for one seat on each AHA and two seats were reserved for representatives of local NHS staff interests.

Unions may also nominate for general seats, i.e. seats not specifically allocated, on the RHAs.

Until 1982 Family Practitioner Committees (FPC) administered services provided by general practitioners, one FPC for each AHA. A trade union seat was reserved on each FPC, nominated by the appropriate county association of trades councils according to the catchment area covered.

Below the Area Health Authorities were Health Districts responsible for local health services and administered by professional officers appointed by the RHA. The services provided in each district are supervised by Community Health Councils (CHC), important bodies which monitor and advise on the quality of local services from the patients' point of view and deal with complaints. Each CHC has at least one trade union representative appointed through the local trades council.

Recent changes leave the Regional Authorities, abolish most AHAs and the FPCs and create new District Authorities to administer all local health services. The changes also alter the powers of the CHCs. These powers, however, include the same right to be consulted by the new District Authorities on proposals for substantial developments of, or variations in, local health services as they had in the previous structure. They also continue to have the right to refer to the Secretary of State proposed closures and changes of use of health buildings where they disagree with the proposal and have put forward a reasonable counter-proposal. The new structure has operated since April 1982. Its object is declared to be to save money on administration which can be spent on clinical services, though this has been questioned by critics of government cuts in public expenditure.

Trade union representatives on health authorities are entitled to reasonable time off work.

**HEIGHT MONEY**   *See* Danger money.

**HOLIDAYS, HOLIDAY PAY**   Britain is the only major European country which has no legal minimum holiday entitlement in industry with certain exceptions: Wages Council and other statutory Wages Board industries and women and young persons under the 1961 Factories Act. Workers in Britain are therefore worse off than those in any other EEC country, apart from Eire, for annual and public holidays.

Normal basic holiday leave in Britain is 15 to 20 days while it is 20 to 30 days in other EEC countries on the continent. Thus, although in Britain four-week holidays are increasing (88 per cent of full time adult males, 81 per cent of women, had annual holiday entitlement of 20 days or more in April 1981), in other EEC countries six-week holidays are not uncommon. It is the policy of the European TUC to achieve annual holidays of six weeks. Proposals for a minimum of four weeks annual paid holiday are under consideration by the EEC Commission. This would considerably improve the position in Britain.

While workers have a minimum entitlement in Wages Council and Wages Board industries and while the Factory Act, 1961, stipulates similarly for women and young persons the entitlement is very small and difficult to enforce.

Trade unions negotiate holidays with pay agreements with employers. For manual workers it is common, if not universal, for more than three weeks to be granted and many have more than four, while for 'white collars' in industry and the public service, between four and five weeks is quite normal. In general manual workers are worse off than staff in all matters concerning holidays. In April 1981, 18.2 per cent of manual male (female 13.4 per cent) workers, as opposed to 42 per cent non-manual male and 30.4 per cent female, had 25 days or more; and the difference is much greater for 30 days or more. The absence of a legal minimum affects workers more in unorganized or poorly-organized industries.

Holiday schemes in Britain are often related to length of service, especially for 'white collar' staff, although the additional entitlement is usually no more than a few extra days. Pay arrangements for holidays vary. Many schemes pay on the basis of a 40-hour week and this of course excludes overtime earnings but some schemes make an extra payment such as a lump sum which may take account of total actual earnings. Sometimes earnings in the previous tax year are the basis of the holiday entitlement. These matters can naturally be the subject of negotiation since lower holiday pay than normal earnings can constitute a serious hardship at a time when expenses may well be higher than usual.

# Homeworkers, Outworkers

Official public holidays in Britain now number 8 days, substantially less than in some EEC countries. There is again, unlike in the EEC, no obligation on employers to pay wages for these days. This is a matter for negotiation or of custom and practice in private industry, as are also extra days. In the public service such holidays are paid and additional days are frequently allowed. Where public holidays are observed it is normal for employers to pay overtime rates if the employee is required to work.

An issue sometimes arises over the timing of public holidays. For example, the management may close the whole factory for a certain period or require no more than a certain percentage to be away at the same time. This should be the subject of agreement between management and unions as should any other arrangement affecting holiday times for individuals or for the workforce as a whole.

**HOMEWORKERS, OUTWORKERS**  These are workers, usually married women with families, who normally undertake work in their homes. Homeworking is prevalent for example in the clothing industry, sewing on buttons, zip fasteners etc. The method of payment is a form of contract piece work e.g. so much for so many, and it is generally uncontrolled. There is generally no effective machinery to prevent exploitation of home work, payments in consequence tend to be very low and working conditions unsuitable. In the Harris Tweed industry however, on the Isle of Lewis, the home-workers (hand-loom weavers) are organized in a trade union and negotiate the payment for the work done. Home or out work has also developed extensively in the secretarial field especially with copy typing. Trade unions see it as a danger in undermining regular employment and collective bargaining and in providing possibilities for exploitation and sweated labour. Wherever they can they seek to bring home working and outworking under some form of control and sporadic attempts have been made to organize the workers concerned.

The term 'outworking' has a different meaning in the engineering industry, where it refers to workers normally employed in a factory who are sent 'outworking' to customers' premises, to install, maintain or repair plant manufactured by their employer.

**HOURS OF WORK**  Most workers are employed under defined weekly hours of work determined by collective bargaining. Until recently these have generally been 40 hours a week for manual workers and 35 hours for non-manual workers. Recent trends in collective bargaining indicate movement towards reduced hours, e.g. 39 in the engineering industry.

There is also growing pressure for harmonization of the working hours of manual workers and non-manual workers partly because of the technological changes taking place in industry.

Since the early nineteenth century there have been legal controls over the hours of work of certain classes of workers. The Factories and Mines Acts provided such protection for young people and women.

Today the Factories Act 1961 limits the normal maximum working hours of young people and women in industrial employment to 48 a week and imposes other restrictions. Similar restrictions apply, under the Shops Act 1950, to young people working in shops. A number of Acts have also restricted hours of work in specific industries. For example the Baking Industry (Hours of Work) Act 1954 was designed to control the night work of male bakery workers and the Hours of Employment (Conventions) Act 1936 restricted the hours of everyone in automatic sheet-glass works. Both Acts are still in force. Under the Sex Discrimination Act 1976 the Equal Opportunities Commission was given the job of reviewing sex-based health and safety legislation, including the various Acts on hours of work. (*See* Shorter Hours.)

# I

**IMMUNITY, LEGAL (TRADE UNIONS)**    Over the years, with ups and downs, a system of immunities has developed whereby the law protects trade unions and trade unionists in carrying out certain activities which could otherwise be actionable in law. It can be said that without this system of legal protection, trade unionism could not function properly. Thus trade union immunities have been the subject of political controversy between those who wish to strengthen and those who wish to weaken the trade union movement. The position, pending the passing of the Employment Bill, 1982, is as follows, according to the Trade Union and Labour Relations Acts, 1974 and 1976:

# Immunity

(1) An act done by a person in contemplation or furtherance of a trade dispute shall not be actionable in tort on the ground only–

(a) that it induces another person to break a contract or interferes or induces any other person to interfere with its performance; or

(b) that it consists in his threatening that a contract (whether one to which he is a party or not) will be broken or its performance interfered with, or that he will induce another person to break a contract or to interfere with its performance.

(2) For the avoidance of doubt it is hereby declared that an act done by a person in contemplation or furtherance of a trade dispute is not actionable in tort on the ground only that it is an interference with the trade, business or employment of another person, or with the right of another person to dispose of his capital or his labour as he wills.

A 'tort' is the breach of a duty imposed by law whereby some person acquires a right of action for damages. And the Act protects trade unions from actions for damages when they commit actions which in other circumstances could be illegal. For example, this can happen every time industrial action is called and pursued, which can be alleged to be a breach of contract. A crucial part of the protection provided is for trade union funds which cannot be sequestered by legal action when the union or its members are engaged in industrial action.

This is the basic immunity provided by the law. As long as the trade union is considering or is actually engaged in industrial action, it may not be sued though it is committing actions (breach of contract) for which, if not part of an industrial action, it could be sued.

There are however important subsidiary conditions to the immunity, laid down in the Employment Act of 1980. Immunity is restricted in three ways. Immunity does not apply to an act done in the course of picketing unless carried out at the picket's own place of work. Nor does it apply to secondary action generally, unless the action is taken by employees of customers or suppliers of the employer in dispute, its principal purpose is to interfere with the supply of goods and services between the employer in dispute and those customers and suppliers during the dispute, and it is reasonably likely to achieve that purpose. Equally it does not apply where the industrial action is to compel workers to join a trade union at a place of work other than where the action is taking place.

It is important to note that these immunities protect the organizers of strikes for inducing breach of contract but do not affect the liability of individual employees for breaking their contracts of employment without due notice. So it is possible for an employer faced with industrial action to sue or dismiss each of his individual workers who have broken their contracts of employment. In practice this rarely happens; and courts will seldom award substantial damages against individual employees, nor will they order the specific performance of a contract of employment.

It should also be noted that immunity is given from actions in tort (with certain minor exceptions) to trade unions or employers' associations for all acts, whether or not they are committed in contemplation or furtherance of a trade dispute. This immunity therefore prevents trade unions, as opposed to individuals, from being sued in tort for an injunction or damages either for their own acts or for acts done on their behalf by their officials or members, and extends to acts outside trade disputes. This is an important protection for trade union funds.

It should be made clear that the immunities provided to *individuals* under the law apply only to actions in contemplation or furtherance of a trade dispute. But the offence itself involved in breach of contract remains under common law and is not abolished. It is also important to note that the immunity does not extend to individuals, whether acting in contemplation or furtherance of a trade dispute or not, who commit acts other than breach of contract which would make them liable to action under the civil or criminal law, e.g. acts of violence. Thus anyone who commits a criminal offence, e.g. an act of violence, is given no protection from prosecution.

*See* Employment Bill, 1982, on page 86 above, for the Conservative Government's proposed changes in legal immunities for trade unions./*See also* Picketing, Secondary Action, Sympathetic Action, Trade Dispute.)

*Appendix: Brief legislative history of trade union immunity*

1871 TRADE UNION ACT – Protected unions from criminal prosecution for action 'in restraint of trade'.

1875 CONSPIRACY AND PROTECTION OF PROPERTY ACT – Protected unions from criminal prosecution for threatening or taking industrial action. Permitted 'acts in contemplation or furtherance of a trade dispute' (the so-called golden formula).

# Import Controls

1906 TRADE DISPUTES ACT – Gave immunity from civil lawsuits if 'golden formula' was observed. Unions not liable for acts of their members.

1927 TRADE DISPUTES AND TRADE UNIONS ACT – Made it a criminal offence to incite a strike which was not industrial or was aimed at coercing the Government.

1946 Repeal of 1927 Act

1965 TRADE DISPUTES ACT – Threatening or inducing breaches of employment contracts became immune from civil suits.

1971 INDUSTRIAL RELATIONS ACT – Repealed the 1906 Act, but kept most immunities. Introduced concept of 'unfair industrial practice'. Aimed at unofficial strikes and strikes by unregistered unions.

1974 TRADE UNION AND LABOUR RELATIONS ACT – Repealed 1971 Act. Restored 1906 position. Attempt to give explicit immunity for breaches of commercial contract failed.

1976 TRADE UNION AND LABOUR RELATIONS (AMENDMENT) ACT – Included above extension.

1980 EMPLOYMENT ACT – Removed immunity from 'secondary' picketing, and from some, but not all, 'secondary' industrial action. Removed immunity for acts of 'coercive recruitment'. Restricted picketing conditions.

**IMPORT CONTROLS**   In the critique mounted by the trade union and labour movement on the Government's deflationary policy a key role is given to the imposition of controls on selected imports from abroad. This was also a feature of left wing criticism of the policies of the 1974–9 Labour Governments, when unemployment began to grow sharply. The proposed controls can take the form either of imposing quotas on certain goods from selected countries or import taxes (tariffs), generally applied to particular goods.

Import controls are seen by the TUC as part of a package, an alternative economic strategy, which by rejecting deflationary policies aims to stimulate the economy, and so employment, by various measures including a major increase in public expenditure acting as a booster to private industry. As industry picks up, it is argued, it must be selectively protected from foreign competition to avoid the bigger spending leading to a flood of imports and a consequent balance of payments crisis.

Among arguments used against import controls it is claimed that prices to the consumer will rise both because cheaper imported goods will be taxed and some producers of goods may use the opportunity to raise the price, thus creating more inflation and reduced living standards if wages failed to keep pace; the policy therefore also requires price controls or other measures to bring prices down e.g. VAT reductions which in turn create a different set of problems e.g. alternative means of taxation. There is also the position of Britain in the EEC which would have to be faced if controls were to be imposed on articles from EEC countries. Imports from these countries are nearly half of our imports.

Yet another argument is the danger, perhaps certainty, of retaliation e.g. from the USA, restrictions on whose goods are very minor. Some countries, however, already operate informal import controls e.g. exceptional safety standards, rapidly changing import regulations. Retaliation, however, is not regarded as a serious issue. There is also the fact that restrictions against other countries which are our markets will rebound on exports by weakening their purchasing power for our goods.

The fact remains that the demand for selective import controls is powerful in its immediacy as a measure to combat unemployment and de-industrialization. But the complexity of the issues involved in widespread import controls would indicate that their successful imposition would need to be part of a more comprehensive economic strategy involving both our membership of the EEC and substantial reflation within a greater public control over the economy.

**INCENTIVE PAYMENTS**    A great deal of local collective and individual bargaining is about financial incentives; this is an all-embracing term for any form of payment aimed at improving performance, however defined and measured. Payment by results is a form of financial incentive. Piecework is one form of payment by results. The principal forms fall under the following headings:

(a) Payment by results, i.e. piecework, work-study based payment by results, high time rate systems, or
(b) other financial incentives, based on job evaluation, merit rating, share of production plans, profit sharing or productivity bargaining.

These systems may be coupled together; for example, a payment by results scheme based on work study might be associated with job evaluation, or profit sharing with productivity bargaining.

A special bonus for achieving a target is used as a form of incentive in some industries. In the road haulage industry there has been a

# Incomes Policy

practice of 'job and finish' which means that if a job is normally expected to take say 8 hours but is completed in 6 hours the payment made is that for 8 hours.

This system was known as 'stint working' in the rubber industry and there have been many variations of it in other industries.

Other financial incentives, usually between management and an individual, may take the form of allowing the worker to put in a great deal of overtime at enhanced rates (either actual or notional); giving a special 'hand-out'; or simply 'paying over the odds' i.e. paying above the recognized rate for the job.

**INCOMES POLICY (PRICES AND INCOMES POLICY)**  This is the policy of a government to influence, direct or control the level of incomes in the community from all sources. In practice it has meant attempted control of the level of wage and salary increases sometimes along with price and dividend but not profit controls.

After the war the Labour Government, 1948–50, called for 'wage restraint' and then for a 'wage freeze' but applied the policy only to public service employees though it received the voluntary support of the TUC for a time until the 1950 TUC Congress when the support was withdrawn. Subsequent Tory attempts to win voluntary trade union support for wage restraint, e.g. through the operation of a Council on Prices, Productivity and Incomes were unsuccessful. In 1961 the Chancellor of the Exchequer in the Macmillan Government imposed the 'Selwyn Lloyd Pay Pause', operating once again on public service employees as an example to the private sector.

Then in 1962 a National Incomes Commission (NIC) was set up to oversee the Government's aim to reduce wage increases to around 2 to $2\frac{1}{2}$ per cent. This effort, however, was opposed by the TUC which also refused to co-operate with the NIC. The latter was abolished when Labour returned to power in 1964. Instead the new Government operated a voluntary policy associated with the name of George Brown, Minister of Economic Affairs, in which the TUC, the employers and the Government jointly issued a 'Declaration of Intent'.

In 1965 the Government followed this up with a National Board for Prices and Incomes, which lasted until 1971, to examine and report on prices and incomes with the object of restraining increases in incomes and prices. Though the government had powers to refer cases to the Board, the Board had no statutory powers, although in 1966 the Government took powers to defer increases until they had been examined by the Board, and imposed a short pay and prices standstill. This was followed by a period of 'severe restraint'.

The Heath Government abolished the Board in 1971 but operated a three-stage prices and incomes policy beginning in 1972 with stage one, a statutory 90 days pay and prices freeze which lasted until early 1973 when stage two began with the Counter Inflation Act. Under this a Pay Board was set up to set norms and a prices code was created, operated by a new Prices Commission with powers to reject or modify price increases. Maximum pay targets were operated in stage three which ended with the fall of the government in which opposition to its incomes policy, especially by the miners, played a large part. Under the Labour Government that followed the Pay Board was abolished and the Social Contract operated within which by agreement with the TUC successive annual maximum wage and salary increases of £6.00, 5 per cent and 10 per cent were operated. Failure to agree with the TUC on a 5 per cent wage and salary increase proposed for the 1979 wage round ended the operation of this phase of incomes policy.

When the Conservative Government came to power in May 1979 it declared a policy of no controls. But in 1980 it announced that only a 6 per cent increase would be allowed for in grant aid to local authorities to pay increases which in effect constituted the imposition of a new incomes policy for the public sector as was evidenced by its own negotiations with the civil servants. However, the policy was not generally applied as was seen in the larger increases won e.g. by the miners.

The declared aim of recent national incomes policies has been to bring inflation down. But such policies have been more successful in restraining wages than prices and although dividends have been controlled profits have not. Again the government's ability financially to control the public sector has meant in practice discrimination against its own and local government employees in controls not necessarily followed by privately owned industry or strong sections of public enterprise. There is powerful feeling within the trade union movement against incomes policies especially the statutory variety.

**INCREMENTS, INCREMENTAL SCALES** Some salary structures, e.g. in local government, the Civil Service and teaching, are based on scales rising from a minimum to a maximum point. The employee progresses from the former to the latter by a series of annual increments, or additions, and can be moved (by promotion) to a higher scale – either to the minimum of the new scale, to the incremental point he had reached on the old one, or to the next higher point, according to the particular circumstances of the scales (e.g. whether they overlap or not) and the agreement within the industry or occupation.

Both the incremental point at which an employee enters the occupation, and the scale, may be linked to age or based on qualifications and experience. There may also be an 'efficiency bar' on progress along a scale or from one scale to another, depending on the employee's performance in the job. Increments may in some cases be paid for 'merit' or for particular additional qualifications.

The tendency in negotiations is for unions, where incremental scales apply, to seek larger increments and shorter scales, i.e. speedier progression from minimum to maximum, as well as to reduce the number of scales.

Incremental scales are in effect a means of providing limited automatic annual wage or salary increases. But they have been criticised as leading to depressed salaries for those at the lower end of the lowest scale. For such employees, increments have been described as 'deferred' wages or salaries.

**INDEPENDENT REVIEW COMMITTEE, TUC** The Independent Review Committee exists to consider appeals from individuals who have been dismissed, or given notice of dismissal, from their jobs as a result of being expelled from, or of having been refused admission to, a union in a situation where trade-union membership is a condition of employment. Although it has been established under the auspices of the Trades Union Congress and its secretariat is drawn from the staff of the TUC its members were originally appointed in consultation with the Secretary of State for Employment and the Chairman of the Advisory, Conciliation and Arbitration Service. The Review Committee is completely independent in reaching its decisions.

The following procedures are also part of the Committee's terms of reference:

(i) The Committee must be satisfied, before considering an appeal, that an individual who has been dismissed has exhausted all internal union procedures;

(ii) The Committee will discuss the case with the union and the individual concerned and will try to resolve the matter by agreement;

(iii) If agreement cannot be reached the Committee will make a recommendation about whether or not the individual should be admitted to the union, or in the case of a member who has been expelled, whether or not he should be taken back into the union and, if so, upon what conditions. There is then a clear responsibility on the part of the union concerned to act upon such a recommendation. (*See* Closed Shop, TUC.)

**INDEX LINKING – PUBLIC SERVICE PENSIONS**  The pensions of a large number of employees in the public service are increased annually in accordance with movements in the Retail Price Index (RPI). The principle was established by the Heath Government in 1972. Public servants involved are those serving in the civil service (non manual), HM armed forces, HM Government Industrial Establishments (e.g. naval dockyards and Royal Ordnance factories), HM prisons and Borstals, Government Ministers and MPs, the Health Services (doctors, dentists, nurses, administrative and ancillary services), Post Office, Local Government services (administrative, professional, technical, teaching, manual and craft work), Police Forces, Fire Brigades. The principle is also applied in many other parts of the public sector including nationalized industries where about 500,000 pensioners benefit from analogous schemes. Today well over six million workers are members of public service superannuation schemes which accept the concept of index linking, and some private industrial and commercial schemes have followed suit.

Index linking operates to provide, in November every year, a percentage increase equal to the Government's estimate of the rise in the RPI for the preceding year if that rise exceeds 2 per cent. This in effect has mean in recent years that the cost of living has risen substantially before the increase is paid. So that it cannot be said that index linking renders the public service pensioner entirely inflation proof.

Concern by the present government at the cost of index linking led to the appointment of a committee under Sir Bernard Scott to 'consider and advise on the value of index-linked pensions and job security'. In its Report (Feb. 1981) however, the Committee enunciated the principle that 'It is a highly desirable social objective that the standard of living of those in retirement should be protected' and indeed went on to suggest ways that the Government might consider for helping to pay the cost. It also recommended consideration of index-linked schemes for the private sector, and ways of paying for them.

Trade unionists point out that in public service schemes where the increases are financed by the Exchequer and which are not in fact 'funded' (e.g. the Health Service and the teaching profession) the Government has every year taken, for the relief of the Exchequer, the net income (contributing by employers and employees minus benefits paid out) and has credited the *notional* funds of these schemes with rates of interest which have compared unfavourably with rates of interest on actually funded investments.

This is clearly relevant when considering the net sum for which the Government is responsible. In the case, too, of the Civil Service who have a non-contributory scheme, the Government has taken the value of index linked pensions into account in wage settlements at a valuation estimated as worth an 8 per cent deduction at source; while for teachers, who pay 6 per cent of salary towards their superannuation, an additional 2 per cent, giving a total of 8 per cent as the value of index linking, was estimated by the Clegg Commission in making their comparability award. So index linking cannot in such cases be said to be given 'free'.

A measure of index linking operates under the Social Security Acts, 1980, in the state retirement pensions scheme but the basic pension is very low. (*See* Social Secuity.)

**INDUCTION**    This term can be used to describe generally the process whereby a worker is introduced either to a new job or to a new way of doing it, implying certain procedures of supervision, advice or training. More particularly it may refer to an organized process of training for a young worker entering his first job; the training may be full-time or part time and can be both on-the-job and off-the-job, e.g. in a college or other centre.

**INDUSTRIAL COURT**    One of the key recommendations of the Whitley Committee of 1919 was the provision of 'a standing arbitration council for cases where the parties wish to refer any dispute to arbitration'. This was put into effect by the Industrial Courts Act 1919 which established the Industrial Court as a permanent and independent tribunal composed of representatives of employers and workers, independent members, and including at least one woman. One of the independent members was to be appointed president, others could act as chairmen in proceedings, and a chairman had a deciding voice where the other members of the Court failed to agree. Its awards were not legally binding, but all were published. Almost any actual or anticipated industrial dispute could be referred to the Court through the Minister of Labour, but only with the consent of both parties. It was normally expected that the agreed negotiating arrangements had been exhausted before a reference was made and it was also usual for the Court to try to secure a resumption of work before proceeding with the case.

Certain additional functions were given to the Industrial Court under the Road Haulage Wages Act 1938 and the Terms and Conditions of Employment Act 1959 – neither of which are now in force. The functions of the Industrial Court are now performed by the Central Arbitration Committee. (*See* Whitleyism.)

**INDUSTRIAL DEMOCRACY** Industrial Democracy is the achievement by employees collectively of a greater control over their work situation. There is growing support for the view that in a democratic society, democracy should not stop at the factory gate or the office door. Yet some of the most basic aspects affecting working arrangements and security of employment, stem from decisions taken at very remote levels. This applies especially to decisions about closures, redundancies, mergers and major redeployment of labour. The White Paper on 'Industrial Democracy' presented to Parliament in May 1978 said: 'People in industry have different interests and differ about objectives and how they are to be achieved. But part of the conflict is due to poor communications, lack of information and lack of trust. One way to change this is to create a framework for employees and their representatives to join in those corporate decisions that affect them and to encourage them to do so.'

Various attempts have been made over the years in the direction of Industrial Democracy. One idea has been the allocation of shares to workpeople, but this does not give any real power or influence to employees. Another idea is the extension of the Works Council system but the experience in British companies demonstrates an almost total lack of real joint decision making. Although a Green Paper published by the EEC in 1975 recommended that works councils should be obligatory in all member countries and this should lead eventually to some form of worker representation on boards of directors, British trade unions tend to oppose this concept because works councils, including those operating in EEC countries, are invariably separate from the trade union movement. More enlightened management has seen the need to make jobs more interesting, improve communication with employees and consult them more. But however good these improvements are they do not in themselves achieve more democratic control.

Developments which have indicated progress towards industrial democracy range from the Joint Production committees of the Second World War period to experiments in 'workers on the board' in the Post Office, Ports and Steel industries. Other instances have included limited legislation on the disclosure of information; the Health and Safety legislation involving safety representatives; and not least the widening scope of collective bargaining and expansion of shop steward representation. Negotiations between trade union representatives and management have in many cases been extended to systems of 'joint control and regulation', *de facto*, over a wide range of issues including manning, dismissals and discipline, output targets, overtime and shift working. Productivity bargaining and negotiation over incentives, job evaluation etc. also provided a major boost in the area of joint decision making.

Since the Labour Party Committee on Industrial Democracy issued its report in 1967, trade union and labour opinion has supported the expansion of collective bargaining as the major means of achieving industrial democracy and has insisted that there should be 'one channel' i.e. the trade union system, through which the workers' point of view should be presented. The argument for this is based on the principle of independence from management control and the avoidance of conflict and differences between competing channels of representation, for example through non-union works councils.

In more recent times trade union pressure has built up for 50 per cent representation on Boards of Directors and based on the trade union system. This found expression in the Committee on Industrial Democracy 1977 (headed by Lord Bullock), as did opposition to the idea of supervisory boards on the continental pattern.

The TUC policy is also to ensure adequate trade union representation in all economic planning agencies, including the NEDC and regional planning agencies, as part of a wider approach to industrial democracy. (*See* Bullock Report).

**INDUSTRIAL INJURIES ADVISORY COUNCIL**   The Industrial Injuries Advisory Council is appointed by the Secretary of State. There is no limitation on the Council's size, but four of the members are appointed after consultation with organizations representing employers and four after consultation with organizations representing workers. The Council considers proposals for regulations and advises the Secretary of State which diseases shall be included in the list of prescribed industrial diseases.

**INDUSTRIAL INJURIES INSURANCE BENEFITS** Industrial Injuries Insurance Benefit (previously known as Workmen's Compensation) is paid under the Social Security Act, 1975, to people who are unable to work because of an accident at work. The system covers all employees but not the self-employed; and there is no requirement to have paid a certain number of national insurance contributions. The benefits are administered by the DHSS at the local offices.

Payment is to employees who have suffered a *personal* injury caused by an accident, although the injury does not need to have been immediate; thus, for example, back strain due to heavy work is normally regarded as an injury. The injury, however, must arise out of and in the course of employment and so does not include accidents in travelling to work, although it does normally cover travelling between different sites in working hours and during breaks; and the victim must be incapable of work as a result.

Although a sick note from a doctor or hospital is normally necessary, it is possible to claim without a doctor's statement but in that case evidence of incapacity to work will normally be demanded, as well as proof that the accident did arise out of and in the course of employment.

Industrial injury benefits are paid instead of sickness benefit and have always been higher. They are paid at a flat weekly rate with allowances for dependents for up to 26 weeks, with each case being treated on its own merits by an Insurance Officer who informs the Department of Health and Social Security (DHSS) of his decision. If absence from work exceeds 26 weeks, industrial disablement benefit may be claimed (see below).

If the Insurance Officer denies benefit there is a right of appeal to the Local Appeals Tribunal on which union and employer representatives sit under an independent, legally qualified chairman. There is a further right of appeal to the National Insurance Commissioner.

# Industrial Injuries

Trade union advice should be sought on the procedure to be followed.

Disablement Benefit may be paid to employees after 26 weeks on Injury Benefit if the employee has suffered a loss of physical or mental faculty as the result of the injury (or disease, see below). Such loss is judged by comparison with a normal healthy person of the same age and sex and is expressed as a percentage of disability for purpose of payment. The disability does not have to be permanent.

If the claimant has returned to work before 26 weeks have elapsed, application should be made as soon as he returns to work, when Industrial Injury benefit ceases, and a medical examination will take place for assessment of the disability.

If the disability is assessed at 20 per cent or over, a weekly pension will be paid; if at less than 20 per cent, a lump sum will be paid. There are additional payments available:

*Special hardship allowance* may be paid in certain cases to people who are unable to do their regular, or a comparable, job because of the disability as a result of the injury, and so lose money.

*Hospital treatment allowance* may be paid to patients who are receiving less than 100 per cent disability pension and are being treated for the injury causing the loss. Increased benefits may be paid for dependants.

*Constant attendance allowance* may be paid where the extent of the disability creates the need for constant attendance although the attendance must involve more than housework. Exceptionally severe disablement allowance may be added to those in this category who are seriously disabled.

*Unemployment supplement* may be paid to those likely to be permanently out of work or unable to earn more than a limited amount through the disability. Increased benefits may be paid for dependants.

Where there is a continuing incapacity for work, sickness, retirement or invalidity benefit is payable in addition to the disability benefit. The benefit is also paid even if there is no wage loss.

*Industrial diseases*: Benefits are payable to people suffering from a list of 'prescribed' industrial diseases arising from having worked in certain industries, if the employee can show that on medical evidence he is suffering from the disease and that he has been employed in one of the jobs prescribed after July 1948. It may be necessary to show that the disease has actually been caused by the job but causation is prescribed where the disease is 'prescribed'. Insurance contributions are not necessary for a claim to be made.

Benefit for the contraction of any other disease arising from an industrial injury may also be paid if the employee is unable to work.

A list of the prescribed diseases and jobs is available in any Social Security office and the TUC has regularly demanded that the list be extended.

There are special arrangements for certain diseases, e.g. occupational deafness, pneumoconiosis, and byssinosis.

Both the TUC and the Industrial Injuries Advisory Council have asked for all diseases due to employment to qualify for benefit.

*Industrial Death Benefit*: This is paid to the dependants and other relatives of the victim of a fatal accident at work or of a prescribed industrial disease. The death need not have been immediate but it must be clearly related to an injury or a prescribed industrial disease arising from, out of and in the course of employment.

*Proposed Changes*: A Review is now taking placce by the Government of the whole system of industrial injuries and disease payments which is very complex as shown above. Under discussion are possible extensions of the system to include travel to work, work abroad for a British or foreign employer, problems relating to occupational diseases and the problem of the self-employed.

A White Paper on the reform of the scheme was published by the Government in November 1981. The changes proposed in this Paper may be summarized as follows: (items v to xii and xx were put forward for discussion)

(i) Injury benefit should be abolished, but sickness benefit should be available without contribution conditions where incapacity stems from an industrial accident or prescribed disease;

(ii) Disablement benefit should not be payable for disablement assessed at less than 10 per cent where this is not expected to be permanent;

(iii) The scale of compensation for disablement should be revised so that a lower percentage payment is made for disablement assessed at 40 per cent or less, and an enhanced payment for assessments between 60 per cent and 90 per cent;

(iv) Disablement benefit might commence after a waiting period

# Industrial Injuries

of say 15 weeks rather than – as now – after 26 weeks or when incapacity for work ceases, if sooner;

(v) Special hardship allowance (SHA) should replace 50 per cent, rather than 100 per cent, of earnings lost through industrial cause;

(vi) Awards of SHA should be subject to a maximum, which should be raised from its current level (equivalent to a 40 per cent disablement pension) to the amount payable for 100 per cent disablement;

(vii) SHA should be available to all recipients of disablement benefit, whatever their level of assessment;

(viii) In the calculation of SHA, pre-accident earnings should be revalued in line with general increases in earnings – as should post-accident earnings where these have ceased for reasons unconnected with the relevant loss of faculty;

(ix) Where however incapacity for work results directly from industrial accident or prescribed disease, SHA should be calculated as though the claimant's national insurance benefit represented his post-accident earnings;

(x) Consideration should be given to a limit on SHA where, together with invalidity pension, it would otherwise result in more than 85 per cent replacement of pre-accident earnings, as revalued;

(xi) SHA should cease at retirement, but previous receipt of the allowance should be reflected in pension entitlement and it would not be withdrawn from those already receiving it.

(xii) SHA, as redesigned, should be known as 'reduced earnings allowance';

(xiii) Unemployability supplement should be withdrawn, in view of the provision of national insurance benefit for incapacity which is industrially caused;

(xiv) Hospital treatment allowance should be withdrawn;

(xv) Constant attendance allowance should be replaced by the main scheme's attendance allowance;

(xvi) Exceptionally severe disablement allowance should be available to industrially disabled people who have qualified for the higher rate of attendance allowance;

(xvii) Industrial death benefit should be withdrawn but not from widows already receiving it.

(xviii) Industrial injuries cover should be extended to employment abroad which gives rise to national insurance contribution liability;

(xix) Industrial injuries compensation should not become available for accidents incurred during self-employment or travel to and from work, or for loss of earnings unaccompanied by loss of faculty;

(xx) There should be legislation to bring about full offset of social security benefits against tort damages, i.e. damages paid in compensation.

The Government's intention is to abolish Injury Benefit with effect from April 1983, with the other changes following later in 1984. It is expected that the new proposals would in due course cost less than the current scheme. A number of the changes involving reductions or withdrawals are likely to be opposed by the unions.

**INDUSTRIAL SOCIETY**   This is an independent, self-financing advisory body specializing in man-management and industrial relations. With some 16,000 member organizations, it has the support of very many industrial and commercial companies, nationalized industries and central and local government departments, as well as forty-eight trade unions. Leading industrialists and trade unionists sit on its Council.

It acts as a centre for sharing experience of what works in practice and thereby helps members to take action themselves to achieve increased efficiency and profitability. It encourages 'proven techniques that are acceptable to trade unions'. It campaigns to get a greater understanding of the importance of creating wealth in industry and commerce, among employees, in education, and in the community.

Its brief on man-management and industrial relations emphasizes effective leadership, productive management–union relations and participation, practical communication and consultation, and relevant conditions of employment and working environment. This message is conveyed through numerous courses and conferences for all levels of management from supervisor to managing director. Courses are also organized for personnel and training officers, for shop stewards and for young workers. Good company practice is disseminated at such meetings; discussion takes place on possible answers to common problems and practical action on management subjects is considered.

The society's own specialist staff, drawn from both sides of industry and the public services, provide advice on training needs as well as

# Industrial Training Boards

practical help. They also carry out, if requested, a thorough examination of a company's industrial relations and practice and make recommendations for action by management and unions. The society also offers its members a mediation and arbitration service geared to solving disputes at company or plant level urgently, to prevent industrial relations being impaired. Its services are widely used to carry out ballots and surveys to assess employees' wishes on matters of consultation and representation.

An information service handles over 9,000 enquiries a year on all aspects of personnel, management and industrial relations. Examples of good company practice are available on loan and immediate specialist advice on employment problems can be given. Help is also given in drafting agreements, procedures and employee handbooks and in negotiating policies. The society specializes in tailoring advice and help to an organization's particular needs.

Educational work is carried on through many conferences for sixth formers, involving young managers and trade unionists as group advisers to bring home to young people the importance of creating wealth. Short, practical books are produced on all aspects of the Society's work including a *Notes for Managers* series and guides to employment legislation. The society's magazine, *Industrial Society*, provides members with the latest developments in management and industrial relations.

**INDUSTRIAL TRAINING BOARDS (ITB)**    Industrial Training Boards were set up under the Industrial Training Act, 1964 to establish minimum standards and improve the quality of training throughout industry as well as to help bring training into line with economic needs and technical development. Boards came into existence for 24 industries covering some 15 million workers. They were appointed by the Department of Employment and consist of an equal number of members representing employers and employees in the industry, with some Further Education representatives, under a Chairman with industrial or commercial experience.

Boards have the responsibility for stimulating vocational training both within the industry and for those seeking to enter it, by organizing courses either in Skillcentres or in Further Education Colleges.

A new Employment and Training Act in 1973 set up the Manpower Services Commission (MSC) and two subsidiary bodies, the Employment Services Agency (now Division), and the Training Services Agency (now Division) to work with the Boards, the Local Education

Authorities and the Agricultural Training Board. The Training Services Division is responsible for training and for supervising the work of the ITBs.

While previously the Boards' expenses were covered by a levy which they were empowered to impose on employers within the industry, most of it being returned to them in grants towards improved training schemes, this was changed by the 1973 Act. While retaining responsibility for vocational training within their vocational sector the Boards are no longer obliged to raise a levy for training purposes though they may do so or can be directed to do so by the MSC, the levy not exceeding one per cent of the payroll. Instead, all proposals are submitted to the MSC and once they have been approved by it the administrative costs of the Board are borne by the Commission. Boards normally exempt from payment of the levy those firms they consider have adequate training schemes or are too small to bear the cost. It should be noted that the Local Education Authorities remain responsible for providing vocational guidance in schools and colleges.

In the Thatcher Government's Employment and Training Act 1981, further amendments of the system were made. Exchequer funding through the MSC of the operating costs of the ITBs ceases in 1982–3 and are to be transferred to industry to be paid from the levy (see above) although some of it may be returned under certain conditions. The Government, too, is abolishing statutory Boards where they consider this to be desirable and is leaving training increasingly to voluntary effort by industry, leaving statutory Boards in a few key industries only. A major criticism of these proposals is that a number of firms will opt out of training to the detriment of the industry as a whole, and if industry is to pay the operating costs of Boards this will reduce the money they are prepared to spend on training.

In preparation for these changes the MSC was instructed to carry out a review of the work of the Boards in consultation with industry. Their findings were published in July, 1981. These recommended that statutory Boards should be retained in seven key sectors and that a decision on seventeen other Boards should be postponed pending further investigation. The seven statutory Boards should also continue to be funded by the Government – these are for rubber and plastics processing, engineering, clothing and allied trades, road transport, hotel and catering, ceramics, glass and mineral products, construction and road transport. New training Boards were also suggested for the insurance and ports transport industries.

# Industrial Training

The Government's decision is to retain six of the above-mentioned Boards, excluding Ceramics (some of whose functions are being transferred to the Constructions Board) and to add the Board for Offshore Oil. Various changes have been made in the scope of other Boards.

Since the Boards have been responsible for most training of craftsmen and technicians the changes proposed are of great importance to unions and the TUC has opposed them as being a retrograde step which will be detrimental to the future employment of essential skilled personnel.

**INDUSTRIAL TRAINING: WHITE PAPER ON GOVERNMENT PROPOSALS 1982–5,**

**A NEW TRAINING INITIATIVE: A PROGRAMME FOR ACTION**   In May 1981 the Government endorsed the Manpower Services Commission's consultative document *A New Training Initiative*. This set out three major national objectives for the future of industrial training:

(i) to develop skill training including apprenticeship in such a way as to enable young people entering at different ages and with different educational attainments to acquire agreed standards of skill appropriate to the jobs available and to provide them with a basis for progress through further learning;

(ii) To move towards a position where all young people under the age of 18 have the opportunity either of continuing in full-time education or of entering a period of planned work experience combined with work-related training and education;

(iii) to open widespread opportunities for adults, whether employed or returning to work, to acquire, increase or update their skills and knowledge during the course of their working lives

In December 1981 the Government set out its decisions on both immediate and longer term action in a ten-point programme.

(i) a new £1 billion a year Youth Training Scheme, guaranteeing from September 1983 a full year's foundation training for all those leaving school at the minimum age without jobs;

(ii) increased incentives for employers to provide better training for young people in jobs;

(iii) development of an "Open Tech" programme to make technical training more accessible to those who have the necessary ability;

(iv) a working group to report by April 1982 on ways of developing the Youth Training Scheme to cover employed as well as unemployed young people, within available resources;

(v) setting a target date of 1985 for recognised standards for all the main craft, technician and professional skills to replace time-serving and age-restricted apprenticeships;

(vi) better preparation for working life in initial full-time education;

(vii) more opportunities for vocationally relevant courses for those staying on in full-time education;

(viii) closer co-ordination of training and vocational education provision nationally and at local level;

(ix) a £16 million fund for development schemes in particular localities or sectors;

(x) examination of longer-term possibilities for more effective, rational and equitable sharing of the costs of training between trainees themselves, employers of trained people and the general taxpayer.

The White Paper points out that nearly one third of the 16- to 19-year-olds are in Full-time education and that £60 millions extra money was being given in 1982–3 to increase this number.

But it is necessary to improve young people's training when they start work and to this end the Unified Vocational Preparation scheme is being expanded to take some 50,000 young people by 1984–5 and the 35,000 places for skill training will be continued in 1982–3.

The young unemployed remain, however, a priority group and for them a new Youth Training Scheme is proposed.

The new scheme will build on the experience gained from the Youth Opportunities Programme and the Unified Vocational Preparation programme. It will aim to equip unemployed young people and adapt successfully to the demands of employment; to have a fuller appreciation of the world of industry, business and technology in which they will be working; and to develop basic and recognized skills which employers will require in the future.

There will be five main elements:

*Induction and assessment.* Individuals will receive a proper induction to the programme and to each element of it. Their skills and attainments will be assessed. This may include opportunities to sample different skills or jobs in order to establish aptitudes.

*Basic skills.* The programme will aim to ensure that basic skills like

# Industrial Training

numeracy and literacy have been acquired; to develop some practical competence in the use of tools and machinery and in some basic office operations; and to foster skills in communication (in interview for example).

*Occupationally relevant education and training*, both on and off the job. This will provide opportunity for personal development and use of the basic skills in a variety of working contexts, adapted to the needs of the local labour market. It will be integrated with planned work experience, with young people being given a minimum of three months off-the-job training or relevant further education. Arrangements will be flexible, so that the training can be given in the form of day or block release and can take place in a company training school or at a college.

*Guidance and counselling.* Young people will receive advice and support throughout the programme under arrangements agreed with their sponsors.

*Record and review of progress.* Each young person's progress will be recorded, reviewed and assessed as he or she goes through the programme. A document of progress will be given to the young person on leaving the programme and will record standards achieved in a way which is recognisable both to the young person and to potential employers.

The scheme will require the co-operation of employers, unions, LEAs, FE Colleges, the Careers Service and voluntary bodies.

Under the new scheme, the Government intends to guarantee an early offer of training to all minimum age school leavers who are unemployed during their first year after leaving school. Unemployed school-leavers will be offered a full year's training course; those who become unemployed after some experience of work will be offered shorter courses which may average six months.

Other young people under 18 who leave school or further education after the minimum age and cannot find a job and others under 18 who have had a job but become unemployed within 12 months of leaving school will be eligible for places. The resources made available for the scheme are intended to be sufficient to provide enough places for these two categories on the same basis as for minimum age leavers, i.e. unemployed school-leavers will be offered a full year's training, and other young people who have had some experience of work will be offered shorter courses. There will not, however, be an absolute guarantee of such places. While resources are limited it seems right to accord priority to minimum age school leavers who find themselves unemployed during their first year after leaving school.

Unemployed 16-year-old school leavers, when they are guaranteed a place in the scheme, will cease to be eligible for supplementary benefit in their own right (they will be treated as dependants of their parents) until 1st September in the year after that in which they leave school. Scottish leavers at Christmas, 1983 will become eligible in September, 1984. Child benefits will continue to be paid to parents so long as the young person is neither at work nor in the scheme.

For those unemployed in their first year after leaving school at 16 there will be an allowance of around £15 a week. Those who join or are on the scheme after September 1st in the year following their minimum school leaving age (16) will be paid an allowance of around £25 a week and will be eligible for supplementary benefit. Those who refuse a suitable training place would have their benefit reduced for six weeks. These allowances will apply from 1983.

Some 300,000 places will be provided in 1983–4 and 1984–5, costing £1 billion in a full year as compared with £400 million for the Youth Opportunities Programme in 1981–2. The Training Opportunities Programme (TOPS) will also be increased from £250 million to £280 million, support for apprenticeships and others at work will amount to £100 million a year and resources will be provided for an "Open Tech" as a new means of encouraging training education through the use of 'distance learning' methods. The MSC will remain the main agency through which the new schemes will operate and the DES and other education interests are to be 'fully involved'.

The new scheme has received sharp criticism from the TUC, youth and educational interests. The chief target has been the inadequacy of the £15 a week allowance as compared to the YOP allowance which is being increased to £25, and the removal of independent supplementary benefit rights, which has been strongly opposed by the TUC as in effect constituting 'coercion' of 'compulsion'. The MSC has advocated substantially larger allowances. Criticism has also been directed against the weak and vague educational element in the scheme particularly in conditions of massive youth unemployment and the question has been asked, 'training for what?'. It has been argued that there is a considerable weakening of the role of both the DES and the LEAs in relation to the MSC in responsibility for young people and that this is not in the interest of youth.

# Industrial Tribunals

Allied to this criticism has been the failure to provide an Educational Maintenance Allowance scheme for those staying on at school – a major disincentive – and the inadequate provision for the employed. To many in the unions the exercise has been seen to have as its major objective the reduction of numbers on the unemployment register without creating genuine conditions for employment after the year's training. The MSC has submitted a more generous alternative scheme.

**INDUSTRIAL TRIBUNALS**  Industrial tribunals were originally established in 1964 to allow more informal handling of cases arising from labour legislation. With the growth of such legislation since then they have considerably extended the range of their activities.

An industrial tribunal can deal with the following:

The right not to be unfairly dismissed

Time off with pay for safety representatives

Right to receive redundancy payment or rebate and questions related to the amount of such payment

Right to receive the same pay or other terms of contract of employment as an employee of the opposite sex working for the same or an associated employer if engaged on like work or work rated as equivalent under job evaluation

Right to have a written statement of terms of employment or any alteration to them

Right not to be discriminated against in employment, training and related fields on grounds of sex or marriage, nor to be victimized for pursuing rights under the Equal Pay and Sex Discrimination Acts.

Right to be paid by the Secretary of State of certain debts owed by an insolvent employer.

Right to be paid by the Secretary of State occupational pensions schemes contributions owed by insolvent employers

Right of the union to be consulted about redundancies

Right to receive payment under a 'protective award' made by an industrial tribunal

Right of an employer to appeal against reduction of redundancy payment rebate for failure to notify proposed redundancies

Right not to be unfairly dismissed for reasons connected with pregnancy and the right to return to work following absence because of maternity. Right to receive maternity pay

Right to receive reasonable time off in the event of redundancy to

look for work or make arrangements for training, or to receive
payment for such time off
   Right to receive guarantee pay (from employer) during lay offs
   Right not to be dismissed on medical grounds relating to health
and safety regulations. Right to receive pay on suspension on
medical grounds.
   Time off for public and trade union duties
   Right to receive an itemised pay statement
   Right to have a written statement of reasons for dismissal
   Right not to be discriminated against in employment, training
etc. on grounds of colour, race, nationality or ethnic or national
origin or victimized for pursuing rights under the Race Relations
Act.

Responsibility for their appointment lies with the Department of
Employment which has built up a panel of experienced people. From
this panel a Chairman is appointed by the Lord Chancellor or Lord
President in Scotland who has legal expertise and two lay members,
one from nominations submitted by the TUC and the other from
various management organizations. Decisions are taken by majority
vote of the three members. Parties to the dispute can either represent
themselves or be represented by e.g., a trade union official, it is not
necessary to employ a lawyer, though many employers do this.
   Though Industrial Tribunals are part of the civil law system they
differ in some ways from the ordinary courts of law in that cases are
expected to be solved by the exercise of common sense based on
experience of good industrial relations rather than rigid application of
legal procedures. In spite, however, of their more informal organization, tribunals operate much like a court of law with witnesses being
cross examined under oath. Witnesses may also be ordered to attend.
Workers who lose a case cannot, however, be ordered to pay the
employer's costs or vice versa unless the tribunal takes the view that
one of the parties acted 'frivolously' or 'vexatiously' – that is without an
apparently reasonable case. There are provisions for review of cases if
reasonable procedures can be shown as not having been adopted by
the tribunal. Application for a review must be made within fourteen
days of the original decision being notified to the parties.
   The TUC has stressed the need for the training of TU representatives on tribunals. The importance of being knowledgable on legal
procedures is underlined by the right of the tribunal to hold a special

preliminary hearing under a 'pre-hearing assessment' procedure introduced in 1980, to decide whether, in effect, it is worthwhile proceeding with the case. If on examination the tribunal thinks that the complaint is unlikely to succeed or that any of the arguments put forward are unlikely to succeed it may warn the applicant that if the case is proceeded with or the arguments concerned are not withdrawn, in the tribunal's opinion the applicant may have costs awarded against him. This sifting-out process weakens the position of workers: it could act as a deterrent to applicants and as a delaying mechanism in settling disputes.

Application forms for use of tribunals may be had at any local employment office, Jobcentre, or unemployment benefit office where there are also leaflets giving information about possible legal assistance. This letter is also available from Citizens Advice Bureaux. Full information about tribunals and their procedures is contained in a pamphlet obtainable from any local employment office.

Payments are made within certain limits for travelling and subsistance during attendance at tribunals. These do not apply to trade union or employer's paid officials or to lawyers. There are also loss of earnings or national insurance benefits allowances.

For ease of access some fifteen Industrial Tribunal Regional Offices including Scotland exist, apart from the central office in London. There are Employment Appeal Tribunal (EAT) offices in London and Glasgow.

It can be seen that tribunals originally intended to be more informal than courts of law have increasingly become more like the courts, which many deplore. Trade unions normally recommend recource to a tribunal only as a last resort. It is essential that trade unionists do not take any action towards bringing a case to the Industrial Tribunal without the backing of their union. This is all the more important since legal aid is not granted for such proceedings though legal advice may be given free in certain cases (based on low income).

Cases that have been heard before an Industrial Tribunal can be referred to the EAT if a party to the dispute feels that the law has been misinterpreted or misapplied, provided that the issue arises under one of the following Acts: Equal Pay, 1970, Health and Safety, 1974, Sex Discrimination, 1975, Employment Protection, 1975, Race Relations, 1976 and Employment Protection (Consolidation), 1978. Such appeals must be brought within 42 days of the notification to the parties of the original decision. The EAT usually consists of a legal chairman and representatives of each side of industry with experience of industrial relations. The EAT has the power to demand the attendance of witnesses or the production of any necessary documents and may hear evidence on oath. When the EAT has made its decision there is still a right of appeal to the Court of Appeal but this can only be on a point of law. If it is desired to pursue the case further, appeal may be made finally to the House of Lords. In the case of these two latter Courts appellants must employ lawyers.

Where the EAT or one of the higher courts has made a decision this must act as a precedent to be followed by industrial tribunals.

**INFLATION**   When prices rise and the value of the money in your pocket therefore falls, there is inflation. More commonly the term is applied when the process is continuing, substantial and rapid. When the rise is very rapid, seemingly out of control, economists speak of 'galloping inflation' or 'hyperinflation' as distinct from the slow steady rise often described as 'creeping inflation'. Great Britain in the 70s experienced periods of high inflation (over 20 per cent); consumer prices rose by 15.5 per cent on average every year between 1971 and 1980. Germany in the 20s suffered from galloping inflation resulting in total loss of confidence in the value of the currency.

While there are many and conflicting views on the causes of inflation there is no doubt about some of the major consequences. People on fixed incomes or savings or incomes controlled by the Government, e.g. pensioners or those living on social security payments suffer, as indeed does everyone whose income rises at a slower rate than the rate of inflation. Hence in periods of inflation the demand for the adequate upgrading of state benefits and pressure for substantial wage increases is powerful. As employers normally respond by increasing prices, further wage demands follow leading to what has been described as the wages/prices spiral. This is a very misleading phrase as it can lead to the false conclusion that rising wages are the cause of inflation whereas wage costs are only one factor in the costs of production. Many factors, national and international, can be involved.

Inflation has consequences for the balance of trade, for exports and imports. Thus the former, becoming more expensive, may fall while the latter which may be cheaper than the inflation-affected prices at home increase so that there can be balance of payments problems. All this depends, however, on what the rate of inflation is in countries with which we trade and on how exchange rates are handled.

Bringing down the rate of inflation has been a major preoccupation of British governments in the 70s and early 80s. Methods of achieving this have been very controversial. The trade union movement has steadily resisted attempts to control wages except during the period of the Social Contract. It has disagreed strongly with the present government's view that wage increases are the decisive factor in the rate of inflation and therefore have to be drastically curtailed, especially in the public sector where government influence is either major or total.

**INJUNCTIONS** (*EX PARTE* **INJUNCTIONS**)    This is a judicial process by which an individual or an organization is either restrained from committing any alleged civil wrong, i.e. from taking an action which it is alleged is wrongful or illegal, or is commanded to restore matters to the position where they stood before action was taken. Application for an injunction is made to a court or judge in chambers. The injunction, if and when granted, operates pending full trial of the issue.

Such decisions of a court can have an important effect on trade union rights in relation to industrial action. Failure to comply with the order is contempt of court and can lead to substantial fines or even imprisonment. Moreover as the union is prevented from using industrial action at what may be the crucial stage of a negotiation the employer who has initiated the injunction process may have no need to pursue the matter further and bring the case to trial.

However, under the law concerning injunctions in the case of trades disputes, courts are expected to grant them only if they think that when a trial takes place it is likely to be shown that the action taken was illegal. And as they would have to recognize that actions taken in contemplation or furtherance of a trade dispute have immunity in law, the grant of an injunction in such circumstances would be unlikely. Judges under the law as it stands have to consider whether the action contested is protected by the relevant immunities provisions.

Injunctions however may concern issues other than trades disputes between employers and unions and can play an important part in the course of industrial relations. They may for example be used in cases of alleged breach of an individual's rights in a union, or of alleged wrongful spending of money by a union.

**INSOLVENCY OF EMPLOYER – EMPLOYEE'S RIGHTS**
Insolvency provisions of the Employment Protection (Consolidation) Act 1978 may enable payment of certain debts owed by the employer, if payment cannot be made because of his or her insolvency on or after 20 April 1976.

The debts covered by the provisions are:

- arrears of pay up to £135 a week and for a period not exceeding eight weeks (pay includes salaries, wages, employees' commissions, guarantee payments, medical suspension payments, payment for time off work and remuneration under a protective award);
- holiday pay up to £135 a week – that is pay in respect of holidays actually taken and accrued holiday pay – up to a maximum of six weeks;
- payment in lieu of notice up to the statutory minimum entitlement at a rate not exceeding £135 a week;
- any payment outstanding in respect of a basic award (by an industrial tribunal) of compensation for unfair dismissal;
- reasonable sums by way of reimbursement of apprentice's or articled clerk's fees.

There is no qualifying period for eligibility nor are there any age limits, but excluded from the provisions are:

- the husband or wife of the employer;
- a registered dock worker;
- a share fisherman who is paid solely by a share of the catch;
- an employee who ordinarily works outside Great Britain;
- a merchant seaman.

(*See also* Redundancy Payments.)

**INSTITUTE OF DIRECTORS**  This is an organization of Company Directors which aims to improve the professional competence of its members through education, training and an industrial relations advisory service. It also has a retirement advisory bureau. In addition it makes public statements reflecting its members' views on economic and industrial relations policy. Such statements have been pro-capitalist and anti-socialist in content with clear political implications. Statements by its officers have been sharply hostile to trade union power, especially the closed shop.

# Institute of Personnel Management

**INSTITUTE OF PERSONNEL MANAGEMENT**   This is an association of people engaged in personnel management in both the private and public sectors, financed by its members' subscriptions, and governed by an annually elected Council. It disseminates information about personnel management practices and aims to encourage high standards of qualification and performance by training and other services. It also promotes investigation and research into personnel management problems.

It publishes a monthly Journal and Digest as well as various reports, gives appointments advice, arranges conferences, courses and meetings and has links with trade unions, employers' associations, government departments, and education authorities, through both its national and regional organization.

**INTERNATIONAL CONFEDERATION OF FREE TRADE UNIONS (ICFTU)**   This was formed in 1949 after the break-up of the World Federation of Trade Unions as then constituted. Led by the AFL/CIO (the 'TUC' of the USA) and the TUC, most of the non-communist trade union centres in the world left the WFTU (World Federation of Trade Unions) and set up the ICFTU. Today there are 127 organizations affiliated from 89 countries, with an individual membership of about 70 million. The TUC is the largest trade union centre affiliated since the AFL/CIO withdrew from the ICFTU over a constitutional disagreement. The headquarters is in Brussels and there are Regional offices in Asia, Africa and the Americas.

There are 16 autonomous industrial trade union federations associated with the ICFTU, covering all major industries including metal working, mining, transport, chemicals, etc. The organization takes a particular interest in the developing countries and plays a special role in the presentation and/or co-ordination of trade union views at the United Nations, the ILO etc. on behalf of its affiliates. It has sharp differences with the WFTU which it regards as being communist-influenced and too closely linked with Governments e.g. the Soviet Government in the case of the ACCTU (the TUC of the Soviet Union). It also has disagreements with the WCL (World Confederation of Labour) because of that body's religious connections.

The full Congress of the ICFTU meets every four years and there are 29 Executive Board members drawn from the different areas where the ICFTU has affiliates.

**INTERNATIONAL LABOUR ORGANIZATION (ILO)**   This is a tripartite body (governments, employers, workers) created under the Treaty of Versailles in 1919 together with the League of Nations. In 1946 it became the first specialized agency associated with the United Nations. Each member country has two government delegates, one employers' and one workers' delegate (in Britain the latter is nominated by the TUC).

One of the ILO's important functions is the adoption, by its tripartite Annual International Labour Conference, of *Conventions* and *Recommendations*, which set international labour standards. Through ratification by member States, Conventions are intended to create an obligation to put their provisions into effect. Recommendations provide guidance on policy, legislation and practice. Furthermore, the ILO conducts an extensive programme of international technical co-operation to help promote national economic and social development.

The ILO has its headquarters in Geneva and offices around the world. It employs more than 3,000 people of some 100 nationalities. About 140 countries are members of the ILO.

**INTERNATIONAL MONETARY FUND (IMF)** Established in Washington in 1947 as a Special Agency of the United Nations following upon an Agreement at an international conference held at Bretton Woods in the USA in 1944, the IMF's aim was to promote international monetary co-operation as a means of promoting international trade. This was to be achieved by removing exchange restrictions, encouraging the full convertibility of all currencies and helping to keep exchange rates of the currencies of its members stable. Members (now around 130 countries) pay into the Fund a quota sum in their own currency related to their share of international trade and the Fund is used to help members suffering from temporary balance of payments difficulties by providing foreign currency in exchange for their own. It also provides a facility for Special Drawing Rights whereby a member may draw credits in foreign currency in proportion to its quota as a means of facilitating the flow of international trade. These amounted to over £14,500 millions in 1980.

In effect the IMF acts as a banker to its members, lending them the currencies they need in return for their own currency. When members draw on the Fund and become in deficit with it (they may borrow beyond their quota within certain limits) they are obliged by its rules to consult with the Fund organization on the measures they intend to take to solve their particular problem. It is here that difficulties may arise. The Fund has been dominated by the United States (the largest shareholder) and the more conservative elements

# Intimidation

of the EEC and the conditions it lays down, and which have to be observed, may well run counter to progressive policies of socialist governments sanctioned by their own electorate.

Thus in 1968 and 1976 these conditions involved for the British Labour Governments a commitment, for example, to cut public expenditure which aroused enormous controversy within the labour and trade union movement. The IMF in fact imposed a deflationary policy on Labour and so seriously interfered with Labour's freedom to operate its own policies. Conservative governments have found less difficulty in dealing with the IMF.

It can be said that the IMF acts as an important part of the international capitalist system. Its highly restrictive rules hamper the economic and social development of countries which have turned to it for aid. In the words of the Deputy Secretary of the US Treasury, lending conditions must be 'very, very rigorous to ensure economic reforms.'

**INTIMIDATION**   This term is used to describe attempts on either side of industry to secure objectives by threats of violence, dismissal or other forms of undue pressure. It is commonly misused by right-wing politicians and opponents of trade unions in connection with picketing during an industrial dispute or on the issue of the closed shop, though intimidation by employers is seldom acknowledged by them. The limits of peaceful persuasion by unions under the law are however laid down in the Trade Union and Labour Relations Act 1974 amended by the Employment Act 1980.

Intimidation may be alleged and difficult to prove because it may be indirect in application e.g. an employer's failure to promote or even appoint an active trade unionist, or the pressure of trade unionists to induce workers to join the union or engage in industrial action. The trade union movement has always condemned intimidation in any form. (*See also* Employment Bill, 1982.)

**ITEMIZED PAY STATEMENT**   Workers employed in manual or non-manual work, whether paid in cash or by cheque, are entitled to receive under the Employment Protection Act a statement giving full details of how their pay is calculated every time they are paid. There are a number of exceptions including merchant seamen and part-time workers who work less than 16 hours a week unless they have been employed continuously by their employer, for five years or more for at least eight hours a week.

The pay statement must include the following items:

(a) The gross amount of the wage or salary
(b) The amounts of any fixed deductions and the purposes for which they are made
(c) The amounts of any variable deductions and the purposes for which they are made
(d) The net amount of wages or salary payable
(e) Where different sums of the net amount are paid in different ways, the amount and method of payment of each part payment; for example, where an employee receives part of his salary in cash and the rest is credited to his bank account.

In respect of (b) above the employer may detail the deductions in an annual statement and simply give the total deducted each pay day. Fixed deductions are likely to include for example trade union subscriptions under 'deduction at source' schemes, and National Savings payments agreed by the worker. If an annual statement is made it must be in writing and give full particulars of each deduction. Any changes must be notified in writing to the worker. The statement must be re-issued at intervals no longer than twelve months.

If the employer fails to issue an itemized pay statement or if the statement when issued is incomplete the worker can refer the matter to an industrial tribunal. Questions, however, relating solely to the accuracy in the amount of any item may not be referred. The tribunal, before proceeding, will try to solve the issue through the use of an ACAS conciliation officer and will only deal with it if this fails. If the tribunal finds the complaint justified it will make a declaration to that effect indicating the nature of the statement the employer must issue. It may also award compensation to the worker up to the sum total of all 'unnotified deductions' made in the thirteen weeks preceding the application to the tribunal.

**INVALIDITY PAYMENTS**     *See* Social Security.

**INVESTMENT**     This term is loosely used to mean the setting aside of income, whether personal, corporate or national in order to receive some future benefit. It is used to describe buying shares in order to receive future dividends or putting money on deposit in banks or placing it elsewhere to earn interest. In general the term includes all uses of money to produce future benefits instead of immediate consumption. However, as generally used by economists

# Investment

it means channelling resources into the production of capital goods such as buildings and machinery or into research aimed at improving 'the means of production'.

In industry funds for investment are derived from both profits and borrowings. As machinery for example gets old or out of date money must be set aside for its replacement or improvement. How much investment takes place and where, e.g. industry or property speculation, is therefore a matter of importance to trade unionists as it can have a crucial impact on employment. The development of new industries and the employment they provide also depends on investment. In times of depression investment has special importance as old industry declines. Investment and the development of new technology are closely linked.

Trade unionists who under the law have certain limited rights to receive company information are therefore well advised to demand as much information as possible on investment policies and the ACAS Code of Practice on Disclosure recognizes this. The trade union movement has taken the view that there should be substantial increases in investment in the long term interests of the economy; British banks have a poor record of long term lending to manufacturing industry. It has been a matter of concern to the TUC that the British level of investment in manufacture has been for a number of years lower than that of our major competitors and it has called for a major boost to investment. In September 1981, the TUC put forward a five year £24 billion programme of public investment to create 500,000 jobs. Public investment has been cut from £16 billions to £10 billions between 1975 and 1981.

In spite of the fact that government taxation policy favours profits being used for investment, the response has been inadequate as far as domestic industry is concerned. According to the Department of Industry, capital investment in manufacturing in 1981 was 13 per cent down on 1980 and in 1980 it was $6\frac{1}{2}$ per cent down on 1979. 1982 is expected to show a further one per cent decline. This is largely due to another feature of government policy, the abolition of all controls on overseas investment in the autumn of 1979 when exchange controls were ended. This has resulted in a huge outflow of money overseas where quicker and better profits can be earned, at the expense of domestic investment.

In the first quarter of 1981 more money was invested abroad than in the whole of 1978 or 1979, mainly in foreign companies or foreign government stocks, and investment in foreign company shares reached a record of £1150 million. In the autumn of 1981 British investment overseas was running at the rate of £8–900 millions a month – in the first nine months of 1981 the figure was nearly £7000 million, almost as large as the amount for the whole of 1980. Institutional investors such as Pension Funds played a large part in this; such investment rose to £2.47 billion towards the end of 1981 – hence the demand of the TUC for more democratic control of the investment policies of Pension Funds made up of the contributions from workers, many of whom could be made unemployed by the Funds' policy.

General control of overseas investment is therefore part of the trade union movement's alternative economic policy to that of the government.

# J

**JOB DESCRIPTION**   This is a statement of the main duties involved in performance of a particular job. In some cases it can be important if transference from one job to another is demanded by an employer and the job descriptions of both jobs differ. Job descriptions must be distinguished from job evaluation and job analysis which serve a different purpose. (*See* Job Evaluation.)

**JOB EVALUATION, JOB CLASSIFICATION, JOB ANALYSIS**   Job Evaluation was originally introduced by some managements arising from strong trade union opposition to individual merit payment systems prevalent in many industries.

It was argued that instead of assessing the merit of individual operators necessary in any individual merit-rating scheme, it was less likely to cause conflict with the unions who argued 'the rate for the job' if *jobs* were graded through 'job evaluation schemes'. In certain cases this is done by mutual arrangement between management and shop stewards. To this extent job evaluation is preferable to 'merit rating' by favour of management.

In practice, job evaluation is a process which purports to assess the relative worth of different jobs being done by workers in a factory or establishment. It claims to relate, in some rational way, the rate of

# Job Evaluation

pay one job merits as compared with another and so help in creating a fair and orderly pay structure. Job evaluation deals with the job a worker does, not with his individual performance of it. It does not therefore decide an individual worker's actual pay, which is subject to the normal procedures of negotiation.

A number of techniques may be used. In the simplest method each job is considered as a whole and is then ranked in relation to all other jobs, thus creating a ranking table in which the jobs may be grouped into grades and pay levels fixed for each grade. The weakness of this approach is that it does not analyse the jobs to explain why one grade is considered to be more difficult than another. Another simple method compares each job as a whole with each other job and makes an assessment of their relative importance on the basis of which points are awarded, which are then totalled creating a ranking order. This method of 'paired comparisons', like job ranking, does not analyse the jobs and does not indicate by how much one job is more difficult than another.

Under 'job classification' a grading structure is established first with a broad description of each grade. Jobs considered typical of each grade are then selected; other jobs are compared to them and then fitted into their appropriate grade. A weakness of the method is that duties and skills may overlap and so create difficulty in grading.

None of these methods analyse individual jobs in order to break them down and determine their various components. They compare whole jobs. 'Job analysis' is on the basis of points assessment, the most common system, if not the simplest. Under this technique jobs are broken down into various elements, e.g. skills, responsibility, physical and mental demands, working conditions, etc. which may then be weighted according to what is judged to be their degree of importance. Whereas the other methods described inevitably involve some subjectivity in assessment, the job analysis points scheme is considered to reduce this possible bias and to be easier to explain rationally. While the method may help workers to understand why one job is rated higher or lower than another, the precise extent of difference is not necessarily able to be quantified with as great precision as may be claimed. And some element of subjectivity must remain in deciding the weighting to be attached to the various elements of the job.

For job evaluation schemes to be acceptable and successful, the backing of both management and unions is shown by experience to be necessary. In the view of ACAS it can help management and unions to:

- establish acceptable differences in the wage rates between jobs, thus removing any existing anomalies and inequities in pay, including any based on pay;
- create simpler, more easily understandable pay structures;
- reduce the number of grievances over relative wages;
- provide a yardstick by which grievances or claims about jobs can be judged and so help avoid arbitary decisions;
- lessen time spent on such grievances and claims;
- fit new jobs into existing pay structures, thus easing technological and organizational change;
- promote better-informed policies for the selection, training, transfer and promotion of workers, a better use of manpower, greater efficiency and the removal of poor working conditions and job hazards.

However, controversy and some opposition has arisen through the actions of those who have sought to elevate this technique to a science. Trade unions have encountered instances where employers have sought to impose completely new wages structures based on job evaluation systems and have opposed trade union efforts to modify the scheme on the grounds that it was developed through scientific job evaluation techniques and left no room for bargaining. Job analysis, classifications and evaluation, it must be emphasized, are not exact sciences whose results are unchallengeable. However, under the conditions of mutual discussion and agreement described above, they can be useful methods of grading jobs on which differentials can be based.

Schemes should be re-negotiable periodically to take account of changing circumstances. It has been argued this is a better method of handling differentials than automatic percentage adjustments. Though job evaluation is commonly accepted there is still some controversy among trade unionists as to the degree of their participation in the preparation and operation of schemes. (*See* Work Study.)

**JOB SPECIFICATION**    *See* Job Description.

# Joint Consultation

**JOINT CONSULTATION**    Joint consultation is the term which tends to be used to describe a degree of workers' participation in considering and in some cases deciding questions of concern to them but which are normally not the subject of collective bargaining. Joint consultation takes a multiplicity of forms. In plants and within Companies it operates in works committees, works councils, joint production and consultative committees, and in many cases through formal or informal meetings between management and shop stewards. Joint consultation machinery also exists, in one form or another, at industry level especially in the case of the nationalized industries. In the last decade or so there has been a tendency to merge the negotiation and consultation functions.

The frequently declared purpose of joint consultation is to bring about greater common understanding by giving workers a chance to know what is going on (communication) and a chance to make a contribution to the running of the enterprise in which they work (participation). Trade Unions have increasingly challenged the adequacy of this approach and have called for greater disclosure of information in companies and more extensive influence by workers over matters affecting their employment and welfare.

**JOINT DECISION-MAKING**    With the growth of the trade unions and the strengthening of representation at the place of work the degree and range of local negotiation has in many cases merged into joint decision making with management. Areas of activity which previously would have been regarded as strictly within the province of management are dealt with jointly between management and trade union representatives, either wholly or in part. Included in this type of decision making are welfare matters, health and safety, grievances and discipline, organization of work and manning arrangements, overtime working, flexibility and transfer of labour, recruitment and deployment of manpower etc.

Often the key to this type of joint decision making has been productivity bargaining, the negotiation of pay incentive systems, the application of *status quo* agreements, and more recently the spread of new technology agreements which cover a wide range of decisions affecting the workplace operations. The extent of this type of joint decision making is uneven in its coverage and tends to be informal, through the collective bargaining process rather than in formal joint committees. British trade unions are divided as to how far the approach should be formalized e.g. through representation on Boards of Directors or through co-determination systems as operated in some continental countries. Generally there is support for the legal right to disclosure of information and participation in decision making through extended collective bargaining. (*See* Bullock Report, Industrial Democracy.)

**JOINT INDUSTRIAL COUNCILS**   In many industries and services there is machinery at industry or national level which brings together representatives of employers associations and trade unions. In a number of instances this machinery is in the form of a permanent (standing) body, with its own secretariat. Such bodies go under a variety of names the most common being Joint Industrial Council (JIC) or National Joint Industrial Council (NJIC) or National Joint Council or Committee (NJC). These bodies are largely based on the model constitution drawn up by the old Ministry of Labour following the report of the Whitley Committee in 1917, although they vary in the range of activities covered other than the negotiation of minimum wages and conditions. (*See* Local Government Pay, Whitley Councils.)

**JOINT MANPOWER WATCH GROUP**   A body representing equally the Department of the Environment and the Local Authority Associations and jointly funded by them which produces accurate figures each quarter of the numbers employed within local government. The statistics are broken down by services and are provided voluntarily by individual local authorities. The object of the exercise is to enable both government and local authorities to monitor staffing numbers in pursuance of government policy of securing reductions in local government staff.

Thus between June 1980 and June 1981 there was a reduction of 36,337 full-time and 22,562 part-time staff, or a full-time equivalent reduction of 42,189 staff. In detail this meant a reduction of 47,685 full-time equivalent staff in general services like education, social services, environmental health, housing and fire brigades and an increase in full-time equivalent staff employed in the Law and Order Services of 5,642.

Joint Manpower Watch figures are closely monitored by the trade unions covering all local government staff in furtherance of their objectives to protect the security of employment of their members and the efficient working of the services.

**JOINT PRODUCTION COMMITTEES** Joint Production Committees were very much part of the war effort in Britain in the Second World War. They were officially introduced in 1942 in the engineering, aircraft and shipbuilding industries and in Government ordnance factories and dockyards. Their introduction followed a strong campaign by the Unions, particularly in the Midlands area, and over 4,500 such committees were formed. It was the first time that the principle of consultative rights on matters relating to planning and the organization of production was conceded to workers. Ideas from the shop floor were taken into account in a new way and a basis was laid for a new era in trade unionism. The experiment was not uniformly good or successful but it widened the horizons of workpeople and sowed the seed of later demands for industrial democracy.

After the war attempts were made to set up Joint Production and Consultative committees with varied results. Trade unionists, however, no longer felt that decisions affecting production were strictly 'managerial functions' and outside their scope.

**JUVENILE (CHILD) EMPLOYMENT** The law regulates the employment of children below the school leaving age, which is sixteen. The actual leaving age is defined legally in relation to two dates. If the age of sixteen is reached between 1st September and 31st January the child may not leave for employment till the end of the spring term just before Easter. If it is reached between 1st February and September 1st he may leave at any time after the Spring Bank Holiday in May though most children wait till the conclusion of their examinations in June or July or till the end of the summer term. A 'child' is therefore legally a person who is not over the school leaving age. A Young Person is defined (under the Employment of Women, Young Persons and Children Act, 1920) as a person who has ceased to be a child and is under the age of 18 years.

Restrictions on the employment of children (juveniles) are based on the provisions of the Children and Young Persons Act, 1933. No child under the age of thirteen may be employed except along with a parent, with his permission, on light agricultural or horticultural work if they are over the age of ten, though in certain cases it may be nine. For all children employment is forbidden on market stalls or on jobs involving the lifting of heavy objects. Employment is limited to a maximum of two hours per day, on non industrial work outside school hours, on any school day or Sunday; and on these days it must not take place before 6 a.m. (though for not more than one hour and at the discretion of the Local Education Authority) or after 8 p.m.

Local Education Authorities have the power to make by-laws governing juvenile employment in their area subject to the approval of the Department of Health and Social Security, but these by-laws may not allow worse conditions than the Act, only better. Thus they can raise the age of employment e.g. to 14, or limit the hours to less than two. Local Education Authorities may also prohibit the employment of children in any specified occupation and prescribe conditions of employment.

Because of the wide divergencies between the by-laws of LEA's different conditions may prevail in different parts of the country and in adjoining areas. A new Act passed in 1973, which has never been put into effect, would have applied uniform conditions throughout the country. Guidance by the DHSS on LEA by-laws was however issued in 1976; it has been generally followed and has ensured greater uniformity than before – it is based on regulations attached to the Act.

It includes provisions that limit employment to one hour between 7 a.m. and 8.30 a.m. and one hour between the end of school and 7 p.m. or two hours between the end of school and 7 p.m.; on non-school days (i.e. Saturdays and holidays) for children under 15 a maximum of 5 hours net per day subject to a maximum of 25 hours a week; for those 15 or over a maximum of 8 hours net a day subject to a maximum of 35 hours a week.

A number of jobs are excluded e.g. in cinemas and dance halls, commercial kitchens, collection and sorting of refuse etc. Provision is also made for rest periods and the issue of employment permits by LEAs.

The duty of enforcement of the law and attendant Regulations lies with the LEA and the major reason given for not applying the 1973 Act by Governments since then has been the additional resources that would be required by local government. The Low Pay Unit has demanded the provision of such resources as well as higher fines for breaches of the law and a campaign to publicise the restrictions on the employment of children which are widely breached, as all reliable evidence shows, through inadequacy of enforcement.

Other Acts of Parliament than those referred to above regulate participation of children in theatrical performances and prohibit employment in licensed or betting premises or on board ships.

Juvenile employment has always been a controversial subject. In 1972 an authoritative survey sponsored by the DHSS drew the 'general inference that pupils who spend more of their out of school time in employment tend to be less able, less industrious, and less well behaved; they attend less regularly, play truant more frequently, are less punctual and wish to leave school at an earlier age than those who work for fewer hours or not at all'. It also made further critical comments including comments on the effects of work before school. (*See* Employment of Women, Young Persons and Children.)

# K

**KEYNESIANISM**   This describes policies associated with the ideas of J. M. Keynes, an economist who died in 1946. Today these policies are associated with active intervention by the government in the economy to control the level of economic activity by fiscal measures, the use of public expenditure and control of credit, to increase employment. They involve measures of reflation, creating increased demand and output. Keynesian policies are generally counterposed to policies such as monetarism and deflation. The policies associated with Keynes have been supported in many respects by the trade union movement.

# L

**LABOUR TURNOVER**   A phrase used to describe the change-over in the labour force in an undertaking i.e. the relationship between the number of employees who leave the employment in the undertaking compared with the number of new entrants.

The balance is normally made over a year although another defined period may be used. The 'labour turnover' may be given as a percentage of the total labour force.

**LAY OFFICIAL**   A member who is an unpaid holder of office in a trade union e.g. branch chairman or shop steward.

**LAYOFFS**   When a company or an industry – because of, for example, shortage of orders or some other reason – decides to reduce its operation, workers are subject to layoffs i.e. the workforce is reduced temporarily or permanently. Layoffs may be full-time or lead to short-time working. The term may be used as synonymous with redundancy. (*See* Redundancy Payments; Dismissal, Notice of; Guarantee Payments.)

**LEAVE OF ABSENCE**   Employees may ask for and receive permission to be absent from work for personal reasons e.g. illness or death of a near relative, the performance of a public duty, the sitting of an examination. Conditions for such leave may be part of an agreement between the appropriate unions and the employers or may be undefined and dependent on the goodwill of the employer. Leave may be with or without pay according to the circumstances. Even when there is an agreement there is sometimes an element of discretion on the part of the employer especially where there are compassionate reasons for the application for leave.

**LEGAL AID**   The official name for a scheme whereby people can get legal advice and help either free or at reduced cost. There are three types of aid: (a) legal advice and assistance which covers any help from a solicitor except for court proceedings; (b) legal aid for civil court proceedings; and (c) criminal legal aid for cases in criminal courts. A means test operates which takes into account a person's 'disposable' savings etc, and income after allowance has been made for dependants, and deductions for income tax, national insurance and, if aid and not just advice is required, other essential expenditure. Although the income limits had hitherto been upgraded regularly this was not done in 1981 so making fewer people eligible to receive aid, though in 1979 a Royal Commission found that services for the less well-off were unsatisfactory.

Help from a solicitor covers not only various personal and family problems including accidents to children, divorce and maintenance, rent and tenancy, debts and hire purchase, but also problems at work such as injuries, redundancy and dismissal, help with industrial tribunals and social security payment difficulties. Help can also be given in the case of criminal charges (where the means test may be less strict) whether at work or outside.

Information on how to get Legal Aid is available at various public offices including Citizens Advice Bureaus, Law Centres, Public Libraries, Town Hall Information Offices etc. For problems arising at work the trade union should be consulted.

The commonly criticised heavy costs of legal action make Legal Aid an important social service which needs major extension if the less well-off are to be adequately served. A report on Legal Aid published jointly by the Law Society and the Lord Chancellor's Advisory Committee in January 1982, sharply criticises the Government for failure to introduce urgently-needed extensions and improvements to the system, even when reforms are agreed to be desirable.

In April 1982 regulations were introduced to increase the financial limits within which civil Legal Aid may be offered, restoring the 1979 position where, it is claimed, at least 70 per cent of households are covered. But rules on contribution to costs have been proposed on criminal Legal Aid, in a Bill which will adversely affect poor families. There is no right of appeal against a refusal. Legal Aid remains unavailable for parents in child care proceedings and for representation before mental health review tribunals.

**LEVIES**  Levies, in the trade unions, are used to raise funds for specific purposes and normally in an emergency situation.

The right of a trade union executive committee to impose a levy on its membership depends upon the union's rule book. Some allow for voluntary levies, others permit compulsory levies. The special circumstances under which a levy might be called for could include: the need for extra financial support in the event of a strike or lock-out; to meet the costs of a big legal action or to help to pay big legal damages; to raise funds for specific projects e.g. a new head office building, an educational/training centre, or to provide international aid.

In exceptional circumstances the TUC might apply a levy on its affiliated unions, if so decided by Congress, but normally the need for extra finance is dealt with by a decision to increase affiliation fees at the Annual Congress.

An example of a regular levy is the political levy which applies to all members (where the rules permit) except those who 'contract out'. (*See* Contracting In and Out, Political Levy.)

**LIABILITY, LEGAL, TRADE UNIONS**  *See* Immunity, legal.

**LIVING WAGE**  After the fall of the 1924 Labour Government the Independent Labour Party, then an important socialist organization affiliated to the Labour Party, produced a series of policies within its general programme of 'Socialism in our Time'. One of these policies advocated a Living Wage which said that the first priority of a future Labour Government should be the achievement of a minimum living income for all and that other policies should centre around this aim.

The policy had a number of forms but its central demand was for a national minimum wage, sufficient to meet all needs, for those in public employment (including government contracts), for legal measures to achieve rising minima in private industry, and for the wage to be supplemented by expanded social services including Family Allowances. The policy was discussed at the 1927 and 1928 Labour Party conferences but strong differences were revealed among the trade unions over Family Allowances on the grounds that they might depress wages and these differences showed up again at the 1929 conference which came to no decision.

The whole issue of the Living Wage became bogged down in a continuing Enquiry by the TUC and the Labour Party, and the attempt to get detailed proposals included in the programme on which the Labour Party fought the 1929 General Election failed. Instead the programme contained more general promises on the standard of living and the social services.

The Living Wage is part of the history of the trade union and labour movement. In one form or another, e.g. the Welfare State, it has persisted and become embodied in a great variety of policies. (*See* Minimum wage.)

**LOCAL AUTHORITIES CONDITIONS OF SERVICE BOARD (LACSAB)**    There are twenty-one national negotiating bodies dealing with the pay and conditions of service of the approximately two million people, both manual and white collar workers, teachers etc., employed by local authorities. For each of these negotiating bodies, LACSAB provides the employers' secretariat in carrying out its role as the manpower service for local government. It is financed by the local authority associations, the Provincial Councils involved in local government negotiations on the employers' side and a variety of other bodies for whom the Board provides a service. LACSAB is a company limited by guarantee, and is non-profit-making.

The Secretary of LACSAB is the designated employers' secretary for more than forty major councils and committees concerned with local government pay and conditions. In addition the Secretariat provides a service to certain bodies that fall outside the strict definition of local government, notably the Whitley Councils for New Towns and Industrial Estates.

LACSAB also provides the employers' component of the Joint Secretariats (employers and employees) which are a feature of the Whitley form of negotiation and whose job is to facilitate the operation of agreements. Its work here includes the promulgation of agreements by circular, the publication of codified handbooks (e.g. the 'Purple Book' for administrative, professional, technical and clerical staff and the 'Burgundy Book' for teachers), advice to employing authorities on the interpretation and local co-ordination of national agreements, and contact with staff side secretariats. Where there are procedures for appeals or disputes at national level, LACSAB services the employers' side and is also available for conciliation if required.

It is thus the major resource called upon by employers in local government for information on pay movements and relevant employment statistics. It also services the Joint Manpower Watch which keeps a check on local government manpower on behalf of local and national government. And it provides for its clients the necessary information for the important discussions between central and local government around the annual Rate Support Grant which involve for example the local government paybill and the imposition of cash limits.

As it is the repository of essential information affecting public policy, a large number of organizations subscribe to the LACSAB Information Distribution Service, particularly those bodies that have chosen to use the local government pay agreements as a basis for their own individual pay structures. Advice and information is provided to local authorities through answers to specific queries, and through Advisory Bulletins which highlight major developments in legislation, regulations and case law and commentaries on pay trends, negotiations and other relevant issues of interest.

LACSAB maintains regular contact with the government departments involved with local authorities and with the relevant trade unions. It also sponsors a pay and Manpower Working Party and provides a continuing forum wherein all types of authorities and central organizations such as the Chartered Institute of Public Finance and Accountancy (CIPFA) work together in the co-ordination of manpower information.

The groups of workers for whom LACSAB services the employers' side are:

White collar workers (APT&C, Chief Officers, Chief Executives);
Manual workers including specialist craft groups;
Education including teachers in primary and secondary schools, lecturers and principals in further education and polytechnics, youth workers, advisers, etc.;
Police, Fire, Probation and Court Staff.

Senior staff at LACSAB either lead at major negotiations, arbitrations and special pay enquiries or play a leading role in assisting the representatives of the employers.

LACSAB's governing body consists of employers' representatives from the Association of County Councils; Association of District Councils; Association of Metropolitan Authorities; Convention of Scottish Local Authorities; National Joint Council for Local Authorities Administrative, Professional, Technical and Clerical Services; National Joint Council for Local Authorities Services (Manual workers); National Joint Council for Local Authorities' Fire Brigades; Burnham Primary and Secondary Committee; Burnham Further Education Committee; National Joint Council for Local Authorities' Services (Scottish Council). (*See* Whitley Councils, Local Government Pay.)

**LOCAL AUTHORITIES' MANAGEMENT SERVICES AND COMPUTERS (LAMSAC)** This provides a computer service for local government, undertakes projects and supplies local government with a consultancy service on work study, organization and methods and other measurement techniques.

**LOCAL AUTHORITY WELFARE SERVICES** *See* Social Security.

**LOCAL GOVERNMENT PAY; NON-MANUAL STAFF IN LOCAL GOVERNMENT OFFICES** A Council on the Whitley model has existed since agreement was reached at the end of 1943 between the employers and unions in local government offices. This is the National Joint Council (NJC) for Local Authorities' Administrative, Professional, Technical and Clerical Services (APT&C), for England, Wales and Scotland. It covers all staff in the above categories with the exception of Chief Officers and those in the highest salary ranges, such as Chief Executives, Chief Education Officers, Chief Architects, etc. There are also thirteen Provisional

# Local Government Pay

Councils and one for Scotland. Below them are local joint committees. Procedures exist for referring disputes from local to district to national level. Similar machinery exists for manual workers. (*See* JICs.)

The NJC and the other two tiers follow the pattern of representation from management and the appropriate trade unions respectively. Thus the NJC has an independent chairman appointed by the Secretary of State for the Environment without the right to vote, thirty-six employer members from the Local Authority Associations – the Association of County Councils (ACC), the Association of Metropolitan Authorities (AMA), the Association of District Councils (ADC) and each of the thirteen Provincial Councils as well as that for Scotland; also thirty-five employees' members from NALGO, GMWU, NUPE, TGWU, COHSE and each of the Provincial Councils and Scotland. On the staff side, NALGO has in practice the majority voice, because of the volume of its membership in the categories concerned.

As an overriding function of the NJC's objective is 'to secure the largest possible measure of joint action for the consideration of salaries, wages and service conditions' of officers within its scope and to consider relevant proposals on these issues from the Provincial and Scottish Councils. More specifically its chief objects are:

(a) provision of machinery for the regular consideration of salaries, wages and service conditions;

(b) measures for securing recognition by all local authorities and officers of agreements relating to salaries, wages and service conditions;

(c) settlement of differences between local authorities and their officers or between both sides in a Provincial Council that are referred to the NJC, the establishment of machinery for preventing disputes and for their settlement;

(d) provision of appeals machinery when the NJC cannot resolve a difference;

(e) collection of statistics and information relevant to its work;

(f) encouragement of the study of methods of administration to improve efficiency;

(g) health and welfare work;

(h) co-operation with the education authorities in matters relating to entry into and training for local government service;

(i) support for Provincial Councils and for the appropriate trade unions and for the observance of collective agreements by them.

Business may be conducted through an Executive and other committees including an important Grading Committee whose constitution is laid down. In the NJC and in committees, decisions can only be made if supported by a majority of those present on both sides.

If there is a dispute over terms and conditions of employment applying to all or particular classes of staff, either side can ask the Secretary of State for Employment to refer the matter to arbitration by the Central Arbitration Committee or some other form of agreed arbitration machinery provided for by law. Any arbitration award must be accepted by both sides.

As in the case of the Civil Service the sanction behind an agreement on, for example, pay is the authority of the Government, so in the case of the NJC the sanction is the authority of the local authority associations effectively representing their members, who will carry out NJC decisions. Similarly the sanction on the employees' side is the authority of the unions to observe agreements. This does not preclude the unions from operating industrial action in circumstances they consider appropriate.

**LOCAL INCOME TAX** The trade union movement takes an active interest in taxation policy. It has long been critical of rates as a regressive tax, that is a tax by which those who are less well off are hit harder than those who are richer. This is due to the nature of rates. Local Authorities which levy rates to pay for local services also complain that rates are too inflexible a means of raising money since rateable values are slow to respond to economic changes.

Local Income Tax has long been suggested both in local government and in the trade union movement as a fairer alternative to rates. In practice this would involve, for most people, the use of the PAYE machinery to collect an additional tax based on the local authority area where the taxpayer lives and at the rate decided on by the local authority. The employer, having been informed of the appropriate levels of tax for his various employees would, after making the necessary deductions, pay the collective sums due to each local authority to the Inland Revenue which would transmit them to the appropriate local authorities. Although the arrangements are complex, local income tax schemes have been successfully operated, for example in Scandinavia.

Arrangements would have to be made for tax on various types of business; although the issues may sometimes be complex they can be administratively and fairly overcome.

# Lock-Out

Abolition of rating or its major modification will remain on the agenda of the trade union movement until it has been successfully achieved. (*See* Rates, Rate Support Grant.)

**LOCK-OUT**    Where an employer closes down a factory or a section of an undertaking as part of an attempt to force employees to accept his terms in an industrial dispute, the situation is described as a 'lock-out'. This sanction is rarely used these days but where it is, if the employees are members of a trade union they would normally be paid 'lock-out pay' (the equivalent of 'strike pay') by the Union.

**LONDON WEIGHTING – ALLOWANCES**    It is quite common for unions to negotiate wages or salaries for their London members above the scales or rates which apply elsewhere. This normally takes the form of a London Weighting or London Allowance. In some cases e.g. the civil service, local government and teachers, the payments vary according to which part of London, inner or outer, the employee works in. London weighting is now an integral part of both wage and salary agreements in the public service and in many industries which have national pay agreements. Nearly all public service employees receive the allowance as do a substantial number of workers in private industry (about one third in 1978).

The allowance is intended to compensate for higher living costs in the capital and so ensure comparable pay as between workers in London and outside. A major survey in 1978 by the then existing Pay Board, which is still the main document of reference in negotiations, used four major items in the cost of living as criteria for estimating the differences in living costs: housing, travel to work, other costs e.g. food and consumer goods, wear and tear e.g. travelling times and London's poor housing standards. The Board also took into account the differences between inner and outer London.

To allow for changes in costs to be calculated from year to year, a set of indices are used for the main relevant items such as interest payments on mortgages of owner occupiers, council house and private rents, public transport fares, costs of running a car etc. The final calculations are complex but they provide the basis for updating the allowance from year to year including the difference between inner and outer London, the former being defined as within four miles of Charing Cross and the latter, the rest of the Greater London Council area. The annual changes are published by the Department of Employment each June.

# Low Paid

In the public services the weighting applies to both manual and non-manual workers and private industry paying it may use the Department of Employment indices.

London weighting has always been a matter of controversy for employees in other big cities who often claim that their costs are no lower than in London and the clearing banks, for example, pay a large town allowance as do some companies. A 'fringe' allowance for areas just outside Greater London may also be paid in certain cases.

The 1980 New Earnings Survey showed that male manual workers in Greater London earned 8 per cent more on the basic rate than the average for the country; women manual workers earned 18.7 per cent more. The 1978–9 Family Expenditure Survey, however, showed an average of 29 per cent greater spending per household in Greater London on housing and 13 per cent on travel than the national averages.

**LOW PAID**    There are different definitions of what constitutes the 'low paid'. In 1971 the National Prices and Incomes Board simply defined them as the bottom 10 per cent of the earnings distribution. Another definition is the level of earnings of those below what a family with two children can draw in Supplementary Benefit. More commonly the group is described as those earning less than two thirds of the national average earnings. An estimate by the Low Pay Unit for mid-1981 on the basis of this definition would be 4¾ million full-time adult workers who were paid £75 or less for a 40-hour week. The New Earnings Survey showed 10 per cent of male manual workers earning less than £50 a week in April 1981.

The distribution of low pay shows a concentration in certain industries regardless of age, race or sex: catering, laundries, clothing, textiles, hairdressing and retailing, agriculture, insurance and banking, the Health Service.

There is also a concentration of low paid workers in Wages Council industries which in many cases, in spite of low statutory minimum rates, still illegally pay less than the rate.

Women suffer proportionally more than men from low pay especially in certain industries. Thus the Child Poverty Action Group estimated (1979) that in Wages Council Industries almost nine-tenths of women are low paid as compared with two-thirds in the economy generally.

Low pay is normally associated with poor working conditions, short periods of notice, unsocial working hours and the absence of fringe benefits. (*See* Wages Councils.)

**LUDDISM, LUDDITES**    An outbreak of machine breaking and destruction occurred in 1811 and 1812 in industrial areas in the midlands and the north under the alleged leadership of Ned Ludd whose real existence is somewhat questionable. Following this, Luddism was the symbolic name attached to other attacks on machinery as a protest against the progress of industrialization in the early nineteenth century, for example by handicraftsmen who found themselves displaced in the new factory system.

In modern times the name has persisted and has been used pejoratively by the media to describe workers who object to the advance of new technology because it will adversely affect their employment or craft, or to what are claimed to be improved methods of work because they would worsen pay and/or conditions.

# M

**MANNING, OVERMANNING**    Manning refers to the quantity of manpower employed in an industry or establishment. Considerable controversy exists as to whether particular establishments or industries are overmanned, that is employ more people than is necessary for the job to be done efficiently. Although overmanning is generally used as a term applied to workers, manual or clerical, to be properly used it should be applied also to management which may also be accused of being overmanned.

Trade union negotiations frequently embrace manning problems which are of great concern because of possible redundancies. Some unions have been criticised for insisting on the maintenance of higher manning levels than are necessary in order to defend their members' jobs, and so for creating financial difficulties for the industry or firm. But maintaining job security is part of a union's function. Moreover the firm's problem may be partly, largely or even entirely managerial in origin. Unions frequently, indeed normally, come to agreements in which manning can be reduced through wastage i.e. not filling vacancies caused by retirement, and voluntary redundancy and early retirement, so avoiding sackings.

# Manpower Services Commission

**MANPOWER SERVICES COMMISSION (MSC)** The Manpower Services Commission was set up in 1974 under the 1973 Employment and Training Act to run the public employment and training services, financed from public funds. It is separate from the Government but accountable to the Department of Employment and the Secretaries of State for Scotland and Wales, through the Exchequer which runs its activities. It has ten members; a chairman and nine others appointed by the Government after consultation with the TUC and CBI (three members each), associations representing local authority (two members) and education interests (one member). Education has been interpreted to mean Further Education but not schools, leaving a major gap in its composition.

Originally the MSC had two subsidiary bodies, the Employment Services and the Training Services Agencies. In 1978 the Commission was restructured and it now operates through the Employment Services Division, the Training Services Division and the Special Programmes Division, along with two support divisions, one for Corporate Services and the other for Manpower Intelligence and Planning.

Four aims have been officially stated for the Commission:

1 to contribute to efforts to raise employment and reduce unemployment
2 to assist manpower resources to be developed and contribute fully to economic well being
3 to help secure for each worker the opportunities and services he or she needs in order to lead a satisfying working life
4 to improve the quality of decisions affecting manpower.

*The Employment Services Division (ESD)* The aim of the ESD is to help people choose, train for and get the jobs they want and employers to get the recruits they want as quickly as possible. Its General Placing Service operates through Jobcentres, which have recently been cut, and Employment Offices and gives jobseekers better access to information about the labour market and about employment and training services. It is also responsible for the resettlement service for disabled people. In addition professional and Executive Recruitment (PER) and rehabilitation services are operated by the Division.

The Sheltered Employment Procurement and Consultancy Services (SEPACS) aims to help 'sheltered workshops' (e.g. for the

171

physically and mentally handicapped) find more work for the people they employ and to give them a general consultancy service.

*The Training Services Division (TSD)* The TSD aims to assist in the development of the national training system, to meet the manpower needs of the economy, to offer training in skills for which there is a demand consistent with the abilities of the individuals concerned and to promote the efficiency and effectiveness of training generally. It has been responsible for providing many new apprenticeships.

Its principal partners are the Industrial Training Boards (ITB) which it helps to finance but it also undertakes activity in public services, nationalized industries and parts of the private sector not covered by ITBs and has a close relationship with the Agricultural Training Board which is responsible to the Ministry of Agriculture and Fisheries and Food.

The major provision of training for those who cannot find training at work is undertaken under the Training Opportunities Scheme (TOPS) which originated before the MSC was established. Courses under TOPS are provided at the TSD Skillcentres or at institutions such as Colleges of Further Education. They cover skilled manual and non-manual occupations through to professional and managerial qualifications, taking in technician and equivalent commercial and clerical, engineering, automotive, construction and HGV (Heavy Goods Vehicles) skills. Priority has been given to technicians and computer related occupations and micro-electronic skills. Trainees under TOPS receive allowances higher than unemployment benefit and which are intended to be sufficient to maintain both single people and a worker and his family during a period of retraining. They can include midday meals and travel allowances. Expenditure cuts have recently caused a considerable reduction in the TOPS effort, to the serious detriment of training opportunities in a number of fields.

The MSC also initiated Training for Skills: a Programme for Action (TSPA) to anticipate skill imbalances and future needs. Its programmes involve both remedial training and job training at semi-skilled level and below. Vocational preparation below craft level has been tried out in the Unified Vocational Preparation Pilot scheme with which the MSC has been closely concerned.

*The Special Programmes Division*: This is responsible for two programmes, the Youth Opportunities Programme, YOP, which has assumed major importance as youth unemployment has escalated, and the Special Temporary Employment Programme (STEP) which has been providing temporary work for youth out of work for six months or more and for adults out of work for twelve months or more in areas of high unemployment. It has been replaced by a Community Enterprise Programme, which was transferred to the Employment Services Division in 1982.

Community Industry (CI) helps disadvantaged and 'difficult to employ' young people (16 to 18) among the unemployed and provides counselling by the Careers Service and work on community projects. Seven thousand places were provided in 1981–82. CI is run by the National Association of Youth Clubs with grant aid by the Government.

*The Corporate Services Division*: Its main objective is to see that the MSC has the resources and services to carry out its work.

*The Manpower, Intelligence and Planning Divison*: This has the aim of developing effective and efficient manpower policies and plans e.g. on the effect of mirco-electronics on employment. (*See* Industrial Traning Boards, Industrial Training White Paper 1982–5, Temporary Employment Programmes, UVP, YOP.)

**MATERNITY BENEFITS**   *See* Social Security.

**MATERNITY: PAY AND EMPLOYMENT RIGHTS**   An employee who is expecting a baby may acquire four rights:
  to receive Maternity Pay,
  certain ante-natal rights,
  not to be dismissed on grounds of pregnancy,
  re-instatement rights in her old job.

*Maternity Pay*  For a woman who has been continuously employed for at least 16 hours a week by an employer for at least two years, or for at least 8 hours a week for 5 years or more, immediately before the beginning of the eleventh week before the expected week of confinement and who continues work at least until that eleventh week date, Maternity Pay is payable under the law. Payment is for the first six weeks of absence because of pregnancy or confinement and amounts to nine-tenths of the gross weekly pay, minus the standard rate of Maternity Allowance (see Social Security, below).

If the woman leaves work earlier than the beginning of the eleventh week before the expected week of confinement she loses her entitlement to Maternity Pay, unless she leaves work earlier with the

# Maternity

employer's agreement to continue the contract. She may continue working beyond the eleventh week up to a date of her own choosing, provided she remains fit. Her Maternity Pay does not begin until she starts her absence.

To receive Maternity Pay, the woman must inform her employer (in writing if requested), as soon as reasonably practicable and at least twenty-one days before the start of her absence that she will be absent from work due to pregnancy.

*Ante-natal care* There is also an entitlement, upon production of an appointment card and a medical statement confirming the pregnancy, for time off with pay, for the purpose of receiving ante-natal care.

*Dismissal on the ground of pregnancy* It is unlawful to dismiss a woman on the grounds of pregnancy or any reason associated with her pregnancy except for one of the following reasons:

(i) that, at the effective date of termination, she is or will have become, because of her pregnancy, incapable of adequately doing the work which she is employed to do;

(ii) that, because of her pregnancy, she cannot, or will not be able to, continue after that date to do that work without contravention (either by her or her employer) of a duty or restriction imposed by or under any enactment.

The Employment Act 1980 also lays down that, not earlier than 49 days after the beginning of the expected week of confinement (or the date of confinement itself), an employer may request written confirmation of the intention of an employee to return to work after an absence for maternity. In order to retain the right of return the employee must normally supply that written confirmation within 14 days of receipt of the request.

*Right to reinstatement* A woman also has the right, regardless of whether she has been dismissed, to return to work, subject to the continuous service qualification, (*see* above), at any time up to the end of a period of 29 weeks beginning with the week in which the date of confinement falls. Subject to the exceptions set out below, her employment must be on terms and conditions no less favourable than if she had not been absent. The employer's failure to permit her to return would be an unfair dismissal, except that the employer is also absolved from liability for unfair dismissal if the employer employs five or less employees and it is not reasonably practicable to give the woman her old job back or offer her a suitable alternative. This, however, sets out only the statutory position and the woman's rights might be improved by some arrangement under her contract of employment.

**MEASURED DAY WORK**  The method of measured day work is applied extensively in the USA and in the last decade or so it has been increasingly used in the UK as an alternative to piecework. This means that the employer continues to use the work measurement systems he would normally apply in connection with direct payment-by-results systems but the rates of pay are all-in, relatively high, time rates. By this process it is argued that managements are able to achieve greater control over workers' earnings and effort.

Some sections of management claim that measured day work is preferable to piecework because the latter system is a major cause of disputes. It is known, however, that difference in performance standards and manning both in the USA and the UK on measured day-work systems have led to a large number of disputes in much the same way as disputes over price bargaining in pieceworking establishments. In addition there is no doubt that where measured day work has replaced piecework in industries such as docks and motor manufacture the incentive to increased output has fallen. In some establishments managements have found it beneficial to re-introduce a bonus element to provide incentive for increased efforts and to modify their authoritarian control over performance standards in favour of negotiated mutuality agreements.

**MEDIATION**  This procedure is sometimes adopted as an alternative to conciliation (i.e. the attempt to get the parties to reach their own settlement) or when conciliation has failed and something less formal than arbitration is desired. Whereas in voluntary arbitration procedures it is normal for the parties to agree in advance to accept the recommendation of the arbitrators, the mediator attempts to conciliate but is also expected to make his own proposals in the hope that they will be acceptable or at least form the basis for further negotiations. Mediation has thus been described as a half-way house between conciliation and arbitration.

Mediation is not used as frequently as arbitration, although the good offices of ACAS are available if a mediator is desired. As in arbitration, the consent of all parties to a dispute is necessary, the agreed procedures for disputes should have been fully gone through and conciliation should have been attempted first.

Mediation procedures tend to be more flexible than those usual in arbitration; they do not follow a set pattern and therefore allow more room for the individual initiative of the mediator in bringing the parties to discussion and keeping them there in the hope of reaching a settlement. The mediator's report is normally first sent to ACAS for transmission to the parties. Such reports may record the terms of a settlement reached or a basis for further negotiations.

**MEDICAL APPEALS TRIBUNAL** *See* Industrial Injuries, benefits.

**MERGERS** *See* Monopolies.

**MERIT RATING** In work where direct incentive payments are considered to be inappropriate, managements traditionally have paid some form of merit recognition. This can describe individual merit payments applied privately to individuals. Usually this method is subjective and contains all the dangers of favouritism and unfairness. In other cases the method used for 'merit assessment' is made known generally and a system of points rating is applied and reviewed by more than one level of management. Even this method has its dangers and in undertakings where trade unionism is strong the 'right of appeal' is insisted upon. Merit assessments are normally applied periodically, e.g. once yearly, and after a merit rate is given it is rarely taken away.

**MINIMUM LENDING RATE (MLR)** This replaced the Bank Rate in 1972 and was itself abolished in August, 1981. It was fixed and announced weekly by the Bank of England under government direction and in practice determined the minimum rate of interest at which banks would lend money. An increase or decrease in the MLR had therefore a very important influence on the availability of funds for business purposes. A high MLR in practice made borrowing more difficult and therefore tended to reduce advances made by banks; it was a key element in the Thatcher government's deflationary policy as a regulating mechanism in controlling economic activity.

Its abolition in August, 1981 will make government control of interest rates and the money supply more difficult. The Bank of England, however, now operates through an unpublished band of short-term interest rates within which it will attempt to exercise control over bank interest rates. Bank rates of interest will become more volatile than under MLR when base rates for borrowing were known.

Under the new system the Bank of England will still have the power to declare minimum rates at which it will lend to the money market if it thinks this desirable in the economic circumstances.

Ending the MLR is part of the Government's policy to free the money market but in practice it will not operate against its deflationary policy. (*See* Deflation, Monetarism.)

**MINIMUM WAGE**     Despite the prevalence of low wages in many industries and occupations and still, particularly, amongst women workers, a legally enforceable national minimum wage does not exist in the UK. Some trade unions and many economists have from time to time put forward demands for a national minimum wage, implying a degree of government enforcement. Most trade unions have, however, for many years opposed the idea of a government regulated minimum wage largely on the grounds that bad employers would tend to make the minimum a maximum wage. Another view is that a legally applied system would detract from the need for union organization and would weaken, rather than strengthen, collective bargaining.

On a number of occasions the TUC has declared the need for a minimum wage compaign and has suggested figures for this. For example in 1975–6 when the flat rate £6 policy was agreed as part of the Social Contract, the TUC insisted, and the Government agreed, that an increase of more than £6 could be paid to workers receiving less than £30 a week, where the higher increase was necessary to achieve £30.

Wages Councils fix minimum wages which are legally enforceable but these tend to be so low that they weaken the case for a legal approach. On the other hand, there is a growing view that in the fight against poverty there should be a clear minimum standard, which should be regarded as a first charge on industry.

At one time it was thought that the Fair Wages Resolution of 1946, the Road Haulage Wages Act and similar legislation, the Equal Pay Act 1970, together with Schedule 11 of the Employment Protection Act 1975, would substantially reduce the problem of low pay. Progress was undoubtedly made, but in 1980 Schedule 11 of the Employment Protection Act (designed to secure observance of the 'recognized terms and conditions') was repealed as was the Road Haulage wages legislation. (*See* Fair Wage Resolution, Going Rate.)

**MOBILITY OF LABOUR**    A term used to describe the movement of labour from one place to another or from one job to another. It can refer to the *actual* movement taking place physically. Or it can refer to economic theories on the subject, its causes, consequences, etc. Although some employees may be contractually obliged to change their places of work, mobility of labour may be an important issue in trade union negotiation, especially in view of rapidly changing technology, or the desire of the employer to move all or part of the operation. In the latter case, questions of allowances, e.g. for travelling, moving, lodging and resettlement, may have to be agreed.

**MONETARISM**    The economic strategy pursued by the Thatcher government is commonly described as monetarist. By this is meant a policy of controlling the supply of money in the economy in order to reduce its rate of growth. Based on the belief that inflation is caused by the money supply in circulation outstripping the volume of production, monetarism purports to provide a solution to the problem of inflation. Means adopted towards achieving the desired end include the raising of the rate of interest to make borrowing more difficult and so limiting the increase in the money in circulation, reducing the Government's own public expenditure and the expenditure of public authorities under its control, a substantial part of which – the Public Service Borrowing Requirement (PSBR) – is raised by loan rather than by increased taxation.

This policy has had certain consequences for the economy. Business has increasingly declined, manufacturing output has fallen sharply and unemployment greatly increased. Moreover the high rates of interest have attracted large foreign funds and created a high exchange rate for the pound. This has reduced British competitiveness in foreign markets by raising prices of British goods while at the same time making imports cheaper and so increasing difficulties for British industry with its further effect on unemployment.

In practice the Government's much publicized target for the money supply has not been achieved; it was greatly exceeded in both 1980–81, and 1981–82. This is because business in its effort to survive and operate in the midst of a heavy recession has had to borrow in spite of the high rates of interest (and the Government was compelled to lower the rates available, though they were again very high in late 1981); and the cost of unemployment, both in reduced income from taxation and in payment of social security benefits, has increased the need to borrow.

At the same time the rate of inflation more than doubled in the Government's first year of office, both for external reasons and because of deliberate Government action (e.g. increase of VAT from 8 per cent to 15 per cent). But inflation also continues, because what some of the Government's measures do is simply transfer burdens from itself to others, e.g. consumers and ratepayers. Although it has since fallen, it has mainly been higher than when the Government took office, when it was running at the annual rate of 10.3 per cent. Since the monetary targets have failed to be achieved, the reduction in the rate of inflation cannot be attributed to the success of monetarism. Monetarism has failed to control the money supply or create real savings.

Monetarism has thus come under severe attack from both sides of industry as an economic strategy which has resulted in major industrial decline accompanied by massive unemployment. The trade union and labour movement has strongly opposed monetarist policies and the 1981 TUC demanded their end and the reflation of the economy to reserve its decline and create employment.

**MONOPOLIES**   A monopoly is said to exist when, in respect of any commodity or service, there is a single, exclusive producer or supplier or trader. It can also exist when a group of producers, suppliers or traders agree to act together as though they were a single unit, e.g. in respect of pricing policy. The consequence of monopoly is that there is no competition in respect of the commodity or service concerned. A monopoly is therefore in a position to dominate the relevant market as regards production, quality and prices. It can restrict or expand output, raise or lower prices as it thinks necessary in order to maintain or expand the profitability of the business. It can also charge higher prices than would be the case under competition.

The term is often loosely used to describe the growth of concentration in trade or industry when, although strictly speaking a monopoly situation is not reached, very large businesses may be in

# Monopolies

a position to control the market. This is largely the case today and 'monopoly capitalism' is therefore one description sometimes given to the ownership of industry in advanced industrial countries.

Clearly the growth of concentration in British trade and industry is a matter of public importance because of the consequences on supply and prices of various commodities and services. There has therefore been an attempt at legislative control of the process operating through the Monopolies and Mergers Commission (MMC). The Commission of 25 members is appointed by the Secretary of State for Trade. The Chairman and his three deputies select a group of the members (about six) to deal with particular references.

Under the consolidated Fair Trading Act, 1973, a monopoly qualifies for investigation by the Commission if one firm has at least 25 per cent of the market or where a group of firms have together 25 per cent of the market and act in a manner to restrict competition. Cases are referred to the Commission by the Director General of Fair Trading (of the Office of Fair Trading) although the Secretary of State for Trade can veto the reference if he thinks fit. He also has power to take the initiative if he thinks it necessary, including the power to split up a monopoly, although this power has rarely been used. The nationalized industries and public sector monopolies also come within the ambit of the Commission, as can special restrictive practices by companies which are alleged to be against the public interest. Indeed the role of the MMC in relation to the nationalized industries has been strengthened in 1982. Monopolies may be attempted or come about through joining one firm with another to become or come under a single organization. This process is called merger. Proposed mergers may be referred to the MMC if the gross value of the assets being transferred exceeds £15 million or the merger would achieve a 25 per cent share of the particular market or more. Decisions on reference to the MMC are taken by the Secretary of State on the advice of the Director General of Fair Trading, who has been criticised because in practice only a small number of cases are referred to the Commission.

Mergers may come about through 'takeover bids', a process whereby a company (or individual) makes an offer to the shareholders of another company to buy their shares at a particular price in order to achieve control of their companies; the term is normally applied when the action is taken without the full agreement of the company to be taken over. Takeover bids, including partial ones, are subject to scrutiny by a Takeover Panel of thirteen members including representatives of, e.g. the Clearing and Merchant Bank, Pension Funds, the CBI etc., with an independent Chairman and Vice-Chairman appointed by the Bank of England. The Panel scrutinizes the bids of UK public companies, particularly as regards the conditions offered to the company to be taken over. It has no statutory powers but its rulings are expected to be observed.

MMC Reports have pointed out that methods used by monopolies have involved actions against the public interest for example by charging high prices to enhance profits, by restrictions on the sale of competitors' goods and by the restriction of supply to particular traders.

**MULTINATIONALS (TRANS-NATIONALS)**    The term used to describe companies which operate across national frontiers. They include trading, finance, insurance, extractive, transport and manufacturing companies. Their growth has been the result of direct overseas investment, that is the setting up in a country of wholly or partly owned foreign subsidiaries, by companies in, for example, the USA as well as the acquisition of enterprises in foreign countries by such companies. This frequently allows them to transfer profits from one country to another in order to avoid government controls and taxation and take advantage of cheaper or more amenable labour unprotected because of weaker trade unionism.

Examples of multinationals operating in Britain include Fords, Rank Xerox, IBM, Standard Telephones and Cables, Unilever, Philips Electrical, Michelin. These are among over two thousand overseas controlled businesses in Britain. A list of fifty British manufacturing multinationals published by the Labour Research Department showed the value of their overseas output in 1980 as 37.5 per cent of their total output, or nearly two fifths. A previous survey of 30 leading multinationals showed that their total overseas production was over four times the value of their exports from the UK, indicating the profitability of their overseas investment as compared with exports from the UK.

New overseas investment in 1980 of British multinationals was about £2,650 millions, about half of which was financed by funds transferred from Britain or by loans raised overseas. Their investment in their foreign subsidiaries was running at about £1,000 million a quarter for 1981, far higher than in 1980.

Large multinationals are very powerful organizations in a position to negotiate with governments regarding, for example, the establishment and maintenance of factories, state subsidies, and various concessions. Their operations can affect the authority and even ability of governments to conduct fully independent economic policies democratically decided. They have intensified the need for international trade union collaboration in facing common problems created by the multinationals in their transnational operations.

# N

**NATIONAL COUNCIL OF LABOUR** This is a body which brings together representatives of the TUC, Labour Party and the Co-operative movement. It meets very rarely and only when one or the other of the organizations asks for the meeting. Its main purpose is to exchange views between the 'three wings of the Labour movement' but to some extent its importance has been overtaken by the TUC/Labour Party Liaison Committee.

**NATIONAL ECONOMIC DEVELOPMENT COUNCIL (NEDC) – NEDDY** The NEDC was set up in 1962 and meets monthly under the Chairmanship of the Prime Minister or in his/her absence, of the Chancellor of the Exchequer. Membership consists of representatives of the Government, the CBI, the TUC, the Nationalized Industries, the Governor of the Bank of England and the Manpower Services Commission plus the Director General of the National Economic Development Office (NEDO).

The principal purposes of the NEDC are to:

(a) examine the economic performance of the nation with particular concern for plans for the future in both the private and public sectors of industry.

(b) consider what are the obstacles to quicker growth, what can be done to improve efficiency, and whether the best use is being made of our resources.

(c) seek agreement upon ways of improving economic performance, competitive power and efficiency, i.e. to increase the rate of sound growth.

The organization is publicly financed, comprises three main elements, the National Economic Development Council (NEDC), the Economic Development Committees (EDCs), and the Sector Working Parties (SWPs) plus the National Economic Development Office

(NEDO). The full Council is the final authority for all the activities of the NEDC and its related bodies ('little Neddies') and the Sector Working Parties etc.

The role of NEDC has been controversial at times and occasionally there have been bitter arguments between the parties but in general there is a reluctance to wind up the organization, which some regard as a talking shop, because of its value in at least bringing the parties together and permitting exchange of views on economic questions.

**NATIONAL ENTERPRISE BOARD (NEB)**    The National Enterprise Board was set up by the Labour Government under the Industry Act 1975 to: develop the UK economy; promote industrial efficiency and international competitiveness; safeguard productive employment by encouraging, maintaining and developing industrial enterprise and reorganization; forward industrial democracy; and extend public ownership into the profitable areas of manufacturing industry. The aims were good but serious financial restrictions and possibly lack of will limited practical progress. Nevertheless, for the first few years of its existence, the Board succeeded in extending public ownership, gave vital aid to ailing industrial concerns and for a period made substantial profits for the nation. The Conservative Government, elected in 1979, severely restricted the operations of the Board and a variety of holdings were sold off. Later the TUC withdrew its support from the Board and trade union members resigned.

**NATIONAL FEDERATION OF PROFESSIONAL WORKERS (NFPW)**    The National Federation of Professional Workers was founded in 1920 to encourage the growth of organization among white-collar and professional workers and to encourage the organizations to link up with the wider trade union movement. These have remained the principal objectives of the Federation.

The Federation, since its formation, has been accepted as an integral part of the wider trade union movement. Like other federations closely associated with the TUC, the NFPW remains, however, an independent body recognized by the TUC, and by government departments as an effective and representative body of its constituent unions.

A total of almost two million members are represented by this Federation.

**NATIONAL    INDUSTRIAL    RELATIONS    COURT (NIRC)**    Under the Conservative Government's 1971 Industrial

Relations Act a new system of industrial relations courts was set up, headed by the National Industrial Relations Court (NIRC) to hear complaints and adjudicate on 'unfair industrial practices' as defined in the Act, with power to award compensation and to make restraining orders.

Most Unions refused to co-operate with the Court or to register under the Act in accordance with decisions by the TUC. Heavy fines on certain trade unions were imposed by the Court which sought to hold trade union leaderships responsible for their members' actions.

NIRC was abolished with the passing of the Trade Union and Labour Relations Act in 1974 under the Labour Government elected that year.

**NATIONAL INSURANCE**   *See* Social Security.

**NATIONAL JOINT COUNCIL FOR LOCAL AUTHORITIES' ADMINISTRATIVE, PROFESSIONAL, TECHNICAL AND CLERICAL SERVICES**   *See* Whitleyism, Local Government.

**NATIONAL RESEARCH DEVELOPMENT CORPORATION (NRDC)**   The National Research Development Corporation is a public corporation which was set up by Act of Parliament in 1949 to promote the development and exploitation of inventions. The Corporation's terms of reference are now laid down in the Degelopment of Inventions Act 1967. The word 'invention' is not precisely defined in the Act and is interpreted by the Corporation to include any technically new product or process.

- The Corporation's activities are not confined to entirely novel products; evolutionary improvements which are significant in their industry can also qualify.
- NRDC may handle inventions from any area of science or technology, including products, processes, know-how and computer software. In practice the only areas of technology which the Corporation does not deal with are defence and nuclear energy.
- NRDC support is not restricted to patented or patentable inventions. The Corporation can deal with confidential know-how, copyright and inventions which cannot be protected.
- The Corporation can support inventions from any source in the public or private sector, and it can also accept inventions originating overseas.

*Principal activities* NRDC's statutory functions have been developed into two main activities:

- the commercial exploitation (normally through licensing) of inventions resulting from publicly funded research; this exploitation activity also applies to inventions made by private individuals and inventions originating overseas;
- the provision of finance (normally risk capital) for innovation by industrial companies, i.e. companies that want to develop their own new products or processes.

The NRDC is an independent body but is ultimately responsible to the Secretary of State for Industry.

**NATIONAL WHITLEY COUNCIL (NWC) FOR THE CIVIL SERVICE (NON-MANUAL WORKERS)** In 1980 Mr. Justice Vinelot defined the NWC as a meeting place where Government and Unions could negotiate and determine the level of remuneration and conditions of service of the main grades and categories of civil servants.

A national joint council on Whitley lines, the NWC, was set up as far back as 1919 for the non-industrial civil service and below. The NWC Whitley Councils were set up in nearly all Government Departments in the year that followed. The National Council deals with matters affecting more than one Department and the Departmental Councils deal with matters under the control of individual Departments and with the application of national agreements e.g. facilities for trade union representatives. Each Council has the power to establish committees to carry out various functions – these committees in practice handle most issues. The Departmental Councils can also establish committees for local offices which are concerned with a range of subjects e.g. leave, accommodation problems, changes in work procedures etc.

Each council and committee consists of an Official (management) Side and a Trade Union Side representing the employees; each side appoints its own representatives, and in the case of the Trade Union Side, decides the number of seats allocated to the various unions involved. All civil service Whitley bodies have the power to take decisions but these must be reached by agreement; the system does not permit of one side out-voting the other. The sanction behind the Official Side is the power vested in it at each level by the Government or Government Department concerned operating current government policy; the sanction behind the Trade Union Side is the authority of the unions involved. The chairman of each council is appointed by the Official Side.

Although the Official Side of the NWC was originally appointed by the Cabinet it is now under the aegis of the Treasury which fills all vacancies. It normally consists of Heads of Department (Permanent Secretaries) plus officials of the Treasury, in order to assure a proper balance between the various Departments. Similarly the Official Side of Departmental Councils is composed of senior civil servants.

*Council of Civil Service Unions* The Trade Union Side, apart from a number of its own officers, is now appointed by the Council of Civil Service Unions (CCSU) formed in May 1980, which is the co-ordinating body for the unions representing non-industrial civil servants and those in analogous employment who are in membership of trade unions representing non industrial civil servants. It is composed of representatives of the recognized Civil Service Associations: the Civil and Public Services Associations (CPSA) , the Inland Revenue Staff Federation (IRSF), the Society of Civil and Public Servants (SCPS), the Civil Service Union (CSU), the Prison Officers' Association (POA), the Institute of Professional Civil Servants (IPCS), the Association of First Division Civil Servants (FDA), the Association of Inspectors of Taxes, and the Association of Government Supervisors and Radio Officers.

The CCSU co-ordinates the views of the constituent unions on all matters included in the constitution of the NWC; it conducts negotiations with and makes representations to the Official Side, Ministers and other Civil Service Authorities and the Civil Service Arbitration Tribunal and it may take such other action as is agreed as a policy decision under its constitution. The main committee of the CCSU is the Major Policy Committee which deals with pay and manpower and liaises with the TUC. The unions in the CCSU are represented on the Trade Union Side of the NWC in numbers roughly proportional to their strength.

The object of the NWC is to secure the greatest measure of co-operation between the state in its capacity as employer and the general body of civil servants, and the scope of its activities therefore covers all matters which affect the conditions of service of staff. Thus, on pay, the NWC is recognized as the body which 'determines questions of remuneration' affecting a class employed in two or more Departments. This in practice means centralized pay negotiations.

Individual unions are however, entitled to negotiate directly with the Treasury or individual Departments on matters affecting the grades for which they have official recognition, although the Government has increasingly preferred to negotiate with the National Trade Union Side. The NWC does not therefore supersede direct negotiations between Government and staff associations where this is thought appropriate.

In practice it has been found expedient to exclude the highest grades from pay negotiations and since 1971 the *Top Salaries Review Body*, appointed by the Prime Minister, considers the pay of those of the rank of Under Secretary and above, normally every two years, along with the pay of certain other highly paid people e.g. Board members of nationalized industries, judges, generals, etc.

Departmental Trade Union Sides are appointed by the associations represented in the Department and are normally working civil servants. Not all departmental Trade Union sides consist solely of representatives of associations recognized by or affiliated to the National Trade Union Side.

The National Whitley Council has met only infrequently. It carries out its business through committees or through individuals representing both sides and committee members may not always be members of the NWC. There are both Standing and Ad Hoc committees appointed for a particular task; the former include committees for superannuation, training, welfare, accommodation, management services, dispersal, computers, and personnel management.

Most of the larger Departmental Councils have regional, local or office committees covering their staffs in particular towns or offices for the discussion of purely domestic matters. (A similar set-up operates for manual workers in government employment.)

**NATIONALIZED INDUSTRIES**  Sometimes described as public sector industries, these are industries owned by the state and controlled by the state in various ways. They are administered by Boards appointed by the appropriate Minister. Though they are each run as independent public corporations they are subject to various government controls as well as Parliamentary scrutiny of their finances. They have no shareholders (though they bear a substantial burden of debt in compensation payments to past shareholders – prenationalization) and cannot therefore raise capital from that source. Money is raised by borrowing from the banks and from the National Loans Fund financed by the Treasury. Limits on capital borrowing

# Nationalized Industries

(an 'external financing limit') are set by the Government and are determined by the Government's policy on the Public Sector Borrowing Requirement.

The industries are expected to do everything possible to pay their way. They have been strongly opposed to the severe restrictions on their right to borrow for development from private sector finance.

The trade union and labour movement have regularly pressed for increased government investment in the industries. In contrast Conservative policy is to sell parts of the industries to the private sector and so reduce the area of the publicly controlled economy. Thus 49 per cent of Government shares in Cable and Wireless were offered for sale following on the hiving off from the Post Office of British Telecommunications. The private sector, too, is allowed to provide telecommunications equipment for use in the telecommunications network and has some freedom to use the network circuits; while the Government (1982) is considering favourably the principle of allowing a competing transmission network.

Similarly, 50 per cent of the shares of British Aerospace have been sold and the corporation has been reorganized as a public limited company. A section of British Rail has been sold off (hotels) and further hiving off (Sealink) is proposed. Powers to sell off part of British Gas (showrooms and appliances) have been taken, its monopoly right of first refusal of all North Sea Gas has been removed, its oil interests in the North Sea are being sold off and the oil companies will be free to supply gas directly to industrial markets, leaving British Gas with the domestic market only. The private sector has been allowed initially a 51 per cent share of the British National Oil Corporation's oil production business in a new company, Britoil. The National Freight Company has been sold off to its employees and more private capital is to be injected into the transport system.

Some of the nationalized industries are monopolies, British Rail, the gas and electricity supply; others e.g. British Steel and the British National Oil Corporation operate alongside private sectors of the industries. As publicly owned monopolies the industries are not immune from investigation by the Monopolies and Mergers Commission. The Chancellor of the Exchequer (July, 1981) outlined steps for dismantling the monopoly powers of the nationalized industries, including, apart from sale to private ownership, breaking them up into smaller, regional units and subjecting them to regulation and efficiency audit by an independent body. In March 1982, the Secretary of State for Industry added to these steps the recruitment of private sector businessmen as non-executive directors.

These measures to weaken the public ownership of the nationalized industries have been strongly opposed by the trade union and labour movement which has pointed out that it is the profitable sectors that have been earmarked for sale.

Highly organized systems exist in the industries for dealing with all aspects of industrial relations, negotiating wages and salaries, conditions of service etc. There are National Joint Committees and Councils or Whitley type councils covering the entire industry as well as committees or councils for various occupational divisions and, as necessary, regions on which management and unions are represented on agreed patterns. Machinery for arbitration also operates as required.

For example the Coal industry is administered by the National Coal Board appointed by the Department of Energy. All questions of wages and conditions of coal miners are dealt with by negotiation between the Board and the National Union of Mineworkers and there are 'Conciliation Boards' both for the industry as a whole, for managerial grades, clerical and junior administrative staff and for deputies, with reference (appeals) tribunals in each case. The rail industry is administered by the British Rail Board appointed by the Minister of Transport. Wages and conditions of railwaymen are negotiated in the first instance in the Railway Staff National Council composed of the management and the three rail unions (the NUR, the ASLEF, and the TSSA with the NUR having half the workers' seats). Arbitration is provided for in the Railway Staffs National Tribunal although its findings are not binding as was evidenced in the 1981 negotiations when management rejected them as they stood.

Not popularly considered as nationalized industries are a number of parts of industries which have become partly or wholly owned and controlled by the Government in recent years, e.g. Rolls Royce, British Leyland. There is also British Petroleum with 51 per cent government shares. In addition a number of companies, although not nationalized, receive government aid through the National Enterprise Board (NEB). Such aid is monitored to a degree by the Industrial Development Advisory Board. Nexos, a consultancy set up by the NEB to export office technology (automation) has been sold to the private sector. (*See* Monopolies, PSBR.)

# Nationalized Industries

*The Nationalized Industries*

Bank of England

British Aerospace
Brooklands House,
Weybridge, Surrey

British Airports Authority
2, Buckingham Gate,
London, S.W.1

British Airways
Speedbird House,
London Airport,
Heathrow,
Hounslow,
Middlesex

British Gas Corporation
59, Bryanston St.,
London, W.1.

The British National Oil Corporation
150, St. Vincent St.,
Glasgow, C.2

British Railways Board
222, Marylebone Rd.,
London, N.W.1.

British Shipbuilders
Benton House,
Sandyford Rd.,
Newcastle upon Tyne, N.E.2.

British Steel Corporation
33, Grosvenor Place,
London, S.W.1.

British Transport Docks Board
Melbury House,
Melbury Terrace,
London, N.W.1.

British Waterways board
Melbury House,
Melbury Terrace
London, N.W.1

Central Electricity Generating Board
Sudbury House,
15, Newgate St.,
London, E.C.1.

Civil Aviation Authority
CAA House,
45–99 Kingsway,
London, W.C.2.

The Electricity Council
30, Millbank,
London, S.W.1.

National Bus Company
25, New St. Square,
London, E.C.4.

National Coal Board
Hobart House,
Grosvenor Place,
London, S.W.1.

National Freight Corporation
Argosy House,
215, Great Portland St.,
London, W.1.

North of Scotland Hydro Electric Board
16, Rothesay Terrace,
Edinburgh, E.H.3.

The Post Office
23, Howland St.,
London, W.1.

British Telecommunications
2, Grosvenor Place,
London, E.C.2.

Cable and Wireless
Mercury House,
Theobalds Road,
London, W.C.1.

South of Scotland Electricity
Board
Cathcart House,
Glasgow, G.4.

Scottish Transport Group
Carron House,
114–116 George St.,
Edinburgh, E.H.2.

United Kingdom Atomic Energy
Authority
11, Charles IInd,
London, S.W.1.

**NEGOTIATING PROCEDURES**    *See* Collective Bargaining.

**NEW EARNING SURVEY**    *See* Earnings, Sources of Information.

**NEW TECHNOLOGY**    Progress in technology is constantly taking place and having considerable impact on the nature of work and the numbers of people employed on any given process. From time to time major breakthroughs in scientific knowledge have led to substantial changes in the means of production and handling processes, from the invention of steam power to advanced mechanisation. Technological change took a massive leap forward during the Second World War and the years that followed saw the development of automation and the computer. The first computers which emerged were large, expensive and inflexible, but in time they became highly efficient, sophisticated and adaptable. Other examples of change ranged from X-ray equipment, automatic machinery, containerization on the docks to the widespread use of electronic equipment. Hardly one industry has remained unaffected, the new technology invaded mining, engineering, aerospace, chemicals, construction, shipping, and many other industries. Offices, shops, warehouses and even schools felt the impact. In the motor car industry a sensational and much publicized development was the introduction of the industrial 'robot' and the term 'robotics' is rapidly becoming part of the language of industry.

New scientific and technological inventions and their application have also led to a recasting of industrial organization, the elimination of whole categories of jobs, and in some cases a major upset in the life of communities e.g. the closure of huge dockland areas.

Perhaps the most significant change, however, is the mass introduction of the microprocessor. Microprocessors – in the form of a silicon chip on which are etched thousands of circuits – can condense an enormous variety of tasks into a tiny machine. Entire ranges of industrial machinery can be replaced; goods handling would be enormously simplified; present day office machinery would become obsolete.

Some of its applications have already been seen. Major changes have taken place in the communications industry, in television, telephones, radios and printing. As the production of microprocessors develops it will become cheaper to make silicon chips, and more applications will be found. It will be possible to automate whole production lines.

It has been calculated that even the high level of current unemployment could be doubled and more, if the changes made possible by the microprocessor are not carefully controlled, as the effect could be substantially to reduce the proportion of labour costs to total costs. In these circumstances the case for a reduction of working time to compensate for general job loss becomes very strong indeed.

*Appendix: Report by TUC General Council to 1979 Congress*

New Technology Agreements: A Checklist for Negotiators

*1* (*a*) The first objective should be: '**change must be by agreement**'. Employers should be committed not to introduce new technology until full agreement has been reached on the whole range of negotiating issues. In practice this will often entail full consultation **before the decision to purchase** – and therefore the choice of actual technology – is taken.

(*b*) In companies or industries where collective agreements already contain **status quo provisions**, governing the introduction of new processes or machinery, there may be scope for unions to actively encourage their more vigorous use in the short term so as to impress on employers the need for earlier consultation, and more active union involvement, if change is to proceed smoothly.

(*c*) The **objectives** which unions wish to see achieved – whether for example on employment levels, hours of work or working conditions – by the introduction of new technology should be clearly specified. Failure to achieve this may lead to technological change being brought about in a piecemeal or ad hoc fashion, and producing undesirable results, so that negotiators are unaware of the significance of these changes until it is too late to alter the employer's investment plans or to place acceptable conditions on the operation of new technology.

(*d*) Having specified these objectives negotiators should ensure that **joint union machinery** exists which is capable of monitoring subsequent developments and reviewing progress against the objectives.

*2 Aspects of Union Organisation and Inter-Union Relations*: Technological change can challenge both traditional union demarcation lines and established occupational and skill categories. An effective trade union response to the challenge of new technology will use the vehicle of collective bargaining – involving the whole workforce through established and tested procedures. For full effectiveness, however, the machinery and procedures of collective bargaining must themselves be subject to close scrutiny and must be developed so that pressure can be exerted at all levels of corporate decision-making, bearing in mind that ultimately new technology will often affect all parts of the workforce throughout an enterprise.

Questions concerning inter-union relations, the development of company-wide union machinery and relations between lay members and full-time officials will have to be resolved on a case-by-case basis but negotiators should bear in mind:

(*a*) that joint union machinery, which can often be developed out of existing but less formal structures, should embrace the largest possible proportion of the workforce since technological developments which initially affect only one work group may eventually have implications for the entire workforce;

(*b*) the need to relate closely such machinery to negotiating bodies so as to emphasise the central role of **collective bargaining**, and the importance of its development, in tackling the problems of technological change;

(*c*) the importance of building up **expertise** on all questions concerned with technology to increase the effectiveness of union involvement. Health and safety representatives are already developing considerable expertise in various aspects of new technology and procedures should be developed to integrate this knowledge and experience into negotiations over technology. On other occasions it may be appropriate to allow for the occasional inclusion of additional representatives in joint bodies – representatives with special responsibilities for, or knowledge of, technology matters.

*3 The Provision of Information*: Securing a full and regular flow of information on which the key decisions taken by companies on new

# New Technology

technology are based is vital if unions are to be in a position to determine change jointly, rather than having to respond to decisions taken solely by management. Guaranteed access to information from the earliest stages of the decision-making process is therefore vital to New Technology Agreements.

(*a*) Agreements should specify that all information which is relevant to decision-making, planning or implementation of technological change should be made **available to union representatives** prior to any decision being taken. Information should also be in a usable and comprehensible form.

(*b*) The provision of information should be linked with **regular consultation** and discussion of the enterprise's plans. This will enable union representatives to identify in advance the likelihood of technological change and thus ensure that they receive the relevant information early enough to exert influence on plans.

(*c*) Where appropriate negotiators may wish to allow technical information to be evaluated by **union nominees** from outside the enterprise. In some cases this could lead to unions appointing, at national level, experts for this specific task.

(*d*) Agreements may specify that union representatives will be provided with paid time-off to attend courses, seminars and conferences by the union's own choosing so as to better equip them for negotiating on issues of technology. This approach is in line both with the recognition that technology issues will be of increasing importance to collective bargaining and with the efforts being made under the auspices of the NEDC and the Department of Industry's microprocessor awareness programme to disseminate knowledge and awareness of new technology throughout industry.

4 *Agreed Plans on Employment and Output*: Trade union strategies towards dealing with technological change will be based on the objective of maintaining and improving employment and living standards. This approach will be followed both through trade union involvement in the industrial strategy and through collective bargaining. Negotiators will be seeking to identify the adoption of new technology with greater security of employment and expansion of job opportunities rather than the negative policy of producing the same output with a reduced workforce. To this end a key demand will be for full union involvement in manpower and production planning within enterprises in order that employment opportunities are maximised.

(*a*) Security of employment for the existing workforce can best be achieved by a guarantee of **no redundancies**, even if this involves individual workers changing jobs within the enterprise.

(*b*) Negotiators should look critically at proposals for using **natural wastage** to change the size of a workforce and should bear in mind the effect which it can have of redistributing unemployment towards young entrants to the labour market. Agreement on manning levels should be a condition for the introduction of new technology, but negotiators will also need to pay attention to manpower developments when the equipment becomes operational to ensure that agreed levels are maintained.

(*c*) If negotiators can succeed in maintaining or even improving the total level of employment in the enterprise then new technology need not be associated with growing unemployment. To achieve this it may be necessary to commit enterprises to pursuing an **expansion of output** and improvement in services so as to maximise alternative employment opportunities. Negotiators can press for exploration by joint union/management teams of new markets for existing products, alternative product ranges, the scope for import substitution and for a commitment that the enterprise will be guided by the recommendations and targets of Sector Working Parties. In the public and private services the aim of trade unionists will be to extract recognition of the principle that new technology provides a timely opportunity to increase the level and quality of service provision rather than to cut staffing levels.

(*d*) Even where guarantees of job security or expansion of employment can be achieved the pattern of labour demand is likely to be changed by new technology. **Redeployment** of the existing workforce is therefore an issue which requires tackling in bargaining about technology. The establishment of redeployment units which enable workers to express a preference about their future deployment, advance counselling of workers and an explicit commitment by enterprises to full consultation before any change is made can all help to avoid the likelihood of forced redeployment.

(*e*) Linked with this is the question of improving **relocation** arrangements for those who move as a result of technological change. Adequate allowances for mobility and relocation are being secured for growing numbers of workers through collective bargaining.

(*f*) Where it is impossible to reach no-redundancy agreements there is a strong case for trying to **improve redundancy payments**.

# New Technology

In some circumstances negotiators may be able to press for continuing arrangements in addition to lump-sum payments.

5 *Retraining*: Many new technological developments will significantly change the pattern of demand for various skills in industry and the service sector. Adequate provision for retraining is therefore crucial in the pursuit of real job security. Although pressure will be needed at all levels on this issue there is much that can be achieved through New Technology Agreements.

(*a*) Agreement can be reached that those sections of the existing workforce whose jobs are most directly affected by technological change should be given **priority both in retraining** in the new skills and in **applying for new jobs**, subject to existing and accepted procedures.

(*b*) At company level employers can be committed to **set up a training scheme** for those who will operate new machinery, with adequate payments for attendance. The operation of schemes should be carefully monitored to ensure that training opportunities are fairly distributed and that the most appropriate skills are being provided.

(*c*) The principle **of maintained or improved earnings** should apply to those who make use of retraining arrangements which are mutually agreed.

(*d*) Redundancy **notification periods**, which should be lengthened, **can be used to provide retraining** to affected workers in skills which will enable them to find employment in other trades or industries.

6 *Hours of Work*: A period in which new technology is being introduced provides great scope for reducing the length of working hours. Because of its effects on the organization of work and production technological change opens up the entire question of the pattern of working time for negotiation, offering the prospect of much greater flexibility. Negotiators will be seizing the opportunities offered and will link agreements on new technology to reductions in working time.

(*a*) Alongside the campaign for **a general reduction in normal hours to the level of 35**, there is scope for achieving **breakthroughs for specific groups** and then generalising them through the collective bargaining system. Negotiators should be aware, however, that this will require attention to be paid to the exchange of information within and between unions.

(b) Negotiators should have regard to the need to *distribute such benefits as widely as possible*. The aim of achieving breakthroughs for individual groups is to use them as levers for progress elsewhere rather than to limit the reduction of hours to those who work with new technology.

(c) Longer holidays, sabbaticals, and early retirement on improved pensions can all be pursued in bargaining about new technology and attempting to reduce working time. The reduction or **elimination of systematic overtime** should be a bargaining priority.

(d) Where new technology produces an increase in shiftworking this should be accompanied by a reduction in hours worked. The flexibility associated with microelectronic technology can be used to **change shift patterns** to bring about a greater intensity of capital utilisation and shorter working hours.

(e) National level agreements can be used to set a **general framework** within which the exact pattern of hours changes can be determined at local level, in line with local conditions and the needs and preferences of individual groups of workers.

7 *Distributing the Benefits of Technology*: By changing skill requirements and, indeed, occupational categories, new technology can present negotiators with potential disruption to existing pay structures. Another danger is of the polarisation of the workforce into a minority of highly paid workers with considerable job satisfaction and a majority of de-skilled workers whose earning power is consequently limited.

This is an important area for negotiators to tackle through New Technology Agreements since the case for accepting technological change rests largely on a fair distribution of the consequent benefits.

(a) A first step is to ensure that present **incomes levels are maintained and improved**.

(b) The **additional skills** required by operatives should be taken into account in assessing their pay grades. Where job evaluation systems exist they may need to be redesigned to reflect changes in skill requirements. Such systems can also be used to safeguard or improve the position of women affected by new technology.

(c) Since new technology will blur, even on occasions transform, established divisions within the workforce – such as manual/non-manual, staff/hourly paid, skilled/semi-skilled/unskilled – bargaining over its introduction offers the opportunity by improving conditions of service for all employees, but recognising the particular progress required for some groups to move rapidly towards single status for the whole workforce. Holidays, sick-pay, pensions, the working environment, and special leave entitlement are all areas where unjustifiable differences still exist between groups of employees.

8 *Control Over Work*: One feature of new technology which has raised considerable fears is related to the ability of some new machines to increase the measurement, regulation and control by management of operatives. If workers are to have confidence that they can share in the benefits of technological change they will need firm assurances on this aspect, and this in turn will require initiative and some expertise on the part of their representatives.

(*a*) It is at the **design stage** for a technological system that decisions will be taken that affect the technology's influence and control over those who work with it. Negotiators should therefore seek full involvement at this stage.

(*b*) Even after a system has been installed, however, microprocessors can be **reprogrammed** at very little cost. Negotiators should therefore be aware that objectionable features of a technological system are not beyond their influence.

(*c*) To enable this to take place arrangements can lay down **procedures** covering, for example, the storage and use of data relating to personal performance, or other details of the workforce.

(*d*) Such procedures can be based on the principle that no information acquired by computer based systems shall be used for individual or collective **work performance measurement**. Any breach of this principle would then allow for re-programming of the system.

9 *Health and Safety*: The implications of new technology for health and safety at work are widespread and profound. Trade unionists will be faced with the prospect of working with machinery and processes, such as Visual Display Units, which place new strains on operatives. The need for stringent standards on health and safety will be greater than ever.

(*a*) Negotiators should ensure that the manning levels for new equipment provide sufficiently for maintenance and running repairs or the operation of the machinery may lead to increased hazards.

(b) Agreements can specify **regular breaks** from working with new equipment which increases the strain on operatives.

(c) Where unions, especially at national level, have produced **detailed guides** on the health and safety aspects of particular equipment, these can be used by negotiators to govern the working conditions associated with new technology.

*10 Procedures for Reviewing Progress*: Even where agreement is reached on the acceptance of new technology, and employers have agreed to proceed on the basis of consent, there will be areas of uncertainty about the precise way in which new machinery and processes will operate in practice. There will therefore be a need to establish procedures to monitor developments and to review progress against the objectives set out in new technology agreements.

(a) An effective way of achieving this is to set up **joint union/ management study teams** with the responsibility for monitoring the detailed effects of the implementation of new technology. This approach has the advantage of highlighting issues which can be tackled at the purchasing and design stage by the same team when considering further changes.

(b) As a further safeguard new technology agreements can specify a **trial period** of operation during which consultation and negotiation can continue in the light of practical experience of working with the new technology.

(c) Problems arising during this period may be processed through established **grievance procedures**, but this may require attention to be given to whether these procedures can work swiftly enough.

**NURSERIES AT WORKPLACE**   Nursery care can be an important factor in determining whether a woman takes a job or not. The demand for comprehensive provision has therefore been an important element in the various programmes for equal rights for women. The fact is, however, that provision is very scarce in Britain. Nursery education in schools covers only a part of the relevant age groups, whether in nursery classes which normally take children at three, nursery schools (a very small number) which can take children at two, or infant schools taking 'rising fives', i.e. before the term in which the children become five, the largest element. Schools normally take children for school hours only which are normally shorter than and do not coincide with hours of work.

Unions in local government and the civil service have gone further than most in developing policies of workplace nurseries and in pressing for their provision.

Local Authorities sometimes provide day nurseries whose hours are closer to working hours but they normally provide only for deprived children and their families are subject to means test for payment of charges. Despite the growth of social services day nurseries have however not been a major growth area.

Nor have the growing demands for nurseries at place of work been very successful and provision is very sparse, indeed minimal, in spite of the legal rights of women to return to their jobs after maternity. Large numbers of women therefore resort to child-minders, registered or otherwise.

Places of work which provide nurseries cover a great variety of establishments including factories, universities and colleges, hospitals and some civil service offices. But the total number is not great in relation to the numbers that could be catered for.

Provision of nursery care in one form or another has long been a demand of the trade union movement. Concern has however also been expressed that nurseries at work can be used as a means of retaining women staff on low rates of pay and with no training and promotion prospects. Nursery agreements should therefore seek to ensure this is not so, as well as ensuring workers' participation in management of nurseries. Current economic difficulties and cuts in public expenditure have in any case seriously affected their availability. What growth there has been has been largely in the field of fee paying private provision.

# O

**OCCUPATIONAL PENSIONS** Both in private industry and in the public sector a number of industries, occupations and jobs have their own pensions schemes over and above the state retirement pensions scheme. In 1979, according to the Government Actuary, there were about 11,800,000 in occupational schemes – about half the workforce, of whom 5,600,000 were in the public sector (about

# Occupational Pensions

75 per cent of public sector employees) and 6,200,000 in the private sector (about 40 per cent of private sector employees). The great majority of those in public sector schemes had better provision than the others. These schemes may be contributory or non-contributory as in the civil service and provide a wide variety of levels of pensions and conditions of payment. The schemes are subject to certain legislative controls and an Occupational Pensions Board, appointed by the Government, administers the legislation affecting them and advises the Secretary of State on questions relating to them.

Employees in occupational pensions schemes that are 'contracted out' of the additional earnings-related pension are entitled to the occupational pension instead of the earnings-related addition. In 1981 10,300,000 of the 11,800,000 in the schemes were 'contracted out'. A requirement of contracting out is that employees should be treated as favourably as in the state scheme.

Because of the difficulty arising when people changed jobs and its effect on the mobility of labour and management, the Occupational Pensions Board was in 1978 asked to look into the problem and to 'consider what further steps should be taken to protect the occupational pensions rights and expectations of employees who change employment including the transfer of rights between pensions schemes'. The board reported in July 1981.

The report recommended the improvement of pension benefits for people who changed jobs. The need for this recommendation arose from the practice of freezing benefits, until they became payable, for employees who left their jobs for new ones, so considerably reducing their value in a time of inflation. Instead the benefits should be increased as far as possible with the movement in average national earnings with a ceiling on the increases of 5 per cent compound interest per annum: though a minority of the Board thought the revaluation should be in line with the movement in earnings but failing that recommended a ceiling figure of $8\frac{1}{2}$ per cent. There should be a legal obligation on employers to pay these increases. The report also recommended other improvements to 'contracted out' members of occupational pensions.

In 1979 the average occupational pension paid was about £20 a week for retired employees and half that for widows and dependants. At the same time the average lump sum payments on retirement have tended to increase. Virtually all occupational pensioners in the public service and three-quarters in private employment received some form of pension protection from inflation although in general less in the private than in the public sector. There has been a very substantial rise in the 1970s in the number of private schemes providing for widows if the employees died in service. About half the women in full-time employment in 1979 were covered by schemes. (*See* Social Security, Index Linking.)

**OCCUPATIONAL PENSIONS BOARD** The Occupational Pensions Board was established in 1973 to administer legislation affecting occupational pension schemes and advise the Secretary of State for Social Services on questions relating to such schemes.

The Board is appointed by the Secretary of State and consists of a chairman, deputy chairman and 12 members.

The Board's functions are:

- To advise the Secretary of State on questions he refers to them affecting occupational pension schemes;
- To decide upon, and issue, contracting-out certificates to employers under the Social Security Pensions Act 1978 and supervise the financial resources of contracted-out schemes;
- To supervise the arrangements for preserving the pension rights of people who leave their employment before pension age;
- To advise whether schemes give men and women equal access to scheme membership;
- To assist occupational pension schemes to adapt to a variety of specified circumstances;
- To report on proposals referred to them by the Secretary of State;
- To consider and report on proposals to make regulations referred by the Secretary of State.

**ORDER 1305** This was the Conditions of Employment and National Arbitration Order made in 1940, primarily to deal with wartime conditions. The main purposes of the Order were to prevent work being interrupted by trade disputes and to supplement disputes machinery already existing by providing an ultimate resort to arbitration at the instance of one party to a dispute even though the agreement of the other party to go to arbitration might not be forthcoming.

The Order established the National Arbitration Tribunal and provided that Awards made by the Tribunal became an implied term of contract between the employers and workers to whom the Award related and could be enforced at law. The Order prohibited strikes and lock-outs unless the difference had been reported to the Minister of Labour and had not been referred by the Minister for settlement within twenty-one days from the date on which the difference was reported to him. A very significant part of the Order was Part III, which made it obligatory on employers in every district to observe terms and conditions which had been settled by collective agreement or by arbitration for the trade concerned in that district. Questions arising as to the terms and conditions which should be observed in particular cases could be reported to the Minister by an organization of employers or a trade union which habitually took part in the settlement of wages and working conditions in the trade concerned and, unless otherwise settled, had to be referred to the National Arbitration Tribunal.

The Order remained in force until it was revoked in August 1951 on the advice of the National Joint Advisory Council (representing both sides of industry), the body which had agreed that the Order should continue in force for a time, after the end of the war period.

The National Arbitration Tribunal issued 1,723 Awards from its inception in 1940 until August 1951 when it was superseded by the Industrial Disputes Tribunal under Order 1376.

**ORDER 1376**  This Order replaced Order 1305 in August 1951 and while it made provision for compulsory arbitration on lines similar to those of Order 1305, it did not contain any prohibition of strikes and lock-outs and there were a number of differences between the two Orders, of which the following were the most important:

(a) The new Order introduced certain restrictions to prevent unrepresentative bodies (e.g. bodies not parties to any established machinery) reporting disputes and using the machinery under the Order.

(b) Certain types of dispute were excluded from the scope of the new Order, which was limited to differences connected with the terms of employment or conditions of work.

(c) A new Tribunal was constituted known as the Industrial Disputes Tribunal.

(d) The new Order provided that a dispute which had been the subject of a decision by joint machinery for the settlement of disputes, or of an award under the Conciliation Act, 1896, or the Industrial Courts Act, 1919, could not be dealt with under the Order. The purpose of this provision was claimed to be to uphold the authority of voluntary machinery.

(e) The general obligation imposed by Order 1305 upon employers

# Organization and Methods Studies

to observe the recognised terms and conditions of employment (or terms and conditions not less favourable) was not continued in the new Order, but provision was made for the reporting of 'issues' concerning the observance of such terms and conditions by an individual employer.

Order 1376 was revoked and the Industrial Disputes Tribunal came to an end in February 1959. During its period of operation it made 1,270 awards.

**ORGANIZATION AND METHODS STUDIES (O AND M)** These are specially arranged studies of the management of an organization or a local or central government department which may be undertaken from time to time or for some special reason. The study would normally cover the work of all administrative staff from clerical to managerial and include administrative procedures and managerial organization. As a result recommendations are made for greater efficiency which the organization or department may or may not implement. O and M studies tend to be quite costly operations.

**ORGANIZATION FOR ECONOMIC CO-OPERATION AND DEVELOPMENT (OECD)** In view of the wide currency of its reports on economic and social issues, trade unionists should be aware of the influence of the OECD established in 1981 with Headquarters in Paris. It replaced a previous organization, the Organization for European Economic Cooperation (OEEC) which was originally set up in 1948 to coordinate the aid provided by the United States under the Marshall Plan – the European Recovery Programme. Sixteen countries were then involved, covering Western Europe and Turkey but excluding the Soviet Bloc, which refused to take part, and Spain. As well as supplying immediate aid the OEEC branched out into wider economic fields, involving co-operation of the member countries, and was ultimately joined by the US, Canada and Spain to create the OECD which was in turn joined by Japan and Australia.

The new Organization has become a prestigious body run by a highly-respected group of specialist officials. Aiming to foster economic development and trade, especially for less developed countries whether or not members, the Organization publishes a great deal of valuable economic and social information about its members as well as studies of important world problems including monetary and technical issues. Its reports are generally regarded as authoritative, but it must be remembered that the Organization reflects the interests of the major capitalist economies. Thus, while giving limited help to the Third World its commitment to unrestricted freedom of trade, for example, has helped to maintain the present world balance between rich and poor countries.

The trade unions in OECD countries are co-ordinated through the Trade Union Advisory Committee (TUAC) whose Headquarters are also in Paris.

**OUTWORKING**    *See* Homeworking.

**OVERHEADS**    Overhead costs are difficult to define precisely but they normally include all costs which have to be met regardless of whether an establishment is actually in production or not e.g. rent, maintenance, depreciation, rates, safety measures and certain management costs. They enter into the computation of the total cost of production. When the establishment is in production the overheads costs calculation may include such items as light and heat and other items apart from wages, salaries and raw materials.

**OVERTIME**    Trade unions and employers are mainly concerned with wages and hours as the chief elements in conditions of work. In the course of time hours of work have been reduced either by law or by negotiation or both. Whereas once in many industries a 40-hour and five-day week was the aim, today sights are often set at a 35-hour working week agreement as the basis of weekly wage rates. This is a major objective of TUC policy, and by August 1982 about 8½ million workers will have achieved a basic under 40 hours a week agreement.

The shorter working week has, however, not eliminated overtime which is the term applied to hours over and above the agreed standard or basic week or the agreed shift on which wages may be based. An *average* of 4.5 hours overtime per week was put in by all male manual workers in April 1981, and the *actual* hours worked by overtime workers is considerably higher. 46.8 per cent of male manual workers worked overtime, with an average of 9.5 hours a week in April 1981. Only 17.5 per cent of male non-manual workers worked overtime, averaging 6.5 hours a week. Such hours are normally paid at higher rates which can vary according to when they are worked, during the ordinary working week or at weekends or during holidays. In making agreements trade unions aim to provide a satisfactory wage but workers frequently have to work overtime to achieve this. Employers, too, can ask, or even demand overtime in order to increase production or complete jobs in progress, for example to

# Package Deal

meet delivery dates. Overtime rates are normally anything from one-and-a-third times the ordinary rate to double the rate.

At best overtime is regarded by unions as a necessary evil and agreements to eliminate unnecessary overtime and control overtime practices, without loss of earnings or earnings opportunity, are normally sought. Unions aim at increasing the workers' leisure as part of a good standard of living. Sometimes time off in lieu of overtime pay is negotiated, principally for white collar workers.

It is a matter of concern to unions that longer hours (including overtime) are worked in Britain by a larger percentage of the workforce than in other EEC countries, taking into account shorter holidays in this country. There is no statutory control in Britain over the amount of overtime working as contrasted with nearly all other European countries except as regards women and young persons in factories. Germane to the issue is the question of spreading work in a time of severe unemployment, and unions may ask for a shorter working week with this in mind. Employers in some cases, however, may prefer overtime working to hiring additional workers.

Whatever the circumstances where overtime is worked or likely to be worked unions will try to negotiate the best possible overtime rates at the same time as securing the shortest possible working week as the basis for wage rates. The fact that overtime working is strongly associated with low pay (e.g. on the railways) complicates efforts to reduce or eliminate overtime. The TUC has under consideration the question of a legal limit.

# P

**PACKAGE DEAL**    Sometimes when wages or salaries are negotiated either side may throw into the discussion arguments concerning other elements in the conditions of work of employees. A package deal may then be negotiated involving more than wages which the union sees *as a whole* to be advantageous. Similarly trade unions may accept what they consider to be a good bargain in one aspect of a negotiation to offset against other parts of the agreement which are not so good. Package deals are a not uncommon result of complicated negotiations. The essence is that the deal must be accepted as a whole.

**PARTNERSHIP**    A business may be organized as a partnership, usually on the basis of a written agreement setting out the terms of the partnership. Partnerships normally comprise from two to twenty people who share the profits on the terms agreed and normally each partner must bear responsibility for any debts incurred by the partnership beyond his share to the full extent of his personal wealth. Thus actions in the name of the partnership are the responsibility of all the partners. There are more limited forms of partnership in which one partner is responsible for debts only to the extent of his share in the business but in that case he is not allowed to share in the management of the business.

Partnerships are common among self-employed professional people such as solicitors and accountants and in businesses with small capital requirements.

Partnerships, unlike companies, do not have the obligation to publish their accounts etc. nor to disclose information to unions. Partnerships must be distinguished from Co-partnership. (*See* Companies, Co-partnerships, Disclosure of Information.)

**PATERNITY LEAVE**    This is the practice (minor as yet but growing due to trade union pressure) of granting leave to the father as well as the mother before, during and after the woman's confinement, for a limited period. It may be with or without pay and has as yet no statutory basis. It recognizes that the father may have to meet additional domestic obligations due to the mother's condition – obligations difficult to fulfil without leave of absence from work. Sometimes workers use their holiday entitlement for this purpose.

Paternity leave granted by firms varied normally from one to ten working days.

**PAY BOARD**    A Board set up by the Heath Government in 1973 under the Counter Inflation Act to set pay norms under the Government's attempted incomes policy. The Board monitored pay in accordance with a Prices and Pay Code and also conducted a number of enquiries into pay anomalies and relativities. An example of a major enquiry was on London Weighting. It was abolished by the Labour Government in 1974.

**PAYE**    Pay as You Earn was introduced during the war as the means of collecting income tax from wage and salary earners through deductions from the employee's pay by the employer. The employee

# Payment by Results

fills in an income tax return in the normal way for the Inland Revenue which then allocates him a code number which is notified to both employee and employer and allows the employer, using tax tables provided by the Inland Revenue, to deduct the correct amount of tax while preserving confidentiality in respect of the employee's income.

**PAYMENT BY RESULTS**   *See* Incentive Payments, Piecework.

**PAYMENT IN KIND**   This is payment, usually in goods but it may be in services provided, instead of payment in part or whole of the cash due in wages. It is governed strictly by the Truck Acts and prohibited save in certain strictly-regulated cases (*See* Truck Acts.)

**PAYMENT ON ACCOUNT**   Sometimes in a wage negotiation a sum may be offered and accepted before the conclusion of a final settlement which may be held up for one reason or another. Such offers are Payments on Account without prejudice to the final agreement. (*See* Subbing.)

**PAY RESEARCH UNIT (CIVIL SERVICE)**   Pay in the Civil Service was for many years, until 1981, determined by the principle of 'fair comparison' with the current pay of outside staffs employed on broadly comparable work but taking into account differences in other conditions of service. To achieve this a Pay Research Unit (PRU) was set up in 1956 under a Director appointed by the Prime Minister and responsible to the National Whitley Council.

The object of the PRU was to find out the facts on which pay comparisons might be based but not to write recommendations; its work, as an independent fact finding body, was such as to command the confidence of both sides in salary negotiations. 'Pay Research' therefore became an integral part of the machinery for determining Civil Service pay, and any refusal by the Government to have regard to the findings of the Unit or to divulge them has been bitterly resented by the Civil Service unions.

The refusal of the Government to release the findings of the PRU for the 1981 pay claim and its unilateral decision to suspend the operation of 'pay research' and arbitration was challenged by the Trade Union Side in the courts on legal grounds but the challenge failed, the High Court Judge declaring the PRU 'an arm of Government' and its Director 'a Government servant'.

In 1981 the Civil Service unions were in dispute involving industrial action with the Government because of its unilateral action contrary to all accepted principles of good industrial relations. Not only was the machinery for negotiating pay – hitherto accepted and recognized – not in operation but also the Government set up an enquiry into the pay of the non-industrial Civil Service which involved proposals for alternative machinery. The Civil Service unions opposed these proposals. Following the settlement of the pay aspect of the dispute in mid-1981 the unions agreed to give evidence to the 1982 Enquiry while the Government agreed to negotiate in advance of fixing cash limits. But the unions protested that in advance of the Enquiry's report the Government had introduced into the 1982 negotiations a new principle linking pay to the staff recruiting position of the various grades.

The absence of the PRU creates a gap in the provision of information; its interpretation of conditions of service for example included such matters as hours, leave, superannuation, luncheon vouchers, assisted travel, house purchase facilities, car allowances, etc.

**PENALTY CLAUSES**    This phrase normally refers to clauses in collective agreements which withdraw agreed payments if other clauses in the agreement are broken (usually by unofficial action).

In general such clauses have not worked successfully and have usually been replaced by undertakings on the part of Executives of trade unions to 'use their best endeavours' to secure observance of agreements. There is a strong view in the trade union movement that penalties and heavy discipline secure little in labour relations and that it is far better for trade union leaders to present proposed agreements to their members in meetings and to distribute detailed explanations, followed by voting. This means that the members know what is involved, and when they indicate acceptance, they are more likely to observe the agreement. In addition, if there is a breach of the agreement the trade union official is likely to gain a resumption of normal working on the grounds that the agreement was democratically approved.

The expression also refers to contract clauses, e.g. in building work, requiring payments of special sums in the event of breach by the contractor. These are enforceable unless they can be shown to be intimidatory.

# Pension Funds

**PENSION FUNDS (OCCUPATIONAL)**    These are the funds accumulated by occupational pensions schemes which have grown in both nationalized and private industry and in local government since the war. Total deposits funded by both employers and employees in over 20,000 schemes with $11\frac{1}{2}$ million members (1980) now amount to some £40,000 millions. The 200 biggest funds are over £20 million each. Since this money is invested by the management of the various schemes the pensions funds are a major element in shareholding in the economy. According to Sir Harold Wilson, Chairman of the Committee on the Functioning of Financial Institutions, the pension funds are so powerful, 'they could very well begin transforming the nature of society more than any Government would ever dare to do . . . .'.

Fund investments are intended to provide security for the future beneficiaries. Difficulties caused by inflation have been met by additional payments by employers into the schemes so as to maintain agreed pension levels.

Management of the funds and where they invest has long been a matter of concern for the trade union movement. Concentration on existing securities and on government securities has been criticised. In particular attention has been drawn to investment in works of art, banks and property. The TUC has been interested and has advocated substantial investment to provide capital for manufacturing industry. It has also been concerned with the large amount of investment, including in property, overseas, which it claims in 1980 exceeded investment in UK securities. Investment policy of the funds has been largely in the hands of a quite small number of merchant bankers and stockbrokers.

Pension Fund management committees may or may not have staff or union representation. Some funds have a Board of Trustees which has control over investment policy but in others employee trustees may be excluded from effective control over investments. About one third of pension fund assets are managed internally by the employers without union participation and the other two thirds by various institutions such as insurance companies and merchant banks. The TUC's aim is 50 per cent trade union representation on Boards of Trustees, an aim which it suggests should be achieved by collective bargaining with employers. But its preference is for this representation to be statutory as was recommended in a Government White Paper in 1976. The Thatcher government is opposed to such legislation.

**PERKS**   As distinct from fringe benefits, which are largely and formally acknowledged as additional emoluments to salary or pay, perks are more informal benefits which accrue from working on particular jobs or in a particular establishment. They may include gifts, tips, the practice of having private work done, material, use of telephone for private calls, food, expense account meals etc. Perks may be taken by custom and practice or they may be taken without authority – or the management may turn a blind eye to the practice. In an industry or establishment they can amount to considerable sums in value and have been criticised accordingly. (*See* Fringe Benefits.)

**PICKETING**   It is customary during a strike for the workers to set up pickets, i.e. place a group of strikers outside the place of work. As described by the TUC, picketing is one of a number of strategies for making industrial action effective. Thus the aim of the pickets may range from simply drawing attention to the strike to persuading other groups of workers to join the action; persuading workers already employed in the workplace not to break the strike or others not to come in to take the place of the strikers; persuading workers to divert supplies of all kinds from entering the factory (e.g. raw materials, components, etc.), not to distribute goods from the factory and not to undertake work transferred from the factory to another location. According to the needs and objectives of the strike as determined by the union, picketing traditionally therefore could take place at a number of locations and involve different numbers of workers as well as others supporting the strike.

A 'legal right to picket' has never existed as such but peaceful picketing has long been recognized as lawful; trade unionists exercising their legal right to 'attend' and 'peacefully communicate information'. But in the course of doing this they can find themselves faced with a variety of charges relating to obstruction of the highway, breach of the peace etc., in making charges under which the police have considerable discretion which can amount to a restriction of picketing in practice. Thus, while there are no exemptions from action under the criminal law, trade unions organizing pickets in furtherance of trade disputes and trade unionists taking part in them – although their aim may be to persuade workers to break contracts, which is a 'civil offence' – are protected by the law from civil action in the courts as long as certain conditions are observed. These conditions, the subject of considerable controversy, are now laid down in

# Picketing

the Employment Act, 1980, and are spelled out in a Code of Practice issued by the Department of Employment. ACAS felt unable to endorse the Code and the TUC has strongly opposed both the Act and the Code as designed to weaken the unions.

For picketing to be lawful it may be undertaken only in contemplation or furtherance of a trade dispute; it may be carried out by the picket only at or near his own place of work; a trade union official may also take part accompanying or representing his member(s); its only purpose must be 'peacefully obtaining or communicating information or peacefully persuading a person to work or not to work'. Workers such as lorry drivers, who do not have a fixed place of work, or workers for whom 'it is impracticable to picket at their own place of work because of its location' are permitted to picket the premises from which they work or from which their work is administered. Where in the course of the dispute the employer has dismissed the worker, the worker may picket at his former place of work provided he has not found a job elsewhere.

These provisions are a considerable restriction on what had long been regarded by unions as normal and legally possible in picketing. Thus, now excluded from lawful picketing are other workers who wish to give support to strikers out of sympathy for their cause; picketing at the head office of an employer except for those who actually work there, except as may be covered above for mobile workers etc; picketing another workplace belonging to the employer in order to secure support; picketing premises involved in supplying goods to or distributing goods from their workplace or picketing another workplace to which their work has been transferred.

Pickets, according to the Code of Practice, may seek to explain their case to those entering or leaving the picketed premises, to ask them not to enter or leave – verbally, by issuing leaflets, or by carrying banners or placards. But the picket cannot compel attention or stop anyone crossing the picket line. The police have a large measure of discretion to determine whether picket behaviour is threatening, violent or intimidating and therefore goes beyond 'peaceful persuasion'. Such behaviour may result in a criminal charge. As an example, the Code cites obstruction of the highway or physically barring the passage of vehicles or persons, lying down in the road, linking arms across or circling the road or jostling or physically restraining those entering or leaving the premises, or obstructing a police officer in the execution of his duty. On the other

212

hand the driver of a vehicle approaching or seeking to pass through a picket line must drive with care and not in a manner which might foreseeably cause a risk of injury.

One of the most controversial features of the 1980 Act limits the number of pickets to not more than six and the Code suggests that frequently a smaller number will be appropriate. The police in any event have considerable discretionary power to limit the number of pickets in any one place where in their judgement there is danger of disorder. This provision is clearly directed against 'mass picketing' and may considerably diminish the effectiveness of picketing in particular circumstances. It has been strongly objected to by the TUC.

Equally controversial are the provisions of the Act concerning 'secondary picketing'. If a worker contemplates picketing at his own place of work in contemplation or furtherance of a dispute between another employer and his workers he is subject to the following conditions. If such picketing interferes only with contracts of employment than they are protected by the statutory immunity described earlier. If however they also interfere with commercial contracts, immunity will apply only if their employer is a supplier to or customer of the employer in dispute, the principal purpose of the picketing is to disrupt the supply of goods or services between their employer and the employer in dispute, and the picketing is likely to achieve that purpose. Employees of an associated employer of the employer in dispute or of a customer or supplier of the associated employer, may also picket with immunity where work has been transferred to the associated employer because of the dispute and the secondary action is aimed at disrupting that work and is likely to achieve that purpose.

The Code of Practice makes various suggestions on the organization of picketing, some of which are reasonable and some of which may well be impracticable or even undesirable and would seriously limit picketing if they were a condition of operation. Thus it is suggested that an experienced person, preferably a trade union official, should always be in charge of the picket line and that there should be advance consultation with the police on the numbers who should take part at any one time. Consultation between unions, where several are involved, is clearly important, as well as knowledge of the complexities of the law as far as possible by those picketing. It is important, too, to note that under the Act it may be considered unreasonable to expel or exclude from a union in a closed

# Piecework

shop a person who has crossed a picket line which the union had not authorized or which was not at the member's place of work.

In a separate section the Code advises pickets to ensure that their activities do not interfere with the movement of essential supplies and services and carrying out essential maintenance of plant and equipment. It lists at some length how it defines essential supplies and services which include for example medical and pharmaceutical products, heating fuel for schools, and the operation of the police, fire, ambulance, medical and nursing services etc.

An employer or employee faced with pickets which he considers are not acting lawfully may start a civil action for damages or seek an injunction from the court stopping the unlawful picketing. A person picketing outside the limits set loses the legal immunity provided for in what may be defined as lawful picketing.

Since civil action cannot be taken (May 1982) against unions as bodies any action alleging unlawful picketing would have to be taken against individuals, who it is suggested by the Code will normally be the persons on whose advice or instruction the picketing has taken place and will apply not only to them but to any others acting on their behalf or on their instructions. Should the action be successful and an injunction made it would be contempt of court to defy it. The TUC warns employers against inflaming the atmosphere of industrial relations by recourse to the law. Employers are reminded that they cannot enlist the support of the police in identifying pickets considered to be acting unlawfully. (*See* Employment Bill 1982, Immunities, Secondary Action, Sympathetic Action.)

**PIECEWORK**    Straight piecework means payment of a uniform price per unit of production. Earnings therefore vary directly with the number of units produced by the individual. This system tends to be used most where the work is of a repetitive character and where it can be divided into similar units. A similar principle can be applied to a group or a gang but the total earnings of the group or gang are divided amongst all its members proportionate to their individual wage rates.

Most collective agreements dealing with straight piecework provide for a minimum time or basic rate to be contained within the piecework price and guaranteed as a minimum payment. It is also normal for piecework prices to be calculated to yield a given minimum percentage above the time or basic rate e.g. $33\frac{1}{3}$ per cent for normal effort.

Some straight piecework systems are operated in conjunction with the payment of a flat rate addition (e.g. a cost of living payment). In such a case if output doubles the piecework element alone doubles, the additional payment remaining constant.

Straight piece-work rates may be expressed in one of two main forms: 'money piece-work' or 'time-piece work'. In the case of money piece-work the worker is paid a money price for each piece or operation completed. In the case of time piece-work there is a time allowed for each operation or piece; if the job is finished in less than the 'time allowed' the worker gets financial advantage from the time saved.

Piece-work 'prices' or 'times' are negotiated between trade union representatives of the workers concerned, with the workers being directly involved, and members of management e.g. rate-fixer or time study engineer. Time and motion studies are often used in the process of negotiating within piecework systems.

There are variations from the straight piecework system operated by some companies; usually these are in the form of premium bonuses. The best-known systems used for this purpose are the Halsey (sometimes called the Weir) and the Rowan. Both systems are based on a standard time allowance and a tapering off of earnings as output increases. They are designed to deal with types of work where the measurement cannot be too precise, and whilst they commend themselves to some employers trade unions generally are opposed to their use because they mean in effect, 'cutting the rate'.

**POLITICAL ACTION BY TRADE UNIONS**   From the earliest days of industrialization in Britain trade unions of necessity engaged in political activity in defence of the right of trade unions to exist, to influence Factories Acts, to seek workmen's compensation in industrial accidents, to fight against sweated labour. Some trade unionists actually secured election to Parliament under the Liberal party label and were known as 'Lib-Labs' in the last century, but their independence from influence by the wealthy interests in the Liberal party was always in doubt. The need for stronger and more direct political representation on such issues as improved housing and education for workers and for pensions and accident prevention and

# Political Action by Trade Unions

compensation, led to the formation of the Trades Union Congress in 1868. Political bodies identified with working-class interests developed soon afterwards, including the Social Democratic Federation (1881), Fabian Society (1884), and the Independent Labour Party (1893).

In 1900, the TUC set up the Labour Representation Committee, a federal alliance of trade unions and these bodies, with the purpose of securing more *independent* working-class representation in the House of Commons. In 1906, twenty nine candidates supported by the Labour Representation Committee were elected to Parliament and the Labour Party was born.

Trade union affiliation to the Labour Party began in these circumstances and the Trade Union Act of 1913 permitted the creation of political funds and the development of a political levy by trade unions.

Legislation on trade unions and industrial disputes in recent times has re-emphasized the trade union involvement in political action. The Industrial Relations Act of 1971 and its repeal in 1974, the Trade Union and Labour Relations Act, 1974, the Employment Protection Act, 1975, of the then Labour Government, followed by the Employment Act 1980 of the subsequent Conservative Government, are examples of the direct connection of the trade unions with the law. Apart from the impact of labour laws on trade unions and trade union activity, it is obvious that workers' lives can be improved by progressive social and industrial legislation and trade unions will continue to involve themselves in political activity accordingly. Many trade unions, with political funds, sponsor Labour members of parliament to promote their cause where issues are before Parliament affecting the industries concerned. Usually such 'sponsored' MPs are drawn from members of the Union who have been elected or appointed to the Union's parliamentary panel. If such a person is adopted by a constituency Labour party the trade union will then give an allowance to the constituency party towards the upkeep of the local organization. Additionally, a grant will be made towards the cost of election expenses of about 80 per cent of the maximum amount of expenses allowed by the law.

Grants from Union political funds are also made by Unions to Union members who are fighting a Parliamentary election but are not on the sponsored panel, to union members contesting local government elections, and to appeals from the Labour Party nationally and locally in addition to the payment of affiliation fees to the Labour Party.

Most trade unions are affiliated to the Labour Party and send delegates to the Annual Conference which consists of delegates from constituency labour parties and socialist and co-operative organizations in addition to those of the Unions. The Conference elects the National Executive Committee of the Labour Party which includes twelve members elected from the unions.

The trade unions also are represented on the Regional organizations of the Labour party and, in general, encourage their members to become individual members of the Labour Party and to participate in the local activity of the party. (*See* Political Levy.)

**POLITICAL DONATIONS BY INDUSTRY**     Trade unions are often attacked from the Right for their subvention of the Labour Party although this takes place under the law. What is less frequently pointed out is that quite a substantial number of companies give donations to the Conservative Party or to organizations pursuing anti-labour and anti-trade union policies. Such donations are revealed in company annual reports. Thus in 1980–1, among the companies giving money, sometimes very substantial sums, to the Conservative Party were General Electric, United Biscuits (Holdings), Trafalgar House, Guest, Keen and Nettlefold, Glaxo, Cadbury Schweppes, Sun Life Assurance Society, George Wimpey, European Ferries, British Commonwealth Shipping, The Beecham Group, Hambro's Bank, Lucas Industries and the Rank Organization etc., etc.

Other right-wing organizations subsidized include the Economic League, Aims of Industry, The Centre for Policy Studies, and British United Industrialists. Total donations under the above headings amounted, according to the Labour Research Department, to nearly £2.2 millions in 1980 as far only as clear information is available. (*See* Political Levy.)

**POLITICAL LEVY**     Under the Trade Union Act of 1913, the right of the unions to act in the political field was recognized provided that political objects were included in the rules after the taking of a special ballot, that a separate political fund was kept and that exemption from the political levy was given to all members who signed a form of objection.

Unions use their political levy to affiliate to the Labour Party and pay affiliation fees both nationally and locally to that Party. In addition financial support is given to Labour candidates in Parliamentary and local elections.

The operation of the political levy by trade unions is overseen by the Certification Officer. (*See* Contracting In/Out.)

**POVERTY TRAP**    When poor families are receiving means-tested benefits which are diminished or entirely lost if their income improves they are said to be in the poverty trap. This is because an improvement in income is offset by a reduction in benefits and the family's poverty remains.

The trap operates because of the combined effect of wage levels, taxation and benefit regulations on net incomes. Thus an increase in gross income (as the result of a wage rise) results in more tax being deducted and bigger national insurance payments contributions. At the same time entitlement to various benefits is automatically reduced under the various provisions governing the payment of e.g. family income supplement, rate and rent rebates and free school meals. In some cases a wage increase can actually leave the family worse off. Though the trap may not operate immediately it does eventually as entitlement to benefits is reassessed.

One of the problems, it is argued, that make this 'anomaly' difficult to solve is the lack of co-ordination between the various government departments responsible for different benefits, the Department of Health and Social Security, the Department of the Environment and the Department of Education and Science and the lack of coordination between them and the Treasury which is responsible for taxation. The result is that a family considered to be poor enough to receive benefits (on different scales) may be considered by the Treasury to have sufficient gross income to be subject to tax. The Low Pay Unit claims that the fiscal measures of the Thatcher Government have actually increased the number of families in the trap substantially.

An improvement in child benefits and lifting the taxation threshold would clearly help to solve the problem for poor families with children. Trade unions in negotiating improvements for their members take the poverty trap into account in their overall strategy.

**PRIVATE ENTERPRISE**    Private ownership, control of and investment in the economy as distinct from state intervention of any kind. (*See* Capitalism.)

# Private Health Schemes

**PRIVATE HEALTH SCHEMES**   The creation of the National Health Service (NHS) did not end private treatment. Doctors may still practice privately for fees, a practice which, although not widespread, is growing; all hospital consultants are permitted to treat private patients; and 2,500 pay beds still exist (1982) in hospitals where the consultants can treat their private patients, making full use of the publicly-owned facilities. Many private clinics exist for wealthy patients as well as for those who, one way or another, are able to pay for the service.

Growing rapidly in recent years have been private medical insurance schemes which in early 1982 covered 6 per cent of the population, a percentage which is steadily increasing, thus creating in effect a two-tier hospital and medical treatment system. Spending on hospital-based private health schemes was estimated to be around £350 million in mid-1981. There are some 1,300 private hospitals and nursing homes with about 32,000 beds (1982) and another 2,000 planned.

The best known schemes are the British United Provident Association (BUPA) with over 2 million members, the Western Provident Association and the Private Patients Plan. Also recently formed is a company, Air Call, a chain of private family doctors' surgeries, each with many more patients than a doctor in the NHS looks after. Individuals or organizations or companies join schemes normally on behalf of their management staff and blue collar participation is growing as a perk, although payment by employees is growing too. Membership gives entry to private treatment facilities and/or the use of public facilities at low cost as well as tax relief for group membership for participating companies. All this has been accompanied by the growing number of consultants doing private part-time work.

The growth of corporate membership of private schemes, companies offering sickness and accident schemes plus private medical insurance has been regarded by the trade union movement as a danger to the NHS. With few exceptions the movement wants the end of private practice within the NHS and of pay beds in hospitals. It is opposed to the use by private clinics of the expensive public facilities in hospitals, a form of subsidy for the rich. The unrestricted growth of private clinics is also regarded as a growing danger to the NHS.

Thus six privately owned hospitals opened in 1980–1 and just after and BUPA has set up an Independent Hospital Group to co-ordinate private facilities outside the NHS. It will open three new hospitals in 1982 and more after that.

Among the attractions of Private Medicine is the avoidance of long waiting periods for treatment, i.e. queue jumping, a problem which greater investment in the NHS would help to avoid; or luxury treatment at heavy cost in private clinics which are flourishing. Among the problems created by private medicine is the attraction to the private service of nursing staff not subject to the government's control of public pay, service and conditions.

In order to limit the growth of private health schemes, supporters of the NHS have demanded its improvement, selective nationalization and expensive licensing systems for the schemes.

**PRIVATE SECTOR**     That part of the economy in private ownership and control. Most British manufacturing industry and commerce is in the private sector, though government intervention has been steadily increasing, even under Conservative governments as in the Heath Government's intervention in the affairs of Rolls Royce and the Thatcher Government's in British Leyland.

**PRIVATIZATION**    This describes the policy of the Thatcher Government aiming to weaken the nationalized industries by hiving or selling off parts of their profitable activities to the private sector or removing part of their monopoly in their particular industrial sphere. Examples are to be found in British Rail and British Gas etc. The Government is also encouraging contracting out of all NHS services (e.g. cleaning and laundry) to private industry. This increased 30 per cent between 1979–80 and 1980–1. The term is also used to describe the actions e.g. of a local authority in contracting out its refuse collection or school cleaning to a private contractor to replace the previous system where the employees concerned were directly employed by the local authority. The most publicized case is Southend where the unions have challenged, as grossly exaggerated, claims of resulting economies as well as pointing out worsened wages and conditions.

A report (No. 207) from ACAS in 1980 concluded: 'workers in contract cleaning are among the lower paid in the labour force'.

**PROCEDURE AGREEMENTS**   *See* Agreements.

**PRODUCTIVITY**    'Producing more, while working less, in order to have a better life' was the description of productivity given by

# Productivity Bargaining

Jean Monnet, the French economist. It recognizes that there should be some purpose for higher productivity and takes in the need to use modern technology. Productivity is not working harder but working efficiently with the most modern methods. Work study, wage and salary incentives, modern techniques, productivity bargaining, all have their part to play in achieving higher productivity but the main factor is adequate investment in machinery and equipment. In Britain too many people are working with out-dated and inefficient machinery and very often in poor conditions in old factories and offices. A British worker according to the TUC (1981) has about £7,500 worth of machinery to work with, but a German has £23,000 worth, and a Japanese £30,000 worth.

To maintain and increase productivity there is a need for high demand so that production can be developed at maximum capacity but the machinery and equipment, combined with a well-trained and well-organized labour force, must be there too.

**PRODUCTIVITY BARGAINING**   The term 'Productivity Bargaining' is usually applied to a situation where higher wages and/or improved working conditions are paid to bring about major changes in working methods, performance standards and in some cases manning levels and arrangements. The approach implies negotiation between management and trade union representatives to improve the means and methods of production and clearly must involve a contribution from both sides.

Management usually wants to cut costs and among its considerations will be: reductions in manning, reduction in number of jobs or grades, elimination of surplus labour, increased flexibility or mobility of labour, removing alleged restrictive practices, introduction of new job assessment techniques and payment systems (e.g. measured day work, work study, job evaluation, incentive systems), use of shift work, reduction of overtime and in some cases elimination of rest periods e.g. tea breaks etc. Trade Unionists in negotiating on productivity not only seek higher earnings but normally insist on assurances about employment security. Improvements sought might include higher basic wages or salaries, shorter working hours and/or longer holidays, retention of status for workers whose jobs or job gradings are changed, adequate re-training opportunities and guarantees against redundancy, together with improvements in workplace health and safety. In the best circumstances productivity

221

# Productivity Schemes

bargaining has had the effect, in some industries and establishments, or raising the level and extent of joint consultation and joint determination and has brought about the increased participation of shop stewards or office and local trade union representatives in the negotiation and operation of agreements. Trade unions will always emphasize the continuous nature of productivity bargaining in which their representatives will want to monitor and mutually agree any changes. This contrasts with the attitude of some managements who want to look upon a Productivity Bargain as a means of establishing authoritarian control over its labour force, an approach which is unrealistic and invariably fails.

Because of the degree of inter-linking between white collar and blue collar workers arising from technological changes, there is a strong view that productivity agreements should cover all types of employee in an undertaking. There is also increasing demand for full information to be provided to the trade unions to enable them to assist in the formulation of sound productivity agreements.

**PRODUCTIVITY SCHEMES**   Apart from the more formal 'productivity bargain' and payment by result systems, there are two well known types of Productivity Scheme, one which links bonuses to company sales revenue and profits and one which ties bonuses to output volume.

Output-linked schemes can be based on units of production or percentage increases of output over the previous year's figures, and can relate to the entire plant, or to particular individuals. Schemes of this kind can be affected by a great many variables e.g. machinery in use, company investment policy, the prevailing economic situation, world markets, etc. Because of these considerations such schemes are generally not favoured by trade unions which favour more direct schemes where there can be a measure of mutual involvement.

Somewhat the same reaction on the part of trade unions applies to 'Profit-sharing' and 'added value' schemes that connect bonuses to sales revenue and company profits. Trade unionists argue that a firm's overall performance is affected by a multitude of factors, such as pricing, marketing, the company budget and investment policy, the range and design of the products offered, over all of which the workers rarely have any control. There may be nil bonuses in a bad year for profits caused, for example, by heavy capital investment or

222

losses on a particular line of products, although worker productivity may nevertheless have substantially increased.

Trade unionists are also cautious where the complex calculation of profit and loss lies largely in the hands of company accountants and there is an inadequate disclosure of information. Generally speaking managements have learned that more simplified schemes worked out in co-operation with the trade unions secure better results and the confidence of the workforce.

**PROFESSIONAL ASSOCIATIONS**  Some professional associations are trade unions whose members consider themselves to be members of a profession, e.g. the National Union of Teachers, affiliated to the TUC or the First Division Association in the Civil Service similarly affiliated. On the other hand members of a particular, recognized profession may try to distinguish themselves from trade unions, e.g. the British Medical Association (doctors) or the Law Society (solicitors). That the boundary lines between trade unions and professional associations are blurred is evidenced by the fact that among doctors, for example, there are a number who belong to a trade union of doctors (part of ASTMS) and among teachers there are associations which do not belong to the trade union movement.

In practice a number of professional associations, even if not part of the trade union movement, perform all the normal functions of a union on behalf of their members, i.e. they participate in salary negotiations and look after the conditions of service of their members. But some perform wholly or partly additional functions including control of entry to the profession and control of examinations for qualifications and administering discipline among members as far as their professional practice is concerned. Even here, however, the distinction between union and professional association may be blurred as some unions influence entry e.g. through apprenticeship schemes and others, e.g. teachers' trade unions, have codes of professional conduct which members must observe.

There are also a number of Professional Institutes which have no trade union functions and are concerned solely with qualifications, standards and status e.g. the Institute of Mechanical Engineers, the Chartered Institute of Transport, etc.

The hallmark of a profession is sometimes declared to be its right to govern itself, i.e. make its own rules for entry, discipline and expulsion; but these rules are rarely, if ever, not subject to some wider control e.g. by law or government regulations. Some bodies which insist on their professional status have little or no powers of self government e.g. teachers and administrative civil servants. (*See* Engineering Council, National Federation of Professional Workers.)

**PROFIT**    There are many conflicting theories of the nature of profit which are the subject of controversy among economists, socialist, marxist and capitalist. In popular terms, however, profit is the surplus accruing to an enterprise when all the costs involved in production or in the provision of a service have been deducted from the income received in selling the product or providing the service. Costs would include labour, management, materials, fuel, capital equipment (machinery etc.), buildings, overheads, depreciation and all other expenses accepted under the law as legitimate. Out of this 'gross profit' money will be set aside to pay taxes due, interest on and repayment of loans, bank charges and transfers to reserves. After these payments the remaining amount is called 'net profit' out of which dividends are paid.

Trade unionists in negotiation should be aware of the distinction in company accounts between gross and net profits and be alert on the factors included in 'legitimate' costs and on genuine transfers to reserves in defining net profit. (*See* Overheads.)

**PROFIT SHARING**    *See* Co-partnership.

**PUBLIC CORPORATIONS**    The name used for all the major nationalized undertakings. They are industries taken over or set up by the state and controlled by a Board appointed by the Government and ultimately answerable to Parliament. They are intended to operate as efficient business units and be self financing. Forms of organization may vary as may the conditions under which public corporations operate and the degree of independence they have in their financial operations. (*See* Nationalization.)

**PUBLIC SECTOR**    This refers (in industry) to nationalized industries as distinct from privately-owned industry. The distinction has become blurred owing to substantial government subvention of and subsidy to a number of industries and establishments.

As far as employment is concerned the term is applied to employees in the civil and local government service, manual and non-manual (including those in schools and further and higher education), universities, the National Health Service and the nationalized industries. Those employed in the public sector, dependent as they are to a greater or lesser degree on public finance, have been specially susceptible to government influence and intervention in wage and salary negotiations which considerably limits freedom of bargaining, normally to the detriment of the employees concerned.

This has occurred notably in recent years in the case of civil servants, teachers, fire brigades, local authority manual workers, etc.

**PUBLIC SECTOR BORROWING REQUIREMENT, PSBR** Public expenditure by central and local government takes two forms: spending on current services, benefits and grants which is mainly financed out of taxation and rates or by specific charges e.g. national insurance contributions; and investment in the public sector which is financed by long-term borrowing on the capitalist money market either directly or through the National Loans Fund and especially for smaller local authorities through the Public Works Loan Board. The amount borrowed over and above current income from the public sector (including nationalized industries and public corporations) or any grant out of taxation is the PSBR.

Exactly where the line is drawn between current and capital expenditure is a political question not an iron law of economics so that there is an element of manipulation, in the interests of political propaganda in support of deflation and cutting public expenditure, in the emphasis government places on the largeness of the PSBR.

Thus in recent years the policies of successive governments aimed at limiting the PSBR has involved stringent control over local authority loans and over the freedom of nationalized industries to carry out their plans, e.g. rail electrification, as well as a general policy of reducing the public sector of industry. All these issues may affect employment and are of importance to unions as well as the large part wages and salaries play in public expenditure.

Trade unionists often argue that the nationalized industries should be excluded from the operation of the PSBR so that their necessary and profitable capital investment should be regulated to operate in the same way as investment in the private sector.

# Q

**QUANGO**    This term is popular usage for *Q*uasi *A*utonomous *N*on-*G*overnmental *O*rganization. It covers a variety of bodies which have a role in the process of government but which are not Government Departments or part of a Government Department.

There are three categories of Quango as officially recognized:

*Executive bodies* carry out a wide range of operational or regulatory functions, various scientific and cultural activities and some commercial or semi-commercial activities. They are sometimes described as fringe bodies, meaning that they function on the fringes of government. Examples are the Arts Council, the Medical Research Council, ACAS, the Manpower Services Commission, the Sports Council, the National Development Research Corporation, the National Enterprise Board, the British Overseas Trade Board.

Executive bodies generally employ staff and spend money, supplied by the government, on their own account though they may be subject to overall government advice or control in policy.

*Advisory bodies* are not normally employers of staff or spenders of money themselves but their expenses and the cost of staff working for them are met by sponsor Government Departments. There are thirteen hundred Advisory Committees, including for example four hundred under the aegis of the Department of Employment.

*Tribunals*, like Advisory Committees have their full expenses covered by the sponsoring Department. These range from the Police Arbitration Tribunal to the system of Agricultural Land Tribunals, National Insurance Local Tribunals and the Supplementary Benefit Appeals Tribunals. (A study on the possibility of the merger of the latter two is in hand by the DHSS.)

Executive quangos are set up either by Act of Parliament or administrative action – in some cases by forming a company under the Companies Act; when this happens parliamentary approval is necessary for any money provided to the company. Most Advisory Committees are set up by administrative action though some have a statutory basis. Tribunals and other judicial bodies are set up to meet a specific statutory requirements.

The common feature of all three types, as the official Pliatzky Inquiry into quangos pointed out, is that they are in some sense part of the apparatus of government without coming under the day-to-day direction of Departmental Ministers or civil servants. In the case of Executive bodies and Advisory Committees they have been set up because the relevant Department's own staff either cannot carry out particular functions or, for reasons of public policy, it is not desirable that they should, or because outside advice in policy-making is essential.

Tribunals are judicial bodies in a specialized field with a limited jurisdiction, and may be necessary because a Department should not be judge and jury in its own cause in dealing with such matters as appeals against its administrative decisions under various statutory schemes; and the appeal role is better carried out by specialist tribunals than by the ordinary courts.

The total expenditure of quangos in 1979–80 was £6,800 million and the work of the Pliatzky Committee resulted in a saving of only £11.6 million in spite of a powerful political campaign for their substantial reduction, thus indicating that most quango expenditure would be incurred whatever other form of organization, if any, could be devised. Since the Pliatzky Report there have been further abolitions, the total in February 1982 amounting to 112 executive and 500 advisory quangos; and a Civil Service Guide requires Departments to carry out reviews on the continuing need for the quangos they sponsor and to exercise detailed financial control over them.

In some quangos the Chairman and/or Board member may receive some payment. Decisions to close down quangos were sometimes arbitrary; a notorious case is the Centre for Information and Advice on Educational Disadvantage, abolished by the Department of Education and Science (DES) as part of a quota of closures agreed by the secret caucus of Permanent Secretaries of Government Departments, although its cost was less than £300,000 and the Centre conformed to the conditions laid down by the Pliatzky Committee. The closure showed the contempt of the DES for the problems of disadvantaged children.

The Thatcher Government, although proclaiming against quangos, had by mid-1981 established 31 new ones necessary under its own legislation.

**QUORUM**    The minimum number of members of the union branch or organization who must be present before the business of the meeting can be conducted. (*See* Branch Life.)

# R

**RACE DISCRIMINATION IN EMPLOYMENT**     That discrimination of one kind or another exists in employment against members of ethnic minorities is attested by authoritative surveys and is hardly any longer a matter of controversy. Thus the House of Commons Home Affairs Committee in mid-1981 reported that unemployment is greater among blacks than whites and this disproportion is growing; that blacks tend to get the worst jobs and that this continues even when qualifications are identical. The Race Relations Act, 1976, makes it unlawful for employers, trade unions, employers' organizations, partnerships, bodies responsible for laying down qualifications e.g. for professions, the Manpower Services Commission and its divisions, vocational training bodies and employment agencies to discriminate directly or indirectly on grounds of race, colour, nationality (including citizenship) or ethnic or national origins.

Direct discrimination is defined as treating an individual on racial (or any other of the above grounds) less favourably than others are or would be treated in the same circumstances. Indirect discrimination involves applying a requirement or condition which adversely affects members of a particular racial (or other – as described above) group considerably more than others and which cannot be justified on non-racial grounds and works to the detriment of people in the group.

Thus employers must not discriminate in:

(a) Recruitment and selection – this includes any system of recruiting workers and the nature of any advertisement for a job as well as the refusal to employ.
(b) Pay and conditions of employment e.g. application of conditions not applying to the other employees including eligibility for any benefits, facilities or services.
(c) Access to training facilities.
(d) Promotion.
(e) Dismissal or redundancy regulations or arrangements.
(f) Any other feature detrimental to an ethnic group.
    Employers must not victimize anyone alleging discrimination in good faith.

Similarly trade unions must not discriminate in conditions of membership, the admission of members, benefits provided, exclusion from membership or any other unfavourable treatment. On the other hand unions may make special efforts to recruit particular groups by arranging meetings and publishing material in ethnic minority languages.

There are a number of special provisions. Thus discrimination in selection is permitted if the employer can show that a job has to be done by members of a particular group (e.g. in the theatre). Also permitted is positive discrimination to train or offer opportunities for work to members of a group which has had no or very little training or opportunity for a particular job. An example of this are classes run mainly to prepare ethnic minority groups for entry into teachers' training courses. A different kind of exception is the exclusion from the consequences of the Act of seamen recruited abroad; the seamen's union have opposed this.

The Commission for Racial Equality (CRE) established under the Act may issue Codes of Practice on race relations in employment. It can also investigate cases of alleged discrimination, compelling the provisions of information and the attendance of witnesses and give help to individuals. After an investigation it may issue a non-discrimination notice which can be enforced in the courts if not complied with. The work of the CRE at local level is chanelled mainly through Community Relations Councils to which the TUC recommends local Trades Councils and trade union branches to affiliate.

Complaints regarding race discrimination in employment can be made to an industrial tribunal following an attempt at conciliation by ACAS (the CRE can help in making the arrangements) and if upheld the tribunal may make a declaration of rights, award compensation for the loss suffered and make recommendations for putting the situation right.

After lengthy consultation with Government, employers and unions, the CRE issued a Code of Practice in 1982 with a view to it being given Parliamentary approval. The Secretary of State for Employment must approve the Code and lay it before Parliament or give his reasons for not doing so. The Code lays down practical guidelines for employers; they are recommended to recruit and train racial groups hitherto under-represented, to appoint senior staff responsible for examining equal opportunity, to examine their criteria for selecting employees to avoid discrimination, e.g. they should not demand higher standards of English than are necessary in the job, etc.

**RATE CUTTING**  Under payment by results systems the tendency for management to seek maximum output at the least cost often leads to management concern when the workers earnings rise substantially. In particular the piecework system encourages the worker to work 'flat-out' in order to achieve high earnings and if these are attained some managements will see it as an indication of 'loose rate fixing'. Management may then seek to 'cut the rates'. To a greater or lesser extent a similar situation may arise with any incentive system of payment. Whatever justification may allegedly exist for 'rate cutting' many experts have warned against its dangers of undermining confidence in payment by results systems. Workers will consider that a bargain is being broken by the employer and tend to be wary in subsequent bargaining. Trade Unions have been able to negotiate safeguards against 'rate cutting' in some industries.

**RATE FOR THE JOB**  The established time rate of payment for the normal week (i.e. exclusive of overtime incentive payments etc.) applicable to the job concerned. This is normally contained in a collective agreement. Sometimes the issue as to what is 'the appropriate rate' is disputed, e.g. in the case of claims for Equal Pay and the Going Rate. (*See* Equal Pay, Going Rate.)

**RATES**  In addition to taxes levied by central government, local government levies a direct tax in the form of rates. This is a tax on the assessed value of property, its 'rateable value', either domestic, industrial or commercial, and is charged at so many pence in the pound of rateable value. Assessment of rateable value is a complicated process and is based on the notional sum the property might fetch in rent in the open market. Rates are described as 'regressive' as they tend to hit poorer householders harder, taking a larger proportion of their lower incomes than they take from the better off. People in rented accommodation may be paying rates either separately or as part of their rent.

Various ideas have been mooted for reform of the rating system or its abolition. One is the payment of a 'poll tax' paid to the council by everyone on the electoral register, with allowances for non-earners and the unemployed. Another is a local sales tax on everything except essentials. Yet another is a centralized system of funding in which all local government services are paid for by the central government and are therefore very tightly controlled. The most canvassed proposal is a Local Income Tax.

A Government Green Paper (December 1981) on alternatives to the present system discusses the above possibilities as well as hiving off education (the most costly local service) from local Government. New proposals may follow a period of consultation in 1982, and it is suggested that a combination of the various alternatives with lower domestic rates may be a possibility. The following are the two opening paragraphs of the Green Paper:

*The scale of local government* Local government in Great Britain is expected to spend about £30,000m in the financial year 1981–2. About 16 per cent of this expenditure will be covered by rents and various other fees and charges. The balance, of some £25,000m, will be borne by rates and Government grants; this will be a quarter of all public spending, and will represent $6\frac{1}{2}$ per cent of the gross domestic product. Currently, local government has an outstanding debt of £37,000m and employs some 2.8 million people, or over one-tenth of the work force.

*The sources of local revenue* Of the £25,000m of local rate- and grant-borne expenditure in 1981/82, some 57 per cent will be provided from the Exchequer by central government in the form of rate support grant, specific and supplementary grants. Of the remainder, about 44 per cent is expected to be contributed by domestic rates and about 56 per cent by industry, commerce and other non-domestic ratepayers.

**RATE SUPPORT GRANT (RSG)**  Grant aid to Local Authorities, to help pay for the services they provide under the law (e.g. education), is paid through the Rate Support Grant (RSG) normally announced in November each year to allow the Authorities time to set their local rates for the following financial year in the light of the grant allocated to them. There are separate settlements for England, Wales and Scotland but the principles underlying payment of the grant are the same although the law operates somewhat differently in Scotland (see below).

The total sum is fixed following very detailed discussions between Government Departments and Local Authorities. No discussions of a similar nature take place with representatives of the unions although the level of grant has an important influence on both employment and pay. Any discussions between Government and unions have tended to be for information and can rarely be said to have seriously influenced decision-making.

From the total sum decided, a fixed amount is earmarked for certain specific purposes, e.g. police, certain transport arrangements – such as 'through' roads – and national parks. A further sum is then allotted in the form of a flat rate subsidy to all authorities as a cushion to enable them to charge less to domestic than to industrial and commercial ratepayers. What remains, the great bulk of the grant, is then allocated to individual local authorities. The total sums involved are based on assumptions the Government makes on the level of inflation and changes in pay for the period concerned, that is to the end of the following financial year. (The financial year runs from April to April).

Such calculations are bound to be speculative. But fixed sums allowing for inflation, irrespective of what actually happens, and allowing for wage and salary increases before negotiations take place, are intended to control the level of local authority spending through the operation of the cash limits policy. The total sum paid to the local authorities was reduced for 1981–2 (for England) from 60.1 per cent in the previous year to 59.1 per cent of what the government decided should be the total volume of expenditure on the various services provided by the local authorities, and for 1982–3 it is reduced to 56 per cent, for England. In Scotland the Government percentage was reduced by 2.5 per cent to 64.2 per cent: for Wales it was cut by 1.4 per cent to 72.5 per cent.

Allocations to individual authorities are in the form of a Block Grant which replaced the previous system of two separate elements in local authority expenditure based on the estimated needs and estimated resources as assessed by each authority. Instead the government now makes the assessment. This it does by assessing how much each authority should be spending in the light of the demand for its services and their cost; this allows it to work out the average national level of rates that should be levied, (grant-related poundage); the amount the authority then receives is the difference between the assessed spending needs and the total it could raise in rates if it charged the national average rate.

The assessment of each authority's needs, known as the Grant Related Expenditure (GRE), is a very complicated process. It involves a decision by the government on the total sum it nationally decides as necessary for the various services (i.e. the total GRE), e.g. education, personal social services, public transport etc. This division is of course based mainly on politically decided priorities. The division of the total between the authorities results from the government's assessment based on various criteria or 'indicators' of each authority's needs and costs, following the detailed discussions referred to above. The 'indicators' take account of the number of people in the area, its physical features, its social and environmental problems, differences in costs of providing services and the special requirements of particular services.

Once the grant is announced the local authority knows how much it will have to raise in rates to maintain its services. This could mean a very large rate increase since grant allocated has been assessed on the basis of the government's decision that local authority expenditure should be reduced. Authorities are therefore faced with the dilemma; either to raise the rate substantially or to reduce the services. If, however, the former decision is made, a new factor enters the scene. When an Authority spends more than the Government has assessed should be spent on various services, its grant is cut. And this is done not just proportionately but at an increasing rate, creating for the Authority a 'Catch 22' situation; the more it tries to do, the less it will receive. The 'support' grant becomes a 'negative grant', a cut, subject only to a small 'threshold of flexibility'. This is the method adopted to secure reduced expenditure whatever the effect on vital services – the greater the 'overspend' the harsher the penalty on local ratepayers. In 1982–3 authorities' spending, for penalty purposes, will be scrutinized against *both* the Government's spending target and the GRE. The process is euphemistically called 'adjustment of grant entitlement'.

In Scotland, however, grants can be cut (and were in the case of the Lothian Authority) on the basis of estimates, not of actual expenditure. The Local Government (Miscellaneous Provisions) Scotland Act allows this and also stops Scottish Local Authorities from making good cuts by increasing rates or in any other way. The expenditure target set for Scotland in 1982–3 involves significant reductions in local authority expenditure and the Local Government and Planning (Scotland) Act, 1982, gives the Government powers to oblige a local authority to redetermine a lower rate where it thinks spending plans are 'excessive and unreasonable'.

Since many urban areas including London have in the past incur-

# Rate Support Grant

red heavy expenditure on what they have regarded as essential social services which they had an obligation to provide under government legislation, the situation has for them been further worsened by another factor, the redistribution of the total grant in 1981–2 from metropolitan areas in favour of shire counties although the process has worked somewhat erratically and has to some extent been made good in 1982–3, e.g. for London. Another change has adversely affected the Inner London Education Authority in that instead of precepting its demands from the GLC, it now receives part of its grant direct, like an LEA, and part through precept.

These arrangements began operating in April 1981 and for the first year certain minor measures allowed of the mitigation of the adverse affects on ratepayers created by the redistribution. The operation of the new system in 1981–2 has been sharply criticised by the Local Authorities' Associations as irrational, unfair, and failing to take into account the actual position in each area because of the method of calculating *nationally* the need for various services and then applying the calculation locally irrespective of current actual provision and need. Secondly it has been even more sharply criticised as undermining the independence of local government in handling its own services and as decisively weakening the functions and role of local government.

From 1982–3 the Government, through the Local Government Finance (No. 2) Act, will control further the power of local authorities to raise rates. The Act abolishes supplementary rates and precepts so that local authorities have to levy rates and precepts for the whole financial year. The abolition is directed mainly at Labour authorities striving to maintain services. If there is an urgent, unanticipated, 'absolutely essential' need for extra revenue, the Secretary of State has power to sanction temporary borrowing by the authority if application is made to him. The Act also leaves power with the Government to impose in the middle of the year a *general* 'holdback' on RSG, in addition to the penalty system for *individual* authorities described above.

It also establishes an Audit Commission to supervise the audit of local authorities in England and Wales to ensure 'value for money'. The conditions of operation of the Commission have been the subject of sharp controversy between local authorities and Government.

These measures amount to a constitutional departure of major significance in the relations between central and local government. Its consequences can materially affect trade unions, which have very many members working for local authorities.

**REAL WAGES (REAL EARNINGS, REAL TAKE HOME PAY)** Wages are paid in money whose value has changed to a greater or lesser extent since the previous agreement was made. In recent times sharp inflation has reduced the value of money substantially. Negotiators must estimate the *real* value of money wages as compared with their value when the last agreement was made. *Real* wages are therefore often contrasted with money wages and negotiations for increases will take into account the movement of inflation since the previous agreement and will normally argue for increases beyond that in order to achieve a *real* increase.

Real earnings are the real value of the total pay packet as compared with the previous position, that is including overtime pay, any bonuses and allowances etc., before deductions are made for tax and insurance.

Real take-home pay as between one period and another involves a calculation not only of the movement of inflation as it affects total money earnings but also of other factors which affect the actual amount in the pay packet. These would include deductions for tax through PAYE and national insurance payments.

**RECESSION** One of the terms used to describe falling economic activity marked by growing unemployment and falling production and profits, temporary rather than long term in which case the term commonly used is 'depression' or 'slump'.

**RECOGNITION OF TRADE UNIONS** The Employment Protection Act, 1975 established procedures under which unions could seek recognition from employers for collective bargaining purposes. The Employment Act, 1980, repealed these provisions so that there is now no legally-established procedure available to trade unions which are refused recognition. This is a matter of considerable contention, since the demand for recognition is now back in the arena of conciliation, in which ACAS may have a voluntary role, negotiation or industrial action.

Recognition is usually demanded for collective bargaining on pay and terms of employment as well as on the many issues that crop up in a workplace where employees wish to be represented by a union of their choice. Under the Act, procedures were available if negotiations to establish recognition in the normal way were unsuccessful. These procedures were as follows.

An independent, certificated union was able to apply to ACAS, either for recognition or for recognition in respect of additional matters. An attempt would then be made by ACAS to settle the matter by conciliation after finding out for itself by any means it considered suitable (e.g. by a secret ballot) the views of the workers and employers concerned. If this failed, ACAS prepared a written report giving its findings and could make a recommendation for recognition or otherwise. If recognition was recommended its scope, purposes, any conditions etc. had to be specified.

If the employer refused to accept the recommendation and still refused recognition or to negotiate genuinely on the issue, the union could complain to ACAS two months after the date from which the recommendation was to operate, following upon which ACAS would make a further attempt to conciliate. Where this still failed the union could then complain to the Central Arbitration Committee (CAC) both on the failure of the employer to carry out the recommendation and claiming specific terms and conditions of employment.

In these circumstances the CAC, having considered the case, could not compel recognition by the employer but could indicate its view of the justice of the claim for recognition. If it considered the claim justified it could make an award that the employer must operate the union's claimed terms and conditions of employment or other terms which it specified. These terms were enforceable and became part of the workers' contract; and if the employer breached them, individual workers, but not the union, could sue for breach of contract in the county courts. The terms could be varied by a subsequent award or by a collective agreement or by individual agreement provided the change was an improvement.

In practice the use of the ACAS procedures under the Act did not lead to substantial results in achieving recognition; the much-publicized Grunwick case is an example. The procedures were not effective enough, the long delays involved being one factor. Nevertheless the existence of the ACAS procedures in the background encouraged the growth of trade union recognition.

**REDEPLOYMENT**    This term may be used in two ways. It can refer to a company shifting its resources or part of them from one activity to another, e.g. from an unprofitable to a profitable or potentially profitable activity, existing or about to be developed. This can have important consequences for the labour force employed, for example leading to layoffs. But it may also lead to shifting, i.e. re-deploying employees to correspond to the new developments from one job to another, which should mean negotiations between unions and management to secure agreement about the moves. Workers may also be redeployed to the same job in another place e.g. as in a number of major civil service moves to sites outside London accompanied by negotiations between management and unions. Redeployment may also be used as a means of preventing redundancies by shifting workers from one workplace or job where there is a surplus of labour, according to the management, to another where there may be a shortage, to fill vacancies. Here again union involvement is essential to overcome difficulties. (*See* Mobility of Labour.)

**REDUNDANCY AND REDUNDANCY PAYMENTS**  Redundancy is the term used when an employee is dismissed or laid off because the business is closed, or is closing, or is being removed to another place, or because the employer no longer requires the particular job to be done either at all or in the present location. The provisions of the law on redundancy are very detailed and precise with the aim of avoiding disputed interpretations.

Under the Employment Protection (Consolidation) Act, 1978, Sections 81–120, employers must make a lump sum compensation payment, called a 'redundancy payment' to an employee who is dismissed because of redundancy and who fulfills other laid down conditions. This may also apply to those laid off or kept on short time for a substantial period.

Employers making redundancy payments under the Act may claim rebate at the due rate from the Redundancy Fund which is financed from Social Security contributions. The rate is 41 per cent (1982). Disputes concerning payment or rebates can be referred to an industrial tribunal.

Employees are not disqualified by volunteering for redundancy. Nor is there dismissal where the employee accepts an offer of alternative employment by the employer, a new owner of the business, or an associated employer. Again, workers are not eligible for payments if they are dismissed for reasons other than redundancy, e.g. inefficiency, unsuitability, misconduct (see below) or health reasons, but

# Redundancy

all entitlement is not necessarily lost if, for example, dismissal for misconduct arises during the period of notice of redundancy. This is also the case if an employee goes on strike during the notice period.

There can be disputes on the 'suitability' of alternative work offered which can be settled by an industrial tribunal which can also determine whether an employee's contract permits layoff without pay and short-time working which does not constitute redundancy.

Of some importance is the provision that if an employee dies before receiving the payment to which he would have been entitled the payment is still due to his personal representative. There are also special provisions concerning employees on fixed term contracts of various terms (see below), concerning apprentices, and employment abroad.

*How Much is Paid*: The amount of payment depends on age, length of service with the employer (up to a maximum of 20 years) and reckonable weekly pay up to a maximum of £135 (Feb. 1982) subject to annual review, with a maximum payment of £4,050. The employer is required to give the employee a written statement of the calculation.

The rate of payment for each complete year of service, up to a maximum of twenty years, is as follows:

1 From age 41 ......................................... $1\frac{1}{2}$ week's pay
2 From age 22 to 40 ................................... 1 week's pay
3 From age 18 to 21 ................................... $\frac{1}{2}$ week's pay

If an employee is past his 64th birthday when his employment ends (59th birthday for a woman), the payment is reduced by 1/12th for each complete month between that birthday and the Saturday of the week in which the employment ends.

*Who is Not Covered?* Nearly all employees are covered by the Act. The principal exceptions are:

1 People with less than 104 weeks' continuous employment since the age of 18 (service before 18 does not count)
2 People who work less than 16 hours each week (except those who have worked for at least five years, when it will be less than 8 hours each week)
3 Men of 65 and over and women of 60 and over.
4 Registered dock workers
5 Share fisherman
6 Merchant seamen

238

7 Crown servants and NHS workers

8 People employed by a foreign government

9 People employed on fixed term contracts of two years or more which specifically exclude the right to redundancy payment

10 Domestic servants employed by a household

11 Self employed people

12 Workers whom the employer is entitled to dismiss instantly because of 'gross misconduct' or who were on strike before redundancy notices were sent out.

*Layoff and Short-Time Working*: Layoff and short time have special meaning under the Act. Layoff means that a worker receives no pay whatever and short-time working means that he receives no more than half of his statutory weekly pay.

A worker may put in a claim for redundancy pay if he is laid off or put on short time working (or a combination of both) for a period of four consecutive weeks or for any six weeks during a period of thirteen weeks.

The following timetable applies when claiming:

1 Not later than four weeks after this qualifying period notice of intention to claim a redundancy payment must be given.

2 Within 7 days the employer must give counter notice that he can offer a resumption of work. He must state that within the next four weeks work will be resumed for a minimum of 13 continuous weeks without any layoffs or short time working.

3 Whether or not the employer gives notice, if there is no resumption within four weeks of the notice, a claim for a redundancy payment must be put in and notice of termination of employment according to the contract must be given.

4 If the employer does not make a redundancy payment, recourse may be had to a tribunal for an award.

*Alternative Employment and Trial Periods*: If the employer can offer certain kinds of new work to workers made redundant he can escape his obligations to make redundancy payments.

The following conditions must be attached to any offer of alternative work:

1 The new employment must take effect immediately after the old employment or within 4 weeks of ending it.

# Redundancy

2 The offer, which can be in writing or otherwise, must be given before the old contract ends.

3 If the new job is not the same as the old job, it must be suitable in relation to the individual concerned.

4 The employee must not have unreasonably refused to do the job.

5 If the new job is on different terms from those applying during the old job the employee must be given a trial period.

Tribunals normally do not regard jobs as reasonable if they are at a lower rate of pay, or at a substantial distance from the previous work, or if there is substantial disruption to the workers' routine.

The trial period lasts for at least four weeks from the date on which the new job is taken up. It can be extended provided an agreement is made that satisfies the following:

(a) it is made between the worker or his union and the employer
(b) it is made before the new work begins
(c) it is in writing
(d) it specifies the date on which the trial period ends, and finally
(e) it specifies the terms and conditions that will apply after the end of the period.

*Time Off*: A 'reasonable' amount of paid time off, for training or to look for new work, must be given to workers with 2 or more years service who face redundancy.

*Procedure for Handling Redundancies*: Any employer who proposes to make part of his work force redundant and who recognizes an independent trade union representing their interests must consult with that trade union at 'the earliest opportunity'.

Minimum periods are laid down for the consultation process, as follows:

90 days for 100 or more dismissals to be made within a 90 day period
60 days for 10 or more dismissals to be made within a 30 day period.

No minimum period is specified for less than 10 redundancies, but consultation must still take place at 'the earliest opportunity'.

*Information disclosure*: In these consultations, the employer must disclose prescribed information about the redundancies, including:

(a) the reasons for his proposals
(b) the numbers and descriptions of workers affected
(c) what selection process he plans to use
(d) the period over which dismissals are to take effect
(e) the method of carrying out dismissals – whether by pre-agreed procedure or not.

The employer must observe the above rules on disclosure and minimum consultation periods as far as is 'reasonably practicable'. He must consider any representations made by the trade union concerned and give a considered reply.

*Complaints against Employer: Protective Awards*: The trade union involved (but not the individual workers) can complain to an industrial tribunal that it has not been consulted by the employer. If conciliation does not solve the problem and the complaint is upheld, the tribunal can then make a protective award. This would require the employer to pay each worker covered by the award for a specified period at the tribunal's discretion, but subject to a maximum of 28 days (or 90 or 60 days in the instances formulated above). If the employer refuses to pay the full amount of the award, the tribunal may order him to do so.

Contractual payments and pay in lieu of notice covering a protected period will be offset against the protected award. Also any worker unreasonably refusing an offer, from the employer or a new owner of the business or an associated employer, for a new contract or a renewal of the old one, will lose his entitlement.

It should be noted that where there is a change in ownership of a business, the old and the new owners are regarded as one and the same employer as far as responsibility for redundancy payments are concerned. Service is also regarded as continuing from the old to the new employer if a trial period is involved (see above) and the employee continues beyond its expiry. But these conditions apply only if the business, or an identifiable part of it, has changed hands as a going concern, not where the premises have been bought and are being used for a different kind of business. In that case the responsibility for redundancy payments rests with the old employer.

*Insolvency of the Employer*: Where an employee claims that the employer is liable to make a redundancy payment and the employer is insolvent and the whole or part of the payment remains unpaid, an application may be made to the Secretary of State for payment from

# Re-engagement

the Redundancy Fund. As soon as the Department is satisfied that the claim is correct, it will be paid.

**RE-ENGAGEMENT**  An Industrial Tribunal may make an order for re-engagement of an employee unfairly dismissed. This specifies the employee's return to a job comparable to the old one and at equally favourable terms of pay and conditions of employment if this is reasonably practicable. (*See* Unfair Dismissal.)

**REGISTERED UNEMPLOYED**  This is the number of people who actually 'sign on' at an Employment Office or Jobcentre as being unemployed. It is generally regarded as an underestimate of the total number of unemployed which includes many, such as married women paying reduced national insurance contributions, who do not sign on. It is no longer compulsory for unemployed persons to register at their Employment Office or Jobcentre to be able to claim Unemployment Benefit. (*See* Unemployment, Unemployment Benefit.)

**REINSTATEMENT**  An industrial tribunal in an unfair dismissal case may make an order for the employee's return to his old job. This is reinstatement. (*See* Unfair Dismissal for examples, including Rights on Maternity etc.).

**RESTRICTIVE PRACTICES**  The really anti-social restrictive practices are those applied in trade by monopolies, cartels and trade associations. Some (though limited) oversight of these practices is provided by the Restrictive Practices Court and the Monopolies Commission.

Restrictive practices associated with the Trade Unions usually take the form of limitation in the number of apprentices or control of particular jobs or machines. Often this 'right to a trade' or 'right to a job' by particular classes of workers or trade unions arises from a background of unemployment, and therefore is a defensive weapon.

Trade Unions do not normally impose direct restrictions on what their members produce or service, except in the form of direct industrial action. For example trade union groups may retaliate against management attempts to 'speed-up' production or to impose new, unacceptable forms of payment, by applying a variety of restrictions in the process.

Occasionally employers have described a 'work to rule' action by workers and refusals to work overtime or to operate shift work as 'restrictive practices'.

**RETAIL PRICE INDEX (RPI) – COST OF LIVING INDEX – TAX AND PRICE INDEX (TPI)**   In all pay negotiations movements in the cost of living play an important, sometimes a decisive part. It is necessary therefore for both sides involved to be able to refer to an acceptable measure of the movement. To provide this is an object of the Retail Price Index, popularly called the Cost of Living Index, compiled by the Department of Employment. This supplies information on the percentage rise in prices during the previous twelve months based on the cost of goods and services on which it is reasonable to expect the 'average' family spends its money.

Its calculations are based on the study in over 230 towns of the prices charged for over 500 items – a considerable collection of data to analyse. This is married up to the 'spending pattern' of a 'typical family', to establish which, information is collected from about 7,000 households. The information includes for example rent, rates, fuel, telephone, food, transport, over a period of fourteen days, but exceptionally high and low spenders are excluded. The pattern which emerges is then used to calculate the proportion of expenditure assumed to go on different groups of items in the family budget. The index is published monthly and the spending patterns every year.

Changes from year to year are measured with reference to the position in 1974 which is indexed as 100. Thus in January 1978 the figure was 189.5, in January 1979, 207.2 and in January 1980, 245.3 indicating rises of 9.3 per cent and 18.2 per cent respectively since 1978. With each month's figures comes a calculation of the 'annual rate of inflation' for that month.

Clearly such important information has to be carefully checked against deliberate bias and an expert committee on which the TUC is represented does this. The index is generally considered to be reasonable but negotiators would take into account that it cannot measure local changes in items, which may be important in a particular negotiation, and that in the case of the lower paid workers the spending pattern for certain items (e.g. food) is likely to be different from the index 'weighting' so that the movement of particular items in the index becomes important in certain cases.

# Retirement Pensions

The Conservative Government, after its election in May 1979, proceeded to prepare a Tax and Price Index (TPI) which aimed at calculating the rise in the cost of living after tax and national insurance contribution changes had been taken into account. It measures the increases in gross income needed to maintain 'take home pay' in real terms. The object was generally understood to be to offset tax reductions against the rise in VAT which had a sharp effect on the RPI.

After the VAT changes had worked themselves through for a year less use has been made of the TPI than before. Thus though the TPI was introduced as a 'truer guide' than the RPI, at a time of tax reductions, it has since, in 1981, exceeded the RPI (in November 1981 by as much as 3.6 per cent). So its usefulness to the Government as a criterion for reducing the demand for wage increases has been removed for the present. In fact its use can be counterproductive in such circumstances.

**RETIREMENT PENSIONS**   Over nine and a half ($9\frac{1}{2}$) million people are now over retirement age, this is the equivalent of over a third of the labour force, and the proportion of old aged pensioners in the population is steadily increasing.

Although the basic retirement pension is increased in amount each year, it is still well below the level which should be set to assure the comfort that retired people deserve. The annual increase is an estimate (made at the time of the Budget) of what the movement of prices will be in the following November – expressed as a percentage; this percentage is then applied to the low basic pension which means the increase is low. Indeed it means that the purchasing power of the pension tends to decline for two reasons: firstly, pensioners tend to buy goods such as foodstuffs in smaller amounts than other members of the population, and the cost of small purchases is known to be relatively greater than the cost of larger purchases. Secondly, pensioners spend a far greater proportion of their money on food and energy (gas, electricity, coal, oil, etc.) and these items have risen faster in price than many other items measured in the Retail Prices Index.

Many pensioners are in such dire need that they have to apply for supplementary benefits (undergoing a means test in the process). Millions of pensioners are in receipt of supplementary benefits, and it is calculated that nearly 700,000 in 1981 were entitled to supplementary benefit but did not claim it. Many of the latter resent the indignity of a means test and regretfully suffer poverty out of a sense of pride. Only an *adequate* basic retirement pension can overcome this problem and the Trade Union movement and all pensioners organizations are united on this demand (see the Declaration of the Pensioners' Convention at the end of this section).

Some pensioners receive occupational pensions from their previous employment in addition to the basic pension but these vary greatly in amount.

From April 5th 1979 a new earnings-related system of additional pensions came into force. This provides for two pensions which all should receive, i.e. a basic flat rate pension and a new earnings related additional pension. The additional pension will be paid along with the basic pension except where the employers 'contract out' of that part of the scheme. Employers who 'contract out' must establish that their scheme is as good or better than the state additional pension.

This new scheme, however, will be introduced over a period of 20 years, so that a full value additional pension will not be paid before 6th April 1998.

Campaigns to improve the condition of the retired population have been conducted for some years by retired workers' organizations supported by the TUC and individual trade unions. A £10 Christmas bonus for pensioners was negotiated in 1973 with the Government by the TUC, and continues; later a major breakthrough came with advances of up to 40 per cent in pension rates in 1974. In 1975 it was decided by Parliament that the pension should be increased annually in line with the movement of earnings or prices, whichever is the greater. In 1980 the link with earnings was abandoned. A number of Local Authorities have agreed to concessions on bus transport for retired people, and in the case of the GLC (Greater London Authority) free transport is provided to retired people both on buses and the underground. Organizations identified with retired people, in conjunction with the TUC, now hold periodical National Conventions which have adopted the following Declaration on which campaigning is currently in progress.

## Declaration of Intent

This Convention declares that every pensioner has the right to choice, dignity, independence and security as an integral and valued member of society.

These rights require an adequate State retirement pension. There must be an immediate commitment to a pension level of not less than one half of average gross earnings for a married couple and not less than one third of average gross earnings for a single person, uprated at six monthly intervals.

**In addition to an adequate income, a pensioner should, as of right:**

—live in accommodation which is appropriate to personal need and circumstance with a reasonable degree of choice including sheltered housing;

—be able to call on the full range of community and personal social services to give full support as need arises, including, for example, home helps, meals on wheels, chiropody, television and telephone;

—be able to use a National Scheme of substantial concessionary facilities on all public transport in all parts of the country;

—have ready access to comprehensive free health care on demand;

—be able to maintain a warm and well lit home with adequate heating allowances covering all fuels;

—have full access to a varied and extensive range of education and leisure facilities;

—be paid a regular tax-free Christmas bonus of £20, adjusted in future in line with inflation;

—be eligible for an adequate retirement pension on ceasing work at any time of his or her choice after the age of 60 years, without being subject to an earnings rule;

—be entitled to an adequate death grant irrespective of age.

**Unanimously adopted by**
**The National Pensioners' Conventions**
**London, June 1979 & November 1980**

(*See* Social Security.)

**RETROSPECTIVE PAY**    *See* Back Pay.


# S


**SABBATICAL LEAVE**    Strictly speaking this means a year off work on full pay after every seven years of work and was intended to give time off for research for academics to pursue their studies. It is now more loosely used to describe time off for study, research, travel or further training for academics or teachers which may be granted after a reasonable period of service. Sabbatical leave may also be given to other groups and may be included in terms of service. Its incidence outside the academic world of universities and polytechnics is very sparse and patchy although the practice does exist in industry for non-manual workers as well as some in top management.

**SAFETY REPRESENTATIVES, TRADE UNION**   *See* Health and Safety

**SALARY**   Another name for wages, normally used in respect of people who are in professional occupations, e.g. teachers, or in management. It can sometimes apply for 'white collar' workers in an establishment as distinct from manual workers, or when wages are paid monthly instead of weekly, or when they are paid into a bank instead of being given in a pay packet.

Some occupations are referred to as 'salaried' and this may be associated too with better conditions of service than are available to weekly-wage paid manual workers e.g. in respect of holidays, hours of work etc.

**SCAB**   *See* Blackleg.

**SCOTTISH TEACHERS SALARIES COMMITTEE**   Under the Education (Scotland) Act negotiations on salaries and conditions of service for school teachers employed by the twelve Scottish Education Authorities take place within the Committee for Teaching Staff employed in Providing School Education. The teachers' side has eighteen members, thirteen of whom are appointed by the Educational Institute of Scotland (EIS), three by the Scottish Secondary Teachers Association, one by the NAS/UWT, and one by the Professional Association of Teachers. On the management side there are seventeen members, fifteen from the local education authorities and two nominees of the Secretary of State for Scotland who, however, as in the case of Burnham, have the major say on the panel, as the Government provides two thirds of the finance. For teachers employed in Further Education there is a separate committee for pay and conditions of service. There are twenty one members on the teaching side in which representatives of the EIS number eight, the Scottish

# Secondary Action

Further Education Association four, the Association of Lecturers in Colleges of Education three, the Association of Lecturers in Scottish Central Institutions two, and ASTMS two. On the management there are also twenty one members, twelve from the Local Authorities, four each from Governing Bodies of Central Institutions and Colleges of Education and two from the Secretary of State.

On each committee, if agreement is reached, the appropriate employers must give effect to it. Provision exists for arbitration, e.g. by ACAS, after consultation with both sides, if negotiations break down; and the result must be accepted by the Secretary of State unless set aside by a negative resolution of either House of Parliament. The Secretary of State can then, after consultation with the appropriate negotiating Committee, make an order promulgating new salary scales. The Educational Institute of Scotland, by far the largest teachers' organization in Scotland, has expressed strong dissatisfaction both with their own proportionate under-representation on the committees and with the inclusion of conditions of service with salaries in a single negotiating body, because of their fear of the imposition by the management of unacceptable conditions to a pay award. (*See* Burnham Committee.)

**SECONDARY ACTION**    This generally means industrial action by employees of an employer who is not party to a trade dispute. It is usually taken either to make more effective an existing strike or simply to express support for employees who are in dispute with their employer. It can be undertaken spontaneously by employees on their own initiative, as sympathetic action, or on instructions from the union. The issue in dispute might be held to involve a principle of general application to employees beyond the immediate parties in dispute and, therefore, to be fought and defended by such employees; or it may be held that the dispute will have repercussions affecting other workers who ought therefore to support it.

Forms of secondary action can vary from outright strike to blacking (boycott) of goods or services of the employer concerned. It can also involve secondary picketing. Unions normally adopt it to put additional pressure on the employer in dispute by interrupting his sources of supply or his sales. The Employment Act, 1980, limits the immunity enjoyed by organizers of secondary action with the aim of reducing its incidence and effectiveness. (*See* Employment Bill 1982, Immunity, Picketing, Sympathetic Action.)

# Secret Ballots

**SECRET BALLOTS (IN UNIONS)**  Voting on any issue or for a candidate in an election can be by either show of hands or ballot. Ballot voting means the expression of the voter's preference in a manner decided by those holding the ballot (e.g. by an X) on a piece of paper. The votes recorded on the papers are then counted and the result declared. If the ballot is held at a meeting the votes are normally handed in to a 'teller', folded, so that the voter's preference is secret. Numbered papers may be sent to members of the organization by post and may be returned by post to a designated address; or the voting papers may be handed out at the place of work and returned to a ballot box, e.g. pithead or factory ballot. Sometimes the voting paper in these circumstances has to be signed (the aim is to prevent fraud) and arrangements may then be made by those counting the papers to ensure the secrecy of the individual vote; there have been criticisms of this method, as potentially allowing breach of secrecy.

The issue of secret ballots has attracted attention recently because of the provisions of the Employment Act, 1980, which allow the Secretary of State for Employment to give unions money for conducting secret postal ballots for various purposes. These include:

- calling or ending of a strike or other industrial action;
- carrying out an election, provided for by the rules of the union, to the principal committee having the executive responsibility for managing its affairs;
- carrying out an election, provided for by the union rules, to any post which the elected person will hold as an officer or as an employee of the union;
- amending the rules of the union;
- obtaining a decision on proposed amalgamations.

Various conditions are laid down on the conduct of the ballot, e.g. regarding secrecy, the right of all eligible to vote without constraint, counting the votes etc., in order to qualify for payment. The scheme will be administered by the Certification Officer. So far no union has made use of the money offered.

The Act makes it obligatory for an employer of more than twenty workers to provide facilities if requested by the union for holding the ballot, ensuring that it is secret and ensuring that all entitled to are enabled to vote. The employer's obligation is limited to providing the facilities; it is the union's responsibility to conduct the ballot.

# Service Increments

Under the Employment Act, 1980, provisions are laid down regarding the use of secret ballots in certain circumstances on the issue of the Closed Shop. Secret ballots are also necessary in the case of union amalgamations. (*See* Amalgamations, Closed Shop.)

**SERVICE INCREMENTS**   *See* Increments, Incremental Scales.

**SEX DISCRIMINATION ACT, 1976**   Sex discrimination applies in employment and in other areas far beyond the question of pay. This Act is intended to deal with such areas. Thus in employment the Act outlaws discrimination against applicants for jobs and against existing employees in respect of issues other than pay. These include conditions of employment, promotion prospects and systems, training opportunities, and the operation of redundancy schemes. It also covers indirect forms of discrimination e.g. by the arrangement of hours in an unnecessarily discriminating way to the disadvantage of others of young children. There are a number of exceptions dictated by common sense (e.g. prisons and certain hospitals). Positive discrimination in training is allowed in favour of women (or men) who in the previous year had very little share in any facilities provided by the employer. Bodies concerned with training e.g. ITBs are forbidden to practice discrimination.

It is also illegal for a trade union or professional association or employers' organization to discriminate against women e.g. by refusing entry or through differential contributions or benefits, with the exception of those concerning death or retirement. On the other hand positive discrimination to ensure that they are adequately represented in running the union is permitted.

In education the Act covers a very wide field, although single sex schools, for example, and single sex sports and physical training are exempt. Otherwise discrimination is forbidden in respect of admissions and of access to the benefits, facilities and services of schools, colleges, universities or polytechnics. This means for example that there should be equality of access to all parts of the curriculum and no discrimination in grants by LEAs and the provision of facilities for social and physical recreation. The operation of the curricular provisions because of custom, tradition, lack of facilities and resources for extending the teaching of various practical subjects etc. will take longer, it seems, than was envisaged when the Act was passed.

The Act also prohibits discrimination in the sale or letting of houses, accommodation in hotels, in banking, insurance and finance and credit facilities, in places of entertainment or refreshment, facilities for transport and travel and in the services of any trade, profession or local or public authority. It also applies to advertisements for jobs. It is very complex and exceptions are allowed in various circumstances requiring careful interpretation. Those wishing to take action under it should therefore consult their union, which should be familiar with the various provisions for enforcement of the law.

Among the most important sections of the Act has been the creation of the Equal Opportunities Commission. This has the duty of working towards the elimination of discrimination, the promotion of equality of opportunity between men and women generally and keeping under review the working of the Act and the Equal Pay Act, as well as dealing with problems of Health and Safety at work.

The Commission reports to Parliament, on its activities and on developments in the progress of equality, and can make recommendations for any necessary changes to promote equality. It may conduct investigations into areas of discrimination, report cases to an industrial tribunal, apply for legal injunctions, provide assistance to individuals or groups with a view to legal proceedings, compel the production of relevant information etc. The field covered is very wide and complex and here again advice should be sought from the union if the assistance of the Commission is desired.

The Sex Discrimination Act has various consequences affecting maternity, redundancy, part-time working, etc.

Both the TUC and the EOC have criticised the Sex Discrimination Act and its unsatisfactory operation. The EOC has asked the government to make a large number of amendments to strengthen its provisions. These include the proposal that part-time workers (about 40 per cent of the female workforce) should be entitled to equal pay on a pro rata basis; that clubs should not discriminate in treatment of women, etc. Its fifth annual report (1980) comments on government discrimination in social security benefits: the housewife's non contributory pension and the invalid care allowance.

Its fifth Research Bulletin (July, 1981) claims that women are still concentrated in low paid, unskilled jobs 'because employers frequently do not operate in the spirit of the law while narrowly keeping to its letter'. Very many firms do not operate an equal opportunities policy and have made no changes in their policies as a result

# Severance Pay

of the Act. The Low Pay Unit confirms some of this critique in pointing out that while there has been a big drop in the number of low-paid full-time women workers in the past decade, of almost 4 million adults classified as low paid sixty five percent are women.

The EOC has prepared a draft Code of Practice for approval by Parliament dealing with consultation with unions, recruitment, training and promotion etc. of workers to ensure that sex discrimination does not occur. And the TUC, among other demands, has made proposals for improved health and safety provisions for women at work. (*See* Equal Pay.)

**SEVERANCE PAY**  These are payments negotiated between a trade union and an employer *or* offered by the employer, inclusive of, or apart from, payments provided for under the Redundancy Payments Act. For example in late 1981 the port employers were offering payments up to £16,000 to dock-workers to accept voluntary severance from the industry. In a number of industries where companies have sought to close undertakings or departments substantial severance payment schemes have been proposed in order to avoid resistance to the closures by the employees. (*See also* Golden handshake.)

**SHIFTWORK**  Most full-time workers work about eight hours a day during the day. Many industrial establishments and some institutions, e.g. hospitals and continuous process industries, however, remain open for work for substantially longer periods round the clock. In such cases workers are employed in 'shifts' of fixed numbers of hours, a first, second or maybe third shift following one after the other in relays. There are a variety of shiftwork patterns. Thus e.g. there may be a day, evening and night shift operating in a factory or hospital. The term may be applied both to the period worked and to the workers employed during the period i.e. 'night shift' may refer both to the time of working and to the group of workers working at that time.

Contracts of employment may require workers to be available for different shifts according to a pattern of work organization agreed between employers and unions. There may be fixed or rotating shifts. Workers may work fixed shifts, (or 'duties') or 'rotated' shifts. In certain industries split shifts or 'duties' are operated where the normal daily hours are worked in two or three stints with unpaid breaks in between e.g. in passenger transport and catering.

Differential payments, under agreements, will normally operate for different shifts, because of the 'unsocial hours' involved.

Nightwork and week-end work are unavoidable in continuous process industries (and institutions) and are often customary in others such as transport, security services etc. With the increasing cost of building and capital equipment, management often seeks to extend shiftwork where it has not been customary in order to obtain the full value for their investment (through reduced overheads and increased production).

The most intensive shiftwork industries include transport, post and telecommunications, the Health Service, electricity supply, coal mining, metal manufacture, chemicals, glass, rubber, textiles, food and drink, and vehicles.

There is concern about the adverse social and health effects of shiftwork outside normal hours on workers. It involves the disruption of the normal routine of family and social life. Trade unions seek to secure compensation for the disadvantages of unsocial hours in increased differential payments and improved conditions e.g. adequate meal breaks and canteen facilities, assistance with transport outside normal hours etc.

Although there is considerable argument about the effects of shifts outside normal hours on health, on balance there is sufficient evidence to show ill effects, for example in stress, accidents, sickness absence, poor digestion and fatigue. Trade unions seek to counter these effects by demanding a range of preventive and compensatory measures.

Another subject of controversy is the participation of women in shiftwork. Exclusion means exclusion also from higher rates of pay and the Equal Opportunities Commission has demanded the repeal of nearly all the legislation which protects women from excessive and unsocial hours. The TUC has, however, opposed this on the grounds that as things stand it could mean levelling down conditions of work instead of levelling up and women might be forced to choose between working unsocial hours against their wishes or being sacked.

Department of Employment figures (1980) for jobs in which shiftwork is most common showed that 15 per cent of all male employees and 9.9 per cent of women received a shiftwork element in their pay.

**SHOP STEWARDS** Most trade unions have officers or represen-

# Shop Stewards

tatives at the place of work. The most common title used for the post is 'shop steward' but various other titles are used related to similar duties e.g. father of the chapel, office representative, delegate, corresponding member, or Whitley representative. There are no precise figures of the number of such representatives in British Industry but it has been estimated that they are in the region of 300,000 to 400,000.

Shop stewards (or their equivalent) are normally elected by their fellow-workers, for a defined area or group, and are usually subject to re-election every twelve months. They are now regarded as the essential arm of the trade union at the place of work and constitute the main training ground for leadership within the trade union movement as well as performing an increasing negotiating role. For many workers they are seen as the effective and visual sign of their union.

The work for which stewards/representatives are elected and recognized by unions involves four main functions: organizing, negotiating, representing members grievances to management and the provision of information. The precise list of duties varies from union to union but normally includes supervising agreements, dealing with members' problems, negotiating piece rates, arrangement of working hours, negotiating on job evaluation, work measurement and similar schemes, union recruitment and reporting to the Union.

There is no doubt that shop stewards/representatives are the instruments for settling thousands of problems at the workplace and most of them work loyally and quickly for their members and the Union they represent. Often they operate under some difficulties and make personal sacrifices, their satisfaction being the service they provide for their members.

Most industrial undertakings now provide facilities for shop steward/representatives to perform their duties e.g. telephone and office facilities for senior shop stewards, meeting facilities for shop stewards' committees and for reporting to members.

A considerable amount of training is now available for shop stewards, provided directly by trade unions concerned or by the TUC. In some cases Colleges of Further Education and other educational institutions provide courses in consultation with trade unions. 'Time off' for trade union duties related to his/her work and for participation in shop steward training and educational courses is now generally recognized as essential for the maintenance of good industrial relations. Provision is made for this under the law, which entitles the steward to payment, and by collective agreement.

Apart from educational activities, some trade unions have periodical shop stewards conferences or quarterly meetings normally held in a locality. Within undertakings, shop stewards usually meet as a joint committee either of one union and/or of the different unions represented.

The desirability of this type of joint activity is obvious, particularly to share experience, and to develop closer relationships and common policies.

Within large-scale undertakings joint committees of representatives/shop stewards have been set up in recent times and are generally known as 'combine committees'. In one or two cases, within multi-national companies, international links have been attempted. These wider approaches have been criticised by sections of trade union leaderships because of possible interference with the policy-making bodies within the trade unions. On the other hand there is some sympathy with the need for co-ordination and speedy communication between groups of trade unionists working within large organizations. This is one of the current problems of the trade union movement and as it is resolved it will mark a further step along the road of shop steward recognition. From the 'unofficial' shop stewards of the First World War period there has been a remarkable transformation in the evolution of this unique British labour institution.

It is now widely accepted that shop stewards will be the key to any progress made towards Industrial Democracy. This was implied in the Labour Party Report on Industrial Democracy in 1967 and in the Bullock Report. (*See* Bullock Report, Industrial Democracy.)

**SHORTER HOURS**    The demand for a shorter working week and a shorter working day has been central in trade union aims since the 1880s. At the present time the case for shorter working hours is stronger and more relevant than ever, with the Western world faced with a massive rise in unemployment. The general view of the trade unions in Europe is that a major reduction in working hours (combined with earlier retirement) is necessary to secure a return to full employment. Currently a number of collective agreements in the UK and Europe have been arrived at, giving a 38 or 39 hour week for manual workers. The general aim is for a 35 hour week and ultimately a reduction for both manual workers and 'white collar' workers to 32 hours, without loss of pay.

The view that the effects of reducing working hours will mean increased labour costs per unit of output and an increase in overtime worked, is strongly contested by the trade unions. They claim that on previous occasions employers and industries concerned met the effect of reduced hours by a mixture of recruiting more labour and increasing both efficiency and productivity.

In the UK 'normal' hours fell in 1959–61 and 1964–6 and this led to a pronounced fall in 'actual' hours worked. It would also appear that wage costs per unit of output rose less rapidly in those periods than in the equivalent years of comparable trade cycles in which hours did not decrease to such a marked extent. Experiences in Austria, Belgium, Denmark, Luxembourg, Norway and Sweden indicate a similar pattern.

The facts show that in 1980 the UK was at the bottom of the league in the EEC for average hours worked by manual workers, with a figure of 43.2. This includes overtime which is associated with low rates of pay. It has been estimated that by August 1982 $8\frac{1}{2}$ million workers will have won a basic working week of less than 40 hours though very many of these are non-manual workers. Throughout industry local and national agreements have been made for basic working weeks of 39, 38, $37\frac{1}{2}$, 36 and 35 hours. (*See* Overtime.)

**SHORT TIME**   Instead of being made redundant, workers may be employed on 'short time' i.e. for part of the week, temporarily, pending a return to fulltime or the operation of redundancy. Sometimes unions try to negotiate this with employers. The Government has operated a number of schemes which encourage employers to organize short-time instead of creating redundancies. (*See* Temporary Employment Measures.)

**SICK PAY**   Payment by the employer of wages or salary (or part payment) to an employee during periods of sickness. This is normally detailed in the collective agreement or contract of employment. This payment is in addition to any Sickness Benefit which may be received under the national insurance scheme. (*See* Social Security, Sickness Benefit, Invalidity Allowances.)

**SICKNESS BENEFIT**   *See* Social Security.

**SIGNING ON**   When an employee is made redundant he normally 'signs on' in the appropriate office of the Department of Employment to become eligible for Unemployment Benefit and at the same time receive information as to suitable vacancies available. (*See* Registered Unemployed.*)*

**SIT-INS (FACTORY OCCUPATIONS)**   The use of the 'sit-in' or 'sit-down' by workers, as a form of industrial action, is not new. It was applied in some instances in the period following the First World War and used as a tactic in trade union struggles in the USA and France as well as occasionally in Britain (for example in the South Wales coalfield), in the inter-war years.

As an action to secure the 'right to work' the 'sit-in' in the Clyde shipyards during 1971–2 was outstanding. The collapse of the Upper Clyde Shipbuilding Consortium threatened the jobs of thousands and the workers responded by occupying their shipyards and appealing to the public and the whole trade union and labour movement to support them. Widespread publicity and financial support followed and the 'sit-in' continued for months until finally the Government of the day announced the decision to grant substantial financial aid to three of the four shipyards which had been reprieved from closing down and to assist Marathon (an American Corporation) to rehabilitate the fourth yard for the construction of oil-drilling rigs.

Similar action was taken at the Triumph motor-cycle works at Meriden which led to the formation of a co-operative there and a measure of (Labour) Government support.

'Sit-ins' over arbitrary dismissals, factory closures and in some cases over wage claims, have become somewhat commonplace in the last decade but are acts of desperation coming out of the workplace itself. Only where the employees themselves feel very strongly about the issue is such action effective. Trade unions are rarely officially involved in such actions because of the legal problems that may be involved.

**SLUMP**   *See* Depression.

**SOCIAL CONTRACT**   The 'Social Contract' was a range of policies formulated between the Labour Party and the TUC in 1972 and 1973 through the medium of the Liason Committee representing both organizations. This committed the Labour Party, when it became a Government, to a wide programme of measures, in indus-

# Social Contract

trial relations (including the repeal of the 1971 Industrial Relations Act)and substantial social and economic improvements, in return for co-operation from the TUC in tackling the country's economic problems. Much of the thinking involved was contained in a statement issued by the TUC–Labour Party Liaison Committee in February 1973 entitled 'Economic policy and the cost of living'.

The economy was in the throes of a severe crisis marked by high domestic inflation, growing unemployment, and industrial obsolescence, against a background of world recession and high costs of oil and other imported raw materials. There was considerable anxiety in the ranks of the working population due to the closure of industrial units, redundancies and lack of prospects for the future. There had been a serious deterioration in industrial relations, an increasing number of strikes and a loss of confidence in the methods of conciliation and arbitration. The TUC–Labour Party Liaison Committee statement claimed that the policies produced by the reigning Conservative Government had induced and encouraged the dire situation and had 'chosen to re-distribute income and wealth, on a massive scale, to the most privileged sections of the community'. The statement put forward an alternative programme of which the main elements were:

- A wide-ranging and permanent system of price controls to cover the main items in the family budget and affect the various levels of activity from manufacturing to retailing.
- A new approach to housing costs and rents.
- A substantial increase in house building and public ownership of all the land required.
- A policy of planned growth to reduce unemployment, provide for training and re-training, and including agreed policies on investment (e.g. investment funds for industry linked to greater accountability).
- A large-scale redistribution of income and wealth, including taxes on wealth and capital transfers.
- Major increases in retirement pensions with yearly upratings related to earnings or prices whichever is the greater. There were also other measures to improve the social wage.
- Development of new public enterprise and public supervision of investment policy.

# Social Contract

- A programme for regional development.
- Measures designed to achieve the extension of industrial democracy and economic democracy.
- The repeal of the Industrial Relations Act and introduction of measures to improve industrial relations.

These and other measures were fashioned into the detail of the Labour Party's manifestoes on which it fought the two General Elections of 1974. In the first two years of the Labour Government substantial elements of the Social Contract were implemented. The Industrial Relations Act was repealed. ACAS was set up. The Employment Protection Act (a workers' charter) was introduced. Improvements in pensions and other assistance were given to the retired and the disabled and later child benefits were brought in. It raised taxes for persons with high incomes and closed evasion loopholes. Control of food prices and rents was established with subsidies being provided in both areas. A Price Commission was established and other measures adopted to keep prices down, although this proved to be a weak aspect of the Governments operations. Steps were taken to nationalize the shipbuilding and aircraft industries and the National Enterprise Board was established. The Community Land Act was enacted to take development land into public ownership. Extensive measures were taken to deal with the energy problem and the British National Oil Corporation was established. Progress was made on Health and Safety at Work and Equal Pay legislation together with the expansion of industrial training. In 1974–75 the social wage increased by over 30 per cent and there was a 32 per cent increase in expenditure on housing. The foregoing does not tell the whole of the story but is sufficient to indicate the progress made in implementing the social and economic measures envisaged by the 'social contract'.

As part of the overall approach the TUC had promised to cooperate with the Government in combating inflation while insisting on the abolition of the legal restraints on collective bargaining which had been applied by the previous Government. Initially, in 1974, a voluntary policy was agreed encouraging unions to restrict wage claims to twelve-month intervals and to restrain the size of claims to '. . . compensate for the rise in the cost of living since the last settlement' or to the anticipated rise for the following year. This,

# Social Contract

however, did not halt the inflationary fever and in May 1975 average earnings had shot up 29 per cent higher than they were a year previously. Price inflation was worse, 33 per cent higher.

With a rapidly deteriorating economic situation the general position was alarming and the TUC acted to prevent the severe dangers involved in hyperinflation. It proposed a flat rate increase of £6 per week to operate for twelve months. The Government agreed to this, and to exempt workers whose wage increase required more than £6 to reach a suggested minimum of £30 a week and women claiming equal pay. In addition people with salaries in excess of £8,500 were not to receive an increase (the TUC had suggested a limit of £7,000). The policy was approved in a full vote of the TUC Congress delegates in 1975 and was loyally supported by the trade union membership throughout the country.

The effect of the £6 policy was spectacular. The rate of inflation was brought down to 12 per cent and there were fewer strikes combined with a general improvement in industrial relations. But the external economic situation worsened with a fall in the value of the pound which led to pressure for a further period of pay policy. This was finally agreed at 5 per cent combined with a package of tax reliefs. The inflation rate fell to 8 per cent but the policy came increasingly under strain. The TUC decided on an ordered return to free collective bargaining but accepted the need for 12-month intervals between increases. For the following year the TUC acquiesced to 10 per cent increases but the inflation rate started to move back to double figures and then up to 15 per cent. Despite this the Government itself called for another year of restraint – limited to 5 per cent – and imposed sanctions on firms which paid more. The consensus between the Government and the TUC visibly crumbled, the TUC did not approve the 5 per cent policy and was highly critical. A 'free for all' situation developed leading to the notorious winter of discontent in 1979.

The early period of the 'Social Contract' had succeeded in uniting the Labour Party and the Trade Unions and in widening the horizons of trade unionists by influencing social and economic policies of the Government. The Government, in the end, however, demanded too much and failed to deliver on certain aspects of its undertakings to the TUC. Restrictions on imports were not introduced and the directives of the EEC prevented an effective control over food and other essential prices. Progress on the industrial democracy front was also minimal.

**SOCIAL SECURITY, BENEFITS AND PAYMENTS** The Trade Union movement is closely concerned with social security benefits and payments which are a central feature of welfare provision in Britain. This provision is governed by legislation and its object is to help people in need when their normal source of income has been interrupted or ended (e.g. by sickness, unemployment, retirement); to assist families with children (e.g. child benefits); to help certain other potentially disadvantaged groups (e.g. widows, pregnant women, the handicapped, people suffering from industrial injuries); to supplement the incomes of very low paid workers and pensioners. Beyond direct aid in these cases the social security system extends into fields such as free school meals, rent and rate rebates, prescription charges, welfare assistance of various kinds, to families and old people, etc. – all issues of Trade Union concern. Many people who are entitled to benefits do not receive them because they fail to apply for them through not knowing the regulations or for other reasons, e.g. mistaken fear of being thought to be 'scrounging'. A reasonable estimate suggests a loss of £500 million a year in benefit entitlement and up to 80 per cent take-up only, except in the case of child benefits. For example, the Disability Alliance in August 1981, claimed that one-third of the most severely handicapped might be losing up to £21 a week by not drawing the Attendance Allowance (see below).

As social security benefits and payments cost a great deal of money their level and extent have always been the subject of acute political controversy. Under the Thatcher government, whether by legislation or regulation, the fabric of the system has been eroded, especially by reducing the value of important elements. It is the view of the Trade Union and Labour Movements that changes recently made are seriously undermining the welfare state. The official estimate is of a 'saving' of some £1500 millions in 1982–3, stemming from decisions taken since 1979.

*National Insurance:* Crucial for the social security system is the National Insurance Scheme, funded by insured persons (mainly employees), employers and a small element of government contribution. The contributions paid by insured persons, who are divided into four classes, give them rights to various benefits, provided that contributions are adequate.

Contributions are paid by employees including apprentices, (Class I); by self-employed persons – that is, those who are in business on their own account and those working for gain but who are not under a contract of service (Class II and Class IV). In addition, certain groups who are not employed may make voluntary reduced contributions and receive a limited range of benefits (Class III). In Classes I, II and IV, contributions are compulsory for everyone, with certain specified exceptions, between the ages of 16 and the age when pensions are received.

Employed married women may pay either the full contribution or a reduced contribution, except that, if married after April 5th 1977, the full contribution must be paid and this is also the case when a married woman who has been paying the reduced contribution returns to work after an absence of two complete, consecutive tax years.

In 1982 contributions were not paid by employees earning less than £29.50 per week, students, and retired people.

Employers' contributions are paid in respect of their employees, while the government makes its payment to the fund out of general taxation. Though the National Health Service is separately financed, it draws on a small part of the National Insurance Fund.

There are four types of contribution: Employees (Class I) pay in 1982 an earnings-related contribution of 8.75 per cent on all earnings from £29.50 a week to an upper limit of £220 a week. Those earning over £220 a week pay the same as those earning £220 a week. The tax is therefore regressive. The self-employed (Class II) pay a flat-rate contribution, although self-employed earners earning more than a certain minimum amount (Class IV) pay at a higher rate. Class III, i.e. non-employed persons and some others, make a voluntary contribution. Employees pay by deduction at source through the PAYE system.

*Benefits:* Class I contributions entitle the contributor to the following benefits:

| | |
|---|---|
| Unemployment benefit | Maternity Allowance |
| Sickness benefit | Maternity Grant |
| Invalidity benefits | Widow's allowance |
| (Invalidity pensions, | Widowed Mother's allowance |

| Invalidity allowances) | Widow's pension |
|---|---|
| Guardian's Allowance | Child's special allowance |
| Retirement pension | Industrial injury and |
| Death Grant | disablement benefits* |

*Industrial Injuries are financed separately entirely by employees and employers and are available for married women paying on reduced rates. (*See* Industrial Injuries.)

Class II contributors receive all these benefits with the exception of unemployment benefits and disablement and industrial injury benefits.

Class III contributors do not receive unemployment, sickness and invalidity benefits, nor the maternity allowance, nor industrial injuries and disablement benefits.

Class IV contributors receive the same benefits as Class II.

To qualify, contributions must have been paid in any one tax year amounting to twenty-five times the Lower Earnings Limit (LEL) which is fixed annually by the Department of Health and Social Security (in April 1982 this was £29.50). For full benefit entitlement, however, (apart from retirement pension) contributions are necessary amounting to fifty times the Lower Earnings Limit in the previous tax year; contributions can, however, be 'credited' for each full week of sickness or unemployment for which the contributor is entitled to maternity allowance. There are exceptions to these conditions to assist young people and women who become widowed or divorced.

Most benefits, apart from retirement pensions, are tax free but, from July 1982, unemployment benefit will be taxed and certain other benefits will be taxed later. The amounts of all benefits are changed annually. The change up till recently has been linked with the Retail Price Index. This may no longer be the case; the Secretary of State has powers (till 1984) to raise benefits by 5 per cent less than the expected rise in prices and in November 1980, short-term benefits (e.g. Unemployment and Sickness Benefit) suffered this 5 per cent cut which has not been restored. Retirement pensions are now increased in line with the rise in prices, whereas, previously, they were related to the rise in earnings if that figure was higher than the rise in prices; in November 1981, the increase was 1 per cent less than the previously estimated rise in prices to 'compensate' for a 1 per cent 'overpayment' the previous year – a reduction which has

# Social Security

clearly caused hardship. In fact, social security benefits went up in November 1981 by 3 per cent less than the rate of inflation, and although there was a promise to make good the shortfall in November 1982 the increase, which allowed 9 per cent for inflation, is 11 per cent not 12 per cent. At the same time dependents' allowances for children are cut by 50p for all on short-term benefits although increased by 25p for those on long-term benefits. These changes will continue and indeed increase severe hardship in many cases.

Some of the main features of the various benefits are described below. Dependants' Allowances are applicable where relevant.

*Unemployment* and *Sickness Benefits* are made up of a flat-rate payment plus allowances for wife or other adult dependant and dependent children. A married woman paying reduced contributions is not entitled to these two benefits. An unemployed wife who has paid full contributions cannot usually claim for a dependent husband.

*Unemployment Benefit* is not paid for the first three 'waiting' days and is payable for two days or more out of six days a week up to a maximum of 312 days. At leas thirteen weeks have to be worked after that before benefit can be claimed again, which means that many unemployed must have recourse to the means-tested Supplementary Benefits Scheme (see below). The fact is that the real value of unemployment benefit for a single person in November 1981 was worth 17.5 per cent of average earnings of male manual workers – the lowest proportion since 1951.

Workers on strike or locked out are not entitled to unemployment benefit. Benefit can also be refused for up to six weeks if the worker was dismissed for misconduct, or left his job voluntarily without good reason, or places 'unreasonable restrictions' on the kind of job he will accept. It can also be withdrawn if the worker fails to accept suitable employment. In such circumstances, union advice should be sought; there is a right of appeal against disqualification from or withdrawl of benefit.

Unemployment benefit is not payable if the worker is receiving Guarantee Payments but is payable while redundancy pay is drawn. Benefit can be paid to part-time workers or, under certain circumstances, to those on short-time for the days not worked. Pensioners over 60 who are receiving an occupational pension now have their unemployment benefit cut by £1 a week for each pound of occupational pension over £35 a week.

*Sickness Benefit* is not paid for the first three days of sickness but is payable for spells of sickness lasting four days or more; from June 1982 doctors will not be required to provide sick notes for social security purposes for illnesses which last less than seven days. The Social Security Bill (1982) proposes to transfer the statutory obligations for the first 8 weeks' payments from the government to the employer. The employer, however, will not have to pay benefit if he is affected by strike action or if the employee is entitled to maternity allowance. Employers' payments will be flat rates of £37 a week to employees earning over £60; £31 to those earning £45 to £60 and £25 to those earning less than £45 a week. This has been bitterly criticised as being unfair to the lower paid, who would receive more under the national insurance payments which provide for dependants. The TUC has attacked the £37 payment too, on the same grounds.

After 28 weeks an *Invalidity Pension* replaces sickness benefit. This was previously paid at the same rate as the retirement pension, but is now subject to the 5 per cent reduction below the rise in prices as in other benefits (see above), as well as losing the earnings link as with retirement pensions (see above). This means a double loss for these disadvantaged people.

An *Invalidity Allowance* is added for the chronically sick who are well below pensionable age.

Any sick pay received from an employer's scheme is additional to Sickness Benefit. It is estimated that some 50 per cent of all full-time employees qualify for sick pay from both employers and the state. Some 80 per cent have some cover for sickness from employers. Sick notes from a doctor (on payment) may still be required for employers' schemes.

*Additional Invalidity Benefits:* Severely disabled adults or children (the disablement can be physical or mental) are entitled to a tax-free *Attendance Allowance* intended to help pay for attention to the invalid during the day or night. There is no means test. Payment is decided by an Attendance Allowance Board which arranges for medical examination – usually by the invalid's own doctor. (*See also* Industrial Injuries.)

# Social Security

There is also a *Mobility Allowance*, payable to the physically disabled unable or those virtually unable to walk, who are likely to remain so for at least a year and are not permanently housebound. From November 1982 this is not subject to tax.

A non-contributory *Invalidity Pension* is payable to workers over 16 who have not been able to work for 28 weeks but who do not qualify for sickness or invalidity benefit because they have not paid enough contributions. The claimant must be under 65 (60 for women) to start getting the pension. If the claimant is a disabled housewife she must be incapable of performing normal 'household duties', although, in fact, most disabled women have been out of work, so the household test is inappropriate and, of course, restricts eligibility. It has been condemned by the Equal Opportunities Commission (EOC) as discriminatory. Additions to the Invalidity Pension are payable to male claimants for a wife or other adult dependant or for dependent children. An *Invalid Care Allowance* is payable to people of working age (16 to 65 or 60) who have to stay at home to look after a severely disabled relative. There are additions for dependants, but a married woman living with her husband or cohabiting with a man as his wife is not eligible. This has been criticised by the EOC as 'obvious discrimination'.

*Maternity Benefits:* A married woman who has a baby or babies is entitled to a single payment of a small *Maternity Grant* for each child; from July 1982, the Grant has become non-contributory and available to every woman expecting a baby after 28 weeks of pregnancy.

In addition, a *Maternity Allowance* is payable, dependent on the woman's own, *not* on the husband's, contributions in the tax year preceding the year in which the baby is born, provided the contributions are on earnings amounting to at least fifty times the Lower Earnings Limit. If this condition is not met, the Allowance may be paid at a reduced rate. The normal payment is for eighteen weeks, starting at eleven weeks before the Sunday of the week in which the baby is expected. It is not payable until the woman has ceased work. Maternity Allowance is only payable if the woman is not already getting an equal or higher rate of sickness, unemployment, widow's or injury benefit. It is advisable to claim Grant and Allowance immediately after the beginning of the fourteenth week before the baby is expected. (*See also* Maternity Pay.)

*Widow's Benefits*: A *Widow's Allowance* is paid for the first 26 weeks after the husband's death. After the allowance ceases, a widow with children receives a *Widowed Mother's Allowance* (WMA). If she does not qualify for this she receives a Widow's Pension (WP), if she was over 40 when her husband died. Similarly, when a woman over 40 in receipt of a WMA ceases to be eligible (because, e.g., her children are over 18, or younger if not in full-time education), she receives the pension. Widow's pensions cease on remarriage or if the woman cohabits with a man as his wife.

*Retirement Pensions*: Some 8½ million people in 1981 received retirement pensions. A man aged 65–69 and a woman aged 60–64 qualify for retirement pension if they have retired from regular employment; even if still in employment they qualify over 70 and 65 respectively. A married woman qualifies for a pension on her husband's contributions when her husband retires if she is then over 60 and has also retired. If she qualifies on both her own and her husband's contributions she receives whichever pension is greater.

A pension is composed of the following elements:

(a) A flat rate or basic pension depending on contributions. A reduced rate may be paid.
(b) A graduated addition based on graduated contributions above a certain minimum between 1961 and 1975.
(c) Extra pension earned by staying on at work after 65 (60 for women).
(d) Additional Earnings Related Pensions dependent on contributions since April 1978. This is also payable to the widow of a pensioner. If she is retired she can add this to her own Earnings Related Pension subject to an upper limit. A man whose wife dies when they are both over pension age will also inherit the additional pension based on his wife's earnings.

Employees in a 'contracted out' occupational scheme may be entitled to the occupational pension instead of the earnings related addition. There may be entitlement to (b) and (c) above even if the employee does not qualify for (a).

If a male pensioner under 70 or a female under 65 earns after retirement over £57.00 in any week from November 1982, the pension is reduced by 50 per cent of all earnings between this sum and £61.00 a week and by all earnings above that.

Those retiring before 65 or 60 (women) who have not paid enough

# Social Security

contributions may need to pay extra voluntary contributions to qualify for the pension. A *Death Grant* is payable to a widow or other relative. The maximum payment is £30 (1982) and has not been changed since 1967. It is now claimed to be so inadequate as not even to cover the VAT on funeral costs. In March 1982 the Government would only promise a consultative document on the issue.

*Child Benefit:*: This replaced the previous family allowance and child tax allowance, is tax free and is paid for all children under 16, or under 19 if still at school. It is not payable in respect of students at college over 19, or apprentices. The benefit is higher for the first child in a single-parent family. Child benefit has not been upgraded adequately in line with the Retail Price Index and it is worth much less than when first introduced. It does not now cover the cost of a child's food and clothes. From 1982, mothers, except single parents or those receiving Supplementary Benefit or Family Income Supplement, claiming benefit for the first time will be paid every four weeks instead of weekly, which is bound to cause hardship in many cases, although mothers already receiving Child Benefit are able to choose between weekly or four weekly payments, as are mothers *proving* hardship.

*Supplementary Benefit*: As it cannot be assumed that benefits are sufficient to keep an individual or a family above levels agreed by Parliament as satisfying minimum requirements, Supplementary Benefits at rates laid down may be paid in certain circumstances after a means test. Supplementary Benefits, paid in 1982 to nearly 4 million households – mainly pensioners, unemployed and single-parent families – are now administered by the Social Security Advisory Committee, a body with no statutory powers, unlike its predecessor, the Supplementary Benefits Commission, which had a considerable amount of independence. Benefits are paid as a right to people over 16 whose resources are insufficient to meet the minimum requirements including housing costs or rent and rate costs which it is proposed (1982) to combine in a new Housing Benefit. It is proposed in 1982 that large numbers getting Supplementary Benfit (SB) but whose SB is necessary only because they cannot pay their housing costs, will be paid a Housing Benefit by their Local Authority (see below). Benefit is confined to those who are not in full-time work (if paid to the employed it is taxable) with certain exceptions, including 'urgent' cases, workers in the first fifteen days after starting or restarting work, disabled people, self-employed people whose earning power is substantially lower than that of others in the same occupation. In fact, the majority of claimants are pensioners.

Supplementary Benefits take account of certain additional requirements. These include:

(a) Heating Allowances for pensioners on Supplementary Benefits who are householders over 70 or for householders with a child under 5 or to certain disabled people
(b) Special diet patients
(c) Blind people
(d) Lump sum payments for certain 'exceptional needs'.

To receive Supplementary Benefit, an applicant's requirements are calculated on levels laid down by Parliament and his resources are estimated by a Social Security Officer, the difference between the two being the sum that should be paid in Supplementary Benefit. The scales are fixed annually and take account of an applicant's dependants and whether the requirement is long or short-term. Estimation of resources depends on a large number of factors, e.g. the amount of savings, and is complicated; there are now many regulations strictly imposed which limit the discretion previously available to social security staff. These have affected, e.g., clothes and furniture grants. This is also the case with the 'exceptional needs' and 'urgent cases' payments, which take account of extreme hardship. Authoritative surveys show that very many families find the basic rates are inadequate to meet their needs, leaving them in dire poverty.

A provision added by the Thatcher Government reduces the Supplementary Benefit available for the family of an employee on strike by £13.00, a controversial feature of current social security legislation because it penalizes children. Such Supplementary Benefit is taxable. The striker's family is also penalized by restrictions on 'exceptional needs payments' (which is intended to take account of extreme hardship). A Church of England report has condemned these measures as wrong, saying that the effect is to put strikers below the moral category of convicted criminals. Unemployed school leavers are now unable to claim supplementary benefit until the end of the school holidays after they leave. This throws an additional burden on the school leaver's family especially if the child stays on to the summer school leaving date, the Spring Bank Holiday, when benefit would not be payable till 1st September. This can have serious educational consequences in encouraging children to leave, if eligible, at Easter, when the holiday period is much shorter, and so preclude them from sitting the summer examinations for qualifications. Young people studying in colleges for up to 21 hours a week can claim Supplementary Benefit. Lunch breaks and private study are not included within the 21-hour limit, although both teenagers and those over 21 must have been unemployed for 3 months before starting a course.

Until recently, too, there was an Earnings Related Supplement to certain benefits which allowed many workers to avoid recourse to the means tested supplementary benefit scheme. This has now been abolished despite a great deal of opposition especially since it was financed by contributions in anticipation of hardship.

Ordinary rates of Supplementary Benefit rise in November 1982 by 10½ per cent, i.e. one half percent less than the increase in other benefits. This reduction is due to the exclusion from the inflation calculation of housing prices which will be paid separately, (see above), and the very questionable assumption that housing costs will rise substantially more than other prices in 1982. In practice the effect will be that the real level of the Benefit is likely to fall.

*Family Income Supplement*: This is a payment aimed at helping families with very low incomes where the head of the family is in full-time work and there are one or more dependent children. It is not intended to make up the full difference between a low income and a 'prescribed amount' which is laid down presumably as needed for subsistence, but half the difference. It is payable for a full year, even if circumstances have changed during the period, and the sum will vary according to the number of children. If a family is eligible for Family Income Supplement it is automatically eligible for the welfare payments available to those receiving Supplementary Benefit. As in the case of Supplementary Benefit recipients of Family Income Supplement are subject to a means test. From November 1982 the income limit below which FIS is paid rises roughly in line with other benefits to £82.50 with similar rises for children.

*Rent and Rate Rebates and Rent Allowances*: Rent rebates and allowances are means tested benefits claimed from the local authority which can reduce the rents of council tenants or pay a cash sum to tenants in private furnished or unfurnished accommodation or to tenants of housing associations. Rebates or allowances should last for six months, or for pensioners for a year.

Rate Rebates are given by the local authority to both tenants and owner-occupiers, subject to a means test.

Neither Rent nor Rate rebates have been available to those receiving Supplementary Benefits, but a new, unified Housing Benefit is proposed to be paid by the local authority, probably in 1983, replacing the above and the housing element of the Supplementary Benefit (see above).

*Free School Meals:* Under the regulations now in operation, if the parent is in receipt of either Supplementary Benefit or Family Income Supplement, an entitlement to free school meals automatically follows. But application can also be made by others whose *net* income is low after a means test. Scales of net weekly income for qualification are reviewed regularly. Head teachers can supply the necessary application forms.

Until the 1980 Education Act, there was a legal requirement on local councils to issue free milk to infants. This no longer applies but many councils, however, still do so.

*Free Prescription Charges, Free Dental Treatment, Free Glasses:* These are available to all in receipt of Supplementary Benefit or Family Income Supplement, and to children under 16. They are also payable to expectant mothers and mothers who have had a child within the previous twelve months, people suffering from certain medical conditions and war pensioners with disablements.

Children of 16, 17 and 18 and people of 'low income' may get these benefits free or at reduced cost under various conditions and means tests. All over 60 (women) or 65 (men) get free prescriptions. Details of the very complex provisions are available at any DHSS office or any Advice Centre. They require careful study to confirm entitlement.

*WelfareMilk andFood:* If in receipt of Supplementary Benefit or Family Income Supplement expectant mothers and any children under school age are entitled to a free pint of milk a day, free children's vitamin drops and mother's vitamin tablets.

*Local Authority Benefits:* Local Authorities are empowered to provide a wide range of other benefits on conditions which may vary

# Social Security

from council to council. These include:

- Essential School clothing and uniform grants
- Grants to young people staying at school after 16
- Free travel within certain distances to school
- Cheap or free fares for pensioners
- Home helps for old people, the disabled chronic sick, mothers before or after confinement.
- Meals on wheels and luncheon clubs for old people.

They also have a duty to provide various services in the home and transport for the blind, deaf and dumb and those permanently handicapped in various ways; and to assist, by making various cash payments, families whose children may otherwise be taken into care.

*Social SecurityTribunals:* Two appeals tribunals exist under social security legislation:

*Local Appeals Tribunals.* These decide on appeals against decisions of the Insurance Officer in the social security office who has dealt with claims for benefit under the National Insurance Acts. The Tribunal is composed of a Legally Qualified Chairman and an employer and an employee representative, the latter being a trade unionist nominated by the local Trades Council and the proceedings are normally conducted informally. Legal aid is not available to appellants who should secure if necessary the assistance of their union in presenting their case. Witnesses can be brought in evidence.

A claimant has 21 days from the date of the decision of the Insurance Officer to appeal unless he can show 'good cause' for delay, usually a medical reason. Appeals should be presented in writing (though this is not legally essential) and should take full account of the fact that the tribunal has to work within the framework of the relevant laws and Regulations and the National Insurance Commissioners' decisions on the interpretation of the law. If facts are in dispute the tribunal has to try to determine the truth and in any case they can use their judgement on issues raised. Trade union representatives should be aware that Insurance Officers' decisions are often based on information given to them by employers.

It is possible to appeal against the decisions of the tribunal to the National Insurance Commissioners' on points of law only.

*Supplementary Benefits Appeals Tribunals* deal with appeals (normally in writing) against refusal to grant any element in supplemen-

tary benefit, e.g. payment of rent in full or payments for 'exceptional
needs'. The Tribunal is composed of a Chairman selected from a
panel appointed by the Lord Chancellor, a person appointed from a
panel for knowledge of living on low income and a trade unionist
from a panel submitted by the County Association of Trades Councils in the relevant area. Two people may attend to assist the appellant. As the Supplementary Benefit regulations are very complicated
expert advice should be sought by the appellant from a trade union
or other knowledgeable body.

The Child Poverty Action Group has criticised the Tribunals for
not being independent of the DHSS (especially their influential
clerks who are seconded from the Department), which is an
interested party; for frequently reviewing the decisions of the benefit
officer rather than making their own decision; and for not being
bound by normal rules of evidence and procedures.

**SOCIAL SECURITY TRIBUNALS**   *See* Social Security.

**SOCIAL WAGE**   This is the name given to the aggregate of social
benefits available to individuals and families which are paid for by
the community in various forms of taxation but which are received
wholly or partly free over and above the money earnings from employment. Such benefits include free education, treatment in the
National Health Service (not wholly free), child benefits. The term
can also be used to include social security benefits for those who
receive them and other benefits available from public authorities or
central government.

Trade unions are concerned with the social wage in their broader
policies and activities including their political activities. The extent
of the social wage has been largely the result of trade union backing
for the policies that have developed it, particularly since the Second
World War. (*See* Social Security, Welfare State.)

**SOCIALISM**   Some trade unions have socialism as their ultimate
objective. This is generally taken to describe a society in which the
means of production, distribution and exchange (industry, commerce and finance) are in public ownership and control and are run
for the common good, not private profit. Socialism is also equated
with 'democratic socialism' in that the publicly-owned and controlled economy would operate within a democratic political system and
according to what are commonly accepted as democratic political

procedures i.e. a Parliament, genuine elections, full freedom of political debate and decision and the existence of different political groupings or parties.

The Labour Party's constitution has socialist objectives and it is commonly described as a socialist party.

Karl Marx described socialism in different terms as a stage in the transition to communism. The socialist stage was a society in which each gave according to his ability and received according to his work. In the communist stage each gave according to his ability and received according to his need.

**SPECIAL TEMPORARY EMPLOYMENT MEASURES**  *See* Temporary Employment Measures.

**SPEED-UP**  'Speed-up' was a phrase used often in the inter-war years when trade union organization was much weaker than it is to-day, to describe management attempts to force workers to work harder. Increasing the 'speed and feed' times on a machine, speeding up the assembly lines, reducing manning scales, increasing the number of machines to be tended, all these and many other methods were used.

In some undertakings the 'speed-up' still operates but trade union organization and representation normally insists on consultation and negotiated agreement before changes are introduced. The use of productivity agreements, measured day rates, job evaluation and similar methods are the modern day version of the 'speed-up' plus the acceptance of technological changes ranging from mechanisation, automation, containerization, the use of the computer through to the application of the 'micro-chip'. The drive to produce or service more with less labour is a never ending process and justifies the insistence by trade unions on 'mutuality' – i.e. the right to agree or disagree.

**SPREADOVER (STAGGERED HOURS)**  This term is used to describe hours of work which are not continuous. They may be arranged within one day-time period or night time period or partly in the day and partly at night. They are not uncommon in the catering and entertainment industries but are not limited to these. They occur for example in transport. Spreadover working is unpopular and trade unions may negotiate special payments when it occurs. Spreadover is sometimes described as staggered hours.

**STAFF ASSOCIATIONS**   This term may be used in two ways. Perjoratively it is sometimes used in the trade union movement to describe an association or union which is not genuinely independent, is the creature of the employer and may be financed by him.

A report, *Staff Associations*, published by the Certification Officer in February 1981 shows that Britain's 126 leading staff associations lost over half their 200,000 membership to *bona fide* trade unions in the previous three years, the largest loss being in the field of banking due to the formation of the Clearing Banks Union in 1960. Losses have also occurred in the field of insurance. The report indicates that two-thirds of the surviving staff associations were founded after an initiative from the employer.

On the other hand, certain bona fide Civil Service unions call themselves staff associations, representing as they may do staff in a particular Department or of a particular grade. (*See* Company Unions.)

**STAND-BY PAYMENTS**   In some industries, especially service industries such as gas, water and electricity, it may be necessary to call out workers in emergencies. At week-ends or during the night, for example, when perhaps a full complement of labour is not at work a special arrangement is made for certain workers to be 'on call' at their homes. A payment is made for this availability entitled 'stand-by payment' and this is provided for in the collective agreement. Where, during 'stand-by' the worker is called out to work then it is normal for additional payment to be made.

**STANDARD RATE**   A 'standard rate' of pay is distinguished from a 'minimum rate' and is expected to be applied without additions. The term was in greater use when wages were rigidly fixed by national agreement. Many national collective agreements these days allow for some local variation or adjustment but where they do not the rates laid down are 'standard rates'.

**STATUS QUO**   *See* Agreements.

**STERLING**   Sterling is the name give to British currency on the international market. One speaks of pounds, sterling to distinguish between British currency and other currencies which have pounds. The Sterling Area is a group of countries, officially known as the Scheduled Territories, who settle most of their international trading accounts in sterling. Once a very large group including the Commonwealth and other countries it now consists of the United Kingdom, including the Isle of Man and Channel Islands, and Gibraltar.

**STINT**  An assessment of an amount of work to be done or in some cases a fixed limit on output. Examples are to be found in the road haulage industry where men might agree to do a fixed number of loads for a day's work; this practice known as 'job and finish' enables the men concerned to finish work earlier than the normal finishing time if they have completed their 'stint'. The principle has also been applied in rubber manufacturing and other industries, and in a variety of occupations. The normal days pay is of course applicable even if the work is completed in less time than the normal day. In piecework shops it is not unusual for the pieceworkers themselves to agree collectively a limit on output and earnings to avoid disparity and the danger of the employer attempting to cut piecework prices.

**STRIKES**  The traditional weapon which workpeople and unions may use to enforce or make meaningful collective bargaining with employers, or in seeking to rectify a grievance. Strikes are caused by a variety of circumstances, the overwhelming majority are due to disputes about wages. Other causes relate to working conditions, manning and work allocation, dismissals and disciplinary matters, hours of work, trade union questions (including trade union recognition and closed shop disputes), 'extra wage and fringe benefits'. This is not a complete list but it gives some indication of the range of industrial problems which are the background to many stoppages.

There are strikes which go on for a very long time, some involve a large number of workers, other strikes may be short and sharp and some strikes may only have a small number of participants. There is also a distinction between 'official', 'unofficial' and 'unconstitutional' strikes. The 'official' strike is called by the Executive of the trade union or supported by them. A strike which occurs without the approval of the Union executive is usually referred to as 'unofficial' – although sometimes this may be converted to 'official' status during the course of a dispute. A strike which occurs in breach of an agreed procedure may be called 'unconstitutional'.

Union leaderships take a responsible view of the strike weapon and seek to ensure that the purpose of the strike is well-founded and is supported by the membership. In most strikes workers suffer financially and unions which pay strike pay (usually well below the normal wage of the people on strike) suffer a drain on their funds; whilst there is always the danger of a loss of membership support if sufficient progress is not made as a result of the strike. Whatever the form of the strike there is no doubt that workers prefer to have their problems resolved by negotiation and without the need for strike action, if at all possible.

The record of strikes in Britain has been comparatively high, but not consistently so, and generally it has been lower than in some other major industrial countries, e.g. USA, Canada and Australia.

Attempts to restrict legally the right to strike in Britain have proved ineffective. In the First and Second World Wars there were restrictions on the right to strike but local stoppages nevertheless took place. Restrictions contained within the Industrial Relations Act of 1971 were resisted strongly by the unions and the Act was eventually repealed in 1974 by the Labour Government.

The variety of conditions under which a strike may take place make it difficult to generalize on their conduct by trade unions. The economic circumstances, the degree of organization, the financial position of both sides, the mood of the workers are all important considerations. Any of the major factors may change during the course of the strike, in which case a review of attitudes would need to take place. Practical tactics which a trade union involved in a strike might be expected to decide would include: the conduct of publicity, the arrangements for regular contact with the people on strike, the organization of pickets, and not least the composition and role of a strike committee at each of the establishments where the strike is taking place.

It is usual for the policies being pursued by the trade unions to be explained continually to the strikers and accurate information supplied, so that there is no loss of confidence throughout. This is especially important at the concluding stages of a dispute when the state of the negotiations and the recommended terms of settlement need to be clearly and carefully explained. The conditions under which a return to work takes place, even if the terms are not as favourable as many of the workers desire, are an essential key to the maintenance of morale. If the strikers do not return to work in good spirits it can be equally dangerous for employer and union. Resentment and disgruntlement may set in which sometimes reflects itself in 'go-slows', refusal to co-operate, and a critical attitude to both management and union. Trade unions usually seek to ensure that

# Strikes

workers feel a sense of achievement as a result of a strike and sensibly make plans for an 'organized return to work'.

Depending on the circumstances, trade unions and their members may determine to adopt methods short of full strike action. These could include: partial strikes of key sections, one day strikes, overtime bans, 'go-slows', 'sit-in' strikes (which mean the occupation of the workplace). 'Sympathetic' strikes i.e. strikes in support of workers in other factories or industries or in solidarity with workers in other countries tend to be short in duration (e.g. a one day strike) or take the form of a boycott (blacking) action.

On rare occasions a 'general strike' may occur i.e. a widespread stoppage of work covering a whole area or group of industries. Such

Industrial disputes – international comparisons 1969–78

| | Working days lost through industrial disputes per 1000 employees in selected industries (mining, manufacturing, construction and transport) | | | | | | | | | | Average for 10 years |
|---|---|---|---|---|---|---|---|---|---|---|---|
| | 1969 | 1970 | 1971 | 1972 | 1973 | 1974 | 1975 | 1976 | 1977 | 1978(a) | 1969—78 |
| United Kingdom | 520 | 740 | 1190 | 2160 | 570 | 1270 | 540 | 300 | 840 | 840 | 897 |
| Australia(b) | 860 | 1040 | 1300 | 880 | 1080 | 2670 | 1390 | 1490 | 700 | 1010 | 1242 |
| Belgium | 100 | 830 | 720 | 190 | 520 | 340 | 340 | 560 | 420 | 650 | 467 |
| Canada | 2550 | 2190 | 800 | 1420 | 1660 | 2550 | 2810 | 2550 | 830 | 1930 | 1929 |
| Denmark(c) | 80 | 170 | 30 | 40 | 4440 | 330 | 110 | 220 | 240 | 90 | 575 |
| Finland | 200 | 270 | 3300 | 520 | 2530 | 470 | 310 | 1310 | 2360 | 160 | 1143 |
| France | 200 | 180 | 440 | 300 | 330 | 250 | 390 | 420 | 260 | 200 | 297 |
| Germany (FR) | 20 | 10 | 340 | 10 | 40 | 60 | 10 | 40 | — | 370 | 90 |
| India | 1270 | 1440 | 1100 | 1300 | 1330 | 2480 | 1450 | 830 | 1310 | 1280 | 1379 |
| Irish Republic | 2170 | 490 | 670 | 600 | 410 | 1240 | 810 | 840 | 1050 | 1630 | 991 |
| Italy | 4160 | 1730 | 1060 | 1670 | 2470 | 1800 | 1730 | 2310 | 1560 | 890 | 1938 |
| Japan | 200 | 200 | 310 | 270 | 210 | 450 | 390 | 150 | 70 | 60 | 231 |
| Netherlands | 10 | 140 | 50 | 70 | 330 | — | — | 10 | 140 | — | 75 |
| New Zealand | 300 | 470 | 350 | 300 | 530 | 360 | 390 | 950 | 810 | 790 | 525 |
| Norway | — | 70 | 10 | — | 10 | 490 | 10 | 70 | 40 | 90 | 79 |
| Spain | 130 | 240 | 190 | 120 | 210 | 310 | 370 | 2540 | 3350 | 1820 | 928 |
| Sweden(d) | 30 | 40 | 240 | 10 | 10 | 30 | 20 | 10 | 20 | 10 | 42 |
| Switzerland | — | — | 10 | — | — | — | — | 20 | — | — | — |
| United States(e) | 1390 | 2210 | 1600 | 860 | 750 | 1480 | 990 | 1190 | 1070 | na | 1282 |

Notes
(a) Provisional figures.
(b) Including electricity and gas; excluding communication.
(c) For Denmark, figures up to 1974 relate only to manufacturing, and are therefore not fully comparable with later figures which include construction and transport.
(d) For Sweden, figures up to 1971 relate to all sectors and are therefore not fully comparable with those for later years.
(e) Including gas, electricity and water.
na Not available.
— Negligible/less than five.

Source: *ACAS Industrial Relations Handbook*, 1981

a strike occurred in Dublin in 1913 and partially in Liverpool in 1911. The most renowned 'general strike' took place in 1926 and was called by the TUC in support of the miners, who had been locked out by the coal-owners. The strike covered a range of industries and lasted for nine days. Such strikes were made illegal by the Trades Disputes Act of 1927 but that Act was repealed by the Labour Government in 1946.

The right to strike is jealously defended by the trade union movement as an essential freedom to be used as a last resort. Effective collective bargaining and the use of voluntary conciliation and arbitration serve to reduce the need for strike action, although the weapon will always be required as a vital means of labour defence and advance, in extremity.

An international comparison of working days lost through industrial disputes per 1000 employees needs to be made with caution, partly owing to differences in the statistical definitions and recording methods used in the different countries and partly because of different national patterns of industrial employment combined with the varying incidence of strikes in the different industries.

In order to reduce the effects of the different industrial patterns and strike frequencies, the International Labour Office publishes the statistics, given on page 278, which limit the overall incidence rates to a broad economic sector consisting of the mining, manufacturing, construction and transport industries.

The incidence rates vary considerably from year to year for most countries shown in the figures. Comparisons between countries are accordingly best made by means of averages over a period of years. Over the decade 1969–1978 it may be seen that the UK was close to the middle of the range of estimates for the nineteen countries. (*See also* General Strike, Sit-ins.)

**SUBBING**   To 'sub' is workplace language and refers to the practice of a worker asking for a payment 'on account' before the normal time for the payment of wages.

For example a newly-employed worker may be expected to agree to the employer 'holding a week in hand' so that he does not receive payment of wages at the end of the first week. In such a case the worker may ask for a 'sub' and be paid some money on account.

Workers themselves may also 'sub' a mate if he is short of cash. It is not an unusual practice in industry for working people to help each other out in this way.

**SUBSIDIES, INDUSTRIAL, BY GOVERNMENT** *See* Nationalization.

**SUPPLEMENTARY BENEFIT** *See* Social Security.

**SUSPENSION (ON MEDICAL GROUNDS ETC.)** When an employee is removed from the job or the establishment temporarily, for reasons of health or discipline – i.e. he is not dismissed – he is said to be suspended. The conditions attending suspension for disciplinary reasons should be laid down in the relevant procedure agreement, e.g. whether pay continues or not and the duration of the suspension.

Under the Employment Protection Act an employee is entitled to normal pay for a limited period during suspension on medical grounds under certain health and safety regulations. The relevant regulations cover jobs involving exposure to ionizing radiation, lead and certain other chemicals where health would be endangered by continued exposure to the substance. The decision to suspend is made by a doctor.

The entitlement to pay operates only if the employee has had at least four weeks' continuous employment with the employer and if he works at least 16 hours a week or at least 8 hours after five years continuous service. There are also certain other limitations which are officially indicated.

A normal week's pay is given for up to a maximum of twenty-six weeks for employees suspended under the health and safety regulations. Employees who have a right to pay under their contract of employment while suspended should continue to receive that pay. The employer will not pay suspension pay in addition but if the actual pay is less than a normal week's pay the employer must make up the difference.

Employees who have been dismissed because they would otherwise have been suspended for medical reasons can complain to an industrial tribunal if they have been continuously employed by their employer for four weeks. They can also complain if they think they have been underpaid. (*See* Unfair Dismissal.)

**SWEATED LABOUR** The term 'sweated labour' was used to describe very low wages in certain industries in the latter part of the last century. A series of reports by a Select Committee of the House of Lords in the 1880s and 1890s exposed terrible conditions which had arisen from cut-throat competition between employers to gain contracts from Government departments and local authorities. Fair Wages Resolutions (the first in 1891) were introduced to alleviate the position in the case of public contracts, and Trade Boards were set up, ostensibly to deal with the position of employers in the private sector cutting wages to the bone to obtain contracts. (*See* Wages Council.)

**SYMPATHETIC ACTION**     Action by a union not directly involved in a dispute in sympathy with another union or unions engaged in action, with the aim of helping them to win by increasing its effect. Sympathetic action is a form of 'secondary action' and legal immunity for those taking part is strictly limited by the Employment Act, 1980. (*See* Employment Act 1980, Employment Bill 1982, Immunity, Picketing, Secondary Action.)

**SYNDICALISM**     This describes a trend in the trade union movement which sees unions as bodies not concerned simply with defending and improving their members' pay and conditions and with providing various benefits (insurance of different kinds) but as a means of waging the class war directly against the capitalist system and for its replacement by a socialist system of society. Syndicalists see the unions mainly as political instruments ultimately taking direct action to transform society by a series of strikes leading to a final general strike. The syndicalist conception of a socialist society involved the unions in one way or another taking control of their sectors of production and through this leading to a form of workers' control of the whole of society.

   Although syndicalism had a certain vogue at various times in the trade union movement in the early nineteenth century and before the first world war it never took hold of the movement and today is not a significant trend and must be distinguished from the current movement for 'workers' control'. Political action among British trade unions followed the line of creating a parliamentary instrument through the Labour Party for wider political objectives than the day-to-day concerns of the unions.

# T

**TAKE HOME PAY**     *See* Real Wages.

# Takeover

**TAKEOVER, TAKEOVER BID**   *See* Monopolies.

**TAX AND PRICE INDEX**   *See* Retail Price Index.

**TAXATION, DIRECT AND INDIRECT**   Central Government taxation policies and local government rate policies play a part in the preparation of wage and salary demands. Taxes are the main means whereby the central government raises money for its various purposes and functions. There are various types of tax. Direct taxes are compulsory payments levied on persons or businesses. The most important personal tax is Income Tax. It is deducted from the employee's pay or salary at source by the employer and is graduated at lower and higher rates according to income. Income can be both earned and unearned and includes income from rent, profits and interest. In certain categories of income, tax may be paid direct. Not all income is taxed; there are various allowances and 'reliefs' deducted from gross income before it becomes taxable, e.g. mortgage payment and occupational pension payment reliefs.

Other forms of direct taxation include: Corporation Tax which is a tax on company profits; capital gains tax which taxes increases in values in capital assets between time of buying and selling; capital transfer tax which replaced what were popularly known as 'death duties' and which taxes wealth given away during the donor's lifetime as well as wealth transferred at death.

National Insurance contributions may be considered a form of direct tax.

Payment of direct taxes is a legal obligation and may not be evaded without breaking the law which provides for penalties. There is, however, a considerable amount of 'tax avoidance' which takes advantage of loopholes or ambiguities or provisions of the law which can be interpreted flexibly. Tax evasion and tax avoidance, usually on the advice of 'tax experts' employed by business concerns reach an estimated total of £4,000 million a year in loss of revenue by the Government, which the rest of the community has to pay for in higher taxation. An authoritative estimate gave a figure of £15,000 million for the 'black economy', i.e. all forms of economic activity illegitimately not paying tax, amounting to about 6 per cent of the Gross Domestic Product. Provisional estimates published by the OECD show total tax revenue in 1980 in the UK as 35.9 per cent of the Gross Domestic Product, eleventh in a league table which shows our major EEC competitors paying higher percentages.

Indirect taxes are taxes on spending or purchases and include Value Added Tax (VAT), a tax levied on sales of most goods or services, customs and excise duties on tobacco, alcoholic drinks, and on certain other categories of imports, various licenses (dogs, television, cars, gambling).

Indirect taxes tend to take a larger share of lower income than of higher and are therefore criticised as 'regressive', hitting the poor more than the rich. Income tax on the contrary is described as 'progressive' because the higher the earnings the greater the tax paid. Yet in the first three budgets of the Thatcher government the direct tax burden has been redistributed to the disadvantage of the low paid and the advantage of the higher paid. (This takes into account National Insurance Contributions, which are regressive in their impact, hitting the lower-paid more than the higher.) The tax burden on wage and salary earners has increased except for the highest paid. Britain's workers also start paying income tax at lower wages than nearly all other workers in the EEC. About one and a quarter million more of the lower-paid now pay direct taxes who did not pay before. Changes in indirect taxation have also been to the advantage of the higher paid. (*See* Company Taxation, PAYE, Rates, Social Security, VAT.)

**TECHNICIAN, TECHNOLOGIST**   These terms are often loosely used. More precisely technicians are within a broad band of personnel who have the technical knowledge to exercise technical judgement, know and understand the principles underlying their work and the purpose of what they are doing and frequently, supervise other staff. It is generally taken to be the level of responsibility above the craft level.

Technologists are generally people with professional and/or higher education qualifications (from university or Further Education Colleges) in a particular technology e.g. engineering. They are expected to be able to understand fully the technical processes involved in their industrial operation, deal with problems that arise, possibly develop new processes and make technical innovations, and plan work with the best use of technical resources.

**TECHNICIAN EDUCATION COUNCIL (TEC)**   This is a council set up by the Government in 1973 following the Haslegrave Committee report on Technician courses and examinations to provide a national unified system of technician education in England,

# Temporary Employment Measures

Wales and Northern Ireland which both meets student needs and industry's requirements. It is concerned with a broad band of personnel who have certain features in common: they have to exercise technical judgement, understand the principles underlying their work and the purpose of what they are doing, and, frequently supervise other staff.

TEC works in partnership with colleges and industry aiming to create a unified range of technician courses previously run by a large number of separate bodies, and replace them with courses in a single national system. TEC programmes replace the previous dual structure of Ordinary and Higher National Certificates and the technician qualifications of the City & Guilds of London Institute.

Courses are approved by a committee consisting of experts drawn from colleges, industrial concerns, professional bodies and training boards. TEC provides course material which colleges can use and this helps to ensure the national currency and standards of its qualifications and the establishment and maintenance of standards of performance. Colleges may use or adapt TEC courses but may also design their own for validation by TEC. It is intended that colleges work closely with local firms in the planning and provision of courses.

TEC courses can be pursued by full-time, sandwich (i.e. students who spend block periods at college and on the job) or part-time students and certificates awarded show the nature of the course undertaken. Its qualifications (Certificate, Diploma, Higher Certificate and Higher Diploma) at different levels are recognized for qualifying or exemption purposes by many professional and technician bodies and they can provide the basis for students who want to go on to degree courses or attain full professional status.

**TEMPORARY EMPLOYMENT MEASURES (PROGRAMMES), SPECIAL** Either through the Manpower Services Commission (MSC) or directly the Department of Employment is responsible for a number of programmes providing temporary employment for the unemployed.

*Community Enterprise (CE)* has replaced the Short Term Employment Programme (STEP) and is run by the MSC. Priority in this programme is given to long term unemployed, primarily those aged 18 to 21 unemployed for more than six months and those over 25 unemployed for over 12 months. Its aim is to promote partnerships between the private and public and community sectors in order to provide jobs for projects of community value. Expenditure cuts have, however, drastically curtailed the possibility of catering for the great majority of the long term unemployed. Thus the aim was to provide 25,000 places by April 1982, not restricted as STEP was to areas of high unemployment, though they are given priority, but nationwide.

Its development is intended to be through private firms sponsoring projects mainly on environmental improvements. Voluntary organizations promoting work for the unemployed are also an element of the scheme. The TUC is concerned at the rates of pay, the relaxation by the government of the rules on financial gain by private sponsors and the need for extended public sector involvement in generating jobs as well as trade union involvement in the approval and monitoring of projects.

In the March 1982 Budget the Chancellor of the Exchequer announced a new programme of community work for the long-term unemployed to run alongside CEP. It is intended to provide temporary work on non-profit-making projects sponsored by local authorities, voluntary organizations, churches, etc. Those participating, up to 100,000 unemployed workers, will be paid 'broadly the equivalent of their benefit entitlement plus an addition for expenses and the like'. The TUC has sharply criticised the scheme as aiming to provide 'a cheap adult labour force for employers to exploit'.

*Temporary Short Time Working Compensation Schemes (TSTWCS):* These are run by the Department of Employment to encourage employers to adopt short time working, to avoid redundancies affecting at least ten workers in jobs which have a 'reasonable' chance of becoming viable. Employers are expected to consult the unions on the arrangements. Under the scheme workers are paid a minimum of 50 per cent of their normal pay for each workless day and employers can claim reimbursement of this 50 per cent of normal wage payments subject to a maximum normal pay of £120 a week for nine months. The TUC has pressed for this to be extended to one year, and eighteen months in certain very hard pressed industries. The take up has been quite extensive (nearly 250,000 jobs in 1980) in the past. Among the disadvantages of the current scheme is that low paid workers may be paid wages near or below unemployment benefit

# Time Off for Union and Public Duties

giving little incentive to avoid redundancy. The scheme does not cover employees who do not qualify for guarantee payments except such employees with less than four weeks service.

*Job Release Scheme (JRS):* Under this scheme, from February 1982 until March 1984, men of 62 (if disabled, 58) can take early retirement and a taxable allowance of £47.50 single person, or £59, married, until they reach their statutory age of eligibility for pension. The scheme also applies to women of 59. This is intended to release jobs (a vacancy must actually be created for an unemployed person to fill) for younger unemployed people. The TUC has pressed for the ages of eligibility to be reduced to 55 for women and 60 for men. Those receiving the allowance are not eligible for other state benefits such as Sickness or Unemployment Benefit, but their entitlement to the retirement pension is not affected.

*Small Firms Employment Subsidy:* This scheme is now abolished but a number of firms are still being paid £20 a week for any new full-time jobs they created. No new scheme has been proposed by the government to replace this attempt to pay employment subsidies to generate new jobs.

*Young Workers Scheme:* Under this scheme employers are paid £15 a week for each school leaver aged 16 and 17 they take on, provided they are in their first year of work, at a wage of less than £40 a week for up to a year. A reduced subsidy of £7.50 a week will be paid for the employment of school leavers at a wage of between £40 and £45 a week. The scheme has been attacked by the TUC as encouraging employers to undermine union rates of pay and encourage employers to take on school leavers, instead of, not in addition to, adults. The Government does not deny that apart from the creation of new jobs an aim of the scheme is to bring down the rates of pay for young people. The scheme's take up is estimated to be 15,000 to 20,000 jobs in a full year.

**TIME OFF AND FACILITIES FOR UNION AND PUBLIC DUTIES**   One of the most important features of the Employment Protection Act (EPA) is to grant time off to union represntatives for union activity in an establishment. The ACAS Code of Practice on Time Off also includes a section on the provision of facilities for Union representatives to do the job properly. The smooth and reasonable operation of these provisions can only make for good industrial relations.

286

# Time Off for Union and Public Duties

Time off is normally with pay at the average earnings rate and covers a variety of activities but excludes any connected with industrial action. They positively include time off for the following purposes: explaining to new workers the advantages of trade union membership, representing members who have grievances, attending shop stewards committee meetings, collective bargaining on pay and conditions, keeping members informed on negotiations and consultations with management. Time off is also available for union representatives to take part in union training at different levels.

The Act also allows for reasonable time off to be given to union members for participation in union affairs during working hours where the union is recognized for collective bargaining purposes and for activities connected with the election or appointment of union officials. Such activities must be at an 'appropriate' time with the employer's permission and apply only in respect of the activities of independent unions.

The amount of time off is subject to negotiation and agreement but must be sufficient to allow the union representative to do his job effectively. And the provisions are not restricted to union officials but extend to a great variety of representatives, including for example, conference delegates, district and national Executive members, members of policy committees, and union members appointed to serve on outside bodies. They also cover arrangements to carry out union activities in tea breaks and lunch hours and can include arrangements for collecting union subscriptions and inspecting members' cards.

The ACAS Code also allows for management to make available facilities within the establishment to enable the union representative's job to be carried out efficiently, and to allow him to communicate effectively with his members, officials, etc. Such facilities may include office space, accommodation for meetings, access to a telephone, office facilities such as the use of a filing cabinet, notice board, use of the internal post, typing, photocopying and duplicating facilities. Management should also provide a list of new workers.

Should there be disputes concerning time off and facilities, or concerning payment involved, every attempt should be made to settle them through existing procedure agreements. If this fails, the matter should be referred to the unions concerned. The Act and Code of Practice are designed to promote good industrial relations by negotiated agreements and this places an obligation on both sides to assume clearly reasonable attitudes. Only in the very last resort, therefore, should application be made to an industrial tribunal.

Time off is not limited to union representatives. It is also available for workers involved in public duties, for example, Justices of the Peace, members of a local authority, members of any statutory tribunal, of Health Authorities or Boards, school or college governors or managers, water authorities, etc. As in the case of union representatives the time off must be 'reasonable' and should take into account the amount of time needed to do the job, the amount of time the employee may have off for trade union duties and the circumstances of the employer's business. There is one important difference between time off for union and for public duties; the employer is not obliged to pay workers who have time off for public duties.

**TIME SERVED**   When an apprentice completes his apprenticeship after the necessary number of years he is said to be time-served.

**'TINA LEA' CLAUSE IN AGREEMENTS**   Under the Industrial Relations Act, 1971, which was bitterly opposed by the trade union movement and which was repealed by the Labour Government in 1974 agreements between unions and employers were legally enforceable unless it was agreed by both sides that this should not be so. In these circumstances a clause was inserted into the agreement that This Is Not A Legally Enforceable Agreement', the initials of the statement being TINA LEA. Such disclaimer clauses were widespread and were normally demanded by unions. This helped in practice to undermine the Act which was also rendered ineffective in many respects by other trade union action.

**TOLPUDDLE**   In 1834 six agricultural labourers in the village of Tolpuddle in Dorset were sentenced to seven years transportation to Tasmania for administering illegal oaths to prospective members of their 'Friendly Society', an early name sometimes used for what was in effect a trade union. The sentence was a savage one, intended as a warning against forming unions. The six labourers became known as the Tolpuddle Martyrs and are frequently referred to as an example of the determination of workers to form trade unions. The Tolpuddle case played a significant part in paving the way for the modern trade union movement. The sentences aroused an enormous mass movement of protest and were remitted after two years though it was not till after another two years that the labourers were released and returned to England.

**TOOL ALLOWANCE**   An allowance provided for in some collective agreements to provide for the upkeep and replacement of tools used by tradesmen etc.

In some cases companies help with the initial purchase of tools and their replacement. There are instances also of companies paying for 'tool insurance' to cover the loss or damage to tools.

**TOP HAT PENSIONS**   The special pension arrangements made for top management on specially favourable terms with very substantial financial advantages. They are an important incentive which companies offer to top management in order to retain its services, being in effect a concealed form of pay subsidized by the rest of the tax paying community. (*See* Fringe Benefits.)

**TOP SALARIES REVIEW BODY**   A group appointed by the Prime Minister which reviews, normally biennially, the pay of the civil servants of the top ranks (under secretary and above) and other high paid public servants e.g. members of Boards of nationalised industries, judges, generals, etc. (*See* National Whitley Council.)

**TRADE CYCLE**   *See* Depression.

**TRADE DISPUTE**   The definition of a Trade Dispute is of great importance for all conducting trade union activity. It is defined in Section 29 of the Trade Union and Labour Relations Act, 1974, as follows (key sections):

Meaning of trade dispute.
29.—(1) In this Act " trade dispute " means a dispute between employers and workers, or between workers and workers, which is connected with one or more of the following, that is to say—

> (*a*) terms and conditions of employment, or the physical conditions in which any workers are required to work;
>
> (*b*) engagement or non-engagement, or termination or suspension of employment or the duties of employment, of one or more workers;
>
> (*c*) allocation of work or the duties of employment as between workers or groups of workers;

(d) matters of discipline;

(e) the membership or non-membership of a trade union on the part of a worker;

(f) facilities for officials of trade unions; and

(g) machinery for negotiation or consultation, and other procedures, relating to any of the foregoing matters, including the recognition by employers or employers' associations of the right of a trade union to represent workers in any such negotiation or consultation or in the carrying out of such procedures.

(2) A dispute between a Minister of the Crown and any workers shall, notwithstanding that he is not the employer of those workers, be treated for the purposes of this Act as a dispute between employer and those workers if the dispute relates—

(a) to matters which have been referred for consideration by a joint body on which, by virtue of any provision made by or under any enactment, that Minister is represented; or

(b) to matters which cannot be settled without that Minister exercising a power conferred on him by or under an enactment.

(3) There is a trade dispute for the purposes of this Act even though it relates to matters occurring outside Great Britain, so long as the person or persons whose actions in Great Britain are said to be in contemplation or furtherance of a trade dispute relating to matters occurring outside Great Britain are likely to be affected in respect of one or more of the matters specified in subsection (1) of this section by the outcome of that dispute.

(4) A dispute to which a trade union or employers' association is a party shall be treated for the purposes of this Act as a dispute to which workers or, as the case may be, employers are parties.

(5) An act, threat or demand done or made by one person or organisation against another which, if resisted would have led to a trade dispute with that other, shall,

notwithstanding that because that other submits to the act or threat or accedes to the demand no dispute arises, be treated for the purposes of this Act as being done or made in contemplation of a trade dispute with that other.

(6) In this section—

" employment " includes any relationship whereby one person personally does work or performs services for another;
" worker ", in relation to a dispute to which an employer is a party, includes any worker even if not employed by that employer.

(7) In the Conspiracy and Protection of Property Act 1875 " trade dispute " has the same meaning as in this Act. (*See* Employment Bill 1982, for proposed changes.)

**TRADE UNION** A trade union is an independent self-regulating organization of workers created to protect and advance the interests of its members through collective action. The Union is responsible to the workers in membership and cannot be directed by any outside agency. Its purposes, practices and policies are continually subject to the wishes of the membership expressed through a democratic organization working the rules it makes itself.

Unions negotiate collective agreements on behalf of their members with employers on pay and conditions of work which include, for example, hours, shift work, hygiene at the workplace, relationships between workers and representatives of management, holidays, sickness arrangements, redundancy and short-time working agreements.

Unions represent their members who individually or collectively may be indispute with management as a whole or its representatives. They strive to reach agreements and make settlements with employers but are organized to apply sanctions if necessary, including the ultimate sanction of the withdrawal of labour.

Unions may also provide legal advice and assistance for their members, insurance, sickness and convalescent benefits of various kinds, and educational facilities. They may also engage in political activities as laid down by their rules and subject to the provisions of Acts of Parliament.

**TRADE UNION AND LABOUR RELATIONS ACTS (TULRA) 1974 AND 1976**    One of the first legislative acts of the 1974 Labour Government was to repeal the 1971 Industrial Relations Act. This resulted in the following main changes:

(a) The National Industrial Relations Court, the Commission on Industrial Relations and the Registry of Trades Unions and Employers Associations were abolished.

(b) The concept of an 'unfair industrial practice' was abolished, and the restricted legal immunities for unregistered unions and employers associations and for actions in respect of a trade dispute were removed.

(c) The guiding principles in the Industrial Relations Act for the conduct of trade unions and employers associations were repealed.

(d) The emergency procedures (e.g. for strike ballots) were abolished.

(e) The provisions dealing with recognition, agency shops and procedure agreements were repealed.

(f) The procedure for registration of trade unions and employers associations were replaced by greatly simplified 'listing' arrangements.

(g) The right not to belong to a union, and the voiding of pre-entry closed shops agreements, were repealed. Closed shop agreements became lawful again in these respects.

The TULRA restored to trade unions the immunity they had previously enjoyed against common law actions based on the doctrine of restraint of trade. The legal protections against actions in tort were restored to what they were between 1906 and the 1971 Act. A person acting 'in contemplation of furtherance of a trade dispute' who induced or threatened a breach of any contract, including a commercial contract or employment contract, or who interfered with the performance of any contract was not liable in tort on the ground only that his actions produced that effect (although they might have been actionable in other respects). Action in contemplation or furtherance of a trade dispute was not to be actionable in tort just because it interfered with trade or business or an individual's free choice of employment. The immunities which existed before 1971 were restored and extended to include threatened and intended future actions of the organisations, and the traditional immunity against liability for civil conspiracy actions was continued. Actions by trade unions (other than those in furtherance of a trade dispute) which resulted in personal injury or affected property were not protected.

TULRA reversed the legal enforceability of collective agreements except where it expressly stated in writing that both parties intended the agreement to be legally enforceable.

With the abolition of registration and the Registry of Trade Unions and Employers Associations, statutory requirements concerning trade union affairs were dealt with again by the Chief Registrar of Friendly Societies, and then taken over by the Certification Officer under the Employment Protection Act 1975.

The provisions on 'unfair dismissal' first enacted by the Industrial Relations Act 1971 were not repealed; instead, the qualifying period before an employee could make a complaint against his employer was reduced from two years employment to six months, and maximum compensation was substantially increased.

The Act introduced the concept of 'constructive dismissal' or forced resignation. An employee was to be considered unfairly dismissed if he resigned in circumstances in which he would be entitled to terminate his contract without notice by reason of the employers' conduct.

During the passage of the 1974 Act, the Conservatives were able, because of their automatic majority in the House of Lords and the Labour Government's minority status in the Commons, to carry a number of important amendments, which eventually necessitated the introduction of further legislation in the form of the Trade Union and Labour Relations (Amendment) Act 1976.

The main wrecking amendments had extended protection against dismissal in a closed shop establishment to those who objected on any 'reasonable' grounds in addition to those who objected on grounds of religious belief. A further clause gave workers protection against dismissal if they joined 'another appropriate independent trade union'. Other clauses removed the immunity from action for inducing breach of contract against commercial contracts, thus restricting blacking and sympathy strikes, and withdrew protection given to workers taking industrial action in support of disputes overseas in which they were not directly involved.

Other amendments gave workers a right not to be excluded from membership of a trade union arbitrarily, and provided a civil remedy if the decisions of industrial tribunals on questions of exclusion or expulsion were not carried out, and laid down regulations for trade

# Trades Councils

union rules on such matters as elections, disciplinary action, eligibility for membership, union funds and financial benefits. And a union member was given the right, on giving reasonable notice and complying with any reasonable condition, to terminate his membership of the union. These amendments were repealed in the TULR (Amendment) Act, 1976.

**TRADES COUNCILS**   In most towns in the United Kingdom there is a Trades Council. In Scotland and N. Ireland Trades Councils are affiliated to the Scottish TUC or the Irish Congress of Trades Unions and send delegates to the Annual Congresses. In England and Wales the Trades Councils act as the local agents of the TUC and are composed of representatives of local trade union branches. They function under the control of the TUC which registers them each year and thus accords recognition to them as local representative bodies of trade unionists. In a few cases the Trades Council is the industrial section of a Joint Trades Council and Labour Party. Trades Councils are financed mainly from affiliation fees paid by affiliated branches but in some cases unions arrange to pay fees on behalf of their branches from district or national funds.

The main objects of Trades Councils are to provide services to branches on a wide range of industrial, civic and educational matters, to help in building up and improving trade union organization in the locality and to nominate representatives of the trade union viewpoint to a large number of local committees and tribunals such as District Advisory Committees covering the Manpower Services (employment and disablement), various Health Authorities etc. Each Trades Council affiliates to one of the county associations of trades councils (CATCs) and in turn the CATCs are represented on the TUC Regional Councils (in Wales, the Wales Trades Union Council). There is an annual Conference of representatives of Trades Councils attended by members of the TUC General Council. There is also the TUCs Trades Councils' Joint Consultative Committee which is composed of six representatives of Trades Councils and six members of the General Council. This Committee is responsible for advising the General Council of the TUC and for compiling a report to the conference of Trades Councils which meets each year for two days to discuss problems within the range of their activities.

**TRADES UNION CONGRESS (TUC)**   The Trades Union Congress was formed in 1868 and has been in continuous existence since that time as a permanent association of independent trade unions. With over 11 million affiliated members it brings together the majority of trade unionists in Britain and is universally recognized as the spokesman for employed people in Britain on a wide range of national issues.

The TUC provides means of co-ordinated and direct access to Governments, employers' organizations, and other important bodies, and plays a crucial role in regulating relations between individual unions. Consultation takes place between the TUC and Government Departments on all aspects of working life and on other national and international problems upon which the TUC has a viewpoint. The TUC also nominates the representatives of the Trade Union movement to numerous national and regional bodies including a variety of statutory committees concerned with social and economic problems.

The Workers' Delegate representing Great Britain at the International Labour Organization (ILO) is nominated by the TUC and is always recognized as a senior representative of the world's workers at ILO meetings. Also, in the international field, the TUC was in 1949 one of the founder members of the International Confederation of Free Trade Unions (ICFTU) and in 1973 it helped to form the European Trade Union Confederation (ETUC) which united trade union federations in the EFTA and EEC countries. It assisted the formation of the Commonwealth Trades Union Council in 1979 which has established useful links with trade union organizations in Commonwealth countries.

In many industrial nations in the western world, trade unions and their national centres are divided on the basis of party politics or on religious grounds. In other countries there is a division as between manual and non-manual workers' unions. In Britain the TUC is the single national centre for the trade union movement and in that respect is the envy of many other trade union movements in the rest of the world.

*Annual Congress*: The Congress, consisting of delegates appointed by the affiliated Unions, meets once a year, normally the first week in September, although special Congresses and conferences of trade union executives may be called if required. Affiliated unions paying a fee of 47½p per member (1982) each year are entitled to send to Congress one representative for every 5,000 members or part

# Trade Union Congress

thereof. At the 1981 Congress, 108 unions were affiliated with a combined membership of 11.6 million. Congress considers the report of the TUC General Council, which is an outline of the work undertaken by the TUC during the year. It also discusses and decides on resolutions and amendments submitted by affiliated unions, who may submit not more than two motions and two amendments each. As many motions cover similar ground, the General Purposes Committee (elected at the previous Annual Congress) may draw up a single composite motion by mutual agreement with the unions involved.

*General Council*: The Annual Congress elects each year the General Council which acts for the TUC between Congresses. For purposes of representation, affiliated unions are divided into 18 different trade groupings each with members on the General Council, roughly according to the size of the group. There is a special 19th Group for women which ensures that women representatives are elected to the General Council. Elections for the General Council are by ballot voting within the Congress of all the affiliated unions.

The General Council is the executive body of the TUC and meets at least monthly. It is responsible for implementing the decisions of Congress, co-ordinates the actions of affiliated unions, overlooks and pronounces on day to day developments affecting the trade union movement of a general character. Much of the Council's work is done through committees which report to it at its monthly meetings for decisions on their recommendations. The major committees are: Finance and General Purposes, Economic, International, Education, Employment Policy and Organisation, Social Insurance and Industrial Welfare, Equal Rights.

Expert departments back up these committees and provide specialist assistance to the TUC Industrial Committees which bring together unions in a number of important industries.

*Regional Machinery*: In England eight TUC Regional Councils and in Wales the Wales Trade Union Council are made up of representatives of all trade unions and County Associations of Trades Councils in the Region concerned and are financed by TUC funds. (Scotland has its Scottish TUC and in Northern Ireland trade unions are affiliated to the Irish Congress of Trade Unions.) Regional TUC Councils are represented on Economic Planning Councils for their Regions, Industrial Development Boards and Regional Health Authorities. They also oversee TUC educational activities in their Regions.

296

Individual members of trade unions have links with these bodies through branch representation on Trades Councils (see Trades Councils).

*TUC–Labour Party Liaison Committee*: This is a major committee set up in late 1971 linking the TUC General Council, the Labour Party National Executive Committee and the Parliamentary Labour Party. Joint statements are issued from time to time on such matters as industrial law, economic policy, industrial relations, social policies, and the cost of living.

*TUC links with major National Bodies*: The TUC has representatives on a number of major bodies which are financed by the Government. These include: The National Economic Development Council (Neddy), ACAS, the MSC and the Health and Safety Commission. This representation and its connection with many other public bodies indicates the wide range of matters on which the TUC is expected to speak on behalf of working people.

For TUC responsibilities in inter-union relations, see 'Bridlington Agreement'. (*See also* Independent Review Body for disputes arising out of closed shops.)

**TUC/LABOUR PARTY LIAISON COMMITTEE**  A Joint Committee of the Labour Party and the TUC set up in 1971 to work out joint policies, particularly in the economic field, and to maintain contact. The Committee meets monthly and consists of representatives of the TUC General Council, the Parliamentary Labour Party and the National Executive Committee of the Labour Party.

**TRAINING OPPORTUNITIES SCHEME (TOPS)**  *See* Manpower Services Commission.

**TRANSNATIONAL COMPANIES**  *See* Multinationals.

**TRUCK ACTS**  The purpose of the Truck Acts, 1831–1940, is to protect the workers to whom they apply from abuses in connection with the payment of wages. These are all manual workers (except domestic servants). They must be paid their wages in cash, or under the Payment of Wages Act, 1960, on written request, by cheque or direct transfer to a bank account. Payment in kind including payment of part of a worker's wages in meals is illegal as well as deductions from the wage packet, e.g. in fines, for damaged goods and materials, or for services provided by the employer, except where these are made by prior agreement with the worker. It is also illegal

# Unemployed Workers' Centres

to require wages to be spent in any particular way e.g. in particular shops such as shops belonging to the employer.

Deductions from wages may however be made as provided for by other laws e.g. for income tax, national insurance contributions, or for medical care, fuel, rent of accommodation let to the worker, food prepared and eaten on the employer's premises, etc. if these are agreed in writing by the worker as well as other requirements. When deductions are made they must be notified to the worker in writing and the worker may demand in writing a copy of the contract containing its terms. All fines or deductions agreed must be 'reasonable' and must not exceed the cost to the employer.

There are many detailed provisions in the various Acts for whose operation the Secretary of State for Employment is responsible. He appoints officers to enforce the Acts and complaints may be made to the Senior Wages Inspector at the nearest Regional Office of the Department of Employment. The Department may institute criminal proceedings for breaches of the Acts. To recover wages due, the worker (who should consult his trade union) can institute civil proceedings before the appropriate court. ACAS will also advise on the matters involved.

# U

**UNEMPLOYED WORKERS' CENTRES**  *See* Unemployment and Union Membership.

**UNEMPLOYMENT**  Although there are several meanings of the term, it is normally applied to a situation where employment is not available to those seeking it. Firms or services may close down or reduce their labour force because of a fall in demand and lack of orders for their products. They may be unable to pay high interest rates or find that the exchange rate makes them uncompetitive in the export market and gives an advantage to imports. Services may lose customers because of inflation and therefore lay off workers. Cuts in public expenditure may cause public authorities to economize in labour by reducing the services they provide. The immediate causes are many. Although economists attempt to classify the various types of unemployment, such as cyclical, seasonal, structural, etc. as resulting from different circumstances, the TUC's view is that today's massive rise

# Unemployment

in unemployment is due to low demand in the economy, of which the main causes are government deflationary policies.

Unemployment has risen sharply in recent years. Figures of those registered as unemployed doubled in the first two years of the Thatcher Government. In January 1982 they increased to over 3 million (well over a quarter of whom had been out of work for more than a year) and it is officially accepted that they will increase further. But it is generally recognized that these are not the total figures as for one reason or another many unemployed do not register, e.g. married women who do not pay the full National Insurance Contribution and therefore do not qualify for Unemployment Benefit. The Department of Employment in mid-1981 estimated 400,000 unregistered unemployed. There are also many on short time (434,000 in April 1981) and therefore not fully employed as they would wish. And there are large numbers of young people on publicly subsidized temporary schemes outside the labour market and on other temporary employment schemes. The TUC estimated that another million should be added to the published figures, making unemployment in March 1982 around 4 million. While unemployment rose by 85 per cent between April 1979 and April 1981, in twelve other European countries the average rise was 30 per cent so that British unemployment has been rising more rapidly than in some of our major competitor countries.

The Treasury's Economic Progress Report (February 1981) estimated that each unemployed worker costs the government some £3,400 in lost tax and national insurance revenue and in extra social security benefits. An updated Treasury Report (February 1982) which remains unpublished, produced figures which suggest the cost of 3 million registered unemployed to be around £15,000 million a year: while the Institute for Fiscal Studies suggested a figure of £13,000 million. These figures do not take into account the cost to the nation in lost output, special employment schemes, etc.

Unemployment has a different impact in different regions and among different sections of the people. Thus, for example, it has been higher in Northern Ireland, Scotland, Wales, the North, the North West, Yorkshire, Humberside and the West Midlands; and among women and young people, general labourers, the semi-skilled, and the ethnic minorities. In April 1981 for example there were 876,000 unemployed under 25, not counting those on temporary schemes like YOP or CEP, and the official, projected figure for

# Unemployment and Union Membership

the 16–18s is over 500,000 for the beginning of 1982. It has been authoritatively estimated that in September 1982, 60 per cent of school leavers will be unemployed.

Unemployed workers receive various payments (benefits) under the social security system which are dependent on family and other circumstances. For the overwhelming majority of the unemployed, the level of these benefits means considerably reduced incomes with consequent hardship. Britain's provision for the unemployed compares unfavourably with that of many other industrialized countries.

The TUC has demanded a major expansion in public spending and public investment, complemented by import controls and the relaxation of the credit squeeze, aimed at both providing work and modernizing industry, as well as supporting union claims for reduced working hours and earlier retirement.

**UNEMPLOYMENT AND UNION MEMBERSHIP**  With the growth of unemployment, union membership has inevitably been adversely affected. Different unions have different policies under their rules for membership of unemployed workers. Many do not allow recruitment of the unemployed although most permit the retention of members who become unemployed and some actively encourage their retention. Rules of unions vary as to contributions payable by the unemployed, some demanding full contributions while others permit reduced contributions. Some unions pay unemployment benefit to unemployed members. Rules also vary on the rights enjoyed by unemployed members, some allowing full rights, others only restricted rights.

In view of the complexity of the situation it is therefore impossible to generalize about unions' attitude to unemployed membership. Each union's position has to be looked at separately.

The TUC has encouraged the growth of Unemployed Workers' Centres under the aegis of the official trade union movement; in the autumn of 1981 these numbered over eighty in towns and cities most affected by unemployment. It is however opposed to unemployed workers being organized separately outside the existing structure of the trade union movement and has urged all affiliated unions to do all they can to retain and recruit more of the unemployed.

According to the TUC, the objects of Unemployed Workers' Centres should be to provide advice and information services for the unemployed and education courses including trade union education.

They should also be able to make representations on behalf of the unemployed locally. The trade union movement locally, including Trades Councils, as well as the local authorities and the Manpower Services Commission, may be involved in both setting up, funding and running the Centres.

**UNEMPLOYMENT BENEFIT**  *See* Social Security.

**UNFAIR DISMISSAL**  The law protects the worker against unfair dismissal. He has the right not to be dismissed unfairly and if he thinks he has been unfairly dismissed, the right to seek a remedy by complaining to an industrial tribunal within three months after the alleged unfair dismissal.

Provisions made under the Employment Protection (Consolidation) Act 1978, Sections 54–80 are:

*Who is eligible to make a claim?* People employed under a contract of employment can claim unfair dismissal. People who work for the House of Commons and for the Crown are also included. The unfair dismissal provisions do not apply to the following:

(a) Anyone who is not an employee, such as people who work under contracts for services (e.g. independent contracts or freelance agents)
(b) Members of the police service or armed forces
(c) Men over 65 and women over 60, or who have attained the normal retiring age for people employed in the business in their position
(d) Workers with less than 52 weeks continuous service or 104 weeks if the business has less than 20 employees
(e) People who normally work outside Great Britain
(f) Part-time employees who normally work less than 16 hours a week (except those who have worked for five years or more for more than 8 hours per week
(g) A person who works for her/his husband or wife
(h) Registered dock workers engaged on dock work
(i) Share fishermen who are paid solely by a share in the profits or gross earnings of a fishing vessel.

*What is 'Fair' and 'Unfair'?* Under the legislation there are a number of reasons for dismissal which are regarded as potentially 'fair'.

# Unfair Dismissal

These are dismissal on grounds:

(a) Of the capability or qualifications of the employee for the job for which he was employed. 'Capability' is assessed by reference to skill, aptitude, health, or any other physical or mental quality, and 'qualification' means any degree, diploma, or other academic, technical or professional qualification relevant to the position which the employee held.

(b) Of the conduct of the employee

(c) Of redundancy. Redundancy has the meaning which was given to it by the Redundancy Payments Act 1965, now repealed

(d) That continued employment of the employee in his position would result in either him or his employer contravening a duty or restriction imposed by law

(e) Of national security

(f) Of some other substantial reason which could justify the dismissal of the employee from that particular position.

*Onus of Proof – employer*: These categories are very wide, and the burden of proof rests on the employer; it is he who has to convince the Tribunal of the reasonableness of his decision.

The employer must also give a written reason for dismissal if the employee asks for one. If he fails to comply with an employee's request, this is also grounds for a complaint to a tribunal where an award of two weeks pay can be made.

*Onus of Proof – employee (Constructive Dismissal)*: The onus on the employee is that he must be able to satisfy the tribunal that he was dismissed directly (i.e. had his contract of employment terminated, with or without notice) or was subject to 'constructive dismissal' i.e. he terminated his own contract in circumstances where the employer's conduct justified such action. If, for example, an employer makes life for an employee so uncomfortable that the employee decides that he has no alternative but to leave the job, an industrial tribunal may judge that the employee was 'constructively dismissed' and make its decision on the case accordingly.

### 'Unfair' Dismissal

(a) *Dismissal for reasons associated with trade union membership or activity*: The Act provides that a dismissal shall be considered unfair if the main reason for it was that the employee:

302

(i) was a member of, or proposed to join, an independent trade union

(ii) had taken part, or proposed to take part at any appropriate time (outside work or during working hours at times agreed in advance with the employer) in the activities of an independent trade union

(iii) refused to belong to a non-independent trade union.

Anyone claiming dismissal under (i) and (ii) above is entitled to an especially speedy tribunal hearing and suspension on full pay until settlement of the case, if the union involved provides its support. The employee in question must appeal to a tribunal within seven days of being dismissed, and support this with a certificate from an official of the relevant union confirming that there are reasonable grounds for suspecting victimization. Unless the employer is agreeable to reinstating, or re-engaging the employee to the latter's or the tribunal's satisfaction, the tribunal must make an order for 'continuation of the employee's contract of employment' if it is satisfied that the employee would win his case at a full hearing. Under such an order, an employee gets full pay, preservation of seniority, pension rights etc. until the case is heard properly by a tribunal. Failure to comply with an order for suspension on full pay may result in the tribunal ordering the employer to compensate the employee for loss suffered through this non compliance and for infringement of the right to re-employment.

(b) *Dismissal in an undertaking covered by a union membership agreement (UMH)*: Where an employer has a union membership agreement with a particular union or unions (or such an agreement is recognized to be in existence) it is not normally unfair for the employer to dismiss an employee who is not a member of an appropriate specified union, or refuses to join, or threatens to resign, from one. Under the Act 'union membership agreement' refers to an agreement or arrangement between an employer and a particular independent trade union or unions which requires that all employees of a certain class (such as all employees who enter a particular occupation or work in a particular undertaking) belong to the union or unions who are parties to the agreement or to another specified independent trade union. This provision does not apply to employees who have genuine objections on grounds of conscience to belonging to any trade union; or in the case of UMAs coming into effect after 1/9/80 where there was not at least 80 per cent support in a secret ballot of those to be covered.

(c) *Unfair selection for redundancy*: While redundancy in itself is a potentially fair reason for dismissal, an employee dismissed for this reason may nevertheless complain of unfair dismissal if he considers that he has been unfairly selected for redundancy because of trade union membership or activities, because his employer has unreasonably disregarded the customary redundancy selection arrangements or agreed redundancy procedure in the undertaking, or for some other reason has selected him unfairly, or because the manner of his selection for redundancy was unfair (due for example, to inadequate warning of the redundancy or his employer's failure to consider the availability of suitable alternative employment within the same or an associated undertaking). This is an important issue because of the effect on payment due.

(d) *Dismissal in a strike or lock-out*: In cases of this kind tribunals shall not determine whether the employee was fairly or unfairly dismissed unless it it proved that:

(i) one or more relevant employees of the same employer have not been dismissed, or
(ii) one or more relevant employees have been offered re-engagement and that the employee concerned has not been offered re-engagement.

A 'relevant employee' is one of those employees who took part in the strike or other industrial action, or, in the case of a lock-out, those employees who were directly interested in the trade dispute which led to the lockout. If a tribunal find that either of the requirements set out in (a) or (b) is satisfied they will consider the employee's complaint in the normal way with the exception of a case where the employee has complained that he was not offered re-engagement although other relevant employees had received such an offer. In such a case the tribunal will consider what was the reason, or the principal reason, for the employee not being offered re-engagement rather than the reason, or principal reason, for his dismissal. Also in this type of case the time limit for making a complaint to an industrial tribunal will not begin with the employee's effective date of termination but the date on which the first offer of re-engagement was made to any of the other employees dismissed during the strike. (*See* Employment Bill 1982 for proposed changes.)

(e) *Dismissal on the grounds of colour, race, nationality or ethnic or national origins:* * Under the Race Relations Act 1976 it is unlawful to dismiss someone on the grounds of his colour, race, nationality or ethnic or national origins. The legislation covers both direct and indirect discrimination. Direct discrimination is where a person is treated less favourably than another would be treated in similar circumstances because of his colour, race, nationality, or ethnic or national origins. Indirect discrimination is where it is claimed that all people are treated equally, but the conditions applied are such that it is much more difficult for a person from an ethnic minority to comply with them than it would be for non-ethnic minority members to comply with them and which cannot be justified. Persons dismissed for racial reasons may claim unfair dismissal under the Employment Protection (Consolidation) Act, 1978 (provided they are under the 'normal retiring age', and are not 'part-time' workers within the meaning of the Employment Protection Act).

(f) *Dismissal on the Ground of Sex;* * It is unlawful to dismiss someone only because of their sex. This applies equally to men and women and all references to women below, apply equally to men. The legislation covers both direct and indirect discrimination. Direct discrimination is where a woman is treated less favourably than a man would be treated in similar circumstances because of her sex. Indirect discrimination is where it is claimed that both sexes are treated equally, but the conditions applied are such that it is much more difficult for one sex to comply with them than it would be for the opposite sex, and which cannot be justified. Also covered is discrimination by way of victimization where, for example, a woman is afforded less favourable treatment than a man, including dismissal because she has taken action under the Sex Discrimination or Equal Pay Acts or has

---

* Protection against dismissal on grounds of union membership, race or sex is given without any qualifying period of service.

alleged that an act has been committed in contravention of either of those two Acts. (But she is not protected if such allegation was wrong and was made frivolously, or if she has assisted some other person to pursue a claim).

(g) *Discrimination on the ground of marriage*: It is unlawful to dismiss someone only on the ground that a person is married unless the procedure is applied equally to both sexes. As for dismissal on the ground of sex, both direct or indirect discrimination and discrimination by way of victimization are covered by the legislation, if a married person is treated less favourably (including by dismissal) than a single person of the same sex would have been treated.

(h) *Dismissal on the grounds of pregnancy*: See Maternity – Pay and Employment Rights.

(i) *Dismissal without proper notice:* Every employee is entitled to a minimum of one week's notice after four weeks continuous employment up to two years and one week for each year of service after that up to a maximum of 12 weeks' notice for 12 years continuous service. The legislation provides that if these statutory requirements are not met, a complaint of wrongful dismissal can be made to an Industrial Tribunal. However, no definite date has yet been established for the implementation of this provision. At present, therefore, complaints that an employer has failed to give proper notice of dismissal should still be pursued through the County Courts (Sheriff Courts in Scotland) unless the complaint is part of an unfair dismissal claim.

(j) *Pressure on an employer to dismiss unfairly:* The legislation provides that a tribunal, in considering whether the main reason for the dismissal was fair and whether the employer was justified in the circumstances in dismissing the employee for that reason, must disregard any evidence that the employer was subjected to pressure to dismiss the employee by means of a strike or other industrial action. This is subject to the provisions of the Employment Act, 1980, on pressure to dismiss because of non-membership of a union.

*Remedies for dismissal:* Tribunals are entitled to make orders for re-employment rather than cash awards, which have become larger and more complicated. An employer, however, may still opt to pay increased compensation rather than comply with a re-employment order.

*Reinstatement or re-engagement:* The tribunal, finding an employee unfairly dismissed, must establish whether that employee wants to be reinstated or re-engaged, and order accordingly although this depends on whether it is practicable to do so. An order for reinstatement requires the employee's restoration to his old job. An order for re-engagement specifies the employee's return to a job comparable to the old one and at equally favourable pay and terms and conditions of employment, if this is reasonably practicable.

Any order for reinstatement or re-engagement of an employee must take into consideration the practicability of the employer complying with the order and whether it is just to make such an order if the employee contributed to some extent to his dismissal. Any such order will specify the sum payable to the employee in respect of arrears of pay and loss of other benefit due between dismissal and re-employment.

An employer who has taken on a permanent replacement for the employee dismissed cannot claim that it is impracticable to comply with a re-employment order, unless he can prove:

(a) that it was necessary to engage a permanent replacement to get the work done, or
(b) that, after a reasonable time, the sacked employee had not told the employer that he wanted reinstatement and it was no longer reasonable to get the work done except by employing a permanent replacement worker.

Failure to comply with a re-employment order will result in an additional award of compensation.

*Awards:* Financial awards for unfair dismissal consist of a basic award, related to the worker's period of service, and a compensatory award of an amount the tribunal considers 'just and equitable' according to the loss sustained by the worker.

*The basic award:* The basic award is reckoned on the same basis as redundancy compensation:

(a) $1\frac{1}{2}$ week's pay for each year of employment from the age of 41
(b) 1 week's pay for each year between the ages of 22 and 40.
(c) $\frac{1}{2}$ week's pay for each year between the ages of 18 and 22.

# Unfair Dismissal

Subject to annual review the maximum weekly earnings that can be taken into account is £135 in 1982 and the maximum number of years, 20 – hence an upper award limit of £4,050. Any compensation received for redundancy must be deducted from the basic award.

*The compensatory award:* The compensatory award may include:

(a) expenses reasonably incurred by the worker as a result of the dismissal (such as loss of pay)

(b) recompense for the loss of any benefit which might have accrued but for the dismissal (such as loss of promotion opportunity).

Subject to review by the Secretary of State for Employment, the maximum amount for a compensatory award is £7,000. Both types of award are subject to reduction if it is found that the employee involved contributed to his dismissal.

*Additional Awards:* Additional awards of compensation due from employers who fail to comply with re-employment orders (unless they show that compliance was not practicable) will amount to not less than 13 and not more than 26 weeks' pay with a maximum payment of £3510. In the case of dismissal for trade union reasons, or on the grounds of race or sex (under the Race Relations Act 1965 or the Sex Discrimination Act 1975), the additional award will be not less than 26 weeks' pay and not more than 52, subject to a maximum of £135 a week (1982) with a maximum payment of £7020.

*The Employment Bill, 1982,* proposes to introduce a minimum payment of £2,000 in the Basic Award in the case of employees unfairly dismissed either because of their trade union activities or membership, or because of their non-membership of a trade union in a closed shop.

Where reinstatement is sought but no order of reinstatement is made by a tribunal, the additional award would be replaced by a Special Award of 104 weeks pay subject to a £10,000 minimum and a £20,000 maximum. Where reinstatement is ordered by a tribunal and the order is complied with, compensation would make good any loss incurred between the dates of dismissal and reinstatement. Where reinstatement is ordered by the tribunal but the order is not complied with, the Special Award would be 156 weeks' pay with a minimum of £15,000 unless the reinstatement was not practicable, when it would be 104 weeks' pay subject to a minimum of £10,000 and a maximum of £20,000.

# Unified Vocational Preparation

These payments may be reduced even below 'minimum' level in certain cases where the tribunal considers the conduct of the employee in the situation justifies it. (*See* Employment Bill, 1982.)

*Taking a Complaint to an Industrial Tribunal:* Application forms and leaflet ITLI giving further information about the tribunals and their procedures may be obtained from any local office of the Department of Employment.

**UNIFIED VOCATIONAL PREPARATION (UVP)**  Launched by the Labour Government in 1976 for school-leavers, aged 16–19, to help them in the transition from school to work, UVP is a pilot scheme aimed at the semi-skilled and unskilled not in apprenticeships or undertaking Further Education courses which would normally lead to craft or technician level qualifications. It is thus a programme of training and education for those below craft level. Its aims, as set out in the initial government statement, are for this target group, to assist them:

(i) to assess their potential and think realistically about jobs and careers,
(ii) to develop the basic skills which will be needed in adult life generally,
(iii) to understand their society and how it works,
(iv) to strengthen the foundation of skill and knowledge on which further training and education can be built.

The scheme is centrally funded by the Manpower Services Commission (MSC) and the Department of Education and Science (DES) and Welsh Office, and is controlled by the InterDepartmental Group (IDG) of UVP on which the DES, Welsh Office, the MSC and the Department of Employment (DoE) were represented, although the DES has since been withdrawn from the direction and management of UVP schemes. Schemes are normally organized by Industrial Training Boards and Colleges of Further Education or voluntary organizations for young people in an industry or occupation. They can last as long as a year and combine specific job training at work with more general industrial training, e.g. in communications skills, personal education and careers counselling in college. Employers receive a payment per place provided.

Most schemes aim to integrate periods of on-and-off-the-job learn-

309

ing and they may include a residential period away from home and work. A Certificate of Attendance is awarded at the end of the courses, which cover quite a wide range of activities within industry and commerce. They have so far been taken by several thousand young workers; 3,500 passed through them in 1980–1. By 1984–5 the scheme is intended to cover 50,000 trainees. (*See* Industrial Training, White Paper.)

**UNILATERAL ACTION**   When action is taken by either party to an agreement, relating to matters involved in the agreement, without consultation with or consent from the other party, it is described as unilateral. It can refer, for example, to the breach of a Procedure Agreement. The term can also be used as a general description of independent action by either side in industry without discussion in advance with the other side.

**UNION MEMBERSHIP AGREEMENT (UMA)**   *See* Closed Shop.

**UNSOCIAL HOURS**   Trade unions, in arguing for special treatment of certain categories of workers, may make a case on the basis that the hours worked depart from the norm of day work in industry. Thus night working, weekend working or spreadover arrangements can be described as 'unsocial' and so merit extra pay for the consequent loss of social amenities or the creation of additional physical, mental or social stress.

# V

**VAT**   This was introduced in April 1973 to replace purchase tax, largely in order to make the British tax system similar to that of the EEC as part of the unification measures required of members of that body. It is an indirect tax (a tax levied on goods and services), as distinct from a direct tax (a tax levied on income). VAT is a tax on the value of goods and services supplied in the course of business. This is how it works:

All businesses over a specified turnover (currently £15,000 per annum) are required to register as taxable persons for VAT. Such businesses must then charge VAT to their customers. They are also entitled to claim back VAT charged to them on supplies of goods and services for their business. In this way, tax paid at every stage in the production and distribution of goods and services is claimed back and does not enter into the costs of businesses. Only the final unregistered consumer pays the revenue obtained by the Government.

Tax returns are made quarterly or in some cases monthly. The tax is administered by a central tax gathering and return processing authority (VAT Central Unit) and local inspection authorities (Local VAT Offices). About 8000 people are employed in administration and the costs of collection are less than 2p in the pound. VAT is now the major source of Government revenue next to income tax.

Currently all supplies of goods and services are dropped into the following VAT categories.

1 *Standard rated* i.e. subject to VAT at 15 per cent.
2 *Zero rated* i.e. subject to VAT in principle but excused by the Exchequer in practice, e.g. food, excluding catering.
3 *Exempt* i.e. specifically excluded by the Finance Act from the operation of VAT, e.g. rents, insurance.
4 *Outside the scope* i.e. usually non-business supplies, such as television licences etc.

**VICTIMIZATION** Dismissal or denial of promotion are two types of action used by employers in retaliation against employees trying to organize for a trade union or to develop opposition to the employer's policy. The word 'victimization' is used to describe such circumstances but victimization can take many forms and is often difficult to prove, for example the transfer of workers to a less favourable job, denial of promotion, unfair dismissal, harassment, etc. Union representatives are expected to be alert in helping members to combat victimization or discrimination.

In the anti-discrimination legislation (Race Relations Act and Sex Discrimination Act) it is suggested that discrimination might occur in the following circumstances:

1 in recruitment
2 in the terms and conditions of employment
3 on transfer and promotion
4 in training
5 in the provision of benefits, facilities and services
6 in dismissals
7 by means of other detrimental activity.

# W

**WAGES SALARIES**     The payment received from employment. The popular distinction between wages and salaries is that the former is the payment to manual workers, usually weekly, while salaries are paid to staff employees monthly. The distinction is lessening as many manual workers go over to salaries (or staff) conditions of employment and the wage or salary is paid into bank accounts; only about half British workers are still paid in cash.

The wage or salary is usually a fixed amount for a period and does not include overtime earnings and other additions and perks of various kinds.

In general, wages or salaries are negotiated and are covered by a collective agreement between the employer and a trade union or unions. (*See* Bonus, Differentials.)

**WAGE CLAIM, SALARY CLAIM**     The demands, or series or package of demands put forward by a union for negotiation with an employer is commonly called the claim. The claim may cover matters other than wages or salaries, e.g. improved hours or conditions of service but is still colloquially referred to as the wage or salary claim.

**WAGES COUNCILS**     Wages Councils grew out of the old Trade Boards which were set up under the Trade Boards Act of 1909 which resulted from the campaign against sweated labour. Initially the powers of the Trade Boards were limited to fixing minimum time rates or piece rates of wages which could be statutorily enforced.

The 1945 Wages Councils Act gave the Trade Boards a new name 'Wages Councils' and broadened their powers. Their responsibility was to 'fix statutory remuneration' either generally or for any particular work and the provision of holidays. The Wages Councils were also required to make reports about their industry when requested by the Government, and were given powers themselves to initiate recommendations to the Government.

The current legislation on wages councils is contained in the Wages Councils Act 1979. This enables the Secretary of State for Employment to establish a Wages Council, either on his own initiative or following an ACAS recommendation. If an application is made for a Wages Council by trade unions or employers' organizations, the Secretary of State for Employment must refer the question to ACAS which may make a recommendation. Similarly, if a Wages Council is to be abolished the Secretary of State may act on his own initiative or following an application from trade unions, employers' organizations or joint bodies. An application for abolition must be on the grounds that a Wages Council is no longer necessary to maintain a reasonable standard of remuneration for the workers concerned.

Wages Councils are serviced by the Office of Wages Councils at the Department of Employment. There are over 30 in existence and they are mainly in the retailing, hotel and catering and clothing industries.

A Wages Council consists of equal numbers of members representing employers and workers, together with a chairman and two other independent persons unconnected with either side of the industry concerned.

Normally the workers' side submits a proposal and after discussion either mutual agreement is reached or a vote is taken and the majority decides. The motion is then passed to the Secretary of State who publicizes the proposals, allowing for objections within a stipulated period. After considering representations, the Wages Council makes an order giving legal effect to the proposals (as amended, if necessary). Employers may be prosecuted for failing to apply Wages Councils Orders. Wages Council inspectors aid enforcement.

In spite of the low minimum wages laid down (in 1981 ranging from £39 to £57 a week), inspectors' reports in 1980 showed that over 35 per cent of the firms visited were paying less than the legally required minimum. It is estimated that a loss of some £25 million occurs to the workers concerned in this way. There has been strong criticism in Parliament of the Government's failure to prosecute offending employers as well as of the low fines imposed, and the demand has been made for automatic prosecution for infractions of the law. (*See* Low Paid.)

## WAGES COUNCILS AT 31 DECEMBER 1979 (GREAT BRITAIN, ENGLAND AND WALES, SCOTLAND):

Aerated Waters (England and Wales)
Aerated Waters (Scotland)
Boot and Shoe Repairing (Great Britain)
Button Manufacturing (Great Britain)
Coffin Furniture and Cerement Making (Great Britain)
*Corset

Cotton Waste Reclamation (Great Britain)
*Dressmaking and Women's Light Clothing (England and Wales)
*Dressmaking and Women's Light Clothing (Scotland)
Flax and Hemp (Great Britain)
Fur (Great Britain)
General Waste Materials Reclamation (Great Britain)
Hairdressing Undertakings (Great Britain)
Hat, Cap and Millinery (Great Britain)
Lace Finishing (Great Britain)
Laundry (Great Britain)
Licensed Non-residential Establishment
Licensed Residential Establishment and Licensed Restaurant
Linen and Cotton Handkerchief and Household Goods and Linen
    Piece Goods (Great Britain)
Made-up Textiles (Great Britain)
Ostrich and Fancy Feather and Artificial Flower (Great Britain)
Perambulator and Invalid Carriage (Great Britain)
Pin, Hook and Eye, and Snap Fastener (Great Britain)
*Ready-made and Wholesale Bespoke Tailoring (Great Britain)
Retail Bespoke Tailoring (Great Britain)
Retail Food and Allied Trades (Great Britain)
Retail Trades (Non-Food) (Great Britain)
Rope, Twine and Net (Great Britain)
*Rubber Proofed Garment Making Industry
Sack and Bag (Great Britain)
*Shirtmaking (Great Britain)
Toy Manufacturing (Great Britain)
Unlicensed Place of Refreshment
*Wholesale Mantle and Costume (Great Britain)

* These have been replaced, 1982, by the Clothing Manufacture Wages Council

**WAGE DRIFT** A phrase mainly used by the economists in the 1950s and 1960s to describe the tendency for workers' earnings to rise faster than the movement of the nationally agreed minimum rates. The widening gap between 'rates' and 'earnings' was due partly to unrealistic basic wages and workers' pressure for higher earnings. The term is now less frequently used as a result of the greater recognition of local bargaining and more comprehensive agreements, together with the negotiation (in most industries) of more realistic basic wages. Redesignation and changing of jobs and promotions are also faster in wage drift.

**WAITING DAYS**    Under the National Insurance scheme, Sickness Benefit and Unemployment Benefit is not paid for the first three days of sickness involving absence from work (Sunday is not counted) or for the first three days of unemployment. An absence of three days or less does not necessarily mean that the worker will not be paid for that time as industry, local or plant agreements may allow for such absences to be paid. Staff, as distinct from manual workers, may be more favourably treated. Non manual employees in the public service are normally paid. (*See* Social Security.)

**WEALTH TAX**    A tax on substantial wealth advocated from time to time by the Labour Party. In 1977 a working party set up by the TUC–Labour Party Liaison Committee recommended that there should be a threshold of £100,000 at which point the tax would be 1 per cent and rise to 5 per cent on fortunes of over £5 million. Relief for owners of productive assets such as farms and small businesses was to have been given along the lines of the capital transfer tax. The tax unit would have been the family. It was estimated that the total yield of the tax at that time would have been up to £550 million per year. (*See* Taxation.)

**WELFARE MILK AND FOOD**    *See* Social Security.

**WELFARE STATE**    The term Welfare State is used for the system of welfare provision established in Britain after the Second World War. It followed the general lines put forward in the Beveridge Report published in 1942. The Beveridge Plan's aim was to provide a system of benefits to cover the main primary causes of need: unemployment, illness or accident, loss of livelihood, old age, marriage needs of a woman (e.g. maternity, widowhood etc.), childhood, physical disease or incapacity, and death (funeral expenses). The finance was to be provided by a system of national insurance payments by employees, employers and the self-employed, supplemented by an element of central government funds.

It was assumed however that the plan could not be satisfactorily operated unless there was also a system of children's allowances, a comprehensive health service available to all, and the avoidance of mass unemployment. A measure of National Assistance based on a means test would still be necessary to cover gaps in the scheme but the scope of such Assistance would be relatively small.

Completing the concept of the Welfare State was the provision of free education and subsidized housing and rent control.

Throughout the post-war years a system of social security on Beveridge lines has operated. But it has always been marked by serious gaps and was subject from the early 1950s to serious erosions. Thus the level and scope of benefits has never been adequate and has had to be supplemented by Assistance (now e.g. in the form of Supplementary Benefit and Family Income Supplement, for millions of people, which are means tested). An originally free National Health Service is no longer universally free in important respects (e.g. prescription charges, optical and dental treatment). Very little was provided for masses of young people in education or training immediately after the school-leaving age, and higher education, never entirely free, has remained largely a middle class preserve. Family Allowances (now Child Benefits) were never adequate. Another criticism has been that the better off benefit proportionally more than those in need from expenditure on, e.g. health, education and housing.

Nevertheless the benefits available are very substantial, compared with pre-war provision, in protecting people from the effects of unemployment, sickness, old age and other causes of need. And a new element has been added in the complex of protective labour legislation introduced by the Labour Government of 1974-9.

Recent and continuing cuts in public expenditure have seriously affected the health and education services, housing aid has been drastically curtailed and new legislation has made inroads into the system of social security benefits. Defence of the Welfare State has therefore become a major issue for the trade union movement in its defence of living standards, especially under the present Government. Welfare and allied services are rightly regarded by the trade union movement as a 'social wage', an essential supplement to earnings and a necessary means of preventing the worst effects of poverty. (*See* Social Security, Social Wage.)

**WHITE COLLAR WORKERS**   A description popularly given to non manual workers, usually clerical and administrative staff as distinct from manual workers.

**WHITE PAPER**   *See* Blue Book.

**WHITLEY COUNCILS, WHITLEYISM**  In popular usage the name Whitley is associated today with the system of organising industrial relations in the Civil Service and Local Government, two very large and important fields of employment. Its significance is nevertheless wider than that and goes back to the First World War when the Government appointed a Committee under Mr J. H. Whitley, MP:

(a) to make and consider suggestions for securing a permanent improvement in the relations between employers and workmen and

(b) to recommend means for securing that industrial relations between employers and workmen shall be systematically reviewed by those concerned with a view to improving conditions in the future.

A series of reports were produced which had a major influence on the structure of industrial relations, throughout large areas of industry, which remains to this day. Whitley recommended the formation in well organized industries of Joint Industrial Councils at national level, to agree the principles governing conditions of service including recruitment, promotion, working hours, wages, etc. Below the national council there should be district committees and works committees representing workers and management to agree on the local application of these principles.

Further recommendations included the statutory regulation of wages in badly organized industries, the setting up of a permanent Court of Arbitration and giving power to the Minister of Labour (now Secretary of State for Employment) to hold enquiries into disputes.

The essence of Whitleyism is joint consultation between management and workers through their representative organizations, with the aim of reaching agreement over a wide range of issues arising between employers and employees and so preventing industrial disputes whether at national, district or local level.

This has not in fact been successfully achieved.

A detailed description is given elsewhere of Whitleyism as applied for the non-manual workers in the Civil Service and local government. Similar provision, however, based on the same general principles, exists for the manual workers in the numerous manual workers' negotiating bodies in the public services, e.g. in government and local government employment, in Joint Industrial Councils etc. The same goes for non-manual employees, e.g. in the NHS, the gas, electricity, water and air transport industries.

**WIDOWS' ALLOWANCES**   *See* Social Security.

**WITHOUT PREJUDICE OFFER**   In an attempt to achieve a settlement, management may sometimes in negotiation make an offer higher than before provided that, if the offer is rejected, it cannot be used as evidence in any arbitration procedure that may follow. Such offers are made 'without prejudice' and are a not uncommon feature of negotiations in certain parts of the public sector. Sometimes the 'without prejudice' offer may be made after consultation by both sides with the independent chairman of a negotiating body in an attempt to prevent breakdown. If the offer is rejected, arbitration (if it exists under the relevant procedures) does not necessarily follow; negotiations may resume at the point they had reached before the offer.

**WOMEN, YOUNG PERSONS AND CHILDREN, EMPLOYMENT**   Certain restrictions controlling working conditions for women, young persons and children were laid down in a 1920 Act, subsequently added to. Children are defined as those not over the school-leaving age, which is currently 16, and young persons as those who have ceased to be children and who are under 18. The restrictions apply to industrial establishments and totally prohibit the employment of children, and the employment of young people at night with some exceptions which were specified in the 1961 Factory Act. Women, too, may not as a general rule be employed on night work. Here again there are certain limited exceptions and women employed in responsible managerial positions, for example, are exempted.

Night is defined as 'During a period of at least eleven consecutive hours, including the interval between 10 p.m. and 5 a.m.'. The TUC wants the definition of night to be extended to cover the period between 6 p.m. and 8 a.m.

Specific restrictions in employment also apply in certain industries and occupations under various statutory regulations. (*See* Health and Safety, Juvenile Employment.)

**WORK EXPERIENCE**   With the onset of large-scale unemployment, the Manpower Services Commission has developed a large number of schemes for the young unemployed to work for arranged periods in industry or commerce. Such schemes are known as WEEP, that is Work Experience on Employers' Premises.

For many years, schemes have been operating in schools whereby pupils, normally in their last year of compulsory education, are given a taste of work in an industrial or commercial establishment for a certain time each week over an arranged period. This work experience is judged to be helpful in the transition from school to work. Arrangements are carefully controlled, normally in consultation with the trade unions concerned, to ensure that advantage is not taken of the pupil-workers to the disadvantage both of himself and the worker in the firm. (*See* YOP.)

**WORK PERMIT**   Certain categories of entrants to this country from abroad are not permitted to take up paid work without a permit granted, on application, by the Department of Employment. Such categories include for example all non EEC citizens apart from Commonwealth citizens with certain exceptions. Some occupations are excluded from the need to obtain a permit, e.g. doctors and ministers of religion. The regulations are complex and employers and prospective workers in cases of doubt should seek information from the Department of Employment.

**WORK STUDY**   This can be divided into two parts; method study and work measurement.

Trade unions, although their criteria as to what is best may be different from that of management, have little quarrel with method study which is designed to ensure that all available resources are planned to the best possible advantage. However, it is in the use of work measurement or time and motion study that differences between Trade Union and management tend to exist.

Time study is a management technique designed to determine the time to be taken to perform a particular task. Normally a stop watch is used to time the individual elements in the study. But this is related to an 'effort rating' which is an estimate made by the 'rate-fixer' of the effort made by the operators being studied.

This, of course, makes nonsense of the claim that time study is scientific. First a scientific instrument, a watch, is used to make an objective assessment of the time taken, then this is qualified by a subjective estimate from the time study engineer.

Frequently when time study is introduced into an establishment for the first time, demands are made for the union concerned to train work study experts to combat the arguments of the employer's time study experts. This can then be taken to the point where, if the employer's expert cannot agree with the trade union expert, a third time study expert is brought in to arbitrate.

This approach is completely to misunderstand the role of the trade union.

Time study is a management technique designed to provide management with an accurate estimate of time taken. This provides the basis for an offer to be made.

Trade union policy is to reach mutual agreement on a time that is fair and takes into account human considerations as well as mechanical factors. (*see* Job Evaluation.)

**WORK TO RULE** 'Working to rule' is a traditional form of industrial action which can cause considerable dislocation and hold-ups in production and servicing. It means keeping strictly to laid down rules or instructions issued by management (e.g. safety rules) or written job descriptions. While workers using such sanctions cannot be accused of a breach of contract their actions can cause chaos. Industries such as electricity supply, railways and emergency services generally have proved particularly vulnerable.

**WORKERS' CONTROL** 'Workers Control' has been advanced over many years by the trade union and socialist movements as an alternative to unilateral control of decision-making in industry by the employers' side. 'Workers' in this sense means all levels of employees. In practical terms it has been attempted perhaps more in Yugoslavia than in any other country. There it takes the form of 'Workers' Self-Management'. The method adopted allows the election of the Management Board from amongst the workpeople (working closely with the Yugoslav trade unions) who in turn appoint the senior management. The whole system has built-in links with the Government and Government industrial policy so that it is distinguished from syndicalism.

The concept of industrial democracy, as advocated by some trade unionists in Britain, is to ensure a substantial measure of worker influence in industrial decision-making by the extension of worker control over practical matters on the shop floor through extended collective bargaining. Examples of such developments in 'workers control' include: the operation of safety representatives, controls over the operation of overtime, negotiating rights on speed of work

# World Federation of Trade Unions

and manning, discipline and the application of the 'status quo' when management proposes changes in working arrangements. Additionally, a section of trade union opinion seeks representation on Boards of Directors. (*See* Industrial Democracy.)

**WORKMEN'S COMPENSATION**    *See* Industrial Injuries Payments.

**WORKS COMMITTEES**    Works Committees or Works Councils in some industries and companies are joint bodies of worker representatives and management, whose purposes may be purely advisory or may cover both negotiating and advisory functions.

In the engineering industry for many years there have been *official* works committees set up by voluntary agreement between the parties and consisting of not more than seven members from each side. They have a specific role under the local procedure. Generally, trade union opinion in this industry, however, favours separate *ad hoc* arrangements and therefore the number of 'official' works committees are few.

The term 'works committee' is also used in some undertakings to describe the joint committee of shop stewards covering most or all of the trade unions in the works concerned.

**WORLD CONFEDERATION OF LABOUR (WCL)**    An international trade union organization based in Brussels. Its affiliates comprise unions with a religious outlook and it is particularly strong in South America. In the past it was occasionally referred to as the 'Christian International'. It has its roots in the old International Federation of Christian Trade Unions, which condemned any liberal, socialist or communist regime and favoured the systematic collaboration of all classes. To-day it has moved somewhat to the left and while maintaining its independent position it has occasional dialogue with both the ICFTU and the WFTU.

**WORLD FEDERATION OF TRADE UNIONS (WFTU)**    Based in Prague, the WFTU is a numerically strong grouping of trade union confederations mainly from communist-led countries. When formed in 1945 the World Federation of Trade Unions was a world wide body, including the TUC, the CIO of America (the AFL remained outside) and other powerful Western trade union centres. Due to political divisions a break-up in the organization occurred and the Western affiliates withdrew and set up the ICFTU.

# Wrongful Dismissal

**WRONGFUL DISMISSAL**   Wrongful dismissal is based on the common law of contract e.g. dismissal without notice, 'summary dismissal' – or in breach of the notice provided in the terms of contract or under the Contracts of Employment Act. The right of claim is to the Courts but it is infrequently used because of the generally wider protection given by the legislation on 'unfair dismissals'. (*See* Unfair Dismissal.)

# Y

**YOUTH OPPORTUNITIES PROGRAMME (YOP)**   The YOP is the responsibility of the Special Services Division of the Manpower Services Commission (MSC). It aims to provide opportunities for training in skills relevant to employment, work (work preparation), work experience to allow the practice of skills in the context of real employment, further education and counselling (vocational advice by responsible people) for young unemployed people aged 16–18, to help them to improve their prospects of finding permanent jobs. It includes a wide variety of schemes ranging in length from two weeks to one year and which allow switching from one scheme to another. This is a major effort; in July 1981 the programme was extended to aim at providing 550,000 places in 1981–2 because of the massive growth in unemployment and the concern this aroused.

The programme is run locally by Area Boards which plan and approve schemes. The Boards represent trade unions, employers, local authorities, the Further Education Service and the Careers Service. Originally intended to cater for school-leavers, it was extended to all unemployed 16- and 17-year olds. The aim was to make it possible for young people leaving school in the Easter and summer of 1981 to have a place in the programme by the end of the year. Any young person still unemployed three months after 'signing on' was to be offered a place on a youth training, work preparation, work experience or other course within the following three months. The programme is ongoing for 1983.

There are basically two types of scheme; work preparation and work experience.

Work Preparation (and youth training) courses include a range of courses devised to help prepare young people for working life and are normally carried on with the co-operation of the education and careers service. They are designed to help young people decide which sort of job suits them best and then train in a range of skills from the most basic up to semi-skilled and operative levels. They should, but often do not, provide 'off-the-job' opportunities in Further Education. They include work introduction courses, short training courses, higher level schemes and employment induction courses.

Work Experience schemes are of four different kinds: (1) Work Experience on Employers' Premises (WEEP) – about two-thirds of the YOP in 1981 – which are schemes within industrial and commercial establishments, are intended to give experience of a real working environment, and are run by a Responsible Officer on behalf of the MSC. (2) Training Workshops, which are set up with MSC approval and financial support, e.g. by a local authority or a responsible voluntary body. (3) Work Experience on Community Projects, which gives groups of young people a chance to acquire training in basic skills. (4) Community Service (a form of Community Project) schemes, giving young people an opportunity to try responsible work in the social services and voluntary organizations serving individuals and the community.

YOP schemes have come under considerable criticism from the trade union movement and outside, in many cases for their quality, (criticisms accepted by the MSC) and strong arguments have been advanced for providing at least a year's programme of vocational preparation. In 1981 some two-thirds of YOP schemes lacked a proper education and training element. Employers have been accused of using the schemes as cheap labour for job substitution – replacing adult workers. Weight is lent to this criticism by the fact that payment for what may be a full week's work (payment being by the MSC, not the employer) is in 1982 £25, quite inadequate sum, which the Government refused to increase. In some cases young people would be better off drawing supplementary benefit while staying at home.

Perhaps an even graver criticism is that, in view of the current unemployment situation, YOP schemes are in fact largely 'dead end'. In early 1981 little more than a third of those completing schemes were getting jobs immediately and not many more five months later.

The 1981 TUC voiced its anxiety at the way the YOP has been developing. The TUC wants WEEP schemes to take place only with union agreement, and union representation for YOP trainees, investigation of employers' abuses of the scheme (e.g. job substitution) and their elimination, and adequate resources for MSC to monitor schemes to prevent abuses. If these measures are not satisfactorily implemented, WEEP schemes will be opposed and trade union co-operation withdrawn.

In a special additional programme for young unemployed, parallel to YOP, the Government announced (July 1981) more funds for long-term training in skills in 1981–3. Thirty Information Technology Centres in Inner Cities, to aid young unemployed training for computer programming, electronics and related skills, are being set up in 1982. In December 1981, the Government produced a White Paper on Industrial Training for young people, to operate from September 1983, to cost £1 billion in a full year, and to build up the experience of YOP and the UVP programme. (*See* Industrial Training: White Paper 1982–5.)

# Z

**ZERO RATING** *See* VAT.

# Appendix 1
# Trade unions at 31 December 1979

(Information from *ACAS Industrial Relations Handbook 1980*)

The list of trade unions is that maintained by the Certification Officer for Trade Unions and Employers' Associations. Membership figures are the latest available; this is normally 31 December 1978. Some figures include classes of members who may not pay contributions but who are members under the rules.

* —denotes a trade union holding a certificate of independence at 31 December 1979
† —denotes a trade union directly affiliated to the Trades Union Congress (branches areas and districts of these unions are not so indicated)
n.a.—membership figures not available or not applicable.

| Name | Membership |
|---|---|
| *England and Wales* | |
| *Abbey National Staff Association | 4463 |
| Accrington and District Power Loom Overlookers Association | 17 |
| Alumasc Employees Association | 137 |
| †*Amalgamated Association of Beamers Twisters and Drawers (Hand and Machine) | 1123 |
| Amalgamated Association of Beamers Twisters and Drawers (Hand and Machine) Preston and District Branch | 204 |
| †*Amalgamated Felt Hat Trimmers Wool Formers and Allied Workers Association | 623 |
| †*Amalgamated Society of Boilermakers Shipwrights Blacksmiths and Structural Workers | 131 099 |
| †*Amalgamated Society of Journeymen Felt Hatters and Allied Workers | 563 |
| †*Amalgamated Society of Textile Workers and Kindred Trades | 5959 |

# Appendix 1

†*Amalgamated Society of Wire Drawers and
    Kindred Workers                                      10784
  *Amalgamated Society of Woolcomb Hackle and Gill
    Makers                                                  76
  Amalgamated Tape Sizers Friendly Protection
    Society                                                 35
  Amalgamated Textile Trades Union Wigan Chorley
    and Skelmersdale District                             1200
  *Amalgamated Textile Warehousemen                       2800
  *Amalgamated Textile Warehousemen (Bolton and
    District Branch)                                      1251
†*Amalgamated Textile Workers Union                     39 864
  *Amalgamated Textile Workers Union—Oldham
    AWA Division                                          1900
  *Amalgamated Textile Workers Union Rochdale
    Todmorden Heywood Bury                                3620
  *Amalgamated Textile Workers Union (Southern
    Area)                                                 1858
  *Amalgamated Textile Workers Union—Staff
    Section                                               1298
†*Amalgamated Union of Asphalt Workers                   2492
  Amalgamated Union of Block Printers of Great
    Britain and Ireland                                     14
†Amalgamated Union of Engineering Workers               n.a.
†*Amalgamated Union of Engineering Workers
    (Constructional Section)                            35 235
†*Amalgamated Union of Engineering Workers
    —Engineering Section                              1 199 465
†*Amalgamated Union of Engineering Workers
    Foundry Section                                     58 728
†*Amalgamated Union of Engineering Workers
    Technical Administrative and Supervisory
    Section                                            200 954
  A Monk and Company Staff Association                    793
  *Anglia Hastings and Thanet Building Society Staff
    Association                                            877
  Arts Council of Great Britain Staff Association         172
  *Assistant Masters and Mistresses Association         n.a.
†*Associated Metalworkers Union                          5262
†*Associated Society of Locomotive Engineers and
    Firemen                                             27 738

# Appendix 1

# Appendix 1

| | |
|---|---|
| *Association of Public Service Finance Officers | 2997 |
| *Association of Public Service Professional Engineers | 2017 |
| †*Association of Scientific Technical and Managerial Staffs | 471 000 |
| Association of Somerset Inseminators | 32 |
| Association of Staff of Probation Hostels | n.a. |
| †*Association of University Teachers | 29 248 |
| Association of Vice Principals of Colleges | 124 |
| Australian Mutual Provident Society Staff Association | 157 |
| | |
| †*Bakers Food and Allied Workers Union | 54 912 |
| Balfour Beatty Group Staff Association | 1790 |
| †*Banking Insurance and Finance Union | 126 343 |
| *Bank of England Staff Organisation | 4715 |
| Bank of New Zealand (London) Staff Association | 172 |
| *Barclays Group Staff Association | 35 517 |
| Beamers Twisters and Drawers Hand and Machine of Blackburn and Bolton Districts | 270 |
| Birmingham and District Association of Club Stewards and Hotel Managers | 74 |
| *Blackburn and District Amalgamated Power Loom Overlookers Association | 400 |
| Blackburn and District Tape-Sizers Society | 49 |
| *Blackburn and District Weavers Winders and Warpers Association | 1750 |
| *Bolton and District Powerloom Overlookers Trade Sick and Burial Association | 269 |
| *Bolton and District Power Loom Weavers Winders Warpers Loom Sweepers and Ancillary Workers Association | 2005 |
| *Bolton and District Union of Textile and Allied Workers | 5045 |
| *Bradford and Bingley Building Society Staff Association | 893 |
| Bradford and District Power Loom Overlookers Society | 649 |
| Britannia Airways Staff Association | n.a. |
| Britannic Assurance Chief Office Staff Association | 587 |
| *Britainnic Field Staff Association | 3305 |

# Appendix 1

# Appendix 1

# Appendix 1

# Appendix 1

# Appendix 1

| | |
|---|---:|
| *Institute of Journalists | 2249 |
| †*Institution of Professional Civil Servants | 99 051 |
| Inter Employees Association | 58 |
| †*Iron and Steel Trades Confederation | 113 432 |
| Jeyes Representatives Association | 80 |
| Johnson Matthey Chemicals Royston Staff Society | 70 |
| Johnson Matthey Headquarters Staff Society | 234 |
| Joint Boots Pharmacists Association | 1026 |
| Joint Industry Board for the Electrical Contracting Industry | n.a. |
| Jones and Shipman Administrative Staff Association | 210 |
| | |
| KDG Industries Staff Association | 110 |
| Kosset Staff Association | 298 |
| | |
| *Lancashire Box Packing Case and General Woodworkers Friendly Relief Sick Superannuation and Burial Society | 642 |
| Leeds and District Power Loom Overlookers Society | 145 |
| *Leek and Westbourne Staff Association | 981 |
| *Legal and General Staff Association | 430 |
| *Leicester Building Society Staff Association | 1000 |
| Leicestershire Overmen Deputies and Shotfirers Association | 414 |
| Leisure and General Holdings Staff Association | 75 |
| *Liverpool Victoria Section of the National Union of Insurance Workers | 3114 |
| *Lloyds Bank Group Staff Association | 21 247 |
| Lloyds Register (UK) Staff Association | 1192 |
| Lloyds Staff Association | 23 |
| London Jewel Case and Jewellery Display Makers Union | 17 |
| *London Society of Tie Cutters | 59 |
| *Lufthansa Staff Association United Kingdom | 177 |
| | |
| Managerial Staff Association of the Provincial Insurance Group of Companies | 104 |
| Manchester Pilots Association | 73 |

333

# Appendix 1

| | |
|---|---:|
| Manchester Salford and District Society of Brewers and General Coopers | 55 |
| †*Merchant Navy and Airline Officers Association | 43 750 |
| †*Military and Orchestral Musical Instrument Makers Trade Society | 220 |
| National Amalgamated Stevedores and Dockers | 3722 |
| †*National and Local Government Officers Association | 729 405 |
| National Association of Chief Housing Officers | 95 |
| †*National Association of Colliery Overmen Deputies and Shotfirers | 19 571 |
| National Association of Colliery Overmen Deputies and Shotfirers (Cannock Chase Area) | 499 |
| National Association of Colliery Overmen Deputies and Shotfirers (Durham Area) | 1810 |
| National Association of Colliery Overmen Deputies and Shotfirers (Midland Area) | 4122 |
| National Association of Colliery Overmen Deputies and Shotfirers (North Staffordshire Area) | 840 |
| National Association of Colliery Overmen Deputies and Shotfirers (Northumberland Area) | 830 |
| National Association of Colliery Overmen Deputies and Shotfirers (North Western Area) | 947 |
| National Association of Colliery Overmen Deputies and Shotfirers (South Wales Area) | 2026 |
| National Association of Colliery Overmen Deputies and Shotfirers (Yorkshire Area) | 8187 |
| †*National Association of Co-operative Officials | 5920 |
| *National Association of Executives Managers and Staffs | 1317 |
| *National Association of Fire Officers | 3924 |
| National Association of Grooms | n.a. |
| *National Association of Head Teachers | 22 330 |
| National Association of Heads and Matrons of Assessment Centres | 108 |
| *National Association of Inspectors and Educational Advisers | 1262 |
| †*National Association of Licensed House Managers | 15 486 |
| *National Association of NFU Group Secretaries | 437 |

# Appendix 1

| | |
|---|---:|
| *National Union of Insurance Workers Royal Liver and Composite Section | 1355 |
| *National Union of Insurance Workers Royal London Section | 2422 |
| †*National Union of Journalists | 30 978 |
| †*National Union of Lock and Metal Workers | 6508 |
| †*National Union of Mineworkers | 371 470 |
| National Union of Mineworkers (Cannock Chase and Pelsall District Midland Area) | 4427 |
| National Union of Mineworkers (Cokemens Area) | 7214 |
| *National Union of Mineworkers (Colliery Officials and Staffs Area) | 20 978 |
| National Union of Mineworkers (Colliery Officials and Staffs Area) Region No. 2 | 4617 |
| National Union of Mineworkers (Colliery Officials and Staffs Area) Region No. 3 | 2230 |
| National Union of Mineworkers (Colliery Officials and Staffs Area) Region No. 4 | 4943 |
| National Union of Mineworkers (Cumberland Area) | 2212 |
| National Union of Mineworkers (Derbyshire Area) | 11 590 |
| National Union of Mineworkers (Durham Area) | 42 965 |
| National Union of Mineworkers (Durham Enginemen Group No. 1 Area) | 826 |
| National Union of Mineworkers (Durham Mechanics Group No. 1 Area) | 6503 |
| National Union of Mineworkers (Kent Area) | 4107 |
| *National Union of Mineworkers (Leicester Area) | 6179 |
| National Union of Mineworkers (Midland Area) | 14 735 |
| National Union of Mineworkers (North Stafford Federation Midland Area) | 5954 |
| National Union of Mineworkers (Northumberland Area) | 17 695 |
| *National Union of Mineworkers (Northumberland Mechanics Group No. 1 Area) | 2800 |
| National Union of Mineworkers (North Wales Area) | 1077 |
| *National Union of Mineworkers (North Western Area) | 8991 |
| National Union of Mineworkers (North Western Area) Pendlebury Branch | 750 |
| *National Union of Mineworkers (Nottingham Area) | 33 580 |

# Appendix 1

National Association of Power-Loom Overlookers   410
*National Association of Probation Officers   4763
†*National Association of Schoolmasters and the
    Union of Women Teachers   140 701
†*National Association of Teachers in Further and
    Higher Education   69 450
†*National Association of Theatrical Television and
    Kine Employees   17 000
*National Association of Unions in the Textile Trade   n.a.
National Federation of Sub-Postmasters   19 649
†*National Graphical Association **   109 904
†*National League of the Blind and Disabled   4250
*National Owner Drivers Association UK   1119
†*National Society of Brushmakers and General
    Workers   1637
†*National Society of Metal Mechanics   50 494
†*National Society of Operative Printers Graphical
    and Media Personnel**   54 786
*National Tile Faience and Mosaic Fixers Society   247
National Unilever Managers Association   3656
†*National Union of Agricultural and Allied Workers **   73 574
†*National Union of Blastfurnacemen Ore Miners
    Coke Workers and Kindred Trades   14 366
*National Union of Club Stewards   2800
National Union of Co-operative Insurance Agents   24
*National Union of Co-operative Insurance Society
    Employees   2863
†*National Union of Domestic Appliance and General
    Metal Workers   5155
†*National Union of Dyers Bleachers and Textile
    Workers **   58 803
*National Union of Flint Glassworkers   2208
†*National Union of General and Municipal Workers   964 836
†*National Union of Gold Silver and Allied Trades   3094
National Union of Hebrew Teachers of Great
    Britain and Ireland   173
†*National Union of Hosiery and Knitwear Workers   72 858
†*National Union of Insurance Workers   20 131
*National Union of Insurance Workers Prudential
    Section   13 212

# Appendix 1

*National Union of Mineworkers (Power Group
    Area)     5000
*National Union of Mineworkers (South Derbyshire
    Area)     5080
National Union of Mineworkers (South Wales Area)     32 086
National Union of Mineworkers (Warwickshire
    District Midlands Area)     5041
*National Union of Mineworkers (Yorkshire Area)     127 233
†*National Union of Public Employees     712 392
†*National Union of Railwaymen     171 411
National Union of Recreation and Sports
    Employees     37
†*National Union of Scalemakers     1960
†*National Union of Seamen     39 000
†*National Union of Sheet Metal Workers
    Coppersmiths and Heating and Domestic
    Engineers     74 116
*National Union of Social Workers     431
†*National Union of Tailors and Garment Workers     116 095
†*National Union of Teachers     293 798
†*National Union of Textile and Allied Workers
    (Rochdale Districts)     1730
†*National Union of the Footwear Leather and
    Allied Trades     61 789
*National Westminster Staff Association     33 906
†*National Woolsorters Society     757
*Nationwide Building Society Staff Association     2200
*Nelson and District Association of Preparatory
    Workers     189
Nelson and District Branch of the Amalgamated
    Association of Beamers Twisters and Drawers
    (Hand and Machine)     196
*Nelson and District Clothlookers and Warehouse
    Association     432
Nelson and District Powerloom Overlookers
    Society     520
Nelson Colne and District Tape Sizers Protective
    Society     111
New Towns Chief Officers Association     120
NFER Staff Assocation     70

# Appendix 1

| | |
|---|---:|
| *Society of Radiographers | 7786 |
| Society of Registration Officers (Births Deaths and Marriages) | 1109 |
| Society of Remedial Gymnasts | 553 |
| †*Society of Shuttlemakers | 103 |
| *Society of Union Employees (NUPE) | 149 |
| *Squibb UK Staff Association | 233 |
| Stable Lads Association | 498 |
| Staff Association of the S W Farmer Group of Companies | 174 |
| Staff Association of the Printing and Publishing Industry Training Board | 77 |
| Staffordshire Building Society Staff Association | 233 |
| *Star Aluminium Managerial Staff Association | 76 |
| *Steel Industry Management Association | 11 702 |
| *Sun Alliance and London Staff Association | 6004 |
| *Sun Life Staff Association | 1533 |
| | |
| *Telecommunications Staff Association | 612 |
| *Telephone Contract Officers Association | 982 |
| Tempered Group (Spring Division) Staff Association | 97 |
| *Teston Independent Society of Cricket Ball Makers | 33 |
| *Textile Manufacturing Trades Federation of Bolton and Surrounding Districts | n.a. |
| *Thames Water Staff Association | 2148 |
| †*Tobacco Mechanics Association | 351 |
| †*Tobacco Workers Union | 20 107 |
| Trade Society of Machine Calico Printers | 223 |
| †*Transport and General Workers Union | 2 072 818 |
| †*Transport Salaried Staffs Association | 72 070 |
| Trebor Sharps Limited Salesmens Association | 77 |
| | |
| *Undeb Cenedlaethol Athrawon Cymru (National Association of the Teachers of Wales) | 2825 |
| †*Union of Construction Allied Trades and Technicians | 325 245 |
| *Union of County and District Secretaries | 414 |
| †*Union of Post Office Workers | 197 157 |
| †*Union of Shop Distributive and Allied Workers | 462 178 |

†*Radio and Electronic Officers Union 4584
Rank Hotels Staff Association n.a.
Redifon Flight Simulation Monthly Staff
    Association 168
*Retail Book Stationery and Allied Trades
    Employees Association 8929
*Retained Firefighters Union 7620
*Retired Officers Association 1528
Robert Hirst Staff Association 160
*Roll-Royce Management Association 600
†*Rossendale Union of Boot Shoe and Slipper
    Operatives 6529
*Rowntree Mackintosh Sales Staff Association 436
*Royal College of Midwives 20 622
*Royal College of Nursing of the United Kingdom 134 389
Royal Insurance Branch Managers Association 81
RSPB Staff Association n.a.
Rumbelows Branch Managers Association n.a.

Schering Chemicals Representatives Association 37
Schweppes Limited Representatives Association 263
†*Screw Nut Bolt and Rivet Trade Union 2524
*Secondary Heads Association 4251
†*Sheffied Sawmakers Protection Society 241
†Sheffield Wool Shear Workers Trade Union 32
*Skipton and District Power-Loom Overlookers
    Association 152
Société Générale Staff Association 130
*Society of Authors Limited 2996
*Society of Chiropodists 4535
†*Society of Civil and Public Servants (Executive
    Directing and Analogous Grades) 106 903
†*Society of Graphical and Allied Trades 1975** 201 665
†*Society of Lithographic Artists Designers Engravers
    and Process-Workers ** 25 561
*Society of Metropolitan and County Chief
    Librarians 238
†*Society of Post Office Executives 22 567
*Society of Public Analysts and Other Official
    Analysts 57

# Appendix 1

| | |
|---|---:|
| National Association of Colliery Overmen Deputies and Shotfirers (Scottish Area) | 2076 |
| National Union of Mineworkers Group 2 Scottish Colliery Enginemen Boilermen and Tradesmens Association | 4850 |
| Professional Staff Association of Scottish Woodland Owners Association (Commercial) Ltd | 28 |
| Scottish Approved Schools Staff Association | 309 |
| Scottish Association of Amenity Supervisory Staffs | 119 |
| Scottish Association of Local Government and Educational Psychologists | 175 |
| Scottish Association of Nurse Administrators | 351 |
| *Scottish Carpet Workers Union | 5039 |
| Scottish Equitable Staff Association | 490 |
| *Scottish Further Education Association | 1732 |
| *Scottish Health Visitors Association | 850 |
| Scottish Joint Industry Board for the Electrical Contracting Industry | 823 |
| †*Scottish Union of Power Loom Overlookers | 250 |
| *Scottish Prison Officers Association | 2553 |
| *Scottish Secondary Teachers Association | 8493 |

*Note:** The National Union of Agricultural and Allied Workers and the National Union of Dyers, Bleachers and Textile Workers, have amalgamated with the Transport and General Workers's Union. There has been a merger between the Society of Lithographic Artists, Designers and Process Workers and the National Graphical Association; and the Society of Graphical and Allied Trades has merged with the National Society of Operative Printers, Graphical and Media Personnel.

††See pages 185–187 above.

*United Association of Power Loom Overlookers     451
*United Friendly Agents Association     3746
*United Friendly Divisional and District Managers
    Association     243
United Friendly Head Office Management
    Association     83
United Friendly Insurance Co Ltd Assistant
    Managers Association     372
*United Kingdom Association of Professional
    Engineers     4883
†*United Road Transport Union     28 371

*Walsall Lock and Keysmiths Male and Female
    Trade Society     144
Whatman Reeve Angel Staff Association     131
Willerby Staff Association     244
Woolwich Independent Staff Association     n.a.
†*Writers Guild of Great Britain     1562

†*Yorkshire Association of Power Loom Overlookers     1252
*Yorkshire Society of Textile Craftsmen     913

*Scotland*
Aberdeen Trawl Officers Guild     161
Association of Directors of Administration in
    Scotland     81
*Association of Lecturers in Colleges of Education
    in Scotland     1193
Association of Lecturers in Scottish Central
    Institutions     588

Distric Nursing Association     n.a.

†*Educational Institute of Scotland     47 056

Glasgow and West of Scotland Power Loom
    Tenters Society     34

Honours Graduate Teachers Association     169

# Appendix 2

Health and Safety Commission
  Regina House, 256/269 Old Marylebone Road, London NW1 5RR
Health and Safety Executive
  Baynards House, 1 Chepstow Place, London W2 4TF
Industrial Society
  48 Bryanston Square, London W1H 8AH
Institute of Directors
  116 Pall Mall, London SW1Y 5ED
Institute of Personnel Management
  Central House, Camp Road, Wimbledon, London SW19 4UW
International Confederation of Free Trade Unions
  37–41 rue Montagne aux Herbes Potagères, 1000 Brussels,
  Belgium
International Labour Organisation
  CH 1211, Geneva 22, Switzerland
Manpower Services Commission
  Selkirk House, 166 High Holborn, London WC1V 6PB
Office of Wages Councils
  12 St James's Square, London SW1Y 4LL
Organisation for Economic Co-operation and Development
  2 rue André-Pascal, 75 Paris 16e, France
Scottish Trades Union Congress
  12 Woodlands Terrace, Glasgow G3 6DE
Trades Union Congress
  Congress House, Great Russell Street, London WC1B 3LS
Union des Industries de la Communauté Européenne
  4 rue Ravenstein, 1000 Brussels, Belgium
Wales Trades Union Council
  42 Charles Street, Cardiff CF1 4SN
World Confederation of Labour
  50 rue Joseph II, 1040 Brussels, Belgium
World Federation of Trade Unions
  Namesti Curieovych 1, Prague 1, Czechoslovakia

# Appendix 2
# Institutions

(Information from *ACAS Industrial Relations Handbook 1980*)

Advisory, Conciliation and Arbitration Service
  Head Office, 11–12 St James's Square, London SW1Y 4LR
British Institute of Management
  Management House, Parker Street, London WC2B 5PT
Central Arbitration Committee
  1 The Abbey Garden, Great College Street, London SW1P 3SE
Central Office of Industrial Tribunals for England and Wales
  93 Ebury Bridge Road, London SW1W 8RE
Central Office of Industrial Tribunals for Scotland
  St Andrew House, 141 West Nile Street, Glasgow G1 2RU
Certification Office for Trade Unions and Employers' Associations
  15–17 Ormond Yard, London SWY 6JT
Commission of the European Communities
  Rue de la Loi 200, 1049 Brussels, Belgium
Commission for Racial Equality
  Elliot House, 10/12 Allington Street, London SW1E 5EH
Confederation of British Industry
  Centre Point, 103 New Oxford Street, London WC1A 1D4
Council of Europe
  Avenue de l'Europe, 67 Strasbourg, France
Department of Employment
  Caxton House, Tothill Street, London SW1H 9NA
Employment Appeal Tribunal
  4 St James's Square, London SW1Y 4JB
  Scottish Divisional Office
  249 West George Street, Glasgow G2 4QE
Equal Opportunities Commission
  Overseas House, Quay Street, Manchester M3 3HN
European Trade Union Confederation
  37–41 rue Montagne aux Herbes Potagères, 1000 Brussels,
  Belgium